Living off the Land

Agriculture in Wales c. 400–1600 AD

Edited by
Rhiannon Comeau and Andy Seaman

WIND*gather*
PRESS

Windgather Press is an imprint of Oxbow Books

Published in the United Kingdom in 2019 by
OXBOW BOOKS
The Old Music Hall, 106-108 Cowley Road, Oxford, OX4 1JE

and in the United States by
OXBOW BOOKS
1950 Lawrence Road, Havertown, PA 19083

Paperback Edition: ISBN 978-1-91118-839-1
Digital Edition: ISBN 978-1-91118-840-7 (epub)

A CIP record for this book is available from the British Library

Typeset in India for Casemate Publishing Services. www.casematepublishingservices.com

For a complete list of Windgather titles, please contact:

United Kingdom
OXBOW BOOKS
Telephone (01865) 241249
Email: oxbow@oxbowbooks.com
www.oxbowbooks.com

United States of America
OXBOW BOOKS
Telephone (610) 853-9131, Fax (610) 853-9146
Email: queries@casemateacademic.com
www.casemateacademic.com/oxbow

Oxbow Books is part of the Casemate group

Front cover photograph: Cwm Graig-ddu on the northern edge of the Epynt
(© Peter Seaman).
Back cover photograph: Llangorse Lake and Llangasty-Talyllyn (© Peter Seaman).

Contents

Acknowledgements

....

The publication of this book has been made possible by grants from the Marc Fitch Fund and from the Scouloudi Foundation in association with the Institute of Historical Research. Many individuals also helped in the production of this book. The conference from which most of the chapters derive was held in the School of History, Archaeology and Religion at Cardiff University, and the editors would like to thank Susan Virgo, Alan Lane and particularly Ben Jervis for their support in organising the event. The sessions were chaired by Stuart Wrathmell, Andrew Fleming, and Nancy Edwards. We are grateful for their insightful comments and discussion. We must also thank the individual authors and the team at Oxbow for their patience, goodwill, and speed in answering queries. Sara Elin Roberts provided advice on the Glossary. Finally, we dedicate this book to Wendy Davies and Heather James, two scholars whose profound influences on medieval Wales (and beyond) are attested throughout its pages.

Rhiannon Comeau and Andy Seaman

List of figures

Colour plates

Contributors

David Austin is Emeritus Professor of Archaeology at University of Wales Trinity St David (Lampeter) where he taught from 1976 to 2015. His principal research interests are in medieval and later historic landscapes in England, Wales and France. Currently he is working on a major project of research and heritage regeneration at Strata Florida, a former Cistercian Abbey in west Wales.

Rhiannon Comeau has recently completed doctoral research at UCL Institute of Archaeology. Her earlier research, which started as a Continuing Education student, is represented by a number of publications. Her work focuses on the Welsh landscape and uses an interdisciplinary approach to identify and contextualise medieval settlement patterns, pre-Norman focal places, and agricultural systems.

Tudur Davies specialises in combining landscape and palaeoenvironmental archaeological approaches, with a specific interest in the early medieval period of Wales. Most recently he has worked at the University of Exeter on the *Manifestations of Empire* project, undertaking pollen analysis to examine patterns of land use associated with the Roman to early medieval transition in south east Wales.

Della Hooke, FSA, formerly a research fellow and lecturer, is an Associate Member of the School of Geography, Earth and Environmental Sciences at the University of Birmingham and a freelance consultant in archaeology and historical landscapes. She edits the journal *Landscape History*. Her numerous books on the early medieval landscape include *Trees in Anglo-Saxon England* (2010) and studies of Welsh historical landscapes.

Andrew Fleming taught at the universities of Sheffield and University of Wales Lampeter between 1967 and 2006. The first recipient of the J. M. Coles Medal for Landscape Archaeology, he has written *The Dartmoor Reaves, Swaledale: Valley of the Wild River,* and *St Kilda and the Wider World.* His current interests include early routeways, transhumance, and wood-pasture.

Thomas Kerr is an archaeologist with the Historic Environment Division, Department for Communities (NI). His doctoral and post-doctoral work focused on settlement within early medieval Ireland. Recent publications have ranged from an overview of early medieval warfare to planning guidance on how to assess impact on the setting of monuments.

Meriel McClatchie is an Assistant Professor in Archaeology at University College Dublin. Her primary research interests are in environmental archaeology, archaeobotany, food, settlement, and later prehistory, and she is currently undertaking research in north-west and south-east Europe. Recent publications have focused on farming systems and foodways in prehistoric and early medieval Ireland.

Finbar McCormick is a Senior Lecturer at Queen's University Belfast. His main areas of research are zooarchaeology, and settlement and economy in early medieval Ireland. He is currently working on faunal remains from prehistoric Malta.

Aidan O'Sullivan is a Professor of Archaeology at University College Dublin. His main research interests are in the early medieval archaeology of Ireland and beyond, wetlands archaeology, and experimental archaeology and material culture. He is also the Director of the School of Archaeology's UCD Centre for Experimental Archaeology and Material Culture.

Stephen Rippon is Professor of Landscape Archaeology at the University of Exeter. His research focuses upon using interdisciplinary approaches to study landscape change over long time perspectives, and understanding local and regional variation in landscape character. Within Wales, he has carried out fieldwork in Monmouthshire and Pembrokeshire, and recent books include *Kingdom, Civitas and County* (2018), *The Fields of Britannia* (2015), and *Beyond the Medieval Village* (2014).

Sara Elin Roberts is a historian specialising in the law, literature, and culture of Wales and the March from the twelfth to the fifteenth centuries. She has published widely on medieval Welsh law, including *The Legal Triads of Medieval Wales* (2007) and *Llawysgrif Pomffred* (2011), an edition of a Welsh law manuscript.

Andy Seaman is Senior Lecturer in Archaeology at Canterbury Christ Church University. His research focuses on Wales and western Britain, and he has particular interests in settlements, landscape and the early Church. He is currently engaged in a number of projects, including the AHRC-funded *Manifestations of Empire: Palaeoenvironmental Analysis and the End of Roman Britain*.

Bob Silvester worked in Devon, Somerset, and Norfolk after graduating from Exeter University, before becoming deputy director of the Clwyd-Powys Archaeological Trust in 1989. Recently retired, he is now affiliated to the University of Chester, is the diocesan archaeologist for St Asaph, sits on the Welsh Cathedrals and Churches Commission, and is reviews editor for the journal *Archaeologia Cambrensis*.

CHAPTER ONE

Introduction

....

Rhiannon Comeau and Andy Seaman

Agriculture lay at the heart of British and Irish medieval (*c.* AD 400–1600) society. In the words of the fourteenth-century Welsh poet Iolo Goch, without the ploughman 'no pope / Or emperor can keep alive / No wine-giving, sprightly king … no living man' (Williams 1973, 59–60). Until coins began to be used regularly in the thirteenth and fourteenth centuries, rents and tribute payments were made up of the produce of cornfields and cattle herds: bread, meat, ale, and honey are stipulated in the eighth-century Llancarfan charters, and much the same is required by thirteenth-century Welsh law (Davies 1982, 46; Jenkins 1990, 128–9; Faith 1997, 104; Charles-Edwards 2013, 280–1). The materiality of food production shaped the world without towns that was pre-Norman Wales. Most people lived in and worked the land from small hamlets, their lives bound up with the seasonal practices of crop-growing and pastoralism that another medieval poet, Dafydd ap Gwilym, worked into his poems: ploughing, the May Day enclosing of ripening corn, summer visits to 'bright-topped meadows of moorland grass', and reaping parties (Davies 1987, 140–2, 149–151; Thomas 2001, 59, 177–8, 187).

It is curious, therefore, that current understanding of the agriculture of medieval Wales is so limited. Despite enjoinders to pay greater attention to the evidence of the environment, relatively little attention has been paid to it (Davies 2001, 16, 18; Edwards *et al.* 2016, 18–30). This book is an attempt to redress this situation, which contrasts sharply with that of England and Ireland. The English medieval landscape is the subject of a wealth of diverse research (*e.g.* Hamerow 2012; Oosthuizen 2013; Williamson 2013; Banham and Faith 2014; Hall 2014; Rippon *et al.* 2015; McKerracher 2018; *cf.* Davies 2004, 200), encompassing field systems, crop usage, animal husbandry, and manorial records in both wide-ranging overviews and detailed studies, which are integrated into narratives concerned with archaeological and landscape history that (particularly for the early medieval period) inform broader socio-economic perspectives. Research into the medieval landscapes and environment of Ireland also surpasses that of Wales, informed by a rich early medieval historical record and the fruits of a considerable amount of excavation undertaken during the 'Celtic Tiger' era (Kelly 1997, McCormick *et al.* 2014).

With certain notable exceptions, research in Wales is comparably limited and less integrated into wider narratives. Some explanation for this lies in the limited availability of charters and manorial records and the sparsity of the archaeological record, though there are other reasons linked to frameworks of scholarship. One of these is the generalised narrative of a nation-based academic tradition, applied to a geographical area that for the earlier part of the medieval period consisted not of a single polity but of a number of small regional kingdoms, which were succeeded by marcher lordships and Edwardian royal shires. This generalised narrative, in turn, drew on a nineteenth- and early twentieth-century discourse that saw nucleated villages and common fields (open fields with communally regulated crop rotation and fallowing) as the defining characteristic of Anglo-Saxon settlers. The open fields and hamlets of Wales were attributed to Anglo-Norman settlement, and dispersed settlements to earlier incomers, semi-nomadic pastoralist Celtic tribesmen (Stuart Piggott's 'Celtic cowboys') who were believed to have enslaved the region's original inhabitants (Rhys 1911, 297–8; Piggott 1958, 25; Fleming 2007, 5–11; Austin 2016, 3–4). Earlier commentators similarly characterised medieval Welsh society as pastoral, often with moralistic overtones. John Leland, describing Brycheiniog around 1540, remarked that '… the Walschmen yn tymes past, as they do almost yet, did study more to pasturage then tylling, as favorers of their consuete idilnes' (Smith 1906, 104). Arable practice is acknowledged by Gerald of Wales' late twelfth-century descriptions of ploughing and reaping, but it is his observation that 'the whole population lives almost entirely on oats and the produce of their herds, milk, cheese and butter. They eat plenty of meat, but little bread' that was selectively used, as late as the 1960s, as evidence for Welsh 'wandering pastoralists' (Parain 1966, 171; Thorpe 1978, 233, 252).

Scholarship has since moved on, and the common fields of the English Midlands no longer define discourse. Together with nucleated villages, they are now understood as developments of the mid- to late Anglo-Saxon and high medieval periods rather than as imports from a Germanic Anglo-Saxon homeland, with a geographical distribution largely restricted to a central belt of England, often termed the 'Central Province' (Roberts and Wrathmell 2002, 123–4, figs 5.4, 5.10; Oosthuizen 2011; Hall 2014, 212, fig. 0.1; Rippon *et al.* 2015, 34–42, 98–9). There is broad agreement among scholars that open fields were a response to pressures for intensification of crop production resulting from the social and economic changes of the middle Anglo-Saxon period, in which technological improvements like the heavy plough, the introduction of new crops, and possibly also the use of crop rotations and folding were instrumental. Further light on the changes signalled by these landscape transformations is provided by research into the crops, animals, technology and the environmental context of the English early medieval landscape (Fowler 2002; Williamson 2003; Moffett 2011; O'Connor 2011; Banham and Faith 2014; McKerracher 2016; Thomas *et al.* 2016;). Earlier, pre-common field arrangements may have involved infield-outfield systems of Romano-British and prehistoric origin, though suggestions that Anglo-Saxon settlers introduced some form of subdivided, communally managed arable fields remain influential (Oosthuizen 2011; Williamson 2013, 82–106; Banham and Faith 2014, 269–292; Hall 2014, 182; Rippon *et al.* 2015, 330–1).

Other ways of exploiting the landscape can also be seen, and variations in regional landscape development are much in evidence outside the 'Central Province' (Rippon 2008; Williamson 2013, 234–5; Hall 2014, 5–6, 212). In the areas of Britain described by Oliver Rackham as 'ancient countryside', less intensive forms of land management are visible in dispersed patterns of settlement, 'irregular' open fields and systems of convertible husbandry in areas where livestock were of greater significance (Rackham 1986, 4–5; Rippon 2008; Banham and Faith 2014, 248–256; Hall 2014, 61–94). Infield-outfield systems were used, in combination with the practice of transhumance, in northern England and Scotland until the early modern period (Fox 1996).

And what of Wales? The myth of the wandering Celtic pastoralist began to be dismantled in academic circles from the late 1950s onwards through Glanville Jones' pioneering recognition of widespread groups of settlements (*trefi* or townships) of dependent tenants (*taeogion* or villeins/bondmen) in twelfth-century north Wales (Jones 1955; 1961; 1964; Davies 2004, 212). His work, and that of his mentor, Jones Pierce, identified the use of small permanently cultivated open fields within systems of infield-outfield and transhumance (Jones 1973; Jones Pierce 1959, 1961). These were regulated by pre-Conquest Welsh law, and organised into territorial structures that Jones drew on to develop his concept of the 'multiple estate' (Jones 1976). This work however was largely dependent on the Welsh lawbooks of the thirteenth century and later, and on records made by the English Crown when it conquered north Wales: elsewhere in Wales, medieval documentation is sparse or non-existent and research must cast a wider net, using maps, place- or field-names, post-medieval documents, field survey and excavation, together with the full range of scientific analyses available (David and Thomas 2016).

The long shadow of the Celtic cowboy can, however, still be felt. Although there are notable landscape studies by, for example Jonathan Kissock and Colin Thomas as well as by contributors to this volume, such work is scarce outside north-west Wales, the Severn Levels and university hinterlands (Silvester and Kissock 2012, 167–8; for other references, see General Bibliography). Studies that place local evidence within a bigger narrative are in particularly short supply. There is no overview of Welsh field systems that approaches David Hall's comprehensive English gazetteer, and understanding of these is largely defined by three regional studies published 50 years ago by Margaret Davies, Glanville Jones, and Dorothy Sylvester, one of which (Davies) focuses heavily on Anglo-Norman influences (Sylvester 1969; Davies 1973; Jones 1973; Hall 2014). An overview of subsequent work is long overdue, as is filling in numerous gaps in research: many landscape studies, for instance, tend to focus on upland areas and transhumance (a legacy of both traditional cultural identifications and of visibility of features on moorland), while the lowland part of the ecosystem is relatively neglected (Davies 2001, 18; Silvester and Kissock 2012, 167–8). At the same time, place- and field-names are remarkably under-utilised, and there has been little attempt to build on the work of Colin Thomas, Glanville Jones, and Della Hooke in using field-names to characterise the medieval landscape. Recent initiatives offer the prospect of change here, with the establishment of the Welsh Place-Name Society, Cymdeithas Enwau Lleoedd Cymru, the creation of a statutory register of historic place-names by the Royal Commission on the Ancient and Historical Monuments of Wales, and – perhaps of most immediate significance to researchers – the digitising of Welsh tithe maps and schedules by the Cynefin project.

Importantly, paleoenvironmental investigations are providing increasing insight into the use of the medieval landscape. Hitherto, pollen analysis has focused on isolated cores covering long time periods from upland sampling sites, but recent studies using multiple cores with fine resolution chronologies from lowland regions have yielded significant insights about land-use and how practices change over time. In addition, the implementation of systematic environmental sampling strategies within programmes of developer-funded and research excavation have yielded plant macrofossil assemblages that provide crucial data on crop growing strategies (Davies 2001, 18; Caseldine 2015, 8; Davies this volume; James forthcoming; see General Bibliography, *e.g.* Carruthers 2010). Much of this data resides within 'grey literature' however, and there is little research and synthesis comparable to Mark McKerracher's (2018) study of agriculture in middle Anglo-Saxon England. Survival of faunal remains is restricted by the prevalence of acid soils across Wales, but some key settlement sites like Dinas Powys hillfort, Llan-gors crannog, and Dryslwyn castle have produced substantial assemblages (Alcock 1963; Gilchrist 1988; Millard *et al.* 2013; Mulville and Powell forthcoming). These offer significant possibilities for improving understanding of animal husbandry practice and the economy. Animal bone assemblages from developer-funded excavation hold considerable research potential, but again much of this data remains unpublished and wider synthesis and comparative research is desperately needed. Isotopic research also has much potential, but to date the number of studies has been limited (*e.g.* Hemer *et al.* 2016).

Research in this arena is thinly spread compared with England and Ireland, since developer-funded archaeological investigations across most of Wales are restricted by poor economic development and extensive areas of upland. Moreover, pre-eleventh-century settlements are notoriously difficult to identify due to a widespread lack of diagnostic material culture (Edwards *et al.* 2016), and the lack of pre-Norman pottery also constrains the effectiveness of key research methods such as fieldwalking and test-pitting. Combined with a long history of under-research, the result is an inadequate platform for new research, with limited comparanda for detailed studies and a diminished scope for and authority of overviews, as Stephen Rippon points out (Rippon *et al.* 2015, 295). Teasing out the relationship between people and land – between settlement, society, and the processes that sustained it – becomes difficult at anything beyond the most superficial level and there are, consequently, few narratives for the early medieval period that link agricultural development with social and political change. Such narratives exist for the post-Conquest period (*e.g.* Davies 1987), but the few detailed medieval landscape studies suggest patchy awareness of how agricultural processes shaped landscape and society away from areas of Anglo-Norman colonisation (for post-medieval overviews see Thomas 1963; Emery 1967).

Against this background, the editors of this volume organised the 2016 conference from which this collection springs. The intention was to rekindle interest in and to explore how an understanding of the Welsh agricultural landscape could illuminate archaeological and historical research. Key questions included: how did the agricultural systems of Wales operate between *c.* 400 and 1600 AD? What light do they cast on the material evidence for life in the contemporary landscape? How similar or different was Wales to other areas or Britain and Ireland? Can we identify change over time? How do we go about researching early Welsh agriculture?

These questions were addressed at the conference via overviews and case studies presented by invited speakers, which were then reviewed in a plenary session where key themes emerged, notably the interdependence of upland and lowland areas, regional distinctiveness, and the importance of a multi-disciplinary approach. Discussants noted in particular the need for greater investigation of lowland agricultural zones and their links with upland areas. The problems of a national 'metanarrative' were noted, along with a need to acknowledge regional distinctiveness within Wales and also relationships between neighbouring Welsh and English regions where the modern border cuts through earlier zones of interaction.

A research wish-list emerged from the conference: a need for both local studies and broader overviews, and the inescapable necessity for a range of approaches from detailed landscape studies to specialised environmental and archaeological research and targeted survey and excavation. Many more detailed local studies of field systems (including more identification of the *penclawdd/* head dyke – muddy boots work!), field-names and associated historical evidence are required, with the dating of field systems a priority. Research must also be set in the context of work in other regions of Britain and Ireland and indeed beyond, and ought to explore what the agricultural landscape reveals about periods commonly identified with change. For instance, exploration of continuity and change within the late- and post-Roman agricultural landscape has the potential to reinvigorate the somewhat stagnated debate surrounding the Roman to early medieval transition (Gerrard 2013, 96–100; Rippon *et al.* 2015). Indeed, exploration of agricultural change during the middle Anglo-Saxon period is contributing significantly to our understanding of the 'long eighth century', a key transitional period across much of Europe (Hansen and Wickham, 2000; Rippon 2010; McKerracher 2018). The Anglo-Norman and Edwardian Conquests are often seen as period boundaries in Welsh scholarship, but a landscape approach allows us to consider continuity/discontinuity across these periods of important socio-political and economic transformation (Davies 1987, 153–9, 399–400, 425–430, 215–222). The impact of Viking trade and settlement, until recently largely overlooked in Wales, warrants attention (Redknap 2006). We must also consider what the agricultural landscape reveals about periods of 'crisis' like the Black Death and the revolt of Owain Glyndŵr. Does the evidence support traditional assumptions focused on abandonment and desertion (*e.g.* Beresford and Hurst 1971)?

In furtherance of this end, this volume presents contributions from speakers at the conference. Most reflect the conference presentations, though two, by David Austin and Andy Seaman, cover different (and new) ground, the former's conference case study having been published in the same year as the conference (Austin 2016), as was that of another conference speaker, Alice Forward (Forward and Hines 2016), whose work is not reflected in the current volume. Our collection of papers begins with assessments by Stephen Rippon and Della Hooke of the bigger picture for England and Wales, and a summary of the current Irish evidence by Meriel McClatchie, Finbar McCormick, Thomas Kerr and Aidan O'Sullivan, before turning to Wales.

Stephen Rippon considers the long-term picture for continuity and change within the early medieval landscape through a comparison of the evidence for Roman and medieval landscapes across the whole of southern Britain. His paper discusses the results of his 'Fields of Britannia' research project (Rippon 2015), and explores what can be learned about the Roman to medieval transition through a synthesis of two datasets: pollen sequences that reflect broad patterns in land-use, and the relationship between excavated Romano-British and medieval field systems. Marked regional and temporal variations are found across the whole of Roman Britain, with some regions showing greater continuity than others. In lowland areas most of this variation will reflect the different ways in which communities responded to the changing socio-economic circumstances that followed Britain ceasing to be part of the Roman Empire, although climate change may have been significant in upland areas. Where there are identifiable discontinuities between Romano-British and medieval landscapes the crucial change may not have come at the end of the Roman period but several centuries later when an intensification of agriculture was seen across much of southern Britain around the eighth century.

Della Hooke's paper considers transhumance, a practice found across much of early medieval Europe. Using English and Welsh case studies, she looks at this long-standing symbiotic relationship between the complementary resources of zones of more intensive agriculture and areas of woodland or upland that were more suited to seasonal pasture. Arrangements can be identified in Anglo-Saxon documents that could have been in place since at least the late Iron

Age, and may have influenced early territorial organisation; in certain regions, especially upland and wetland areas, transhumance continued into medieval times. Hooke's case studies examine midland and south-eastern England in the early medieval period, and north Wales in the high and later medieval periods. In the area that by the eleventh century became Warwickshire, transhumant activity disappears over the course of the early medieval period but is fossilised in links between medieval manorial and ecclesiastical units and their isolated dependent outliers. In Kent, the practice of moving stock to Wealden *dens* (seasonal woodland swine pasture) appears to have survived into the twelfth century and seems to be related to early territorial arrangements. In north Wales, the thirteenth-century Edwardian Extents record the transhumance arrangements of both the Welsh prince (his *hafotir*) and free kin-groups, which linked the coastal plain of Gwynedd with the hills of Snowdonia; the proximity and availability of hill-pasture meant that transhumance was often conducted across relatively short distances, with cattle dominant. Field- and place-names can be used to identify different zones of the landscape, in conjunction with surviving landscape evidence.

The picture for Ireland is presented by Meriel McClatchie, Finbar McCormick, Thomas R. Kerr, and Aidan O'Sullivan, who review the extensive body of archaeobotanical, zooarchaeological, and archaeological evidence recently available for early medieval Ireland and its role in social and economic transformations during this period. Agriculture formed the basis of the economy and played a key role in the organisation of society for the period AD 400–1150, and this material provides new understandings that complement written evidence presented in Kelly's magisterial 1997 survey. The importance of animal husbandry during this period has long been recognised from such sources: cattle formed a basic unit of wealth in this rigidly hierarchical society, where an individual's social status was dependent, to a large extent, on the number of cattle at their disposal. More recently, it has been recognised that arable production also played an important role in agricultural systems and new evidence reviewed in this chapter indicates that during the early medieval period both animal husbandry and crop production began to be undertaken on a larger scale than ever before.

Following these considerations of the wider supra-regional context we turn to Wales, starting with an examination of the evidence of medieval Welsh law, the single greatest source of information about medieval agricultural practice in the region. Sara Elin Roberts provides an introduction to the provisions for ploughing and animal husbandry in the medieval Welsh law texts, which exist in a number of regional versions. Her chapter provides those new to the subject with an overview of the law-texts – what they were, when they were written, and their nature and purpose – before turning to focus upon their references to hunting and agriculture. The importance of these texts to studies of medieval agriculture is highlighted by discussions of their regulation of animal compensation values, food renders, communal herdsmen and herd sizes, the farming year, winter and summer dwellings, pannage rights, animal damage to crops, and the organisation of ploughing.

The remainder of the book is devoted to studies of different aspects of living off the land in medieval Wales. Regional perspectives are provided by Bob Silvester for north Wales, David Austin for west Wales, Rhiannon Comeau for south-west Wales, and Andy Seaman for south-east Wales. An examination of the pollen evidence across early medieval Wales by Tudur Davies rounds off the Welsh contributions.

Bob Silvester discusses the medieval field systems of north Wales, taking as his starting point a paper on north Wales that the late Glanville Jones contributed to Baker and Butlin's landmark 1973 volume, *Studies of Field Systems in the British Isles*. He notes that while Jones' contribution did not provide a comprehensive synthesis, it remains the most influential assessment of Welsh field systems of the last forty years. Bob Silvester's overview looks at the current state of understanding for north Wales and Powys and – incorporating extensive work undertaken in recent years by Clwyd-Powys Archaeological Trust and Gwynedd Archaeological Trust – presents a new classification of the field systems that have been identified in this region. He commences with an examination of open field systems of English form in Wales before turning to identify evidence for the small open fields or sharelands (*rhandiroedd*) of medieval Welsh practice. The significance of ridge and furrow is carefully examined. His paper continues with a consideration of Jones' 'nucleal lands' (infields), the re-use of later prehistoric and Roman field systems, and evidence for the processes of enclosure that saw the development of medieval closes in more low-lying areas. Given the lack of published overviews of the medieval field systems of Wales, this synthesis is timely and pertinent.

The next three papers present new research on different aspects of medieval agriculture in south and west Wales, and – in varying proportions – integrate documentary records, place-names, landscape, archaeological, and environmental evidence. David Austin's examination of the landscape setting of the west Wales Cistercian abbey of Strata Florida is a classic piece of retrogressive analysis that challenges established interpretations of this iconic site. He focuses on the '*milltir sgwâr*', the metaphorical square mile of local life which identifies people with locality and a sense of close belonging. Carefully disentangling and peeling back the layers of evidence, he shows how the landscape of nineteenth-century mining and eighteenth-century estates developed from the Abbey lands recorded in twelfth-century charters. Using archaeology, place-names and charters, he characterises the landscape of the medieval abbey, identifying the locations of 'ancient' (pre-1184) farms made up of the best agricultural land, meadow, valley pasture, and rights to mountain pasture. He argues that the specialist farms of the later medieval Abbey represent a transformation of these earlier arrangements which probably reflect those of a pre-Conquest Welsh royal estate rather than a 'colonial replacement' typifying the organisational structures of English and continental Cistercian monasteries. In essence, then, he suggests that the medieval Abbey took over and adapted an earlier, longstanding agricultural and administrative landscape. The analysis reveals the detailed fabric of landscape structure and social meaning, and an interplay between the continuity of place and agrarian action and the discontinuity of political and economic structures.

The second case study considers the medieval and pre-Conquest agricultural practices of south-west Wales. Rhiannon Comeau presents new research into the medieval Welsh lands of north Pembrokeshire that sets post-medieval descriptions of longstanding local Welsh agricultural practice in the context of references to infield-outfield agriculture in twelfth- and thirteenth-century Welsh law. Welsh law can be seen to provide a template for the north Pembrokeshire practices, which include periodic cultivation of the outfield via methods of convertible husbandry and beat burning that are known in other areas of medieval and early medieval Britain. The local use of a light plough is noted, and correlates with cultivation of spring-sown crops and minimal medieval ridge and furrow. Three localised case studies provide evidence for a consideration of the seasonal and spatial patterning of the landscape, one of which focuses on a recently excavated upland house whose date and moorland context mark it as the earliest firmly dated *hafoty* or summer dwelling in Wales.

South-east Wales provides the setting for Andy Seaman's study, which considers the comparatively small but significant corpus of early medieval charters in the Book of Llandaff. The 'Llandaff charters' are complex sources, but they offer valuable evidence for what is otherwise a poorly documented part of Wales. Most of the 158 Llandaff charters refer to properties within the southern kingdoms of Gwent, Glywysing and Morgannwg, and have been subject to detailed examination by Wendy Davies (*e.g.* 1978) and others, but this chapter focuses on a group of charters that relate to properties and individuals within the poorer understood region of Brycheiniog. Detailed analysis of the properties and their boundary clauses alongside examination of place-names and archaeological evidence allows us to explore patterns of settlement and agriculture. Two of the charters relate to territories associated with a lowland royal estate centre at Llan-gors, whilst the third provides evidence about an upland estate that was associated with the exploitation of Mynydd Epynt.

The final paper by Tudur Davies indicates a potentially fruitful direction of future research in its examination of environmental evidence, providing a review of Welsh palynological data for the early medieval period. Davies finds that although numerous pollen studies exist across Wales, few have well-dated sequences relating to the middle ages, and there are large gaps in geographical coverage, with the majority of well-dated studies located in the uplands of north-west Wales. Despite these limitations, temporal and possible regional patterns can be identified, showing distinct variations throughout the period. The immediate post-Roman period shows a widespread decrease in pollen taxa indicative of pastoral and arable land use, likely to represent a combination of climatic deterioration and decreased demand for farming produce. In contrast, the seventh and eighth centuries show evidence for agricultural activity recovering substantially, possibly in association with an increasingly powerful church. From the ninth to mid-twelfth century, fluctuations in arable and pastoral indicators are observed across the country with increased regional diversity in farming intensity; changes specific to north-west Wales may, however, reflect the growing influence of the rulers of Gwynedd on farming practices and tribute systems within the kingdom at a time of increased conflict both within Wales and beyond its borders. These observations provide considerable food for thought, both as a contextualised background to the landscape and historical evidence of local studies, and for the construction of narratives that set Welsh developments in the wider context.

Taken together, this collection of studies represents a starting point rather than a definitive statement. Authors do not all agree in their interpretations. Different approaches are taken, and varying methodologies used. The book aims to inform, suggest, inspire, and point the way forward for further work, and the final chapter by Andrew Fleming reflects on this. He identifies the need for more holistic models that integrate perspectives of both continuity and change, and acknowledge the role of multiple stakeholders and the 'annual rhythms of the agrarian calendar' in structuring life on the land. To assist with this process of exploration, we have provided a bibliography of key Welsh work and glossary of key terms. We hope that this book provokes further studies that challenge and overtake existing understanding. Over to you, readers.

References (see also the separate General Bibliography)

Adams, I. H. (1976) *Agrarian Landscape Terms: a glossary for historical geography.* London, Institute of British Geographers.

Austin, D. (2016) Reconstructing the Upland Landscapes of Medieval Wales. *Archaeologia Cambrensis* 165, 1–19.

Baker, A. R. H. and Butlin, R. A. (eds) (1976) *Studies of Field Systems in the British Isles.* Cambridge, Cambridge University Press.

Banham, D. and Faith, R. (2014) *Anglo-Saxon Farms and Farming.* Oxford, Oxford University Press.

Beresford, M. W. and Hurst, J. G. (eds) (1971) *Deserted Medieval Villages.* Woking, Lutterworth Press.

Butlin, R. A. (1961) Some Terms Used in Agrarian History: A Glossary. *The Agricultural History Review* 9(2), 98–104.

Carruthers, W. (2010) Charred Plant Remains. In P. Crane and K. Murphy, An Early Medieval Settlement, Iron Smelting Site and Crop-processing Complex at South Hook, Herbranston, Pembrokeshire. *Archaeologia Cambrensis* 159, 117–196 at 164–181.

Caseldine, A. (2015) Environmental Change and Archaeology – A Retrospective View. *Archaeology in Wales* 54, 3–14.

Cavill, P. (2018) *A New Dictionary of English Field-Names.* With an Introduction by Rebecca Gregory. Nottingham, English Place-Name Society

Charles-Edwards, T. M. (1989) Early medieval kingships in the British Isles. In S. Bassett (ed.) *The Origins of Anglo-Saxon Kingdoms.* London, Leicester University Press, 28–39.

Charles-Edwards, T. M. (2013) *Wales and the Britons, 350–1064*. Oxford, Oxford University Press.

Charles-Edwards, T. M., Owen, M. E. and Russell, P. (eds) (2000) *The Welsh King and his Court*. Cardiff, University of Wales Press.

Coredon, C. and Williams, A. (2004) *A Dictionary of Medieval Terms and Phrases*. Cambridge, D. S. Brewer.

David, B. and Thomas, J. (2016) *Handbook of Landscape Archaeology*. London, Routledge.

Davies, E. (1980) Hafod, hafoty and lluest. *Ceredigion: Journal of the Cardiganshire Antiquarian Society* 9(1), 1–41.

Davies, M. (1956) Rhosili Open Field and Related South Wales Field Patterns. *The Agricultural History Review* 4(2), 80–96.

Davies, M. (1973) Field Systems of South Wales. In A. R. H. Baker and R. A. Butlin (eds) *Studies of Field Systems in the British Isles*. Cambridge, Cambridge University Press, 480–529.

Davies, R. R. (1987) *Conquest, Coexistence and Change: Wales 1063–1415* (published in paperback in 1991 as *The Age of Conquest: Wales 1063–1415*). Oxford, Oxford University Press.

Davies, W. (1978) *An Early Welsh Microcosm: Studies in the Llandaff Charters*. London, Royal Historical Society.

Davies, W. (1982) *Wales in the Early Middle Ages*. Leicester, Leicester University Press.

Davies, W. (2001) Thinking about the Welsh environment a thousand years ago. In G. Jenkins (ed.) *Cymru a'r Cymry 2000. Wales and the Welsh 2000*. Aberystwyth, Centre for Advanced Welsh and Celtic Studies, 1–18.

Davies, W. (2004) Looking Backwards to the Early Medieval Past: Wales and England, a contrast in approaches. *Welsh History Review* 22(2), 197–221.

Edwards, N., Davies, T. and Hemer, K. A. (2016) *Research Framework for the Archaeology of Early Medieval Wales c. AD 400–1070*. Unpublished report: http://www.archaeoleg.org.uk/ (accessed 07.01.19).

Emery, F. (1967) The Farming Regions of Wales. In J. Thirsk (ed.) *The Agrarian History of England and Wales, Volume IV, 1500–1640*. Cambridge, Cambridge University Press, 113–161.

Everitt, A. (1977) River and Wold: reflections on the historical origin of regions and pays. *Journal of Historical Geography* 3(1), 1–19.

Faith, R. (1997) *The English Peasantry and the Growth of Lordship*. London, Leicester University Press.

Fleming, A. (2007) 1955 and All That: Prehistoric Landscapes in The Making. In A. Fleming and R. Hingley (eds) *Prehistoric and Roman Landscapes*. Macclesfield, Windgather Press, 1–15.

Fleming, A. and Ralph, N. (1982) Medieval Settlement and Land Use on Holne Moor, Dartmoor: the landscape evidence. *Medieval Archaeology* 26, 101–137.

Ford, M. J. (1976) Some settlement patterns in the central regions of the Warwickshire Avon. In P. H. Sawyer (ed.) *Medieval Settlement: Continuity and Change*. London, Edward Arnold, 274–94.

Forward, A. and Hines, J. (2016) Cosmeston, South Wales: Conquest, colonisation and material culture change. In J. Klápště (ed.) *Agrarian Technology in the Medieval Landscape, Ruralia X*. Turnhout, Brepols, 125–141.

Fowler, P. (2002) *Farming in the First Millennium*. Cambridge, Cambridge University Press.

Fox, H. S. A. (1996) Introduction: transhumance and seasonal settlement. In H. S. A. Fox (ed.) *Seasonal Settlement*. Leicester, University of Leicester Department of Adult Education, 1–23.

Gerrard, J. (2013) *The Ruin of Roman Britain: An Archaeological Perspective*. Cambridge, Cambridge University Press.

Gilchrist, R. (1988) A Reappraisal of Dinas Powys: local exchange and specialised livestock in fifth-seventh century Wales. *Medieval Archaeology* 32, 50–62.

Hall, D. (2014) *The Open Fields of England*. Oxford, Oxford University Press.

Hamerow, H. (2012) *Rural Settlements and Society in Anglo-Saxon England*. Oxford, Oxford University Press.

Hansen, I. L. and Wickham, C. (2000) *The Long Eighth Century*. Leiden, Brill.

Hemer, K. A., Lamb, A., Chenery, C. A., and Evans, J. A. (2016) A Multi-isotope Investigation of Diet and Subsistence Amongst Island and Mainland Populations from Early Medieval Western Britain. *American Journal of Physical Anthropology* 162(3), 423–440.

Hooke, D. (1982) Pre-Conquest Estates in the West Midlands: preliminary thoughts. *Journal of Historical Geography* 8(3), 227–244.

Howells, B. (1967) The Distribution of Customary Acres in South Wales. *National Library of Wales Journal* 15(2), 226–233.

James, H. (forthcoming) The early medieval evidence. In *An Overview of the Results of the South Wales Gas Pipeline Excavations 2005–2007, Cotswold Archaeology*. Cirencester, Cotswold Archaeology.

Jenkins, D. (ed.) (1990) *The Law of Hywel Dda*. Llandysul, Gomer Press.

Jones, G. R. J. (1955) The Distribution of Medieval Settlement in Anglesey. *Transactions of the Anglesey Antiquarian Society*, 27–96.

Jones, G. R. J. (1961) The Tribal System in Wales. *Welsh History Review* 1(2), 111–132.

Jones, G. R. J. (1964) The Distribution of Bond Settlements in North-west Wales. *Welsh History Review* 11, 19–36.

Jones, G. R. J. (1972) Post-Roman Wales. In H. P. R. Finberg (ed.) *The Agrarian History of England and Wales, Vol. 1, AD 43–1042*. Cambridge, Cambridge University Press, 283–384.

Jones, G. R. J. (1973) Field Systems of North Wales. In A. R. H. Baker and R. A. Butlin (eds) *Studies of Field Systems in the British Isles*. Cambridge, Cambridge University Press, 430–479.

Jones, G. R. J. (1976) Multiple Estates and Early Settlement. In P. H. Sawyer (ed.) *Medieval Settlement: Continuity and Change*. London, Edward Arnold, 15–40.

Jones, G. R. J. (1989) The Dark Ages. In D. Huw Owen (ed.) *Settlement and Society in Wales*. Cardiff, University of Wales Press, 177–197.

Jones Pierce, T. (1943) Ancient Welsh Measures of Land. *Archaeologia Cambrensis* 97, 195–204.

Jones Pierce, T. (1959) Agrarian Aspects of the Tribal System in Medieval Wales. *Géographie et Histoire Agraires, Annales de L'Est*, Nancy, Université de Nancy, 329–37.

Jones Pierce, T. (1961) Pastoral and Agricultural Settlements in Early Wales. *Geografiska Annaler* 43, 182–189.

Kelly, F. (1997) *Early Irish Farming*. Dublin, Dublin Institute for Advanced Studies.

Loveluck, C. (2013) *Northwest Europe in the Early Middle Ages, c. AD 600–1150*. Cambridge, Cambridge University Press.

McCormick, F., Kerr, T., McClatchie, M. and O'Sullivan, A. (2014) *Early Medieval Agriculture, Livestock and Cereal Production in Ireland, AD 400–1100*. BAR International Series 2647. Oxford, British Archaeological Reports.

McKerracher, M. (2016) Bread and Surpluses: the Anglo-Saxon 'bread wheat thesis' reconsidered. *Environmental Archaeology* 21, 88–102.

McKerracher, M. (2018) *Farming Transformed in Anglo-Saxon England: Agriculture in the Long Eighth Century.* Oxford, Windgather Press.

Millard, A., Jimenez-Cano, N., Lebrasseur, O. and Saki, Y. (2013) Isotopic Investigation of Animal Husbandry in the Welsh and English Periods at Dryslwyn Castle, Carmarthenshire, Wales. *International Journal of Osteoarchaeology* 23(6), 640–650.

Moffett, L. (2011) Food Plants on Archaeological Sites: The Nature of the Archaeobotanical Record. In D. A. Hinton, H. Hamerow, and S. Crawford (eds) *The Oxford Handbook of Anglo-Saxon Archaeology.* Oxford, Oxford University Press, 346–60.

Mulville, J. and Powell, A. (forthcoming) The Animal Bone. In A. Lane and M. Redknap *Llangorse Crannog: The excavation of an early medieval royal site in the kingdom of Brycheiniog.* Oxford, Oxbow Books.

O'Connor, T. (2011) Animal Husbandry. In D. A. Hinton, H. Hamerow, and S. Crawford (eds) *The Oxford Handbook of Anglo-Saxon Archaeology.* Oxford, Oxford University Press, 361–376.

Oosthuizen, S. (2011) Anglo-Saxon Fields. In D. A. Hinton, H. Hamerow, and S. Crawford (eds) *The Oxford Handbook of Anglo-Saxon Archaeology.* Oxford, Oxford University Press, 377–404.

Oosthuizen, S. (2013) *Tradition and Transformation in Anglo-Saxon England: Archaeology, Common Rights and Landscape.* London, Bloomsbury.

Owen, G. (1994) *The Description of Pembrokeshire (1603).* Llandysul, Gomer Press.

Parain, C. (1966) The Evolution of Agricultural Technique. In M. M. Postan (ed.) *The Cambridge Economic History of Europe: Volume I: The Agrarian Life of the Middle Ages.* Cambridge, Cambridge University Press, 126–179.

Piggott, S. (1958) Native economies and the Roman occupation of North Britain. In I. A. Richmond (ed.) *Roman and Native in North Britain.* Edinburgh, Nelson, 1–27.

Rackham, O. (1987) *The History of the Countryside.* London, Dent.

Redknap, M. (2006) Viking-Age Settlement in Wales: some recent advances. *Transactions of the Honourable Society of Cymmrodorion* 12 (new series), 5–35.

Rhys, J. E. (1911) *A History of Wales from the Earliest Times to the Edwardian Conquest.* London, Longmans, Green and Co.

Rippon, S. (2008) *Beyond the Medieval Village.* Oxford, Oxford University Press.

Rippon, S., Smart, C. and Pears, B. (2015) *The Fields of Britannia: Continuity and Change in the Late Roman and Early Medieval Landscape.* Oxford, Oxford University Press.

Roberts, B. K. and Wrathmell, S. (2002) *Region and Place.* London, English Heritage.

Silvester, R. J. and Kissock, J. (2012) Wales: Medieval Settlements, Nucleated and Dispersed, Permanent and Seasonal. In N. Christie and P. Stamper (eds) *Medieval Rural Settlement: Britain and Ireland, AD 800–1600.* Oxford, Windgather Press, 151–171.

Smith, T. L. (1906) *The Itinerary in Wales of John Leland In or About The Years 1536–1539.* London, George Bell and Sons.

Sylvester, D. (1969) *The Rural Landscape of the Welsh Borderland: a study in historical geography.* London, MacMillan.

Thirsk, J. (1966) The Origin of the Common Fields. *Past & Present* 33, 142–147.

Thomas, D. (1963) *Agriculture in Wales during the Napoleonic Wars: A Study in the Geographic Interpretation of Historical Sources.* Cardiff, University of Wales Press.

Thomas, G. (trans.) (2001) *Dafydd ap Gwilym: His Poems.* Cardiff, University of Wales Press.

Thomas, G., Mcdonnell, G., Merkel, J. and Marshall, P. (2016) Technology, Ritual and Anglo-Saxon Agriculture: the biography of a plough coulter from Lyminge, Kent. *Antiquity* 90, 742–758.

Thorpe, L. (trans.) (1978) *Gerald of Wales: The Journey Through Wales and The Description of Wales.* London, Penguin.

Williams, G. (trans.) (1973) *Welsh Poems: Sixth Century to 1600.* London, Faber & Faber.

Williamson, T. (2003) *Shaping Medieval Landscapes: Settlement, Society, Environment.* Oxford, Windgather Press.

Williamson, T. (2013) *Environment, Society and Landscape in Early Medieval England: Time and Topography.* Woodbridge, Boydell Press.

CHAPTER TWO

The Fields of Britannia: continuity and change within the early medieval landscape

Stephen Rippon

The traditional view of what happened when Britain ceased to be part of the Roman Empire is one of social and economic collapse: the supply of money ceased, the market-based economy and manufacturing industry collapsed, and large parts of the countryside were deserted. Within a few decades, so the traditional story goes, mass immigration from the continent by peoples known as the Angles and the Saxons led to the native British population being largely replaced, and this was followed by the establishment of a new political order. This culminated in the emergence of a series of kingdoms that in places are still commemorated in modern names such as East Anglia (from the East Angles), Essex (from the East Saxons), and Wessex (from the West Saxons). There may, also, have been some continuity in western regions where the county-name of Devon, for example, is derived from that of the British kingdom and Roman *civitas* of the Dumnonii (Watts 2004, 186), and the name of the early medieval kingdom of 'Gwent' is derived from *Venta Silurum*, the Roman name for Caerwent (Charles-Edwards 2013, 17; Knight 2013, 32).

This traditional view of a catastrophic end to Roman Britain has been challenged on many fronts, although there remains a fundamental division within contemporary scholarship between those who study the Roman and the early medieval periods (and even more specifically the archaeology of the Anglo-Saxon eastern regions, and the surviving native communities in the west; *e.g.* Esmonde-Cleary 1989; 2014; Faulkner 2000; Hills 2003; Hamerow 2012; Gerrard 2013). We have, therefore, a Society for the Promotion of Roman Studies and a Society for Medieval Archaeology, and journals for *Britannia* and *Medieval Archaeology*. Period specialisations such as these are inevitable – we cannot all study all periods of archaeology – but they are also unhelpful in creating boundaries in our understanding of the past. This paper therefore focuses on the results of a project – *The Fields of Britannia* – that explicitly set out to explore the significance of the transition between the Roman and the medieval periods. It attempted to do this in three ways: firstly, through an analysis of palaeoenvironmental sequences (notably pollen) that allow us to reconstruct broad patterns of land-use; secondly, through an analysis of the relationships between Romano-British and medieval field systems; and thirdly, a study of how settlement patterns evolved across three contrasting regions. The results have all been published, in a major book (Rippon *et al.* 2015, *The Fields of Britannia*), a paper on the palaeo-economic evidence from animal bones and charred cereals (Rippon *et al.* 2014), and Fiona Fleming's (2016) PhD. This paper will review the results of that project, and reflect on its implications for Wales.

A regional approach to studying landscape change

There have been many studies of what happened at the end of Roman Britain (*e.g.* Esmonde-Cleary 1989; 2014; Higham 1992; Dark 1994; 2000; Faulkner 2000; Gerrard 2013) but the scarcity of well-dated archaeological evidence often leads to an approach based upon individual site biographies from widely scattered places. Until relatively recently, there was – for example – a small canon of classic sites where it was thought that the occupation of Roman settlements continued into the early medieval period such as Rivenhall in Essex (Rodwell and Rodwell 1986), Latimer in Buckinghamshire (Branigan 1971), Barnsley Park in Gloucestershire (Webster *et al.* 1985), and Wroxeter in Shropshire (Barker *et al.* 1997; Gaffney *et al.* 2007). Discussing these sites, however, involved traversing three regions of the British landscape – the South East, the Central Zone, and the West – that we now know were very different in character in the later medieval, early medieval, and Roman periods (Roberts and Wrathmell 2000a; 2000b; 2002; Smith *et al.* 2006; Wrathmell 2017). In periods with relatively little data, there is no alternative but to write narratives based upon the scraps of evidence that we have, but it is questionable what the fate of a Roman villa in a region that experienced extensive Anglo-Saxon influence tells us about landscape history in areas further west.

Archaeologists have, however, been surprisingly slow to recognise the complexity and significance of regional variation in landscape character in the Roman and early medieval periods. An early start was made with Fox's (1932) recognition of the upland/lowland divide, which amongst Romanists became an equally simplistic binary division between 'military and civilian' zones (*e.g.* Rivet 1964, fig. 9). Dark and Dark's (1997) substitution of the term 'villa landscape' for 'civil zone', and 'native landscape' for 'military zone', simply perpetuated this over-simplification and added a new and misleading dimension in suggesting that all lowland areas were characterised by villas when even a cursory examination of a distribution map shows that this is obviously not the case. Taylor's (2007) *Atlas of Roman Rural Settlement in England* was an important step forward, although it used twenty-first-century local government regions rather than divisions within the Romano-British landscape itself.

In *The Fields of Britannia* an attempt was made to identify a set of broad regions within which variations in landscape history could be studied in a more meaningful way. As the aims of that project were to cut across the traditional boundary between the Roman and the medieval, a set of regions had to be devised that would be relevant to both periods. Datasets such as the distributions of Roman villas, temples, mosaics, pottery kilns, and the urban hierarchy, were mapped alongside evidence for Anglo-Saxon burials and settlements associated with halls and *Grubenhäuser* as well as the well-known tripartite division of the English landscape based upon the significance of villages and open fields most recently mapped by Roberts and Wrathmell (2000a; 2002) as their South Eastern, Central, and Northern & Western Provinces (Fig. 2.1). The result was that the whole of Roman Britain south of Hadrian's Wall was divided into

FIGURE 2.1. Data sets indicative of regional variation in landscape character in the Roman and medieval periods. (A) the distribution of Romano-Celtic temples; (B) the numbers of mosaics in rural and urban buildings; (C) the products of regional mosaic schools; (D) Romano-British pottery kilns; (E) Anglo-Saxon cemeteries; (F) the Midland system of open field farming; (G) Rackham's countryside character types; (H) Roberts and Wrathmell's provinces with (shaded) the area of predominantly nucleated settlement extended into Wales; (I) the regions identified in *The Fields of Britannia* (after Jones and Mattingly 1990, maps 8.23, 6.24, 6.39, and 6.41; Hines 1990; Gray 1915, frontispiece; Rackham 1986, fig. 1; Roberts and Wrathmell 2000a, fig. 1.1, extended into Wales using Roberts 1987, fig. 1; Rippon *et al.* 2015, fig 2.11; drawn by Mike Rouillard and Stephen Rippon).

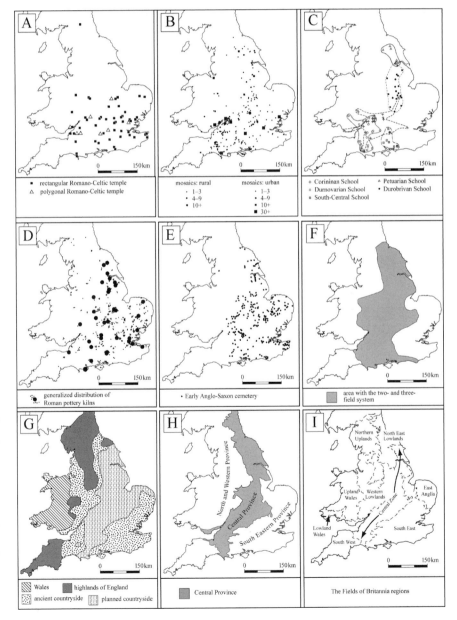

nine regions, each of which appear to have had a broad coherence in their character during the Roman and early medieval periods. This desire to identify regions which were meaningful in the past resulted in marked differences in their size which was particularly the case in Wales. 'Lowland Wales' comprised the coastal districts in the far south which were relatively Romanised, with a small number of villas and urban centres, and which in the medieval period saw the development of some villages and open fields along English lines. To the north lay 'Upland Wales' that was far less Romanised and saw little settlement nucleation or large-scale open field development.

Across most of Britain, the increase in archaeological survey and excavation following the introduction of PPG16 meant that satisfactory numbers of both palaeoenvironmental sequences and excavated Romano-British field systems were available in most regions, although unfortunately this was not the case in Wales. Whilst there were a large number of pollen sequence from upland areas, there had been very little analysis in the lowlands, although an initial assessment of the landscape immediately west of Cardiff has suggested that there are suitable sites for analysis (Davies *et al.* 2015) which the *Manifestations of Empire* project will be exploring further (see Davies this volume). At the time that *The Fields of Britannia* project was undertaking its work there was unfortunately also very little data available on the relationship between Romano-British and medieval field systems, and although the *Roman Rural Settlement Project* (Smith *et al.* 2016) has added some more sites to the Archaeology Data Services' Grey Literature Library, including some in Lowland Wales, there is still far less data from the two Welsh regions than the rest of Roman Britain (http://archaeologydataservice.ac.uk/archives/view/romangl/map.html). The discussion below will therefore summarise the results of *The Fields of Britannia* project as a whole, consider how Wales fits into this national picture, and consider some key data that has become available since *The Fields of Britannia* was published.

Changing patterns of land-use

Such is the scarcity of datable material culture in early medieval Wales that palaeoenvironmental research will always be of particular importance in understanding landscape change. It has been recognised for some time that the relatively few pollen sequences which straddle the Roman and early medieval periods in lowland areas of Britain did not support the traditional view that there had been an extensive woodland regeneration (*e.g.* Bell 1989; Dark 2000). Since then there has been a huge increase in data brought about by development-led archaeology and university research projects, and *The Fields of Britannia* sought to pull this together in the context of a regional comparison. The aim was to study broad regional differences in the major types of land-use at particular periods of time, and see how these patterns of land-use changed as Britain moved from the Roman through to the early medieval period. This was a piece of work that required generalisations to be made so that the 'big picture' could emerge, with the result that pollen was divided into species indicative of just four major land-use types: woodland, arable, improved pasture, and unimproved pasture. The Roman and early medieval periods were divided into four eras (AD 43–410, AD 411–499, AD 500–849, and AD 850–1066), and sites were grouped into the nine regions (South East, East Anglia, Central Zone, South West, Western Lowlands, North East Lowlands, Northern Uplands, Lowland Wales, and Upland Wales). It is recognised that within such broad areas there will have been very great differences in the land-use histories of different *pays*, but there are simply insufficient pollen sequences at present to study land-use at that more localised scale.

The results showed that in the Roman period there were some markedly different patterns of land-use (Fig. 2.2; Rippon *et al.* 2015, table 3.1). The Central Zone and East Anglia were the least wooded regions, with just 14% and 16% respectively of the pollen coming from trees and shrubs. It is important to

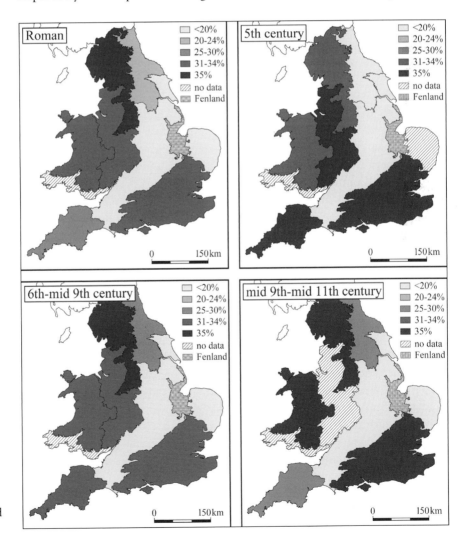

FIGURE 2.2. The percentage of Total Land Pollen from trees and shrubs in the Roman and early medieval periods.

appreciate that this does not mean that 14–16% of the landscape was covered in woodland as different plant species produce very different amounts of pollen: tree and grass pollen, for example, are always over represented, while arable pollen is always under represented (Fyfe *et al.* 2013). What these pollen percentages do show, however, is that the Central Zone (14%) and East Anglia (16%) were far less wooded in the Roman period than the South East (31%) and the Western Lowlands (33%). Unfortunately there was very little data from Lowland Wales, but for Upland Wales the figures for woodland (32%), improved pasture (44%), and unimproved pasture (23%) were comparable to the uplands of northern England.

There was also very marked regional variation in how land-use changed in the fifth century. In the Central Zone the proportion of tree pollen barely changed in the fifth century, and while unfortunately there are no pollen assemblages dated to the fifth century in East Anglia the figures for the Roman period and AD 500–849 are virtually identical, making it unlikely that there was a large increase in woodland in the fifth century that was entirely cleared by the sixth century. Indeed, very small increases in tree pollen may simply have been due to a failure to maintain laid hedges and coppiced woodland (Rippon *et al.* 2015, tables 5.2 and 6.2). In the Western Lowlands tree pollen increased marginally (from 33% to 37%), although in the South West the increase was somewhat greater (27% to 38%: Rippon *et al.* 2015, tables 7.2 and 8.2). Again, there is a lack of data from Lowland Wales, although when data from the 31 sites from Upland Wales are aggregated tree pollen was virtually unchanged, arable was constant, improved pasture fell only very slightly, and unimproved pasture rose very slightly (Rippon *et al.* 2015, table 11.3).

Two studies from upland Wales have appeared since *The Fields of Britannia* was published, and they confirm its conclusions for both the Roman and early medieval periods. Tudur Davies (2015; this volume) carried out an exemplary piece of multi-faceted geoarchaeological and palaeoenvironmental analysis in the landscape around Llyn Tegid (Lake Bala) in north Wales. The immediate post-Roman period saw firstly an expansion in heathland and then some woodland regeneration, alongside a decrease in pollen indicative of arable and pasture and a decline in sediment being washed into Llyn Tegid. Pollen analysis in the Carneddau Mountains above Penmaenmawr, also in North Wales (Caseldine *et al.* 2017), suggests that the Late Iron Age and Roman periods saw an increase in woodland clearance and an increase in pasture, whereas the early medieval period saw an increase in woodland and heather (although large amounts of grassland pollen show that there was still significant grazing activity). Unfortunately, this study's sampling intervals and very limited number of radiocarbon dates make it impossible to examine the Roman and early medieval periods in any more detail.

Traditionally the causes of land-use changes such as these have been attributed to simplistic monocausal factors, most notably climate change. In Upland Wales it is striking that many palaeoenvironmental sequences do

FIGURE 2.3. Compiled palaeoclimatic proxies for the first millennium AD. The Crag Cave speleothem indicates palaeo-temperature, while the northern Britain water table variability is a palaeo-precipitation record. Values for the compiled European summer temperature and Greenland ice core record are expressed as anomalies from the twentieth-century average. Vertical lines indicate the first millennium AD average. Sources: A: McDermott *et al.* (2001); B: Luterbacher *et al.* (2016); C: Vinther *et al.* (2009); D: Charman *et al.* (2006); E: Büntgen *et al.* (2011) (drawn by Ralph Fyfe).

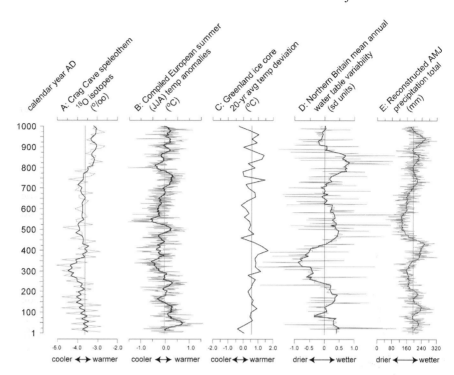

indeed show an increase in pollen indicative of increased wetness at this time, and this tallies with a wide range of other palaeoenvironmental evidence that the Late Roman and earliest post-Roman periods saw increased precipitation (*e.g.* Charman *et al.*'s (2006) synthesis of testate amoebae assemblages from ombrotrophic (*i.e.* rain-fed) bogs across northern Britain: Fig. 2.3). This period of increased wetness also appears to correspond to declining temperatures, seen for example in oxygen isotopes from a speleothem (stalagmite) in south-west Ireland (McDermott *et al.* 2001), Greenlandic ice cores (Vinther *et al.* 2009), and in Luterbacher *et al.*'s (2016) synthesis of a wide range of proxy records from across mainland Europe (see Rippon and Fyfe 2018 for a general discussion of the palaeoclimate data from this period). Although some have argued that climate change was a major driver in the decline of Roman Britain as a whole (*e.g.* Jones 1996), this is unlikely to have been the case. Climate change will affect different regions in different ways and the physically more marginal environments within Britain, where precipitation is higher and temperatures lower – making growing seasons shorter – are far more vulnerable than lowland areas. A slight increase in rainfall, or shortening of the growing season, in Upland Wales for example could have had serious implications for subsistence based farmers, whereas in the fertile lowlands of Wales' coastal plain – and indeed the other lowland areas that made up the majority of Roman Britain – the growing season was far longer than necessary for growing crops and so a slight reduction will have had relatively little impact.

In fifth-century Britain there was, however, another factor at work – the collapse of the tax-driven and market-based economy – and this will also have affected different regions in different ways. The impact of Britain ceasing to be part of the Roman Empire will have been felt hardest in those regions where society was most dependent on the Roman socio-economic system, which in the case of Wales will have been the southern lowlands that were the most highly Romanised (reflected for example by a series of villas scattered across the countryside including in the vicinity of towns such as Caerwent). In these areas, communities were acquiring manufactured goods from across Roman Britain: at Biglis, Llandough, and Whitton, in the Vale of Glamorgan, for example, pottery came from as far afield as Gloucestershire, Dorset, Oxfordshire, Mancetter-Hartshill in Warwickshire, and the New Valley (Jarrett and Wrathmell 1981, 111–45; Owen Jones 1988; Parkhouse 1988). It was in Romanised regions such as these, where farmers were producing a surplus in order to sell it at market, pay their taxes, and buy manufactured goods, that the collapse of the Roman economy will have had its greatest impact, and without these drivers for producing an agricultural surplus we might expect a decline in the intensity of agriculture in these more Romanised regions. It is, therefore, extremely frustrating that we do not as yet have good palaeoenvironmental sequences from these lowland districts in order to explore what impact the collapse of the Roman economy had on those more Romanised areas. In contrast, in the uplands – where the economy was more subsistence-based – the impact of Britain ceasing to be part of the Roman Empire may have gone almost unnoticed and here it is possible that climate change was a factor in the declining agricultural intensity.

Recent palaeoenvironmental studies are also shedding important light on an agricultural revival that is evident several centuries later. A number of early pollen studies suggest that there was some clearance of woodland and increase in agriculture around the later seventh to early ninth centuries, a period that historians have referred to as the 'long eighth century' (Hanson and Wickham 2000; Wickham 2005; Rippon 2010). Tudur Davies' (2015) work around Llyn Tegid shows that – in common with many other areas across Upland Wales – the post-Roman decline in agriculture was reversed around the seventh and eighth centuries with a reduction in woodland and heathland, and an increase in arable and pasture. There is other evidence for an intensification of agriculture around this time, such as the construction of corn driers (*e.g.* West Angle Bay in Pembrokeshire: Groom *et al.* 2011) that appears to be contemporary with changes in land-holding reflected in documentary sources, such as the granting of land to the Church by non-royal individuals (*e.g.* the Llandaff charters: Davies 1978). This was happening at the same time as large estates were fragmenting, and the smaller units so created were increasingly associated with specific settlements and named persons (Davies 1978, 10–13). The climatic data for this period are also fairly clear in showing that the mid-seventh through to the early ninth centuries saw increased wetness (*e.g.* Charman *et al.* 2006;

Büntgen *et al.* 2011), although the temperature data are contradictory with the broad trend across Europe appearing to be for warmer conditions (Luterbacher *et al.* 2016) but Ireland (Fig. 2.3; McDermott *et al.* 2001) and Greenland seeing cooler conditions (Vinther *et al.* 2009; and see Rippon and Fyfe 2018).

This trend towards agricultural expansion during the 'long eighth century' in Wales is also seen elsewhere (Rippon *et al.* 2006; Rippon 2017). It manifests itself in a wide variety of ways including investment in infrastructure such as watermills, crop processing facilities, causeways, and fish-traps that are found right across southern England from the Thames Estuary to the West Midlands and the West Country (summarised in Rippon 2010; 2012; 2017). Another manifestation of this intensification may have been the move towards the nucleation of settlement patterns into villages, and the associated laying out of open fields, but this was restricted to England's Central Zone and East Anglia which covered just part of the far wider area that saw agricultural intensification during the 'long eighth century'. The reasons why communities in England's Central Zone and East Anglia decided to restructure their landscapes in this way – and equally why communities living outside these regions did not – has been much debated (*e.g.* Williamson 2003; 2013; Partida *et al.* 2013; Williamson *et al.* 2013; Hall 2014; Rippon 2014), and the possible reasons need not concern us here. What is important in the context of this paper, and indeed the volume as a whole, is that Wales shared in the underlying factors that lay behind this period of economic growth and social innovation that led to agricultural expansion during the 'long eighth century'.

The relationship between Romano-British field systems and the historic landscape of today

The second strand of research within *The Fields of Britannia* project was an exploration of the relationship between excavated Romano-British field systems and the historic landscape of today. This sprang from various observations that in places there appeared to be a relationship between Romano-British and medieval field systems, and in particular Romano-British ditches running underneath the headlands of medieval open fields (*e.g.* Taylor and Fowler 1978; Upex 2003; Gerrard with Aston 2007). Following Williamson's (1987) pioneering work on 'co-axial' landscapes that appeared to have been overlain by, and so pre-date, Roman roads there was also the possibility that continuity in field systems existed outside those areas with open fields (*e.g.* White 2003; Bryant *et al.* 2005; and see Hinton 1997; Williamson 1998; 2008 for alternative views).

The Fields of Britannia set out to explore how widespread the evidence is for the potential survival of Romano-British field systems through a review of the published and unpublished literature across Roman Britain (note that the project took place before the Roman Rural Settlement Project's database was available, and enhancement of the ADS Grey Literature Library that it brought about). This was done in two ways: firstly, by establishing where there is excavated stratigraphic evidence for late Romano-British ditches having been maintained (*e.g.* recut) into the medieval period, and secondly – where there were no excavated medieval field boundaries – by establishing the relationship between the Romano-British field systems and the historic landscape of today. The analysis set some clear parameters. Only Romano-British boundaries dated broadly to the Roman period, or specifically to the Late Roman period were included: any that were abandoned during the first to third centuries were excluded from the analysis as their relationship to any overlying medieval field systems tells us nothing about what happened in the fifth century as they had already been abandoned. Similarly, field systems revealed through aerial photography, geophysical survey, and/or earthwork survey were only included if they were positively dated to the Roman period through excavation.

Another important parameter in *The Fields of Britannia* project was that the analysis only included Romano-British sites that were overlain by field systems of medieval character, and so sites in areas that became woodland or unenclosed pasture in the medieval period were excluded. It is also important to appreciate that while a Romano-British field system on a different orientation to the overlying medieval one is clear evidence for a discontinuity, this need not have happened in the fifth century, and may not have been associated with a prolonged period of abandonment: while the Romano-British field system may have continued in use until, for example, the eighth century, and then have been swept away as part of a replanning of the landscape, it may equally have been deserted in the fifth century and the area only recolonised several hundred years later. Where a Romano-British field system shares the same orientation as its medieval successor it is also important to remember that this does not automatically mean that the two are related. It is possible, for example, for a field system to be abandoned, and when the area was recolonised for a new field system to have been established on the same orientation as the first one because the latter was influenced by surviving earthworks from the earlier landscape. This is, however, most likely where the area had not been totally abandoned as that will have resulted in woodland regeneration, and the clearance of that woodland will have been an extremely destructive process (*e.g.* the dragging away of tree trunks and grubbing out of tree stumps, is likely to have severely damaged the ephemeral remains of any relict field systems). Experiments have shown that woodland will regenerate within 30 years if land is not grazed by animals (Harmer *et al.* 2001), and so the common orientation of Romano-British and medieval field systems does suggest that there was not a prolonged period of abandonment (although there could have been a change in land-use from arable to pasture).

It is also possible that a Romano-British field system was on the same orientation as a medieval one due to topographical considerations (*e.g.* field boundaries sometimes run perpendicular to contours). This is, however,

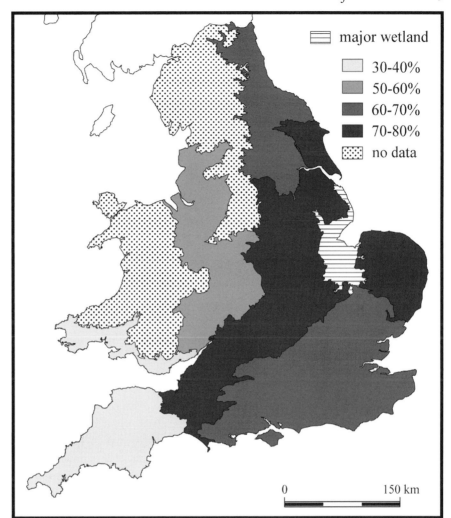

FIGURE 2.4. The extent to which excavated Romano-British field boundaries across the different regions share the same orientation and/ or alignment as historic landscapes characterised by former medieval open fields or closes: *The Fields of Britannia* Figure 12.7 amended in the light of this study (drawn by Chris Smart).

likely to have been equally significant across all regions, and the fact that the correlation between Romano-British and medieval field systems is so much stronger in some areas compared to others suggests that other factors were at work. In East Anglia (73%), England's Central Zone (70%), and the North East Lowlands (67%), for example, there is a relatively strong correlation between Romano-British and medieval field systems and this fits with the pollen evidence in suggesting that these regions had been the most extensively cleared of woodland in the Roman period and saw the least post-Roman woodland regeneration (Fig. 2.4). The potential continuity between Romano-British and medieval field systems is slightly lower in the South East (63%) which also fits with the pollen evidence which shows a greater increase in trees and shrubs. The lowland region with the lowest figure for the correlation between Romano-British and medieval field systems is the South West at just 38% (Rippon *et al.* 2015, table 3.7), although pollen evidence suggests that the discontinuity may have occurred around the eighth century rather than the fifth century.

The Fields of Britannia in Wales

Unfortunately, although a number of Romano-British rural sites have been excavated in Lowland Wales – and a lot more data is available following the Roman Rural Settlement Project compared to when *The Fields of Britannia* was published – relatively few of them fulfil the criteria for analysis outlined above. The distribution of sites on the Roman Rural Settlement Project map looks promising, although some were only occupied in the Iron Age (*e.g.* Woodbarn in Wiston, Pembrokeshire: Vyner 1986), and in other cases reports lack plans, which means that the excavated Roman features cannot be related to the historic landscape (*e.g.* Williams 1996). Several sites were abandoned before the fourth century (*e.g.* Mynydd Bychan: Savory 1954; 1955), or were in locations where the orientation of both the Romano-British and medieval fieldscapes are clearly determined by very strong topographical influences such as being adjacent to the coast (*e.g.* Cold Knap in Barry: Evans *et al.* 1985). Other sites with Romano-British occupation lay within Iron Age hillforts that are not overlain with medieval field systems making it impossible to carry out a *Fields of Britannia*-type analysis *(e.g.* Bulwarks in Porthkerry: Davies 1973; Castle Ditches in Llancarfan: Hogg 1976; High Pennard on Gower: Williams 1941; Porth y Rhaw near Solva: Crane and Murphy 2010). The continued tradition of curvilinear enclosures – stronger in western districts than in the east – is problematic as they give the impression of discontinuity when the overlying medieval field systems are rectilinear in character, but this may be misleading as the form of any field systems associated with the Romano-British settlement are unknown (*e.g.* Walesland Rath in Pembrokeshire: Wainwright 1971). Although Lowland Wales was an area that was extensively settled in both the Roman and medieval periods there were still areas of unenclosed land, and a number of Romano-British settlements lie in these areas where there are no medieval field systems with which their orientation can be compared (*e.g.* Dinas Powys Common: Evans 2001, fig 12; Llawhaden: Williams and Mytum 1998; Stackpole Warren: Benson *et al.* 1990; Whitton: Jarrett and Wrathmell 1981; Wyndcliff near Porthcasseg: Evans 2001, fig. 10; Wiston: Meek 2017). While is it tempting to argue that this represents discontinuity, *The Fields of Britannia* methodology only included sites where there was clear evidence of boundaries in both periods so that they could be compared, rather than speculating on whether the absence of field systems in one period or another was due to abandonment or simply a change in land-use.

There are, however, a number of places across Lowland Wales where Romano-British landscapes do appear to have been on the same orientation as excavated medieval field systems and/or the historic landscape as depicted on the earliest maps. At Crickhowell Road in Trowbridge, near Cardiff, for example, a sequence of three early Romano-British ditches, all oriented NW–

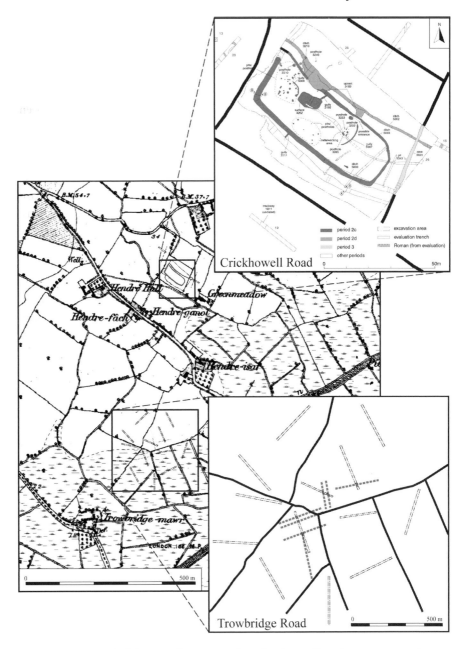

FIGURE 2.5. Two Romano-British landscapes on very similar orientations to historic landscapes whose character is suggestive of a medieval date: Crickhowell Road and Trowbridge Road in Trowbridge, near Cardiff, on the edge of the Wentlooge Level (after Brett 2005; Brett *et al.* 2009).

SE, were succeeded by a sub-rectangular third- to fourth-century enclosure associated with a series of field boundary ditches that were either on the same orientation or at right angles to it and which also contained Romano-British pottery (Fig. 2.5; Brett 2005; Brett *et al.* 2009, figs 3 and 5). This Romano-British landscape was cut by an excavated post-medieval ditch that was at right angles to the late Roman landscape, while field boundaries that appear on the nineteenth-century Ordnance Survey First Edition Six Inch map share the exact same orientation as the late Romano-British enclosure and associated field system. To the south, by Trowbridge Road, a series of evaluation trenches revealed another Romano-British landscape (Fig. 2.5; Havard 2004). It can be difficult to accurately determine the orientation of linear features in relatively narrow evaluation trenches, but when the projected lines of the Romano-British features are plotted it can be seen that they share the same orientation as a series of rectangular fields within the historic landscape in the southern half of the site.

Trowbridge lies on the edge of an extensive reclaimed wetland – the Wentlooge Level – south-west of the Roman legionary fortress at Caerleon. The historic landscape of the Wentlooge Level is characterised by a series of very long, straight-sided fields and a series of excavated late Romano-British ditches at Rumney Great Wharf have been shown to share the same orientation to these medieval/modern fields (Fulford *et al.* 1994). More recent work in the northern part of the Wentlooge Levels has similarly found a series of ditches that conform in orientation to the historic landscape at Great Pencarn (Yates 1998). This apparent continuity on the Wentlooge Level contrasts with the neighbouring Caldicot Level where the smaller-scale Romano-British drainage ditches were all abandoned (Meddens and Beasley 2001).

Potential continuity is also seen elsewhere across Lowland Wales. At Upper Neeston in Herbrandston, Pembrokeshire, a rectilinear field system dating to the third and fourth centuries was on the same orientation as the adjacent parish boundary (Fig. 2.6; Barber 2014), while the enclosure and field system at Thornwell Farm near Chepstow is on the same orientation as the historic landscape of today (Hughes 1996). Elsewhere the evidence is far from conclusive. At Sudbrook Road in Portskewett and Newhouse Farm near Chepstow the late Roman landscapes were on the same orientation as the medieval, although this may have been due to their proximity to the fen-edge (Brett *et al.* 2004; Ponsford and Robic 2008). At Llantwit Major the modern field boundaries closest to the site are on the same orientation as the excavated villa and an associated enclosure complex revealed through a recent geophysical survey (Nash-Williams 1952; Young 2016), although slight changes in orientation as they approach the site suggest that they were respecting an extant earthwork: the orientation of boundaries within the surrounding historic landscape is different to that of the villa. At RAF St Athan (Barber *et al.* 2006) the evidence is also difficult to interpret: most of the Romano-British enclosure ditches were on a different orientation to the medieval and post-medieval field boundary pattern, although the Romano-British Trackway 1 was on the same orientation suggesting that it may have survived in some form to influence the layout of the later landscape. The villas at Ely (Wheeler 1955) and Llandough both near Cardiff (Owen-John 1988), Five Lanes near Caerwent (Evans 2001, fig. 11) as well as the enclosures/field systems at Biglis (Parkhouse 1988), Caldicot Quarry (Vyner and Allen 1988), Church Farm in Caldicot (Insole 2000; Corney 2009) and Ifton (Ellis and King 2012), however, appear to be on a different orientation to the overlying historic landscape.

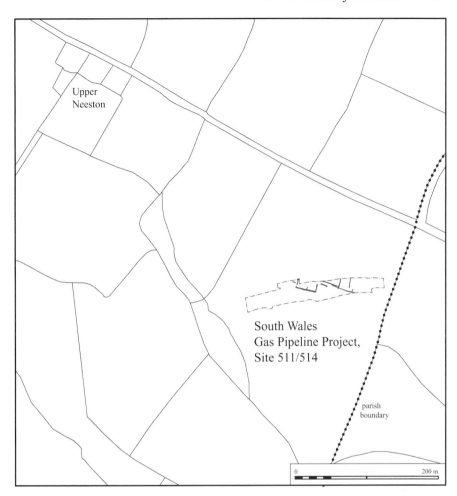

FIGURE 2.6. Romano-British features on a very similar orientation to the historic landscape at Upper Neeston in Herbrandston in Pembrokeshire (after Barber and Hart 2014).

The enclosure complex at Trewen, near Caerwent, is similarly on a different orientation to the historic landscape, although typologically these cropmarks could be Iron Age or Romano-British and so cannot be included in this analysis (Coflein: NPRN 302142).

When *The Fields of Britannia* undertook its analysis there were too few sites with available reports to make any analysis worthwhile, although subsequent data collection and enhancement of the ADS Grey Literature Library by the Roman Rural Settlement Project has now improved the situation. While the number of sites that meet the criteria for this analysis is still very small, 9 out of 21 sites suggest that the Romano-British landscape might be related to that of the medieval period, a figure (43%) that is comparable to the South West of England (38%) but far lower than the Central Zone (70%) and the South East (63%). This does not mean that there was necessarily a major dislocation in the landscape in the late fourth or fifth centuries, as it may have occurred at a later date, for example following the Anglo-Norman Conquest.

Discussion

There have been several major research projects in recent years that have sought to exploit the huge increase in data brought about by development-led archaeology. Some have focused just on England (*e.g.* the EngLAID Project: Gosden 2013) or a single period (*e.g.* The Roman Rural Settlement Project: Smith *et al.* 2006), whereas *The Fields of Britannia* explicitly set out to cut across a traditional period boundary (the Roman to early medieval transition) and to embrace both England and Wales. The project as a whole has suggested considerable continuity across most lowland areas in broad patterns of land-use and the extent to which field systems may have continued in use. There does appear to have been a decline in the intensity with which the landscape was exploited, something that is to be expected as the taxation-driven market-based economy collapsed, and some more marginal areas of the landscape were deserted. There does not, however, appear to have been a widespread woodland regeneration. Where discontinuities between Romano-British and medieval field systems have been identified it may have been the intensification of agriculture during the 'long eighth century' that was more significant than the socio-economic changes of the fifth century. In parts of southern Wales and northern England the decades following the Norman Conquest also saw major transformations of the landscape following the Flemish colonisation of south Pembrokeshire and 'Harrying of the North' respectively (Austin 2005; Rippon 2014; Creighton and Rippon 2017).

Unfortunately, it is difficult to establish the degree of potential continuity between Romano-British and medieval field systems in Wales due to a lack of sites that meet the necessary criteria, and the same is true of land-use due to a lack of suitable pollen sites. In upland areas palaeoenvironmental analysis has, however, been very successful in establishing broad patterns of land-use change, and the decline in intensity seen in the immediate post-Roman period is not a surprise. That this was reversed during the 'long eighth century' in Wales is particularly interesting as this confirms a wide range of other evidence that this intensification of agriculture was seen right across southern Britain both in areas that saw the transformation of landscapes through the creation of villages and open fields, and those that did not. It is to be hoped that in due course more suitable sites will be found for pollen analysis in the more densely settled and Romanised lowland areas so that their response to the collapse of the Roman economy can be explored.

Acknowledgements

The Fields of Britannia project was generously funded by the Leverhulme Trust (award F/00 144/B1). The synthesis of the palaeoenvironmental data was undertaken by Ben Pears, and the analysis of the field systems by Chris Smart. I would like to thank Ralph Fyfe for permission to reproduce Figure 3, and for discussing recent developments in climate change data, and Neil Holbrook for permission to reproduce the plan of Crickhowell Road in Figure 2.5.

References

Austin, D. (2005) Little England Beyond Wales: re-defining the myth. *Landscapes* 6(ii), 30–62.

Barber, A. (2014) South Wales Gas Pipeline Project, Site 511/514, Land South-East of Upper Neeston, Herbrandston, Pembrokeshire. Cotswold Archaeology Report 13254 https://doi.org/10.5284/1035246 (accessed 06.01.19).

Barber, A., Cox, S. and Hancocks, A. (2006) A Late Iron Age and Roman Farmstead at RAF St Athan, Vale of Glamorgan. Evaluation and Excavation 2002–03. *Archaeologia Cambrensis* 155, 49–115.

Barker, P., White, R., Pretty, K., Bird, H., and Corbishley, M. (1997) *The Baths Basilica Wroxeter: Excavations 1966–90*. London, English Heritage.

Bell, M. (1989) Environmental archaeology as an index of continuity and change in the medieval landscape. In M. Aston, D. Austin and C. Dyer (eds) *The Rural Settlements of Medieval England*. Oxford, Basil Blackwell, 269–286.

Benson, D. G., Evans, J. G., Williams, G. H., Darvill, T. and David, A. (1990) Excavations at Stackpole Warren, Dyfed. *Proceedings of Prehistoric Society* 56, 179–245.

Branigan, K. (1971) *Latimer: Belgic, Roman, Dark Age and Early Modern Farms*. Bristol, Chess Valley Archaeological and Historical Society.

Brett, M. (2005), Land Between Crickhowell Road and Willowbrook Drive, Trowbridge, Cardiff: Archaeological Evaluation. Cotswold Archaeology Report 05084 http://reports.cotswoldarchaeology.co.uk/content/uploads/2014/07/1945-Crickhowell-Rd-Cardiff-Eval-05084-complete.pdf (accessed 06.01.19).

Brett, M., Holbrook, N., McSloy, E. (2009) Romano-British and Medieval Occupation at Sudbrook Road, Portskewett, Monmouthshire: Excavations in 2009. Cotswold Archaeology https://doi.org/10.5284/1035241 (accessed 06.01.19).

Brett, M., McSloy, E. R. and Holbrook, N. (2009) A Roman Enclosure at Crickhowell Road, Trowbridge, Cardiff. Evaluation and Excavation 2005–6. *Archaeologia Cambrensis* 158, 131–166.

Bryant, S., Perry, B. and Williamson, T. (2005) A 'Relict Landscape' in South-East Hertfordshire: archaeological and topographical investigations in the Wormley area. *Landscape History* 27, 5–16.

Büntgen, U., Tegel, W., Nicolussi, K., McCormick, M., Frank, D., Trouet, V., Kaplan, J. O., Herzig, F., Heussner, K.-U., Wanner, H., Luterbacher, J. and Esper, J. (2011) 2500 Years of European Climate Variability and Human Susceptibility. *Science* 331, 578–582.

Caseldine, A. E., Griffiths, C., Roberts, J., Smith, G., and Williams, J. (2017) Land Use and Environmental History of Waun Llanfair, an Upland Landscape Above Penmaenmawr, North Wales. *Archaeologia Cambrensis* 166, 89–140.

Charles-Edwards, T. M. (2013) *Wales and the Britons 350–1064*. Oxford, Oxford University Press.

Charman, D. J., Blundell, A., Chiverrell, R. C., Hendon, D. and Langdon, P. G. (2006) Compilation of Non-Annually Resolved Holocene Proxy Climate Records: stacked Holocene peatland palaeo-water table reconstructions from northern Britain. *Quaternary Science Reviews* 25, 336–50.

Coflein NPRN 302142: National Monuments Record of Wales database at http://www.coflein.gov.uk/en/site/302142/details/trewen-caerwent-enclosed-settlement (accessed 06.01.19)

Corney, M. (2009) Archaeological Investigations Off Church Road, Caldicot, Monmouthshire. *Archaeology in Wales* 49, 11–24.

Crane, P. and Murphy, K. (2010) The Excavation of a Coastal Promontory Fort at Porth y Rhaw, Solva, Pembrokeshire 1995–98. *Archaeologia Cambrensis* 159, 53–98.

Creighton, O. and Rippon, S. (2017) Conquest, colonisation and the countryside: archaeology and the mid-11th- to mid-12th-century rural landscape. In D. Hadley and C. Dyer (eds) *The Archaeology of the Eleventh Century: Continuities and Transformations. SMA Monograph 38.* Abingdon, Routledge/The Society for Medieval Archaeology, 57–87.

Dark, K. (1994) *Civitas to Kingdom: British Political Continuity 300–800.* London, Leicester University Press.

Dark, K. (2000) *Britain and the End of the Roman Empire.* Stroud, Tempus.

Dark, K. and Dark. P. (1997) *The Landscape of Roman Britain.* Stroud, Sutton.

Dark, P. (2000) *The Environment of Britain in the First Millennium A.D.* London, Duckworth.

Davies, T. (2015) *Early Medieval Llyn Tegid: An Environmental Landscape Study.* Unpublished PhD Thesis, University of Sheffield.

Davies, T., Davis, O. and Seaman, A. (2015) The Eastern Vale of Glamorgan Palaeoenvironmental Resource Assessment Project: summary report. *Archaeology in Wales* 54, 164–167.

Davies, J. L. (1973) An Excavation at the Bulwarks, Porthkerry, Glamorgan, 1968. *Archaeologia Cambrensis* 122, 85–97.

Davies, W. (1978) Land and Power in Early Medieval Wales. *Past and Present* 81, 3–23.

Ellis, P. and King, R. (2012) Prehistoric, Roman and Medieval Features at Ifton Manor, Rogiet, Monmouthshire. *Archaeology in Wales* 51, 79–92.

Esmonde-Cleary, S. (1989) *The Ending of Roman Britain.* London, B. T. Batsford.

Esmonde-Cleary, S. (2014) Introduction: the Roman Society and the study of AD 410. In F. K. Haarer (ed.) *AD 410: The History and Archaeology of Late Roman and Post-Roman Britain.* London, Society for the Promotion of Roman Studies, 1–12.

Evans, E. (2001) Romano-British South East Wales Settlement Survey: Final report. Swansea: Glamorgan-Gwent Archaeological Trust Report 2001/023 https://doi.org/10.5284/1037299 (accessed 06.01.19).

Evans, E., Dowdell, G. and Thomas, H. J. (1985) A Third-Century Maritime Establishment at Cold Knap, Barry, South Glamorgan. *Britannia* 16, 57–125.

Faulkner, N. (2000) *The Decline and Fall of Roman Britain.* Stroud, Tempus.

Fleming, F. (2016) *A Persistence of Place: A Study of Continuity and Regionality in the Roman and Early Medieval Rural Settlement Patterns of Norfolk, Kent and Somerset. BAR British Series 626.* Oxford, British Archaeological Reports.

Fox, C. (1932) *The Personality of Britain: its Influence on Inhabitant and Invader in Prehistoric and Early Historic Times.* Cardiff, National Museum of Wales.

Frere, S. (1967) *Britannia: A History of Roman Britain.* London, Routledge Keegan and Paul.

Fulford, M. G., Allen, J. R. L. and Rippon, S. (1994) The Settlement and Drainage of the Wentlooge Level, Gwent: survey and excavation at Rumney Great Wharf, 1992. *Britannia* XXV, 175–211.

Fyfe, R. M., Twiddle, C., Sugita, S., Gaillard, M-J., Barratt, P., Caseldine, C. J., Dodson, J., Edwards, K. J., Farrell, M., Froyd, C., Grant, M. J., Huckerby, E., Innes, J. B., Shaw, H. and Waller, M. (2013) The Holocene Vegetation Cover of Britain and Ireland: overcoming problems of scale and discerning patterns of openness. *Quaternary Science Reviews* 73, 132–148.

Gaffney, V., White, R. and Goodchild, H. (2007) *Wroxeter, the Cornovii and the Urban Process: Final Report of the Wroxeter Hinterland Project 1994–7. Volume 1: Researching the Hinterland*. Portsmouth, R. I., Journal of Roman Archaeology Supplementary Series 68.

Gerrard, C. with Aston, M. (2007) *The Shapwick Project, Somerset. A Rural Landscape Explored*. Leeds, Society for Medieval Archaeology.

Gerrard, J. (2013) *The Ruin of Britain: An Archaeological Perspective*. Cambridge, Cambridge University Press.

Gosden, C. (2013) Landscapes and Scale: some introductory thoughts. *Landscapes* 14(i), 3–6.

Gray, H. L. (1915) *English Field Systems*. Cambridge, Mass., Harvard University Press.

Groom, P., Schlee, D., Hughes, G., Crane, P., Ludlow, G. and Murphy, K. (2011) Two Early Medieval Cemeteries in Pembrokeshire: Brownslade Barrow and West Angle Bay. *Archaeologia Cambrensis* 160, 133–203.

Hall, D. (2014) *The Open Fields of England*. Oxford, Oxford University Press.

Hamerow, H. (2012) *Rural Settlements and Society in Anglo-Saxon England*. Oxford, Oxford University Press.

Hanson, L. and Wickham, C. (2000) *The Long Eighth Century: Production, Distribution and Demand*. Leiden, Brill.

Harmer, R., Peterken, G., Kerr, G. and Paulton, P. (2001) Vegetation Change During 100 Years of Development of Two Secondary Woodlands in Abandoned Arable Lands. *Biological Conservation* 101, 291–304.

Hart, J. (2014) South Wales Gas Pipeline Project, Site 508, Land at Conkland Hill, Wiston, Pembrokeshire. Cotswold Archaeology Report 13251 https://doi.org/10.5284/1035245 (accessed 06.01.19).

Havard, T. (2004) Areas 9–12, Trowbridge Road, St Mellons, Cardiff. Cotswold Archaeology Report 04066. https://doi.org/10.5284/1035239; NB the plans are only available from the Cotswold Archaeology website: http://legacy-reports.cotswoldarchaeology.co.uk/report/st-mellons (accessed 06.01.19).

Higham, N. (1992) *Rome, Britain and the Anglo-Saxons*. London, Seaby.

Hills, C. (2003) *The Origins of the English*. London, Duckworth.

Hines, J. (1990) Philology, archaeology and the *adventus Saxonum vel Anglorum*. In A. Bammesberger and A. Wollmann (eds) *Britain 400–600: Language and History*. Heidelberg, Carl Winter Universitätsverlag, 17–36.

Hinton, D. A. (1997) The 'Scole-Dickleburgh system' examined. *Landscape History* 19, 5–12.

Hogg, A. H. A. (1976) Castle Ditches, Llancarfan. *Archaeologica Cambrensis* 125, 13–39.

Hughes, G. (1996) *The Excavation of a Late Prehistoric and Romano-British Settlement at Thornwell Farm, Chepstow, Gwent 1992. BAR British Series 244*. Oxford, British Archaeological Reports.

Insole, P. (2000) The Archaeological Excavation of a Romano-British Farmstead at Church Farm, Church Road, Caldicot, Monmouthshire. *Archaeology in Wales* 40, 20–33.

Knight, J. (2013) *South Wales from the Romans to the Normans*. Stroud, Amberley Publishing.

Jarrett, M. G. and Wrathmell, S. (1981) *Whitton: An Iron Age and Roman Farmstead in South Glamorgan*. Cardiff, Cardiff University Press.

Jones, B. and Mattingly, D. (1990) *An Atlas of Roman Britain*. Oxford, Blackwell.

Jones, M. E. (1996) *The End of Roman Britain*. Ithaca, Cornell University Press.

Luterbacher, J., Werner, J. P., Smerdon, J. E., Fernández-Donado, L., González-Rouco, F. J., Barriopedro, D., Ljungqvist, F. C, Büntgen, U., Zorita, E., Wagner, S., Esper, J., McCarroll, D., Toreti, A., Frank, D., Jungclaus, J. H., Barriendos, M., Bertolin, C.,

Bothe, O., Brázdil, R., Camuffo, D., Dobrovolný, P., Gagen, P., García-Bustamante, E., Ge, Q., Gómez-Navarro, J. J., Guiot, J., Hao, Z., Hegerl, G. C., Holmgren, K., Klimenko, V. V., Martín-Chivelet, J., Pfister, C., Roberts, N., Schindler, A., Schurer, A., Solomina, O, von Gunten, L., Wahl, E., Wanner, H., Wetter, O., Xoplaki, E., Yuan, N., Zanchettin, D., Zhang, H. and Zerefos, C. (2016) European Summer Temperatures Since Roman Times, *Environmental Research Letters* 11(2), 1–12.

McDermott, F., Mattey, D. P. and Hawkesworth, C. (2001) Centennial-Scale Holocene Climate Variability Revealed by a High-Resolution Speleothem δ¹⁸O Record from SW Ireland. *Science* 294, 1328–1331.

Meddens, F. M. and Beasley, M. (2001) Roman Seasonal Wetland Pasture Exploitation Near Nash, on the Gwent Levels, Wales. *Britannia* 32, 143–184.

Meek, J. (2017) The Newly-Identified Roman Fort and Settlement at Wiston. Pembrokeshire. *Archaeologia Cambrensis* 166, 175–212.

Nash-Williams, V. E. (1952) The Roman Villa at Llantwit Major, Glamorgan. *Archaeologia Cambrensis* 102(i), 89–163.

Owen-Jones, H. S. (1988) Llandough: the rescue excavation of a multi-period site near Cardiff, South Glamorgan. In D. M. Robinson (ed.) *Biglis, Caldicot & Llandough: Three Late Iron Age and Romano-British Sites in South-East Wales.* BAR British Series 188. Oxford, British Archaeological Reports, 123–178.

Parkhouse, J. (1988) Excavations at Biglis, South Glamorgan. In D. M. Robinson (ed.) *Biglis, Caldicot & Llandough: Three Late Iron Age and Romano-British Sites in South-East Wales.* BAR British Series 188. Oxford, British Archaeological Reports, 1–64.

Parkhouse, J. and Evans, E. (1996) *Excavations in Cowbridge, South Glamorgan, 1977–88.* BAR British Series 245. Oxford, British Archaeological Reports.

Partida, T., Hall, D. and Foard, G. (2013) *An Atlas of Northamptonshire: The Medieval and Early-Modern Landscape.* Oxford, Oxbow.

Ponsford, M. and Robic, J. Y. (2008) Newhouse Park, Chepstow, 1995–2007: A prehistoric and Roman site on the Severn Estuary. Cardiff, Cardiff Archaeological Consultants https://doi.org/10.5284/1035946 (accessed 06.01.19).

Rackham, O. (1986) *The History of the Countryside.* London, J. M. Dent and Sons.

Rippon, S. (2010) Landscape change during the 'long eighth century' in southern England. In N. J. Higham and M. J. Ryan (eds) *The Landscape Archaeology of Anglo-Saxon England.* Woodbridge, Boydell Press, 39–64.

Rippon, S. (2012) *Making Sense of a Historic Landscape.* Oxford, Oxford University Press.

Rippon, S. (2014) *Beyond the Medieval Village: The Diversification of Landscape Character in Southern Britain* (2nd edition). Oxford, Oxford University Press.

Rippon, S. (2017) Marshlands and other wetlands. In M. Clegg-Hyer and D. Hooke (eds) *Water and Environment in the Anglo-Saxon World* (*Volume III of the material Culture of Daily Living in the Anglo-Saxon World*). Liverpool, Liverpool University Press, 89–106.

Rippon, S. and Fyfe, R. (2018) Variation in the Continuity of Land-Use Patterns Through the First Millennium A.D. in Lowland Britain. *Late Antique Archaeology Journal* 11, 135–154.

Rippon, S., Fyfe, R. M. and Brown, A. G. (2006) Beyond Villages and Open Fields: the origins and development of a historic landscape characterised by dispersed settlement in South West England. *Medieval Archaeology* 50, 31–70.

Rippon, S., Smart, C., and Pears, B. (2015) *The Fields of Britannia.* Oxford, Oxford University Press.

Rippon, S., Wainwright, A. and Smart, C. (2014) Farming Regions in Medieval England: the archaeobotanical and zooarchaeological evidence. *Medieval Archaeology* 58, 195–255.

Rivet, A. L. F. (1964) *Town and Country in Roman Britain* (2nd Edition). London, Hutchinson University Library.

Roberts, B. and Wrathmell, S. (2000a) *An Atlas of Rural Settlement in England*. London, English Heritage.

Roberts, B. and Wrathmell, S. (2000b) Peoples of wood and plain: an exploration of national and regional contrasts. In D. Hooke (ed.) *Landscape: The Richest Historical Record*. Birmingham, Society for Landscape Studies, 47–62.

Roberts, B. and Wrathmell, S. (2002) *Region and Place*. London, English Heritage.

Roberts, B. K. (1987) *The Making of the English Village*. London, Longman.

Rodwell, W. J. and Rodwell, K. A. (1986) *Rivenhall: Investigations of a Villa, Church and Village 1950–1977*. CBA Research Report 55. York, Council for British Archaeology.

Savory, H. N. (1954) The Excavation of an Early Iron Age Fortified Settlement on Mynydd Bychan, Llysworney (Glam) 1949–50, Part I. *Archaeologia Cambrensis* 103, 85–108.

Savory, H. N. (1955) The Excavation of an Early Iron Age Fortified Settlement on Mynydd Bychan, Llysworney (Glam) 1949–50, Part II. *Archaeologia Cambrensis* 104, 14–51.

Smith, A., Allen, M., Brindle, T. and Fulford, M. (2016) *The Rural Settlement of Roman Britain. New Visions of the Countryside of Roman Britain Volume 1*. London, Britannia Monograph 29.

Taylor, C. C. and Fowler, P. J. (1978) Roman fields into medieval furlongs? In H. C. Bowen and P. J. Fowler (eds) *Early Land Allotment*. BAR British Series 48. Oxford, British Archaeological Reports, 159–162.

Taylor, J. (2007) *An Atlas of Roman Rural Settlement in England*. CBA Research Report 151. York, Council for British Archaeology.

Upex, S. (2003) Landscape Continuity and the Fossilization of Ancient Fields. *Archaeological Journal* 159, 77–108.

Vinther, B. M., Buchardt, S. L., Clausen, H. B., Dahl-Jensen, D., Johnsen, S. J., Fisher, D. A., Koerner, R. M., Raynaud, D., Lipenkov, V., Andersen, K. K., Blunier, T., Rasmussen, S. O., Steffensen, J. P. and Svensson, A. M., (2009) Holocene Thinning of the Greenland Ice Sheet. *Nature* 461, 385–388.

Vyner, B. E. (1986) Woodbarn, Wiston: A Pembrokeshire Rath. *Archaeologia Cambrensis* 135, 121–133.

Vyner, B. E. and Allen, D. W. H. (1988) A Romano-British settlement at Caldicot, Gwent. In D. M. Robinson (ed.) *Biglis, Caldicot & Llandough: Three Late Iron Age and Romano-British Sites in South-East Wales*. BAR British Series 188. Oxford, British Archaeological Reports, 65–122.

Wainwright, G. J. (1971) The Excavation of a Fortified Settlement at Walesland Rath, Pembrokeshire. *Britannia* 2, 48–108.

Watts, V. (2004) *The Cambridge Dictionary of English Place-Names*. Cambridge, Cambridge University Press.

Webster, G., Fowler, P., Noddle, B. and Smith, L. (1985) The Excavation of a Romano-British Rural Establishment at Barnsley Park, Gloucestershire, 1961–1979: Part III. *Transactions of the Bristol Gloucestershire Archaeological Society* 103, 73–100.

Wheeler, R. E. M. (1955) Roman Buildings and Earthworks on the Cardiff Racecourse. *Transactions of the Cardiff Naturalists' Society* 55, 19–45.

White, P. (2003) *The Arrow Valley, Herefordshire: Archaeology, Landscape Change and Conservation*. Herefordshire Studies in Archaeology Series 2. Hereford, Herefordshire Archaeology.

Wickham, C. (2005) *Framing the Early Middle Ages*. Oxford, Oxford University Press.

Williams, A. (1941) The Excavation of High Penard Promontory Fort, Glamorgan. *Archaeologia Cambrensis* 96, 23–30.

Williams, D. (1996) Archaeological Field Evaluation, Housing Allocation H2R01, Rogiet, Gwent. Glamorgan-Gwent Archaeological Trust Report 96/060. https://doi.org/10.5284/1037292 (accessed 06.01.19).

Williams, G. and Mytum, H. (1998) *Llawhaden, Dyfed: Excavations on a Group of Small Defended Enclosures, 1980–4*. BAR British Series 275. Oxford, British Archaeological Reports.

Williamson, T. (1987) Early Co-Axial Field Systems on the East Anglian Boulder Clays. *Proceedings of the Prehistoric Society* 53, 419–432.

Williamson, T. (1998) The 'Scole-Dickleborough field system' revisited. *Landscape History* 20, 19–28.

Williamson, T. (2003) *Shaping Medieval Landscapes*. Macclesfield, Windgather Press.

Williamson, T. (2008) Co-axial landscapes: time and topography. In P. Rainbird (ed.) *Monuments in the Landscape*. Stroud, Tempus, 123–35.

Williamson, T. (2013) *Environment, Society and Landscape in Early Medieval England. Time and Topography*. Woodbridge, Boydell.

Williamson, T., Liddiard, R. and Partida, T. (2013) *Champion: The Making and Unmaking of the English Medieval Landscape*. Liverpool, Liverpool University Press.

Wrathmell, S. (2017) Woodland in Roman Britain: some hypotheses. *Britannia* 48, 311–318.

Yates, A. M. (1998) Excavations at Great Pencarn Farm, Newport, Monmouthshire. Glamorgan-Gwent Archaeological Trust Report 98/003. https://doi.org/10.5284/1037288 (accessed 06.01.19).

Young, T. 2016, Geophysical Surveys at Caermead Roman Villa, Llantwit Major, Vale of Glamorgan. GeoArch Report 2016/07. http://www.geoarch.co.uk/reports/2016–07%20Caermead%20geophysics%202016.pdf (accessed 06.01.19).

CHAPTER THREE

Resource management of seasonal pasture: some English/Welsh comparisons

Della Hooke

Transhumance was a common practice across most of Britain in the late prehistoric, Roman, and early medieval periods, as in much of Europe (see Roberts this volume). The links between regions of more intensive agriculture and more marginal regions of woodland or upland which were more suited to seasonal usage may even have influenced early territorial organisation (Hooke 1986). Such practices not only made use of complementary resources but they helped to remove domestic stock away from hay meadows and from agricultural land when crops were growing. The antiquity of such arrangements is often uncertain – some have argued for them having been in place since at least the late Iron Age (Cunliffe 2005, 56, 212, 259, 437). In England and Wales, the links eventually became broken by the increasing fragmentation of folk territories or commotes into estates, townships, and parishes (and in Wales, later, into individual farms). In some regions, especially in upland and wetland areas, transhumance continued well into medieval times. Even today, farming practices often entail the movement of stock from lower lands to the hills in summer.

Several case studies are presented below. In midland and south-eastern England, in the early medieval period, such links are frequently apparent in contemporary documents. These links are visible across the whole of these regions and seem to fall within folk territories which may have originated in pre-Anglo-Saxon times. The marginal lands of both uplands and lowland woods were utilised in this way. All kinds of domestic stock were involved but in lowland woods it was pigs which were dominant.

In north-west Wales a number of Extents, instigated by Edward I in 1283 (Davies 1987, 367), record the long-established practice of transhumance arrangements between the coastal plain and the hills, not only between the *maerdref* and its *hafotir* but also between other landholdings. With so much upland available in north Wales, the distances covered for transhumance were often, but not always, rather less than in many other regions and cattle seem to have been the dominant stock involved. Much of this can be traced through field-names. Sharelands or *rhandiroedd*, the local-level communal land units of

Welsh law, were probably initially cultivated as small open arable fields, giving rise to such names as *talar* 'a headland' etc., while *hafod* and *lluest, llety* sites represent the upland dwellings occupied only in summer, often on the *ffridd* just below the open mountain (Davies 1973, 1980, 1984; Sambrook 2006, 99–104). The evidence here often remains clear on the ground today.

Transhumance links

Some English examples

In midland England, pre-Conquest documentation, especially charters recording grants of land and estates, clearly indicates estate linkages which developed out of early patterns of transhumance. As noted above, the movement of animals not only made use of the resources of marginal areas but removed stock away from the hay meadows and growing crops in areas of intensive agriculture. Such links are visible across the West Midlands and Staffordshire and seem to fall within folk territories which may have originated in pre-Anglo-Saxon times. Certainly the Staffordshire to north Worcestershire links pre-date the seventh-century boundary of the Hwiccan kingdom, with the territories of the *Pencesætan* and the *Tomsætan* extending southwards across the seventh-century boundary into the wooded uplands of the Lickey Hills. These are recorded in a mid-ninth-century charter which recorded the point where the southern boundary of these two Staffordshire folk groups met that of a Church of Worcestershire estate of *Coftune* (Cofton Hackett and Alvechurch) (Sawyer 1968, S 1272 – hereafter referred to only by the S number; Hooke 1990, 135–42). In what was to become Warwickshire, links existed between the less fertile Arden in the northern part of the county and the more intensively cultivated Feldon to the south, again revealed in early medieval documents (below). Here the clay or drift-covered soils of Arden initially supported a wood-pasture landscape utilised for the seasonal grazing of stock from the more heavily cultivated zones, which were often more than 36 km away (Hooke 1985, 78–88, fig. 22) (Fig. 3.1).

In midland England it was indeed largely woodlands that offered such resources; pigs, foraging on acorns, seem to have been the most important domesticated animal pastured in such a way in the early medieval period, with cattle a close second. Recent studies have suggested that stock rearing remained as important as crop growing in the early medieval economy (Banham & Faith 2014, 142–4). It seems that the stock were driven to the summer pastures to be managed by cowherds and swineherds and there appears to be little evidence here for the mass movement of communities (*e.g.* S 1437 below and Comeau this volume). It is swineherds too that are mentioned in association with Kentish documents (see below, Robertson 1956, Appendix II, IX, 252–5).

The transhumance links were to become broken as estates were granted out to the church or lesser lords after the seventh century, which led to the increasing fragmentation of folk territories and eventually to the establishment of townships and parishes. Permanent settlement was gradually established

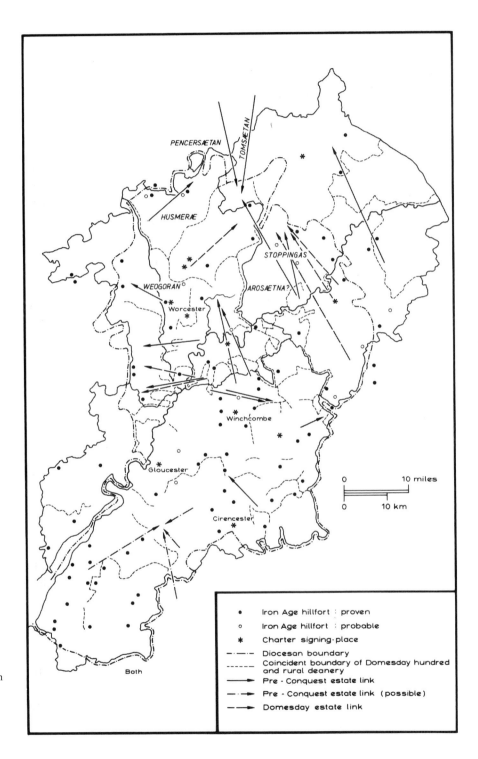

FIGURE 3.1. Territorial links in the Anglo-Saxon West Midlands (from Hooke 1985, fig. 22): estate linkages for resource management.

within the more heavily wooded regions, many of them incorporating the place-name term *lēah* indicative of wood-pasture (Hooke 2008), although many ensuing estates continued to owe the obligation of providing swinemast (forage for pigs). Rights to wood-pasture are recorded in several pre-Conquest charters in west Worcestershire, part of the kingdom of the Hwicce, by then associated with specific estates. Some record that estates were to be freed from such an obligation, as at Bentley in Holt, Worcestershire, freed in 855 from *Pascua porcorum re[g]is quod nominamus fearnleswe* 'the pasturing of the king's swine which we call "fern-pasture"' (S 206), but occasionally disputes arose, as at Leigh Sinton on the Malvern foothills where the king disputed with the Church of Worcester rights to mast in 825: 'the reeves in charge of the swineherds wished to extend the pasture farther, and take in more wood than the ancient rights permitted', but had to settle for the initially agreed mast for 300 swine (S 1437; Hooke 1990, 96–7).

One example of a charter link in the eastern part of the Hwiccan kingdom is that between the estate of Shottery near Straford-upon-Avon (where the Church had an early minster) which was granted by Offa to the Church of Worcester in the eighth century along with holdings in wooded countryside at *Hellerelege* and Nuthurst (S 64; Hooke 1999, 27–30) (Fig. 3.1). The bishop also retained a deer park at Bushwood, another estate nearby in Arden, in the thirteenth century and later. Such long-distance links again often became broken by the increasing fragmentation of folk territories in pre-Conquest times into estates and parishes, with wood-pastures appropriated by particular estates.

It has been noted above how these regions were being actively settled on a permanent basis during the early medieval period (Hooke 1982; 2003a), and by the time of the Domesday survey permanent settlement was firmly established. Indeed, within Arden, by the medieval period, hamlets and farmsteads (many moated) dominated the settlement pattern, practicing mostly a pastoral economy. Small areas of open field had been introduced around manorial centres or hamlets but were rarely extensive. More settlement took place in the twelfth and thirteenth centuries within the Warwickshire Arden as manorial lords readily granted land on the margins of the woodland and waste in order to increase their revenue (Roberts 1965). However, many of the earlier links became fossilised in medieval manorial and ecclesiastical ties with dependent manors and 'daughter' churches. The estate of Brailes in the south of the Feldon, for instance, possessed a dependent manor at Tanworth-in-Arden. These linkages were also frequently fossilised in later hundred boundaries (Hooke 1985, 96–7). Other such links in south Worcestershire existed between estates in the western parts of the Avon valley and the foothills of the Malvern Hills: an estate at Overbury was linked to Pendock in AD 967 (S 216) and Berrow was probably included in the Domesday assessment of Overbury, Welland in that of Bredon. Redmarley, further south, was to be granted to St Peter's at Bredon, while the church of Pershore was to acquire large estates in the Malvern area (Hooke 1985, 83), but it is those estates which were direct

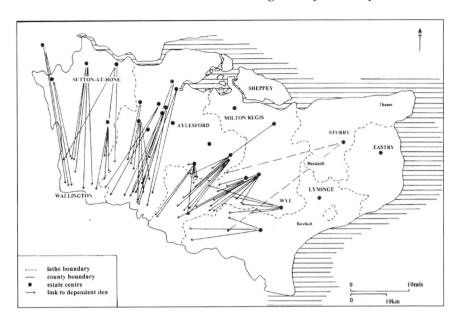

FIGURE 3.2. Links to
Wealden dens.

dependencies that provide the surest evidence for early territorial linkages
(Fig. 3.1).

Once the large-scale and long-distance movement of stock diminished, to be
replaced by permanent, largely pastoral, settlements in the more marginal areas,
products could be exchanged at the markets which were being established in
later Anglo-Saxon or medieval times within the intermediary zone.

A similar picture emerges in the Weald of Kent where the early charter
evidence is particularly rich. Herds of swine, cattle, and even sheep were taken
each summer to the woodland. Here, the transhumant practices appear to have
been closely related to the lathes, pre-Conquest administrative divisions, some
of which appear to have been similar to folk regions, before being appropriated
by individual manors. Thus, an eighth-century charter granting land beside the
River Lympne to Milred, abbess of Minster, probably in 724, included land in
the Wealden woodlands – the *Limenweareawalde* 'the wood of the men of the
Limen region/district'. *Limen* was the name of the old East Rother River that
flowed out to the sea at Lymne and the district became recognised as the [*regio*]
lathe of Lympne, *i.e.* the lathe of the *Limenwara* (Sawyer 1968, S 1180; Kelly
1995, no. 47, 163) (Fig. 3.2). Similarly, the *Weowerawealde* was the woodland
of the men of Wye, with again a lathe recognised in Domesday Book (Hooke
2012). By the time of Domesday Book, however, many lathes took their name
from capital manors. Initially it was again swineherds who spent the pannage
season in their forest lodges or shielings but gradually these were to develop into
permanent settlements, a process beginning before the end of the Anglo-Saxon
period with a few recorded as established settlements in 1086 in Domesday Book
(Everitt 1986, 54–5). The actual practice of moving stock to seasonal pastures in

the Weald, here referred to as dens (Old English *denn*, *denbære*, more specifically 'swine-pasture') appears to have survived well into the twelfth century.

Similar links can be recognised across England, although in northern and south-western England the seasonal pastures lay in hilly or moorland regions. Thus, in Devon, holdings on Dartmoor were used by coastal settlements, but here transhumance gave way to the guardage of stock with the lowland manors paying the officials of the moor to care for their stock during the summer season; cattle were still being summered on Dartmoor in the early fifteenth century (Fox 1989). In Cornwall, 'transhumance origins may be pursued back beyond the seventh century AD and into later prehistory' (Herring 2012, 94–5). Scores of small rectangular houses which could not have housed whole families were clustered into groups of between two to a dozen huts, similar 'in scale and form to shielings, bothies, boolies and hafotai known elsewhere in upland Britain'; these have been located on Bodmin Moor in Cornwall (Herring 2012, 92–5). It is probable that the upland activities were labour-intensive and not confined to watching over cattle but involved the 'twice daily gathering in of livestock, then milking, and butter and cheese making, and carding, spinning and knitting wool sheared on the summer grounds' (Herring 2012, 93). Yet in Cornwall the seasonal movement of people does not seem to have lasted long after the seventh century and subsequently many of the summer pastures were to be overseen by professional summer-only herders (Herring 2012, 101). However, the summer pasturing of cattle on hills, cliffs, and marshes here has continued into the twenty-first century.

In the uplands of northern England and the Scottish borders, transhumance continued well into the sixteenth and seventeenth centuries, with the herdsmen dwelling in huts referred to as 'shiels' or 'shielings' (Winchester 2000, 85–90). Again the remains of these dwellings can still be identified on upland pastures but many were to be replaced by permanent farms in the thirteenth century (Winchester 2012, 134). In the fenlands of East Anglia, settlements sought out pastures on the wetlands as they dried out in summer, often with intercommoning between parishes (Neilson 1920; Darby 1940, 62, 66–7; Silvester 1988; Oosthuizen 2016, 13–14, fig. 4; Oosthuizen 2017).

Where they can be reconstructed, patterns of drove-ways linking the agricultural regions with the woodland pastures often appear to bear little relation to later Anglo-Saxon or medieval settlement foci and may have risen rather earlier through the need for access by communities over a long period of habitual use. They often underlie today's pattern of routeways and even in Kent, where the system persisted for many centuries, only a few survive today close to their original state.

Such a drove-road pattern underlying the later road pattern both in Warwickshire and west Worcestershire (Fig. 3.3) strongly suggests the initial actual movement of herds, accompanied by herdsmen, especially of the pigs to be fattened on the acorns available in late summer and early autumn. Today's over-bred pigs could not cover such distances but in medieval times a pig was

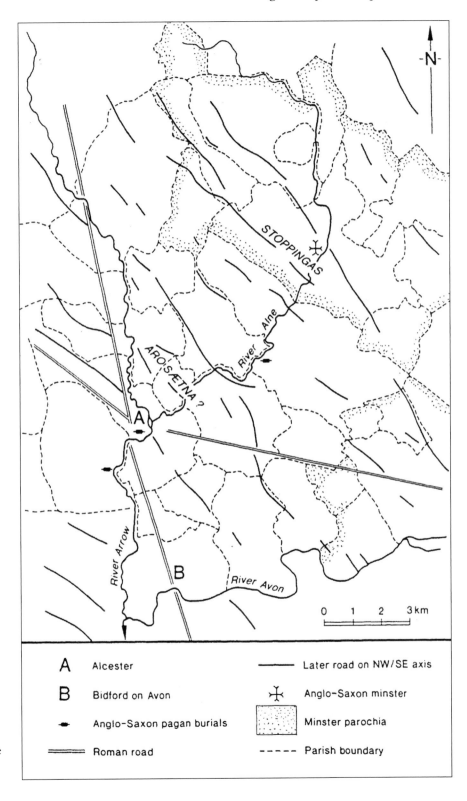

FIGURE 3.3. Warwickshire drove-ways and folk groupings.

expected to be able to cover six to ten miles a day (Bonser 1970, 56) and could therefore manage considerable distances, feeding en route.

Domesday Book records that the woods of northern Warwickshire could support thousands of swine. Here again the drove-road pattern appears to be ancient – might it pre-date the donation of a territory across the headwaters of the River Alne to a group known as the *Stoppingas*? In 716x737 a minster was to be established at Wootton Wawen *in regione quae antiquitus nominatur. STOPPINGAS* 'in the territory which from ancient times is called the *Stoppingas*' (S 94). The drove-way pattern appears to cut through this territory (Fig. 3.3; Hooke 2003a, fig. 2).

Again a pattern of parallel routes can be identified to the west of the River Severn running westwards to the north and south of the River Teme. The southern routes ran across the area which was to become the Forest of Malvern. There may well have been points where cattle could have forded the River Severn before it was deepened for river transport in historical times. To the north of the River Teme the routes ran westwards into and across the woodlands of *Weogorenaleah*. In the pre-Conquest period some routeways here were already documented as charter routes, including the *wudu herpað* 'the way to the wood', 'the westerly way', *ætincweg*, *sylweg*, and *gerdweg* 'yard way', and even several *stræt* routes (often made-up roads) such as the 'south', 'market', and 'old, streets', all running through the wooded area of *Weogorenaleah* (Hooke 2012, fig. 4.2).

The Welsh evidence

There is far less early documentary evidence available in Wales but here again one seems to find longer-distance links giving way to much shorter ones, although the practice of moving stock to seasonal pastures was to remain an integral part of the farming pattern. Although there was considerably more woodland in north Wales until late medieval times, it was largely upland pastures that were the focus of seasonal grazing, as in much of northern England. Also, given the amount of upland pasture available, the distances covered were generally much shorter. Whereas in many parts of England there was in the intensively cultivated regions a serious shortage of pasture, especially for the plough oxen, in many parts of north Wales it was usually crop-growing land that was scarce. Nevertheless both countries seem to have been affected by the fragmentation of early territorial groupings. According to thirteenth-century north Wales law (Jenkins 1990), kingdoms were divided into *cantrefi* which were subdivided into commotes (*cymydau*) and in each of these two *trefi* were held by the king. The one held by the most servile tenure (*tir cyfrif*, a term found only in north Wales) was the *maerdref* where the occupants were obliged to maintain the royal *llys* (court) when the king visited (Jones Pierce 1972, 276; Charles-Edwards 1993, 402). To it was appended the other royal *tref* – the *hafotir*, the summer pasture. The commotes were the earliest administrative districts laid out in Gwynedd with fixed boundaries (Rees 1959; Bowen 1967, 276–9; Jones Pierce 1972, 39). The Edwardian Extents record the long-established practice of transhumance arrangements between the coastal plain and the hills in which stock would be removed from crop-growing areas to seasonal pastures in more remote areas (see below).

The commote of medieval Ardudwy in Gwynedd, part of the *cantref* of Dinodyn/Dunoding, was further divided into Ardudwy Is Artro and Ardudwy Uwch Artro by the Afon Artro (Rees 1959, plate 28; Bowen 1967, 277, fig. 110), to be amalgamated into the new shire county of Merioneth in 1284. At that time the 1284 Extent names the king's pastures and vaccaries of Ardudwy Uwch Artro (not so-named in that extent but attached to the manor of Prysor in Trawsfynydd) as Brincogh, Pressor and Eboydyock (*Extent of Merionethshire*, 190–1) on the barren land to the south-west, lying to the east of the Rhinogau, and on land to the east of the Afon Eden which ran up to the hill range stretching south from the Arenigs (later recorded as *ffrith y bryno3, ffrith Prissor*, and *ffrith y Veidiog*: Ffridd Bryn Coch, Ffridd Prysor, and Fridd y Veidiog: Ellis 1838), plus the 'green island' called *Glaccuns* (Glasynys) – these could have sustained over 200 head of stock if they had not been devastated by war (Fig. 3.4) (there was also a cluster of bond holdings on the west bank of the Afon Eden near Trawsfynydd: Thomas 1970). The later Record of Caernarvon, compiled for Merioneth in 1420 (Ellis 1838), notes that these *Havotreffrith/ hafod y ffrith* of Ardudwy Uwch Artro had also provided pasture, *herbag fforeste* 'herbage of the forest', for the Prince's stallions (literally, *Havotreffrith/hafod y ffrith* is the 'summer pasture of the *ffridd*', the latter term discussed below). The royal vill, the *maerdref* or 'reeve's *tref*', of Ardudwy Is Artro (the bond community supporting a royal *llys*), as in 1284, lay on the coast at Ystumgwern (given as *Stinguerne* in 1284) in Llanenddwyn parish with its summer pastures, the royal *hafotir*, recorded again as the *Havotreffrith*, in *Nancoyl* (Nantcol), over 7 kilometres distant.

Further south, within the *cantref* of Meirionnydd, were the commotes of Ystumanner and Tal-y-bont, located between the estuaries of the Mawddwy and Dovey/Dyfi. The *maerdref* of Tal-y-bont had *hafotreffrith* some 11 kilometres away on *ffrith Pennant*, likely to be on Mynydd Pennant to the south-west of Cader Idris; *ffrith Wanas Ffridd Gwanas*, perhaps on the open mountain between Hafod-oer and Waun-oer to the east of that range some 21 kilometres away; and a third, *ffrith Pennatigi*, possibly, if the identification is correct, as much as 24 kilometres away, even further to the north-east (Fig. 3.4). In Ystumanner, only the herbage of the forest at *ffrith y Voeldrys* 'the ffridd of the thorny hill' (possibly Foel-y-ffridd) is mentioned in 1420.

As noted, with so much upland available in north Wales, the distances covered for transhumance were often, but not always, rather less than in many other regions, and cattle seem to have been dominant. Apart from the royal vills, other landholdings, whether bond or free, had their own summer pastures in medieval times. These holdings were to fall into township units, closely

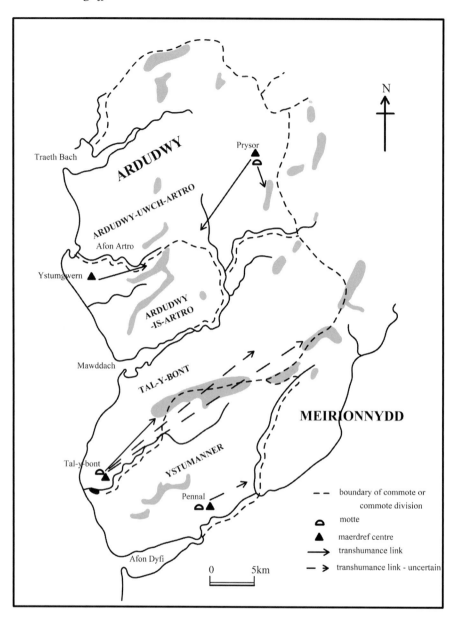

FIGURE 3.4. Ardudwy and Meirionnydd showing transhumance links.

related to the ecclesiastical parishes in the twelfth century, with territorial fragmentation at work here in Wales as in England (possibly before the Edwardian conquest 1277–1283). Over most of England and Wales the township was the smallest administrative unit recognised, a community often with its own agricultural land (Hooke 1985, 111–113). Thus, in Ardudwy Is Artro, the lowland hay pastures were especially protected in the parish of Llanaber near Barmouth in 1326, for instance, when a clansman of Llanaber was fined 'for keeping his animals "in the common pasture of the old settlement" (*in communi pastura del hendreve*) after the community of the township (*communitas villate*) had moved, early in May of that year, with its animals to the mountains' (Jones 1972, 297–8). Winter and summer houses are also mentioned in the Laws of Hywel Dda but these laws in their present form are of twelfth- and thirteenth-century date (Owen 1841, 92–3, 101; Jenkins 1990; Roberts this volume). This confirms that, as in many parts of Europe, transhumance involved whole sections of the community (Fox 1996, 5–6). In Dalarna in Sweden it was the girls and young women who moved with the animals to the hills, spending much of their time there making butter and cheese, but leaving the men folk below to carry out agricultural work.

The Edwardian Extents of the late thirteenth century and the Record of Caernarvon name free and bond holdings, grouped into townships. It may have been a genuine fact – rather than just a refusal to give information to the commissioners – that the boundaries of eight *gwelyau* (hereditary lands) in Llanaber, Llanddwywe, and Llanenddwyn recorded in the Record of Caernarvon were declared as unknown. Their lands may indeed have been intermingled, in Ardudwy Is Artro, making use of the narrow coastal strip which lies here between the Rhinogau and the sea. Some, especially the free holdings, gave their names to later amalgamated farms both on the coast or inland – in Llanaber these included Llecheiddior, Bron-y-foel, and Bennar, all on the coastal strip, plus the free holdings of Egryn, Talwrn, and Taltreuddyn, with Golodd inland in Cwmsylfaen. Taltreuddyn was a township of thirteen households in 1293 but again the name became attached to a single farm, the original *tyddynnod* lost without trace (Thomas 1970, 130, n. 5; Hooke 1997a). Some holdings were appropriated (Gresham 1986; 1987/1988) and given to villein families displaced by the building of Edward I's borough of Harlech.

As already mentioned, sharelands were probably initially cultivated as open arable fields, and this appears to have been the case in Castell in Caerhun in the Conwy valley. Field-names may indicate the open field arable – names including *talar* 'headland', perhaps *dryll* 'strip or ridge', *lleiniau* 'quillets', occasionally *maes* which perhaps usually meant 'open field', and *cyfar* and *erw* referring to measures of land. How early such names originated is a matter of conjecture, but they are likely to be earlier than most of the documents which refer to them. (Around Harlech, English 'acre' names associated with rectilinear fields may represent the open fields of the fourteenth-century burgesses.) Occasionally remnants of terracing have been noted but this has usually been eradicated by later ploughing.

On the Ardudwy Is Artro coastal strip, the Welsh names are concentrated on the more fertile lands along the coastal strip below the 500 ft/150 m contour where a belt of well-drained loams surely indicates the areas initially preferred for crop growing (Fig. 3.5; Hooke 1975; 2003b). Patches of meadowland (*dôl* – not shown) indicate the common meadowland of the township. Development inland across the Rhinogau range seems to have occurred somewhat later as wood names are so much more prolific there apart from in some of the valleys draining down to the Mawddach.

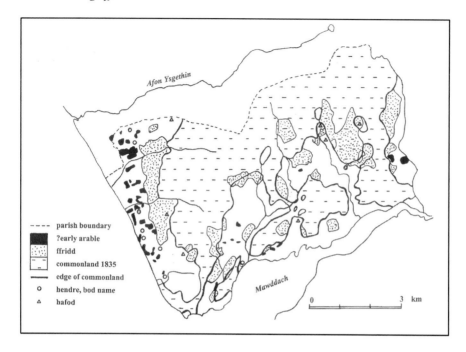

Legend:
- - - - parish boundary
▨ ?early arable
⬚ ffridd
▬ commonland 1835
▬ edge of commonland
○ hendre, bod name
△ hafod

Afon Ysgethin

Mawddach

0   3 km

FIGURE 3.5. Llanaber historical land use; arable, meadow, and *hafodydd* in Llanaber: the field-name evidence.

It was in the 1970s that the present author mapped as well as possible the old medieval settlement sites found on the hillside above – long before aerial photographs became available for this region (Fig. 3.6) (Hooke 1975; 1983; 2003b; these have subsequently been examined by air photography with plots produced based upon this: Snowdonia National Park 1986). These probably represent the seasonal settlement sites on the then open pasture, the *hafodydd* of medieval documents. In Llanaber, above the farmsteads of Egryn and Llwynwcws, they lie on shelves of land at about 650–700 ft/180–210 m and seldom far from streams. The individual houses were rectangular in shape, averaging some 8×4 m, frequently with an internal dividing wall. The upper ends are almost always cut into the slope and the lower ends frequently built upon an apron of spoil and boulders (*i.e.* 'platform houses'). On Egryn land they were often associated with irregular enclosures. Only the foundations of the houses remain but even allowing for the robbing of stone to build later field walls their upper parts may always have been constructed of turves (Plate 3.1a; Fig. 3.7a). Such remains are found less frequently in the parish inland beyond the Rhinogau range rising above the Mawddach. Similar houses are found on the summer pastures in parts of Snowdonia, as in Cwm Brwynog and Cwm Dwythwch in Llanberis, both within the division of Is Gwyrfai in the *cantref* of Arfon, appendant to the vill of Dolbadarn and noted in the Record of Caernarvon in 1352 (where they appear as the *hafodau* of *Combroinok* and *Havot Grynwothok*) (RCHAMW 1960, II. 164, 170).

But Welsh methods of land tenure were to become weakened under English rule and sharelands were being converted into enclosed fields and lowland farms becoming consolidated. Field patterns often indicate the irregular fields around

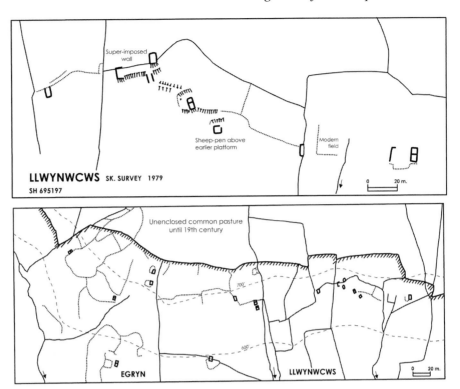

FIGURE 3.6. Medieval *hafodydd* sites in Llanaber (from Hooke 1983, fig. 4).

such consolidated lowland farms (Hooke 1975), some of which bore names related to the earlier *gwelyau*. The rise of farm names such as *hendre* and *hafod* show the system of seasonal movement becoming increasingly localised by later periods (Fig. 3.5). Some *hafod* sites were instead noted as *lluest, llety* 'a lodging, dairy house' (Davies 2000, 7–8; Sambrook 2006), but only a few correlate with known earlier hut sites (Fig. 3.7b).

Expansion and enclosure upwards is revealed in the sixteenth-century list of encroachments onto the hillside common pastures (many recorded as encroachments on to supposedly Crown waste of the so-called 'Forest of Snowdon' in 1575: TNA SC 12/30/24; Thomas 1967; Hooke 1975, 227). Most were represented by substantial intakes of as much as 20 acres but were not usually equated in Ardudwy with upland settlement sites. They appear to have been intakes to established farms: at this time lowland farms were expanding upwards onto the fringes of the commons as livestock farming flourished in Tudor England and Wales (the same process can be seen along the hill ranges of western Herefordshire). The resultant fields in Ardudwy often bear the *ffridd* name, usually interpreted as 'hill pasture' or, in the first instance, 'summer pasture', likely to be unenclosed (Sylvester 1955–6, 21; Adams 1976, 95) (Fig. 3.5). Hywel Wyn Owen and Richard Morgan in their *Dictionary of the Place-Names of Wales* (2007, xliii) prefer to translate *ffridd* or *ffrith* as 'mountain pasture; moorland; recently cleared land'. The term is largely restricted to north Wales (Dixon 2012). Later, *ffridd* was used

FIGURE 3.7. a) Long huts above Egryn, Llanaber. b) Former 'lodging/dairy house' site: Buarth Lluist above Hendre Mynach, Llanaber.

in a quasi-legal sense of 'forest' (Adams 1976, 80). Whether there was any relationship to the Old English *fyrð* is unclear – this appears to have meant land covered with brush wood, and there is a clear indication in some areas that shrubby growth was once found on many such fields on the Welsh hills; this indeed often returns if grazing by sheep is curtailed. Such encroachments ran for some 3 kilometres along the coastal strip of Ardudwy Is Artro and occurred intermittently above the Mawddach (Hooke 1997a, fig. 5). Prior to enclosure, the *ffridd* was a useful buffer zone between the summer grazing of the mountain pastures and the winter grazing on the lowland fields. Ewes with young lambs might graze the open spaces and browse the various tree and shrub species – open scrub with some mature trees characterised well-managed *ffridd* – finding additional shelter in the shrub layer before the weather became sufficiently reliable to move them higher onto the mountain (Dixon 2012).

Well managed ffridd has the appearance of open scrub with some mature trees. It forms a usefull [sic] buffer zone between the wintering of livestock on the fields and the summer grazing of mountain pasture. Ewes with young lambs were moved up from the fields onto the ffridd in late spring or early summer. Here they grazed the open spaces and browsed the various tree and shrub species. If the weather was still undecided and there were late frosts, the ewes and lambs benefit from the additional shelter provided by the shrub layer, often gorse. When the weather was sufficiently reliable, the animals would be moved up onto the mountain. Autumn saw the reverse of the process; with the mountain grazed to a close lawn and little left in the way of fodder, the animals would be brought back down into the ffridd where they would graze the open areas again and take advantage of browse. As the weather worsened they would be brought closer to the farm building, back into the field system (Dixon 2012).

The building techniques of the different periods of stone walling also show differences, those of the newly enclosed upland on to the *friddoedd* often running directly across the medieval settlements (Fig. 3.8a). Most of the enclosure walls associated with the medieval *hafodydd* were robbed to create sheepfolds or later field walls and are now rarely above one course in height but they often incorporated the huge boulders gathered from field clearance which have been too difficult to remove. The walls associated with the consolidated farmsteads are haphazard and of random stone construction, comprising stones of variable size – in other words, again using any stones that were readily to hand – although they are still effective. As time went on, later walls were carefully constructed following the improved techniques of the time. The walls of nineteenth-century enclosure are easily detected – enclosing straight-sided geometric intakes, the walling is particularly strong, high and stable, with through-stones consistently used – built often by experienced gangs and so consistent over wide areas (Fig. 3.8b). Local fashions can also be detected. Returning to the period under discussion, Figure 3.5 shows the inroads that had been made before the upland commons were eventually mapped in 1835. Expansion had also taken place onto the coastal marshes.

A similar picture is seen in the Conwy valley where groups of long huts survive at remote upland altitudes, as on the Bwlch y Ddeufen at 400 m OD, others above 518 m OD, and yet others in a remote situation within Cwm Eigiau (Hooke 1997b, 88–9 and fig. 7.6). In the Conwy valley in the parishes of Caerhun and Llanbedrycennin such long hut groups (often platform houses) are more widely dispersed across the upper moorlands with the main clusters lying along the margin of the hill commons, some on land known to have been enclosed only in the sixteenth century (Hooke 1997a and 1997b). They may represent a type of dwelling also constructed in medieval times at lower levels around areas of rough ground and common but they have usually only survived at the upland *hafod* sites (Hooke 1983). These, however, do not correlate as well as in Llanaber with *hafod* field-names and some may here represent settlement expansion onto the commons in medieval times (Hooke 1997b). The Baron

FIGURE 3.8. a) Medieval site cut by later field wall. b) A nineteenth-century enclosure wall.

Hill manuscripts (Bangor, MS 39) show estate owners buying, leasing and enclosing sections of the mountain pastures, the *ffriddoedd*, in the later sixteenth century as newly emerging large estates took every opportunity to extend their holdings at the expense of the common waste. In the Conwy valley some of the *hafod* settlements named in documents were to become permanent farms in the subsequent centuries but as part of the Baron Hill estates these did not necessarily need to be self-sufficient; however, many were, as in Llanaber, to be later abandoned.

Conclusions

Although long-distance transhumance involving the movement of animals on the hoof has entirely died out in Britain, the movement of stock by road vehicle continues in many places, usually involving the fattening of cattle or sheep on lowland farms prior to slaughter. Modern farming also often makes use of indoor cattle and pig barns, especially in winter. However, sheep and some cattle are still moved short distances to upland pastures in many parts of northern England and Wales, and flocks of sheep remain a common feature on most Welsh hills in summer.

The history of these early farming techniques has left little impression in the English lowlands, apart from perhaps a few drove-ways in places like the Weald that have not been entirely absorbed into modern road patterns. In many parts of Wales, however, such methods have left an impression on the landscape that has survived to the present day. Although some archaeological sites, such as the foundations of long huts and other settlement platforms, have almost disappeared over the last forty years or so, many are now being recorded by air photography, new archaeological techniques such as LiDAR (Light Detection and Ranging), or further field survey such as that carried out by the Gwynedd Archaeological Trust between 1995 and 1999 (Longley 2006) before they disappear almost without trace. This rich history can be deciphered by looking at today's landscape even when documentary evidence is thin – the landscape, especially in Wales, is indeed a palimpsest of historical development (Plate 3.2).

References

Adams, I. H. (1976) *Agrarian Landscape Terms: A Glossary for Historical Geography*. London, Institute of British Geographers, Special Publication No. 9.

Banham, D. and Faith, R. (2014) *Anglo-Saxon Farms and Farming*. Oxford, Oxford University Press.

Bonser, K. J. (1970) *The Drovers*. London, MacMillan and Co. Ltd.

Bowen, E. G. (1967) The Dark Ages. In E. G. Bowen and C. A. Gresham (eds) *History of Merioneth, Vol. 1. From the Earliest Times to the Age of the Native Princes*. Dolgellau, Merioneth Historical and Record Society, 264–279.

Charles-Edwards, T. M. (1993) *Early Irish and Welsh Kinship*. Oxford, Clarendon Press.

Cunliffe, B. W. (2005) *Iron Age Communities in Britain* (4th Edition). London, Routledge and Kegan Paul.

Darby, H. C. (1940) *The Medieval Fenland*. Cambridge, Cambridge University Press.

Davies, E. (1973) Hendre and Hafod in Merioneth. *Journal of the Merioneth Historical and Record Society* 7, 13–27.

Davies, E. (1980) Hafod, Hafoty and Lluest: their distribution, features, and purpose. *Ceredigion* 9(1), 1–41.

Davies, E. (1984) Hafod and Lluest: the summering of cattle and upland settlement in Wales. *Folk Life* 23(1), 76–96.

Davies, R. R. (1987) *The Age of Conquest*. Oxford, Oxford University Press.

Dixon, C. (2012) *Ffridd, Traditional Welsh Agro-forestry*: http://www.konsk.co.uk/cymru/adnoddau/Traddodiad/Ffridd/Fridd.htm (accessed 04.01.19).

Ellis, H. (ed.) (1838) *The Record of Caernarvon* (based upon Harleian Manuscript 696). London, Record Commission.

Everitt, A. (1986) *Continuity and Colonization: The Evolution of Kentish Settlement.* Leicester, Leicester University Press.

Extent of Merionethshire, 1294, Archaeologia Cambrensis, 3rd series (1867) 13, 183–192.

Fox, H. (1996) Introduction: transhumance and seasonal settlement. In H. S. A. Fox (ed.) *Seasonal Settlement, Papers Presented to a Meeting of the Medieval Settlement Research Group*. Vaughan Papers in Adult Education, Department of English Local History, University of Leicester, 1–24.

Fox, H. S. A. (1989) Peasant farmers, patterns of settlement and pays: transformations in the landscapes of Devon and Cornwall during the later Middle Ages. In R. Higham (ed.) *Landscape and Townscape in the South West* (*Exeter Studies in History 22*). Exeter, University of Exeter Press, 41–74.

Gresham, C. (1986) Ystumgwern and Prysor – medieval administrative districts of Ardudwy. *Journal of the Merioneth Historical and Record Society* 10(ii), 100–118.

Gresham, C. (1987/1988) Addendum: 'Vairdre alias Vaildre'. *Journal of the Merioneth Historical and Record Society* 10(iii), 221–6.

Herring, P. (2012) Shadows of Ghosts: early medieval transhumance. In S. Turner and B. Silvester (eds) *Life in Medieval Landscapes, Life in Medieval Landscapes: People and places in the Middle Ages, papers in memory of H. S. A. Fox*. Oxford, Windgather Press, 89–105.

Hooke, D. (1975) Llanaber, a Study in Landscape Development. *Journal of the Merioneth Historical and Record Society* 7, 222–230.

Hooke, D. (1982) The Anglo-Saxon landscape. In T. R. Slater and P. J. Jarvis (eds) *Field and Forest. An Historical Geography of Warwickshire and Worcestershire*. Norwich, Geo Books, 79–103.

Hooke, D. (1983) The Ardudwy Landscape: relict landscape features in southern Ardudwy. *Journal of the Merioneth Historical and Record Society* 9(3), 245–260.

Hooke, D. (1985) *The Anglo-Saxon Landscape. The Kingdom of the Hwicce*. Manchester, Manchester University Press.

Hooke, D. (1986) Territorial organisation in the Anglo-Saxon West Midlands; central places, central areas. In E. Grant (ed.) *Central Places, Archaeology and History*. Sheffield, Department of Archaeology and Prehistory, University of Sheffield, 79–93.

Hooke, D. (1990) *Worcestershire Anglo-Saxon Charter-Bounds*. Woodbridge, Boydell.

Hooke, D. (1997a) Place-names and vegetation history as a key to understanding settlement in the Conwy valley. In N. Edwards (ed.) *Landscape and Settlement in Medieval Wales*. Oxford, Oxbow Monograph 81, 79–96.

Hooke, D. (1997b) The effect of English settlement in medieval north Wales. In G. De Boe and F. Verhaeghe (eds) *Rural Settlements in Mediaeval Europe*. IAP Rapporten 6, Zellik, 331–344.

Hooke, D. (1999) *Warwickshire Anglo-Saxon Charter Bounds*. Woodbridge, Boydell.

Hooke, D. (2003a) Names and settlement in the Warwickshire Arden. In D. Hooke and D. Postles (eds) *Names, Time and Place, Essays in memory of Richard McKinley*. Oxford, Leopard's Head Press, 67–99.

Hooke, D. (2003b) Place-names and land use in coastal Ardudwy, with comparisons with the Conwy valley in North Wales. In T. Unwin and Th. Spek (eds) *European Landscapes: From Mountain to Sea*. Proceedings of the Permanent European Conference for the Study of the Rural Landscape, Conference 2000. Tallinn, 139–145.

Hooke, D. (2008) Early medieval woodland and the place-name term *lēah*. In O. J. Padel and D. N. Parsons (eds) *A Commodity of Good Names. Essays in Honour of Margaret Gelling*. Donington, Shaun Tyas, 365–376.

Hooke, D. (2012) *Wealdbære* and *swinamæst*: wood-pasture in early medieval England. In S. Turner and B. Silvester (eds) *Life in Medieval Landscapes: People and places in the Middle Ages, papers in memory of H. S. A. Fox*. Oxford, Windgather Press, 32–49.

Jenkins, D. (1990) *The Law of Hywel Dda* (2nd Edition). Llandysul, Gomer Press.

Jones, G. (1972) Post-Roman Wales. In H. P. R. Finberg (ed.) *The Agrarian History of England and Wales, Vol. I(ii) A.D. 43–1042*. Cambridge, Cambridge University Press, 281–382.

Kelly, S. E. (ed.) (1995) *Charters of St Augustine's Abbey, Canterbury and Minster-in-Thanet*. Oxford, British Academy, Oxford University Press.

Longley, D. (2006) Deserted rural settlements in north-west Wales. In K. Roberts (ed.) *Lost Farmsteads: Deserted Rural Settlements in Wales*. CBA Research Report 148. York, Council for British Archaeology, 61–82.

Neilson, N. (ed.) (1920) *A Terrier of Fleet, Lincolnshire*. London, British Academy.

Oosthuizen, S. (2016) Culture and Identity in the Early Medieval Fenland Landscape. *Landscape History* 37(1), 5–24.

Oosthuizen, S. (2017) *The Anglo-Saxon Fenland*. Oxford, Windgather Press.

Owen, A. (ed.) (1841) *Ancient Laws and Institutes of Wales*. London, Record Commission.

RCHMW, Royal Commission on Ancient Monuments Wales and Monmouthshire (1960). *Vol. II: Central. The Cantref of Arfon and the Commote of Eifionydd*. London, HMSO.

Rees, W. (1959) *An Historical Atlas of Wales from Early to Modern Times*. London, Faber.

Roberts, B. K. (1965) *The Forest of Arden, Warwickshire, 1086–1350*. Unpublished PhD thesis, University of Birmingham.

Robertson, A. J. (ed. and trans.) (1956) *Anglo-Saxon Charters* (2nd Edition). Cambridge, Cambridge University Press.

Sambrook, P. (2006) Deserted rural settlements in south-west Wales. In K. Roberts (ed.) *Lost Farmsteads: Deserted Rural Settlements in Wales*. CBA Research Report 148. York, Council for British Archaeology, 83–109.

Sawyer, P. H. (1968) *Anglo-Saxon Charters, An Annotated List and Bibliography*. London, Royal Historical Society.

Silvester, R. (1988) *The Fenland Project, 3: Norfolk Survey, Marshland and the Nar Valley. East Anglian Archaeology Report 45*. Dereham, Norfolk Archaeological Unit.

Sylvester, D. (1955–1956) The Rural Landscape of Eastern Montgomeryshire. *Montgomery Collections* 54, 3–26.

Thomas, C. (1967) Enclosure and the Rural Landscape of Merioneth in the 16th Century. *Transactions of the Institute of British Geographers* 42, 153–162.

Thomas, C. (1970) Social Organization and Rural Settlement in Medieval North Wales. *Journal of the Merioneth Historical and Record Society* 6(ii) 121–131.

Winchester, A. J. L. (2000) *The Harvest of the Hills: Rural Life in Northern England and the Scottish Borders, 1400–1700*. Edinburgh, Edinburgh University Press.

Winchester, A. J. L. (2012) Seasonal settlement in northern England: shieling place-names revisited. In S. Turner and B. Silvester (eds) *Life in Medieval Landscapes, Life in Medieval Landscapes: People and places in the Middle Ages, papers in memory of H. S. A. Fox*. Oxford, Windgather Press, 125–149.

Wyn Owen, H. and Morgan, R. (eds) (2007) *Dictionary of the Place-Names of Wales*. Llandysul, Gomer.

Unpublished sources

Bangor, Bangor University Archives and Special Collections, MS 39 (Baron Hill).

TNA SC 12/30/24, The National Archives (TNA), Rentals and Surveys, Portfolios (Rental, Merionethshire, 1558–1603).

Snowdonia National Park (1986). Photographic archive.

CHAPTER FOUR

Changing perspectives on early medieval farming in Ireland

*Meriel McClatchie, Finbar McCormick, Thomas R. Kerr
and Aidan O'Sullivan*

Introduction

Agriculture in early medieval Ireland (AD 400–1150) formed the basis of the economy and played a key role in the organisation of society. Previous investigations into agriculture from this period have often focused on animal husbandry rather than crops. The prominence of animals in early documentary sources has undoubtedly influenced this trend. In an early study, Duignan (1944, 141) noted that 'our early literature, historical, legal, hagiographical, and romantic, is full of the sound of cattle', highlighting the prominent role of cattle in early textual sources. Cattle formed a basic unit of wealth, and dairy cattle were particularly important. In this rigidly hierarchical society, an individual's social status was, to a large extent, dependent on the number of cattle at their disposal (McCormick 2008, 211). Animals, particularly cattle, played a very important role, therefore, in both society and economy.

The zooarchaeological record from the preceding Iron Age (700 BC–AD 400) is still rather poorly understood (although this issue is being tackled currently; Becker *et al.* 2016). Only a small number of animal bone assemblages have been published, and most are associated with high-status ceremonial sites from the earlier half of the period (McCormick and Murray 2007). Variation is apparent in the zooarchaeological record – at some sites (*e.g.* Dún Ailinne), cattle are dominant, while at others (*e.g.* Navan Fort) pig is dominant. The high incidence of pork at Navan Fort may reflect the high status of pork – perhaps regarded as suitable for feasting – during this period (McCormick and Murray 2007, 32; McCormick 2009). Sheep, horse, dog, and wild animals appear in much smaller quantities than cattle or pig, although it should be noted that horse is more prevalent in the Iron Age when compared with the Bronze Age in Ireland (McCormick and Murray 2007, 33).

By contrast, the livestock economy in early medieval Ireland has been interpreted as much more uniform that that of the Iron Age. Several reviews of zooarchaeological assemblages have been undertaken. McCormick and Murray (2007) identified temporal patterning in faunal remains and the wider livestock economy, highlighting a difference in the period from AD 600–800 when compared with later centuries. During the earlier period, they proposed that cattle were dominant throughout Ireland, followed by pig and then sheep, while goat played a minor role. During this earlier period, cattle formed a key unit of wealth (McCormick 2008, 211). After AD 800, McCormick and Murray (2007) identified more diversity in the zooarchaeological record. Cattle were less often dominant, coinciding with a time when other currencies, especially silver, become more important as a currency standard. Although they suggested a decline in cattle for the later period, dairying did persist, as demonstrated by analysis of age-slaughter pattern and sex distribution, which were broadly similar to data recorded at earlier sites (McCormick and Murray 2007, 109). Any shift away from cattle may reflect changing social and economic roles of the cow.

It is increasingly understood that arable agriculture also played an important role during the early medieval period. Few published reviews of archaeobotanical evidence are available from the preceding Iron Age, but agricultural activity has been recorded, if somewhat sporadically (Becker *et al.* 2016). By contrast, there is extensive archaeobotanical, archaeological, and documentary evidence for early medieval Ireland to indicate that cereal production began to be carried out on a larger scale than ever before (Monk 1986; McCormick *et al.* 2014). Tools for ploughing, hand tilling of soil, harvesting, and food processing are often found, and many structures associated with water mills, drying kilns, and suspected retting pits have also been discovered (Rynne 1998; Monk and Kelleher 2005; McCormick *et al.* 2014). Law texts, saints' *Lives* and other documentary sources mention the growing, harvest, and exchange of cereals, including the use of cereals as a form of currency in food-rent (Kelly 1997). Cereals were cultivated primarily for use in food products, including breads, gruels, and porridges, as well as in brewing and as animal fodder (Kelly 1997; Sexton 1998; McClatchie 2015). By-products, such as cereal straw, also provided a valuable resource for structures, roofing, and bedding.

Reviews of early medieval archaeobotanical evidence have previously been undertaken (for example, Monk 1986, 1991; Monk *et al.* 1998), but they were based upon the relatively small quantity of evidence available. Drawing upon archaeobotanical evidence (usually charred remains) from up to 23 sites, it was established that *Hordeum* spp. (barley) and *Avena* spp. (oat) were the dominant cereals, with less evidence for *Triticum* spp. (wheat) and *Secale cereale* L. (rye). Where identified to species level, barley was most often of the six-row hulled variety (*Hordeum vulgare* ssp. *vulgare*). A variety of oat species was recorded, often *Avena sativa* L. (common oat) and also *Avena strigosa* Schreb.

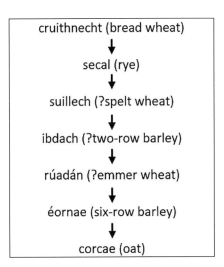

FIGURE 4.1. Order of cereal types in the eighth-century Irish law tract *Bretha Déin Chécht*, reflecting the relative prestige of each cereal.

(bristle oat) and *Avena fatua* L. (wild oat) (Monk 1991). Wheat remains were dominated by *Triticum aestivum* L. (bread wheat). Other crops – including *Linum usitatissimum* L. (flax), *Pisum sativum* L. (pea) and *Vicia faba* L. (broad bean) – have also been found.

The primary crops of early medieval Ireland appear, therefore, to have been oat and barley. Contemporary documentary evidence supports the assertion that oat and barley were more often a feature of daily life than other cereals. An eighth-century law tract *Bretha Déin Chécht* provides a list of cereal types and places them in the following order: bread wheat, rye, ?spelt wheat, ?two-row barley, ?emmer wheat, oat (Kelly 1997, 219; Fig. 4.1). There are question marks attached to several cereal types because the translation of Old Irish words is uncertain. This order represents the relative prestige of each cereal type, correlated with a specific ranking in society. Early medieval legal texts also describe land, trees, and other items in a hierarchical fashion – this was a society fixated on social ranking and power. While it should be considered that these are 'idealised' rankings, and possibly somewhat over-stated, it does appear that each cereal type was accorded a specific social value. In *Bretha Déin Chécht*, bread wheat was equated with the rank of a superior king, bishop, or chief poet; conversely, oat was equated with the commoner. Other documentary sources similarly ascribe more value to bread wheat than other cereals, for example mentioning the restriction of bread-wheat food products to holy days and higher strata of society (Kelly 1997, 219–220). Oat and barley are recovered more regularly from early medieval archaeological deposits in Ireland, perhaps reflecting both the lower status of these cereals and their prevalence as foodstuffs (Monk 1991). The status of bread wheat and rye was perceived as being higher, and they are rarer in the archaeological record. It appears that cereals were regarded not just as a source of sustenance, therefore, but also as cultural symbols that could distinguish social classes or situations (Fredengren *et al.* 2004). Legumes such as pea and bean were ranked below the cereals in *Bretha Déin Chécht*, suggesting that they were of lesser social importance (Kelly 1997, 248).

Many large-scale excavations have taken place in Ireland over the past three decades, associated with the recent boom period of infrastructural, housing, and industrial development. Excavations often included environmental analyses and radiocarbon-dating programmes, resulting in enlarged high-quality archaeobotanical and zooarchaeological datasets. Analysis of these datasets has the potential to transform our understanding of many aspects of past societies in the prehistoric and historic periods throughout Ireland. Pertinent to this paper is the wealth of new data now available from excavations of early medieval sites. The Early Medieval Archaeology Project (EMAP) was established with the support of the Heritage Council in 2007 and subsequently its INSTAR programme in 2008 to lead the way in identifying, collating, interpreting, and disseminating the massive volume of new early medieval archaeological data in Ireland. EMAP has published reports on dwellings and settlements (O'Sullivan *et al.* 2014b), and crafts and production (Kerr *et al.* 2015), as well as a general synthesis on early medieval Ireland (O'Sullivan *et al.* 2014a). This paper will detail results from EMAP's study of agriculture (McCormick 2014; McCormick *et al.* 2014; McClatchie 2015) to provide new understandings on the organisation of agriculture in early medieval Ireland, and its role in social and economic transformations during this period.

Methods

Archaeobotanical data were collated from published and unpublished sources, most often from excavation reports. Unfortunately, no central digital archive of excavation reports exists in Ireland. As a result, considerable time was spent checking through excavation reports – often only available in hard copy – to assess if relevant data were present. For the purposes of this project, archaeobotanical data from 'rural' sites (those located outside the main towns in early medieval/Hiberno-Norse Ireland) were targeted. Urban excavations, such as those from the Hiberno-Norse towns of Waterford and Dublin (Geraghty 1996; Tierney and Hannon 1997), were omitted from the archaeobotanical study because they have produced rather limited evidence for crop remains when compared with rural sites.

Certain sites were prioritised – those where all archaeological analyses had been completed and a final excavation report was available – because a full record of archaeobotanical remains, including contextual and chronological information, was required for analysis. Analysis of data was not undertaken by site, because some individual sites were occupied over several centuries, and discrete phases of activity identified. Instead, analysis was undertaken by phase where radiocarbon dates and stratigraphic information were available. If discrete activity areas could be discerned, these were also analysed as separate 'phases' of activity. Most of the data were derived from charred remains, with occasional examples of waterlogged remains. While charring does enable preservation of organic remains, it is not a complete record of people's engagement with plants in the past. Charred plant remains are often biased in favour of plants that are more likely to come into contact with fire, such as cereal grains being dried before storage, or nutshell being used as fuel or burnt as waste. Plants that are less likely to come into contact with fire, such as fruits eaten raw, are less apparent in the archaeological record.

This formed the largest dataset of archaeobotanical remains ever collated from early medieval Ireland, so research questions were focused on discovering what categories of plants were recorded in different locations and at different times. Archaeobotanical analyses investigated the relative occurrence and frequency of different plant categories, across both space and time. Presence/absence analysis was undertaken for all sites, but due to the absence of quantified data from several phases, investigation of which cereal type was dominant in each phase could not always be carried out. In a significant number of archaeobotanical reports, the raw numbers of plant components were not recorded; instead, these reports provided a scale of abundance (rare, occasional, abundant, *etc.*), but it was found that different workers use different methods, for example for calculating what is rare and what is occasional. This 'scale-of-abundance' approach prevents inter-site comparisons beyond presence/absence analyses. Similarly, radiocarbon dates were available for most, but not all, phases, which restricted investigation of temporal change. Despite these issues, broad trends in the dataset were identified, which can be tested and refined through future analyses.

Zooarchaeological data were also collated from published and unpublished sources, again mainly excavation reports. Significant variation in recording and reporting of zooarchaeological data was encountered. Early methods, for example, were based on estimations of bulk, for example 6,096 kg of animal bone was recovered from Carraig Aille, Co. Limerick (Ó Ríordáin 1949), and 22,700 kg of animal bone was recorded for Lagore, Co. Meath (Hencken 1950). This approach tends to favour recording of larger species with heavier bone mass, such as cattle, rather than being truly representative of the variety and quantity of all bone in deposits. In other cases (for example Stelfox 1941), lists of species were recorded, but detailed, quantifiable data were often absent. By the 1950s, tables were being produced to record fragment frequencies by species and element, as well as 'approximate number of animals' – what we would now term MNI or Minimum Numbers of Individuals. In these early studies, the methods used to determine MNI calculations were often not explicit, but by the 1970s, more modern methods of quantification were being applied in Ireland. Van Wijngaarden-Bakker's 1974 report on the faunal remains from Beaker deposits at the passage tomb of Newgrange, Co. Meath paved the way for future studies. Her approach grouped identifiable bones by species and element, and then counted these to provide a 'number of identifiable fragments' total (now known as NISP). Each group of elements is then sorted to calculate the number of proximal and distal epiphyses, which can be used to estimate the minimum number of elements and subsequently the MNI.

This approach is well suited to large bone assemblages from a limited number of deposits, but such assemblages are not always available in Ireland, where soils tend to be rather acidic and may not support preservation of bone. Aggregation of data from multiple samples is sometimes undertaken, therefore, but this can impact the ratio of one taxon to another. Relying solely on individual fragment values can be problematic. Butchery and taphonomic processes may affect fragmentation of bone and hence the numbers of individual specimens counted. Broadly speaking, the bones of large animals produce more fragments than those of small animals, thus creating a bias in favour of large animals. In Ireland, retrieval strategies are further likely to result in over-representation of larger bones, because sieving of deposits to recover bone is not standard practice, and smaller bones will be missed. Analysts are aware of these limitations, and several different recording methods have been developed (*e.g.* Ringrose 1993; Moreno-Garcia *et al.* 1996; O'Connor 2000). The use of a variety of approaches does result in challenges, however, when comparing different assemblages recorded and quantified using different methods. Issues are therefore apparent when attempting a large inter-site analysis, as has been undertaken here.

Sites that had yielded securely dated early medieval assemblages with adequate quantities of bone were targeted for analysis. It was decided to test an argument put forward by McCormick and Murray (2007), who identified temporal patterning in faunal remains and the wider livestock economy – during the earlier period, cattle were dominant throughout Ireland, while after AD 800, more diversity is apparent in the zooarchaeological record. This argument was based on a relatively small dataset – the current project provided an opportunity to test this argument on a much larger dataset.

Age/death trends in the data were determined to assess slaughter patterns and farming practices. Age of death can be determined through analysis of toothwear (Highham 1967; Payne 1973; 1987; Grant 1982). While there is the benefit of teeth being more hardy than bone and often surviving better in the archaeological record, if loose teeth are analysed, there is the possibility of replication of data because several examples may be analysed from one individual. In order to determine survival rates (rather than death rates), the presence/absence of fused epiphyses at the ends of bones can be assessed. Standardised fusion rates have been established (Silver 1969), for example the distal end of a cattle humerus usually fuses between 10 and 18 months, while the same element on sheep is usually fused by 10 months. Replication of data can also occur in assessing the ratio of fused to unfused epiphyseal specimens. Skeletal elements are usually divided into 'early', 'mid', and 'late' fusion groups because different bones of different animals fuse at different times. Fused cattle femurs, for example, are placed into the 'late' group because they fuse during the fourth year of life, but this means that unfused specimens could belong to any age prior to four years, so could fit into an 'early' or 'mid' fusion group. Each fusion band should therefore be analysed as an individual dataset (O'Connor 2000), which can make creation of an age-slaughter profile for an individual site rather difficult. Fusion data highlights younger animals versus mature animals, whereas toothwear continues through an individual animal's life, and can therefore identify the presence of mature and elderly animals. Separation of dairy herds and beef herds may also be determined through analysis of age-of-slaughter data. According to early medieval documentary sources and comparative ethnographic sources (McCormick 1983; 1992), the milk cow requires the presence of a calf before she will let down her milk, which meant that early medieval dairy herds were unlikely to kill off calves before the calves had reached six to nine months of age.

A range of information can therefore be gleaned from detailed analyses of the newly collated archaeobotanical and zooarchaeological data, and the results of these analyses are detailed below.

Results of analyses: archaeobotany

Archaeobotanical data were collated from 60 excavation sites in total. Analysis was undertaken by phase/area of activity, rather than by site. A total of 165 discrete phases were identified. Sites were located across the island (Fig. 4.2), with 19 sites in Leinster (eastern region; 82 phases of activity), 20 sites in Munster (southern region; 40 phases of activity), 14 sites in Connacht (western region; 31 phases of activity), and 7 sites in Ulster (northern region; 12 phases of activity). Concentrations of activity are apparent in several regions, for example in Meath in the east, and Galway in the west – these concentrations reflect particularly intensive road-building activity in these regions over the past few decades, which was accompanied by archaeological excavations.

Presence/absence analysis of the cereal remains identified clear trends in crop preferences (Fig. 4.3). Barley and oat were dominant, being recorded at 88% and 80% of phases of activity respectively. Wheat was close behind, being recorded at 65% of phases of activity. Rye was found at far fewer phases of activity – only 25%. The exact species of barley, oat, and wheat was not always determined, reflecting preservation issues and component recovery, rather than any deficiencies in identification. Most of these cereals can be identified to species level only when chaff is present. Chaff is, however, less robust than cereal grains and may be underrepresented. Chaff is also usually removed from human foods, so it may have been separated from the grain soon after harvesting, depending on storage availability and food preferences. Where species level was determined, a range of crops was revealed. In the case of barley, hulled barley was more common than naked barley, and six-row was more often recorded than two-row. Common (cultivated) oat was dominant where oat was identified to species, with bristle oat and wild oat also recorded. In the case of wheat, naked wheat was dominant (*Triticum aestivum/durum/turgidum*; bread

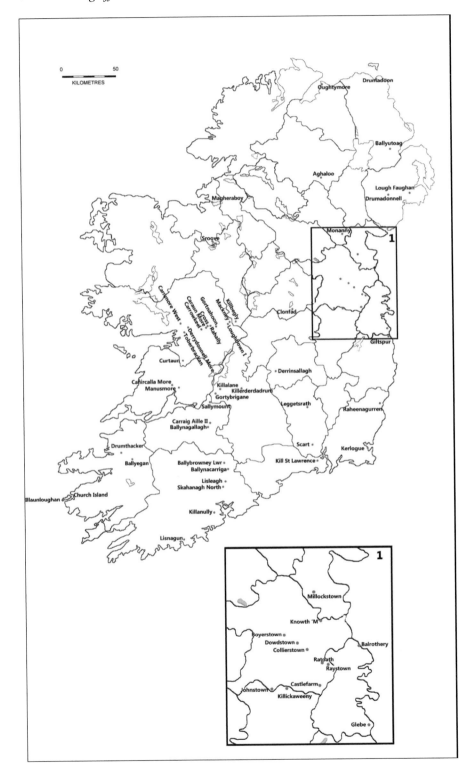

FIGURE 4.2. Distribution map of examined early medieval sites producing archaeobotanical evidence (total sites n=60) (after McCormick *et al.* 2014).

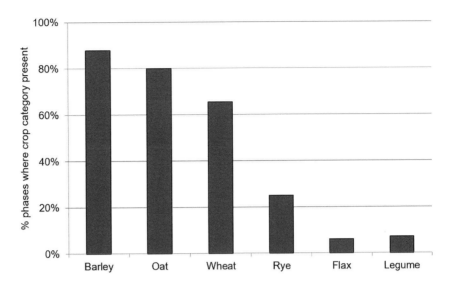

FIGURE 4.3. Relative occurrence of crop types (total phases of activity n=165).

wheat, durum wheat, and rivet wheat), identified as bread wheat where species could be determined. Hulled wheat finds comprised einkorn wheat (*Triticum monococcum*), emmer wheat (*Triticum dicoccum*), and possible spelt wheat (*Triticum spelta*), but these identifications were based on grains rather than chaff. The identification of wheat species by grain alone is generally unreliable (Hillman *et al.* 1996); well-preserved chaff (such as rachis fragments, spikelet forks and glume bases) is instead a more reliable indicator of wheat varieties. The recovery of einkorn in particular should be treated with caution, given the rarity of this crop in Ireland (McClatchie *et al.* 2014).

Determination of which cereals were dominant in each phase of activity produced even clearer patterns of crop preferences. Analysis was focused on the number of cereal grains present in a single phase (with at least 25 grains present). It was deemed that a cereal category (barley/oat/wheat/rye) was dominant when it represented more than 50% of the assemblage and at a level at least 10% higher than the next nearest cereal category. A 'mixed' category reflects an assemblage where one cereal category did not comprise at least 60% of the assemblage, or where for example an assemblage consisted of 54% barley and 46% oat (although barley was in the majority, it was not recorded at a level at least 10% above oat). Barley was the dominant crop in most phases (Fig. 4.4), as it was in the presence/absence analysis. Oat was the second most common crop on a presence/absence basis, and it was also second in terms of dominance. Although wheat was recorded in many phases of activity on a presence/absence basis, it was rarely the dominant crop in any individual phase. Rye was even less well represented in dominance calculations – although present in 25% of phases of activity, rye was not the dominant crop in any of these phases.

Other cultivated crops were also represented, including flax and legumes, but in small numbers (Fig. 4.3). Flax and legumes were present in less than 10% of phases of activity. Pea was present in 3% of phases, bean in 1% and lentil (*Lens*

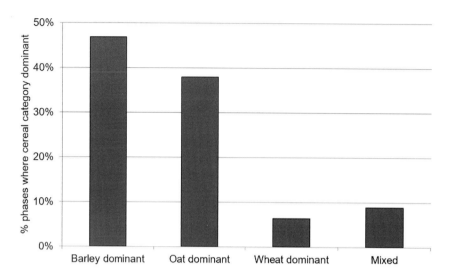

FIGURE 4.4. Relative dominance of cereal types (total phases of activity n=79).

culinaris) in 1%. Lentil – potentially an import – was recorded in two phases of activity at one site. It may be significant, however, that only a small quantity of lentil seeds was recorded in early medieval deposits at this site, while a larger quantity was present in medieval deposits. It is possible that the few lentil seeds in early medieval deposits may be intrusive, having become incorporated during the medieval period.

Chronological analysis was undertaken through investigation of associated radiocarbon dates. Unfortunately, in many cases the calibrated dates spanned several centuries, and clear categories (*e.g.* on a century level) could not be easily determined. It was decided, therefore, to create two broad categories: fourth to seventh century AD and seventh to tenth century AD. There is crossover between these two categories (during the seventh century), but more rigid separation would have resulted in too few dates for analysis. A larger number of phases (42 phases) was dated to the later period, when compared with the earlier period (28 phases). On a presence/absence level, there appears to be little change in the types of cereals appearing in each period. A different picture emerges, however, when analysis of cereal dominance was undertaken. Barley was more often dominant during the earlier period (in 64% of phases of activity, compared with 44% of phases in the later period). While oat was dominant in some locations during the earlier period (in 27% phases), it was more often dominant during the later period (36% of phases). Other cultivars – such as flax, pea, and bean – were also more often found during the later period.

Geographical patterning in the data is apparent, with a clear concentration of material in the east. Data were grouped into four regions: east (Leinster), south (Munster), west (Connacht), and north (Ulster). Analysis of cereal dominance was hampered by small datasets in some regions, but the emerging picture is that barley was more often dominant in the east and west, while oat was more often dominant in the south and north. Wheat is more often associated with eastern and western locations (>60% phases), when compared with northern and southern locations (<50% phases). Rye is rarer, but present in all regions. Flax is found in several regions, but most often in the north. Legumes are more often associated with the east. Both flax and legumes were absent from western locations. It seems, therefore, that the east was a hub of farming activity in early medieval Ireland, including a wider variety of crops than other regions, such as wheat and legumes.

Results of analyses: zooarchaeology

Zooarchaeological data were collated from 115 excavations (Figs 4.5 a, b, and c). A secure chronology – based upon radiocarbon dates or stratigraphy – was evident at around three-quarters of these excavations. Faunal assemblages were sometimes rather small, however, probably reflecting underlying geologies in many cases. In terms of quantification, NISP calculations (number of identified bone fragments) were more often provided than MNI (number of individual animal species, based on specific skeletal remains), while some reports provided both. NISP figures were available from 76 reports, in which 119 phases contained material that fulfilled the size and dating criteria. MNI figures were provided for 49 excavations, representing 84 phases.

A concentration of evidence was located in the eastern region, around counties Meath and Dublin. While this may represent a 'hot-spot' for agricultural activity in early medieval Ireland, it should also be noted that this region was the location of intensive road-building by the then National Roads Authority (now Transport Infrastructure Ireland) in recent decades, which uncovered much archaeological new evidence. A concentration of activity was also identified in the seventh to ninth centuries AD – 42% of sites were dated to this period.

Three domesticated animal categories were found to be dominant: cattle, sheep/goat, and pig (Fig. 4.6). Sheep and goat can be difficult to separate based upon their morphological features, and they have therefore been combined into one category. Cattle were often found to be dominant in NISP figures when compared with NMI, which is likely to reflect better survival of skeletal remains from a large animal when compared with a small animal. While there is variation in the data at an individual site level, cattle are broadly dominant in MNI calculations throughout the early medieval period, with sheep/goat and pig roughly equivalent with each other. Cattle MNI figures are usually at around 40% throughout the period, with sheep/goat and pig usually at around 20% each. There does seem to be a decrease in cattle around the tenth/eleventh century, when cattle dips below 40% and pig increases – it should be noted, however, that these data derive from only a small number of sites, one of which is urban (Hiberno-Norse Dublin), and another of which is a 'monastic town' (Clonmacnoise). Data from another stratigraphically late site (Moynagh Lough crannog) provide further evidence for deviation from the broader trend.

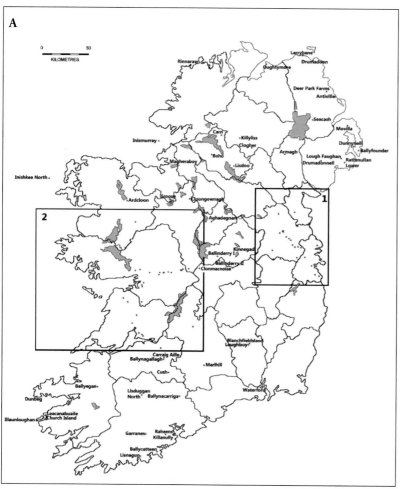

FIGURE 4.5.
a) Distribution map of examined early medieval sites producing zooarchaeological remains (total sites n=115) (after McCormick *et al.* 2014). b) Distribution of early medieval sites with zooarchaeological remains in Meath/Dublin region (after McCormick *et al.* 2014).

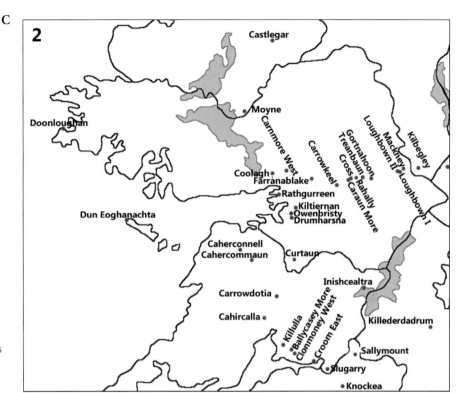

FIGURE 4.5.
c) Distribution of early medieval sites with zooarchaeological remains in Galway/Clare region (after McCormick et al. 2014).

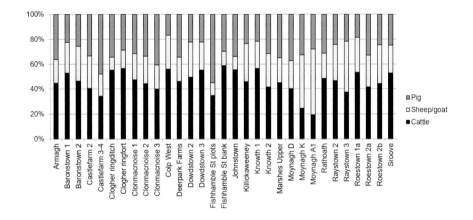

FIGURE 4.6. Minimum numbers of individuals (MNI) percentages for sites where MNI total is >40 (after McCormick 2014).

In an attempt to determine regional patterning, three study regions were established with the zooarchaeological data: north (Ulster), east (Dublin and Meath only), and west (Galway, Clare, north Limerick, and south Mayo; McCormick *et al.* 2014). Only the northern and eastern regions could be compared using MNI data, while sites in the west were compared using NISP data. In the northern region, MNI counts for cattle peak in the sixth/seventh century and then reduce, while pig and sheep/goat increase. In the western region also, cattle NISP calculations decline over the course of the early medieval period, while pig and sheep/goat calculations increase. This contrasts sharply with the MNI data from the eastern region, where cattle are dominant throughout the early medieval period. It appears, therefore, that it is the large dataset from the eastern region that is driving the national picture.

A total of 42 phases from 24 sites produced cattle toothwear data that could be securely dated and an age of death established. The data indicate that cattle deaths did not occur in substantial numbers until the third year of an animal's life. This can be interpreted as reflecting widespread dairying. Analysis of a small sample (five sites/phases) suggests intensive production in the eighth/ninth and ninth/tenth centuries, when very few specimens are dated to less than 24 months. Age profiles were also determined to assess if sites could be determined as 'consumer' or 'producer' sites (Payne 1973; Davis 1987; Soderberg 2003; McCormick and Murray 2007). Producer sites are more likely to have a spread of ages, while consumer sites are dominated by older animals. This assessment is best suited to cattle, since they have a longer life span than sheep, and ill-suited to pigs, who are bred only for meat. At urban sites, such as Hiberno-Norse Dublin and Waterford, the profile of a consumption site was recognised, and a similar profile emerged at the major ecclesiastical (and potentially 'proto-urban') site of Clonmacnoise, Co. Offaly. In the case of sheep, it has been suggested that where young animals are dominant, the sheep are being raised for meat, whereas where mature animals are dominant, this may indicate the importance of secondary products, such as wool and milk (Davis 1987). An increase in older animals is noticeable from the ninth/tenth century in the dataset, possibly to provide wool in emerging urban markets.

A total of 47 phases from 29 sites produced cattle epiphyseal fusion data, which complements some of the findings from toothwear analysis. For example, the toothwear analysis found that there was a low death rate for young cattle in the eighth/ninth century, and the fusion analysis similarly found a high survival rate for cattle at this time. For other sub-periods, however, the fusion data are less clearly aligned with the toothwear data. Interestingly, as well as established 'consumer' sites such as the Hiberno-Norse towns, several substantial enclosure settlements in Co. Meath – including Baronstown, Roestown, Dowdstown, and Ratoath – also produced an age-slaughter pattern that would fit into an urban or consumer pattern.

Discussion

The original EMAP study and this paper represent the largest and most comprehensive analyses of plant macro-remains and animal bones from early medieval Ireland. Analysis of the new dataset indicates that the remains of domesticated crops and animals have been found at many sites across the island, with potential 'hot-spots' in the east and, to a lesser extent, the west. Although farming is well established in these societies, evidence for wild plants and animals is also recorded, reminding us that past societies often did not choose either farming or hunting/gathering, but instead created lifeways that incorporated elements of both.

Analysis of the plant remains highlighted the importance of barley and oat in early medieval Ireland. Regional variation is apparent in crop choices – oat, for example, was more significant than barley in northern and southern areas. Many assemblages were dominated by either barley or oat, with few mixed assemblages, perhaps indicating some level of specialisation. Wheat – often bread wheat – was recorded at many locations, but rarely as the dominant cereal. Rye was a minor crop, being recorded at around one-quarter of all phases of activity, but never dominant.

The predominance of barley and oat may reflect their ecological and cultivation requirements. Oat will thrive in the humid, wet climate of Ireland and will tolerate poorer soils when compared with bread wheat, for example. Barley will grow on both light and heavy soils, and is a relatively low-risk crop because it will often yield at least part of its crop after a poor season. Wheat, particularly bread wheat, requires an increased input of labour and a better quality of soil than other cereals because it is ecologically far more demanding. By contrast, rye can grow on rather marginal soils and seems to be a minor crop because of cultural choice, rather than environmental constraints. Given that naked wheat and rye were accorded a higher social status in early medieval Ireland, according to the legal text *Bretha Déin Chécht* (Kelly 1997, 248), it is unsurprising that these cereals were rarely dominant in the archaeological record. At the small number of sites where wheat was dominant, further indicators of high-status activity were sometimes recorded, for example at the ecclesiastical site of Clonfad, Co. Westmeath, where high-status craftworking (the production of monastic bells) was undertaken. The presence of wheat should not, however, be interpreted as reflecting high-status activity in all cases. Rather it reflects engagement with a more unusual crop that may have been limited to special social or religious occasions. The recovery of flax and legumes extends the variety of crops being farmed in early medieval Ireland, particularly during later centuries and in eastern areas.

The potential for chronological variation has previously been explored, for example in an analysis of cereals from drying kilns at 18 early medieval sites in Co. Kildare (Timpany *et al.* 2011). This kiln study indicated that barley was the dominant crop until around AD 600, when it decreased in importance and oat became more significant (Timpany *et al.* 2011, 79). This apparent shift in crop choice relates to a limited area and one site category, but the larger study detailed in this current paper also suggests temporal patterning in the dataset. A larger number of plant assemblages date to the later period (seventh to tenth centuries) when compared with the earlier period (fourth to seventh centuries), and a wider variety of crops are recorded in the later period also. It is possible that this increase reflects a greater focus on arable production in the later period, as has been suggested previously (McCormick 2008). It may be the case, however, that this increase reflects more broadly the increase in overall settlement activity dating to the later period (Kerr and McCormick 2014; O'Sullivan *et al.* 2014a; although note that rural settlement activity appears to drop off in the tenth century). Perhaps it is this increase that is resulting in more archaeobotanical assemblages being recovered. While there is a relative decrease in the construction of drying kilns during the later period (McCormick *et al.* 2014, 28), it coincides with a peak in the construction of horizontal water mills (Brady 2006, 49). Changes are also apparent in the types of crops being cultivated over time. Barley appears to have been more often dominant during the earlier period (fourth to seventh centuries), while oat became increasingly important during the later period (seventh to tenth centuries). It seems, therefore, that changes in agricultural production did take place during various sub-phases of the early medieval period in Ireland.

Whilst barley and oat are the dominant crops of early medieval Ireland, a different picture is apparent in several other regions of western Europe during this period. Naked wheat (including bread wheat) and barley are the dominant cereals in the Mediterranean area of southern France. In parts of northern France, bread wheat and rye are dominant, with barley also important (Ruas 2005). Oat did not become important in areas of north-western France until the eighth to ninth centuries AD (Ruas and Zech-Matterne 2012). A study comparing data from northern France and the southern Netherlands (Bakels 2005) suggests that rye, oat and barley are dominant on sandy soils, while bread wheat is more often associated with loess soils. In the case of Anglo-Saxon England, bread wheat and rye are common, with barley and oat also regularly recorded (Moffett 2011). A recent reassessment of the archaeobotanical record from mid-Saxon England (AD 650–850) found that barley and naked wheat were common throughout the fifth to ninth centuries, while rye and perhaps oat became substantially more important from the seventh and eighth centuries (McKerracher 2016). In northern Britain, barley and oat are dominant, which is interpreted as representing less favourable field conditions (Greig 1991, 317).

Similarly, the overall trend of cattle dominance throughout the early medieval period in Ireland is not reflected in other regions of north-west Europe at this time. Zooarchaeological studies from Anglo-Saxon England and early medieval south-west France display some similarities, where sheep are abundant in the earliest phases, with cattle becoming more important at a later date, and sheep returning to dominance by the end of the early medieval period (O'Connor 2011, 367; Rodet-Belarbi 2011). Rather than reflecting different food preferences in Ireland when compared with elsewhere in Europe, the emphasis on cattle in Ireland throughout the early medieval period may reflect the special role of cattle in society as a symbol of wealth and prestige.

This focus on cattle in Ireland contradicts earlier studies by Kerr (2007; 2009) and McCormick and Murray (2007), who suggested a shift away from cattle farming at AD 800. The current study suggests that cattle remained important throughout the early medieval period of Ireland. The earlier studies were based upon smaller datasets, although it should be noted that there is regional bias

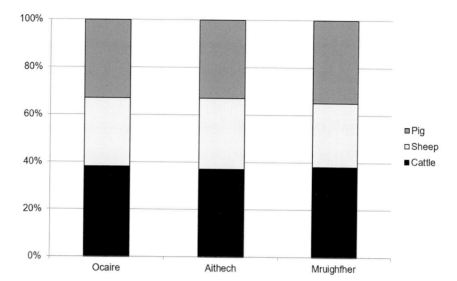

FIGURE 4.7. Percentages of cattle, sheep and pig by grade of farmer, according to *Críth Gablach*.

within the new enlarged dataset, where there are particular concentrations in the east and to a lesser extent in the west.

Early Irish law tracts, such as the *Críth Gablach*, outlined the number of cattle, sheep, and pig an individual should manage to maintain their social status (Fig. 4.7). The relative proportions of the three major domesticates in the eastern region changed little through the early medieval period and appear to correlate with livestock requirements found in the *Críth Gablach*. Western and northern regions are more variable, with sheep/goat, and to a lesser extent pig, becoming more important over time. Environmental conditions may play a role in this variation – the grasslands in the eastern region are well suited to raising cattle, whereas those of areas in the north and west are better suited to sheep grazing. Social impacts of law tracts on status may also have played a role, with more of a focus on following the *Críth Gablach* requirements in the eastern region to maintain social status. Pig does not, however, play an important role in most assemblages, despite its role in the *Críth Gablach*. It seems therefore that attempts to create a uniform farming economy, as outlined in texts such as the *Críth Gablach*, had mixed success and endured only in the eastern region. This may be because there was a shift away from established social hierarchies or perhaps because of ecological constraints in each region.

Mixed results were obtained from analysis of age-death patterns in cattle. Toothwear analysis (age of animal at death) and epiphyseal fusion analysis (survival rates into adulthood) were determined. Toothwear is better at identifying age of death for adult/mature cattle, but possibly weaker at identifying juvenile deaths when compared with fusion data. The data for Ireland suggest that there are clear markers for low death rates among younger cattle (pointing to a dairying economy), but the fusion data are not as clear. Where they do agree is for older cattle, suggesting that cattle were killed at a later age in the later centuries of the early medieval period when compared with the earlier centuries, suggesting an increasingly 'urban' environment, or at least the increasing presence of consumption sites.

Age-death patterns in sheep suggest a shift from treating sheep as producers of meat to treating sheep as primarily producers of wool. This is particularly evident in the northern and western regions. Woollen textiles were created for domestic use and perhaps also for export.

Conclusions

Analysis of extensive new archaeobotanical, zooarchaeological and archaeological evidence from early medieval Ireland reveals that both animal husbandry and crop production were being undertaken on a larger scale than ever before. The evidence derives from excavations in Ireland over the past few decades, often associated with infrastructural developments. This study has provided a more robust basis for understanding farming systems in early medieval Ireland. The primary crops are hulled barley and oat, with the potential for regional preferences. Wheat was present at many sites, but rarely as the primary crop. Rather than being an 'everyday' cereal, wheat may have been associated with particular social or religious occasions. Rye was a minor crop. As well as cereals, evidence was occasionally found for flax and legumes. Crops were more often found at 'later' sites in early medieval Ireland, both in relation to the number of sites where they were recorded and the variety of crops cultivated, perhaps reflecting an increased emphasis on arable farming. Cattle was the dominant animal at many sites, with smaller numbers of pig and sheep/goat usually recorded. Dairying appears to be prominent throughout the island. The major findings from the study of faunal remains are a strong element of regionalism in the farming landscape of early medieval Ireland, and the identification of possible 'proto-urban' sites, with changing patterns of consumption. Both of these findings require further research to test them more fully, but, if valid, they have profound implications for our understanding of early medieval Ireland.

Acknowledgements

This research was undertaken as part of the Early Medieval Archaeology Project (EMAP). Detailed data can be found in McCormick *et al.* 2014. We gratefully acknowledge that EMAP and the research for this paper were supported by the Heritage Council under the Irish National Strategic Archaeological Research (INSTAR) programme, funded by the National Monuments Service of the Department of Culture, Heritage and the Gaeltacht. The following archaeologists and archaeobotanists are thanked for drawing our attention to relevant sites, and for providing access to excavation and specialist reports: Edward Bourke, Lisa Coyle, James Eogan, Ann Frykler, Lorcan Harney, Susan

Lyons, Jerry O'Sullivan, Orlaith Egan, Rónán Swan, Richard O'Brien, Gill Plunkett, Martin Reid, Matthew Seaver, Michael Stanley, and Scott Timpany.

References

Bakels, C. C. (2005) Crops Produced in the Southern Netherlands and Northern France During the Early Medieval Period: A Comparison. *Vegetation History and Archaeobotany* 14, 394–9.

Becker, K., Geary, B., Eogan, J., McClatchie, M., Nagle, C. and Armit, I. (2016) Seeing beyond the site – an innovative approach to examining later prehistoric Ireland. In M. Stanley (ed.), *Above and Below: the archaeology of roads and light rail*. TII Heritage 3. Dublin, Transport Infrastructure Ireland, 13–20.

Brady, N. (2006) Mills in medieval Ireland: looking beyond design. In S. Walton (ed.) *Wind and Water, the Medieval Mill*. Tempe, Arizona State University Press, 39–68.

Duignan, M. (1944) Irish Agriculture in Early Historic Times. *Journal of the Royal Society of Antiquaries of Ireland* 14, 124–145.

Fredengren, C., McClatchie, M. and Stuijts, I. (2004) Reconsidering Crannogs in Early Medieval Ireland: alternative approaches in the investigation of social and agricultural systems. *Environmental Archaeology* 9, 161–6.

Geraghty, S. (1996) *Viking Dublin: botanical evidence from Fishamble Street*. Dublin, Royal Irish Academy.

Grant, A. (1982) The use of tooth wear as a guide to the age of domestic ungulates. In B. Wilson, C. Grigson and S. Payne (eds) *Ageing and Sexing Animal Bones from Archaeological Sites*. BAR British Series 109. Oxford, British Archaeological Reports, 91–108.

Greig, J. (1991) The British Isles. In W. Van Zeist, K. Wasylikowa and K. E. Behre (eds) *Progress in Old World Palaeoethnobotany*. Rotterdam, Balkema, 299–334.

Hencken, H. O'N. (1950) Lagore Crannóg: an Irish royal residence of the seventh to tenth century A. D. *Proceedings of the Royal Irish Academy* 53C, 1–248.

Higham, C. F. W. (1967) Stock Rearing as a Cultural Factor in Prehistoric Europe. *Proceedings of the Prehistoric Society* 33, 84–108.

Hillman, G. C., Mason, S., De Moulins, D. and Nesbitt, M. (1996) Identification of Archaeological Remains of Wheat: the 1992 London workshop. *Circaea* 12, 195–209.

Kelly, F. (1997) *Early Irish Farming*. Dublin, Institute for Advanced Studies.

Kerr, T. (2007) *Early Christian Settlement in North-west Ulster*. BAR British Series 439. Oxford, British Archaeological Reports.

Kerr, T. (2009) The Height of Fashion: raised raths in the landscape of north-west Ulster. *Journal of Irish Archaeology* 18, 63–75.

Kerr, T. R., Doyle, M., Seaver, M., McCormick, F. and O'Sullivan, A. (2015) *Early Medieval Crafts and Production in Ireland, AD 400–1100. The Evidence from Rural Settlements*. BAR British Series 2707. Oxford, British Archaeological Reports.

Kerr, T. R. and McCormick, F. (2014) Statistics, Sunspots and Settlement: influences on sum of probability curves. *Journal of Archaeological Science* 41, 493–501.

McClatchie, M., Bogaard, A., Colledge, S., Whitehouse, N. J., Schulting, R. J., Barratt, P. and McLaughlin, T. R. (2014) Neolithic Farming in North-western Europe: archaeobotanical evidence from Ireland. *Journal of Archaeological Science* 51, 206–215.

McClatchie, M., Kerr, T. R., McCormick, F. and O'Sullivan, A. (2015) Early Medieval Farming and Food Production: a review of the archaeobotanical evidence from archaeological excavations in Ireland. *Vegetation History and Archaeobotany* 24, 179–186.

McCormick, F. (1983) Dairying and Beef Production in Early Christian Ireland, the faunal evidence. In T. Reeves-Smyth and F. Hammond (eds) *Landscape Archaeology in Ireland*. Oxford, Oxford University Press, 253–267.

McCormick, F. (1992) Early Faunal Evidence for Dairying. *Oxford Journal of Archaeology* 11(2), 201–9.

McCormick, F. (2008) The Decline of the Cow: agricultural and settlement change in early medieval Ireland. *Peritia* 20, 210–225.

McCormick, F. (2009) Ritual feasting in Iron Age Ireland. In G. Cooney, K. Becker, J. Coles, M. Ryan and S. Sievers (eds) *Relics of Old Decency: archaeological studies in later prehistory*. Bray, Wordwell, 405–412.

McCormick, F. (2014) Agriculture, Settlement and Society in Early Medieval Ireland. *Quaternary International* 346, 119–130.

McCormick, F., Kerr, T. R., McClatchie, M. and O'Sullivan, A. (2014) *Early Medieval Agriculture, Livestock and Cereal Production in Ireland, AD 400–1100*. BAR International Series 2647. Oxford, British Archaeological Reports.

McCormick, F. and Murray, E. (2007) *Knowth and the Zooarchaeology of Early Christian Ireland*. Dublin, Royal Irish Academy.

McKerracher, M. (2016) Bread and Surpluses: the Anglo-Saxon 'bread wheat thesis' reconsidered. *Environmental Archaeology* 26(1), 88–102.

Moffett, L. (2011) Food plants on archaeological sites: the nature of the archaeobotanical record. In H. Hamerow, D. A. Hinton and S. Crawford (eds) *The Oxford Handbook of Anglo-Saxon Archaeology*. Oxford, Oxford University Press, 346–360.

Monk, M. A. (1986) Evidence From Macroscopic Plant Remains for Crop Husbandry in Prehistoric and Early Historic Ireland: a review. *Journal of Irish Archaeology* 3, 31–6.

Monk, M. A. (1991) The archaeobotanical evidence for field crop plants in early historic Ireland. In J. Renfrew (ed.) *New Light on Early Farming: recent developments in palaeoethnobotany*. Edinburgh, Edinburgh University Press, 315–328.

Monk, M. A. and Kelleher, E. (2005) An Assessment of the Archaeological Evidence for Irish Corn-drying Kilns in the Light of the Results of Archaeological Experiments and Archaeobotanical Studies. *Journal of Irish Archaeology* 14, 77–114.

Monk, M. A., Tierney, J. and Hannon, M. (1998) Archaeobotanical studies and early medieval Munster. In M. A. Monk and J. Sheehan (eds) *Early Medieval Munster: archaeology, history and society*. Cork, Cork University Press, 5–75.

Moreno-Garcia, M., Orton, C. and Rackham, J. (1996) A New Statistical Tool for Comparing Animal Bone Assemblages. *Journal of Archaeological Science* 23, 437–453.

O'Connor, T. (2000) *The Archaeology of Animal Bones*. Stroud, Sutton Publishing.

O'Connor, T. P. (2011) Animal husbandry. In H. Hamerow, D. A. Hinton and S. Crawford (eds) *The Oxford Handbook of Anglo-Saxon Archaeology*. Oxford, Oxford University Press, 361–376.

Ó Ríordáin, S. P. (1949) Lough Gur excavations: Carraig Aille and the 'Spectacles'. *Proceedings of the Royal Irish Academy* 52C, 39–111.

O'Sullivan, A., McCormick, F., Kerr, T. R. and Harney, L. (2014a) *Early Medieval Ireland, AD 400–1100. The evidence from archaeological excavations*. Dublin, Royal Irish Academy.

O'Sullivan, A., McCormick, F., Kerr, T. R., Harney, L. and Kinsella, J. (2014b) *Early Medieval Dwellings and Settlements in Ireland, AD 400–1100*. BAR International Series 2604. Oxford, British Archaeological Reports.

Payne, S. (1973) Kill-off Patterns in Sheep and Goats: the mandibles from Asvan Kale. *Anatolian Studies* 23, 281–305.

Payne, S. (1987) Reference Codes for Wear States in the Mandibular Cheek Teeth of Sheep and Goat. *Journal of Archaeological Science* 12, 139–147.

Ringrose, T. J. (1993) Bone Counts and Statistics: a critique. *Journal of Archaeological Science* 20, 121–157.

Rodet-Belarbi, I. (2011) Viandes animales dans le Languedoc-Rouissillon rural médiéval: bilan 2010. *Ruralia* 8, 91–112.

Ruas, M.-P. (2005) Aspects of Early Medieval Farming From Sites in Mediterranean France. *Vegetation History and Archaeobotany* 14, 400–415.

Ruas, M.-P. and Zech-Mattern, V. (2012) Les avoines dans les productions agro-pastorales du nord-ouest de la France: donnés carpologiques et indications textuelles. In V. Carpentier and C. Marcigny (eds) *Des hommes aux champs pour une archéologie des espaces ruraux du Néolithique au Moyen Age*. Rennes, Presses Universitaires de Rennes, 327–365.

Rynne, C. (1998) The craft of the millwright in early medieval Munster. In M. A. Monk and J. Sheehan (eds) *Early Medieval Munster: archaeology, history and society*. Cork, Cork University Press, 87–101.

Sexton, R. (1998) Porridges, gruels and breads: the cereal foodstuffs of Early Medieval Ireland. In M. A. Monk and J. Sheehan (eds) *Early Medieval Munster: archaeology, history and society*. Cork, Cork University Press, 76–86.

Silver, I. A. (1969) The ageing of domestic animals. In D. Brothwell and E. Higgs (eds) *Science in Archaeology*. London, Thames and Hudson, 283–302.

Stelfox, A. W. (1941) Animal Bones, The excavation of Leacanabuile Stone Fort, near Cahirciveen, Co. Kerry. *Journal of the Cork Historical and Archaeological Society* 46, 95–6.

Tierney, J. and Hannon, M. (1997) Plant remains. In M. F. Hurley, O. M. B. Scully and S. W. J. McCutcheon (eds) *Late Viking Age and Medieval Waterford Excavations 1986–1992*. Waterford, Waterford Corporation, 854–893.

Timpany, S., Power, O. and Monk, M. (2011) Agricultural boom and bust in medieval Ireland: plant macrofossil evidence from kiln sites along the N9/N10 in County Kildare. In S. Conran, E. Danaher and M. Stanley (eds) *Past Times, Changing Fortunes*. Dublin, National Roads Authority, 73–83.

van Wijngaarden-Bakker, L. H. (1974) The Animal Remains from the Beaker Settlement at Newgrange, Co. Meath. First Report. *Proceedings of the Royal Irish Academy* 74C, 313–383.

CHAPTER FIVE

Living off the land in medieval Welsh Law

Sara Elin Roberts

The laws of medieval Wales are a rich and valuable mine of information on all aspects of life and society in Wales in the middle ages, and as such are one of the most important historical sources available for examining any aspect of society in medieval Wales and beyond. As they discuss all aspects of medieval life at every level the laws are a comprehensive source. Agriculture features prominently in the lawbooks, which have specific detailed provisions devoted to it. While, to modern eyes, it may seem a surprising topic for law to consider, for medieval society farming was an essential and critical activity. The laws of Wales dealt with a rural society and could not avoid considering a subject which was central to the lives of the people to whom the laws applied. The laws reflect the social organisation of a largely agrarian society; there is no evidence of towns in archaeological and historical sources of early medieval Wales (Davies 1982, 57), although the surveys, which post-date the lawtexts, suggest that towns were beginning to develop after the conquest of Wales in 1282 (Beverley Smith 1998, 243–4). There are no direct references to commerce or markets in Welsh law, although there are implications such as the references to buying and selling animals (Wade-Evans 1909, 220, 216, 221–3; Jenkins 1986, 177); but in general the focus in the laws is on a society where people live in the countryside and live off the land. Sustenance – food – is central to life, and therefore if the law is intended to cover every aspect of life, as was indeed the case with the Welsh laws, farming could not be neglected. The consequence of this is a preoccupation in the Welsh lawtexts with the farming year; everything is structured around the requirements of ploughing, sowing, harvest, and animal husbandry – which would most likely be true of life itself in medieval Wales. A considerable amount of the material on agriculture in the laws is often mentioned in passing, as parts of discussions on other topics rather than as tractates on 'farming law' per se. The sections discussing contract, tenure, claims and accidents, and property and theft, all discuss matters related to agriculture. The primary focus of the laws may not have been on farming, but the way that farming is found in the laws suggests that it was very much a part of everyday life and points to the centrality of the land, and of living off the land, to all of society.

Medieval Wales had its own system of law, separate to that of England. It was a home-grown system, different to English Common Law and also to the Canon Law of the church, and it is often described as a *volksrecht* system, a law of the people (Jenkins 1977, 63); although perhaps it would be more accurate to describe it as lawyer-made law. The body of law contained within the Welsh lawbooks was attributed to a tenth-century king, Hywel ap Cadell, or Hywel Dda ('Hywel the Good', d. 949/950), but there is no evidence other than the Prologues to the lawbooks to link Hywel to any legal activity. As ruler he held a large part of Wales (if not 'all of Wales' as is stated in the lawbooks) and, following early conquests and consolidation, enjoyed a period of relative stability. He was in contact with the English king Athelstan of Mercia, a well-known lawmaker, which may have inspired Hywel's own lawmaking activities (Jenkins 1986, xi–xvi; Halloran 2011, 299–300). There is, however, no independent evidence to prove the link between Hywel and the laws. None of the extant lawbooks date to the tenth century, and the account of Hywel's legal activity in the Prologues was most likely a story, concocted to give the Welsh laws imagined royal and ecclesiastical origins as a defence against the criticisms of the laws by Norman clerics (Jenkins 1986, xiii, and see p. 1 for an example of a prologue; Pryce 1993, 71–3).

The texts

Cyfraith Hywel ('The Law of Hywel') survives in some forty manuscripts, the majority written in middle Welsh but some in Latin. All the manuscripts date from the mid-thirteenth century to the sixteenth century, but there are elements in the texts which point to some sections being earlier than the date of the manuscripts in which they are contained. Each manuscript text is unique, but the order and content of the Welsh language manuscripts show that they form three groups or redactions. Each redaction is named after a lawyer given pre-eminence in the prologue to that redaction. The Cyfnerth redaction (Wade-Evans 1909; Roberts 2011) contains seven manuscripts, with much variation in the order of the tractates or sections within the lawtexts. This is a very loose group and has its origins in south Wales, with some parts of the text possibly dating to the twelfth century; it appears to be an early text of the laws although the manuscripts are not the earliest in date.

The Iorwerth redaction (Wiliam 1960; Jenkins 1986) has the earliest manuscripts, dating to the mid-thirteenth century, and the manuscripts form a close group of eight with little variation between the order and content of the sections within the text. Iorwerth ap Madog, after whom this group of manuscripts is named, was a jurist who may have edited or reorganised some sections of the lawtexts. Iorwerth ap Madog is credited in the Iorwerth texts themselves as being responsible for the Justices' Test Book, the third section of the lawtexts said to contain the material which a justice or lawyer needed to know in order to practice law (Jenkins 1953, 164–170). In the prologue to the

Test Book it is stated that '... this book was gathered together by Iorwerth ap Madog ... and this book is called "The Test Book"' (Jenkins 1986, 141), but it is not at all clear whether the book which Iorwerth ap Madog collated was the Test Book, a part of the Test Book, or the entire book of the laws (Jenkins 1986, 274; Charles-Edwards 1989, 23, 30). The laws in the Iorwerth redaction are divided into three parts, the Laws of Court, the Laws of Country, and the Justices' Test Book, and the latter was comprised of the sections known as the Three Columns of Law, the Value of Wild and Tame, and other sections on *cyfar* (co-tilling) and Corn Damage (Jenkins 1986, 141–2). This redaction is associated with north Wales and may reflect the law in the kingdom of Gwynedd in the thirteenth century under the two well-known rulers Llywelyn ab Iorwerth, *c.* 1194–1240, and Llywelyn ap Gruffudd, 1246–1282, particularly the former (Charles-Edwards 1989, 38).

The Blegywryd redaction (Williams and Powell 1942; Richards 1954; Richards 1990) contains the most manuscripts, and the texts originate from south Wales. The manuscripts are later in date and several of them are lengthy, including a large variety of legal material which was clearly circulating in some regions (Charles-Edwards 1989, 20–1; James 1993, 152–4). The Blegywryd redaction was originally a Welsh translation of a Latin manuscript similar to one of the extant Latin manuscripts.

This brings us to the Latin texts (Emanuel 1973, 163–4). The Latin manuscripts are often grouped together but their main common feature is the language, and they do not form a single group. Their origin is very uncertain: they may be derived from some sort of Welsh legal text, although there is no extant early Welsh original with which they can be compared. Several of the Latin manuscripts are early and similar in date to the Iorwerth redaction. They were most likely intended for a different audience and probably allowed access to the texts for the Normans in Wales and the March; in addition they had the added benefit of elevating the Welsh laws and placing them in the long European tradition of writing legal texts in Latin (Emanuel 1967, 12).

The lawbooks form lengthy manuscripts, made up of a collection of subject-specific sections. Several of the sections are always present in any complete text of the Welsh laws. For example, the complete manuscripts start with the Prologue, giving the story of Hywel Dda and the creation of the Welsh laws, and then present the Laws of Court, a lengthy section looking at the officers of the royal court and the duties of those serving the king (Pryce 1986, 151–182; Charles-Edwards, Owen and Russell 2000). The Laws of Court clearly reflect an earlier period and were probably obsolete by the time of the earliest Welsh law manuscripts. The Laws of Country contained several other sections on all matters which were not included in the Laws of Court. These include subjects such as land law; contract (suretyship); the law of women, which considered sexual unions and inheritance; the Three Columns of Law on homicide, theft, and arson; and various tractates on damages, accidents and injuries, and governing society, including common agricultural situations and farming.

Every individual was to be responsible for his own actions, and also had a responsibility to society as a whole. Compensation was to be paid for acts, whether deliberate or not, which caused loss or injury to others (Jenkins 1986, xxx–xxi). The social structure revealed by the laws was that of a hierarchical system, with a contrast between the unfree bondmen (*taeogion*, or *bilain*, from 'villein', and also *aillt*; see Jenkins 1986, 310–311) and the freemen, sometimes called *uchelwyr*, 'noblemen' or *bonheddig*, 'noble, men of lineage' (Jenkins 1986, 243). The bondsmen were expected to support the king and his entourage on circuit, and also paid renders twice a year and had other burdens, but the freemen were exempt from payments apart from the 'great circuit of the household in winter' (Jenkins 1986, 121–2, 124–5). The lawbooks reveal a highly developed and still-evolving system, and are crucial for the study of society in medieval Wales and beyond; they also offer evidence, indirectly, for various aspects of life in the middle ages.

Farming in the laws

References to agriculture can be divided into references to animals and animal husbandry, and to arable farming and the crop season. Morfydd Owen's discussion of animals in Welsh law notes that the Welsh lawtexts are unique in their details on animals and husbandry for the period, and appear to reflect the circumstances of the twelfth or thirteenth century (Owen 2009, 24). She also asks an interesting question regarding where the writers or compilers were getting their information, and whether they were reading a text giving the details or whether they had their own practical experience of rearing animals (Owen 2009, 24). While some of the material may have come from written sources, it is tempting to suggest that the centrality of farming and animal husbandry to everyday life meant that the writers of the Welsh lawtexts probably experienced personally at least some of the aspects they discussed in their work.

The two main sections of law which consider arable farming are 'themed' tractates looking at animal damage to crops ('Corn Damage') and the organisation of ploughing (*Cyfar*, 'Co-tillage'), but consideration will first be made of other discussions and references to agriculture in the laws. The most notable of these other discussions is a lengthy tractate called The Value of Wild and Tame which looks at the characteristics of animals 'of which man may make use', and as such is the only piece of writing in medieval Welsh law on animal husbandry. The inclusion of this tractate in the Justices' Test Book of the Iorwerth texts – a key section that every lawyer needed to know in order to qualify (Charles-Edwards 1989, 31) – emphasises the importance of farming and animals in both legal and everyday life. The tractate is also included in the Cyfnerth and the Blegywryd redactions, as well as in the Latin texts (Wade-Evans 1909, 65–83, where the section is followed by Corn Damage; Williams and Powell 1942, 87–94, preceded by Corn Damage; Emanuel 1967, 152–7,

233–6, 358–362, 484–8); in these texts the tractate is included in the Laws of Country, but the texts do not have the same clear tripartite structure which is evident in the Iorwerth redaction. In the tractate, each animal discussed has its own paragraph, sometimes rather lengthy. The word 'value' in the title of the section is not used in the sense of market prices, but rather lists the characteristics of animals, what they should and should not do (with an emphasis on human use of animals), and when they should be doing it: these are the *teithi*, 'characteristics' (Owen 2009, 6).

> *Guerth porchell, o'r nos y ganher ene el y tonuoy, i.k'; hyt tra uo en dynu, o henne allan, ii.k': sef hyt e dele bot en denu, try mys. Ac o henne allan ene el e moch e'r coet, banv uyd, a iiii.k' y werth. Ac o vyl Yeuan yd a e moch e'r coet hyt y kalan, xv, yu e werth; o'r kalan hyt uyl Yeuan em pen e uluydyn, iiii.k' arnau, ac ena en xxx. adan e coet ual e uam.*
>
> *Teythy huch: na bo baedredauc, ac nat esso y perchyll, a'e goruot teyr nos a thry dyeu rac e uynyglauc.* (Wiliam 1960, 86–7; Iorwerth)

The value of a piglet from the night it is born until it goes grubbing, a penny. While it is sucking from then on, twopence. The length it is right for it to be sucking, three months; and from then on until the pigs go to the woods, it will be a pigling and its value is fourpence. And from St John's Day [29 August, the Feast of the Decapitation of St John the Baptist] when the pigs go to the woods until the New Year its value is fifteen pence. From the New Year until St John's Day at the end of a year, fourpence added to it, and then thirty pence under the trees like its mother.

The properties of a sow is that she is not always on heat and that she does not eat her piglets, and that she is guaranteed against quinsy for three nights and three days. (Jenkins 1986, 178–9)

The values given to the animals in the tractate were not for buying and selling – they are not a reflection of the market price at the time of writing the lawtexts, for example, and the values are unchanging in the lawtexts – but rather for compensation purposes, to be paid if an animal was stolen, or killed; animals without the complete legal characteristics listed would not be worth the full amount (Owen 2009, 6). As well as the detail on the animals, their periods of growth and development, and their characteristics, there is some detail found here on the care of animals, and the knowledge of animal diseases. While the section includes both the wild and the tame in its title, the main focus is on the domestic animals (Jenkins 1993, 2). Horses, cattle, pigs, sheep and goats, poultry – geese and hens but not ducks – and cats and dogs all have a section, some lengthier than others, and sheep and goats are discussed together. Dogs occur twice, both as farm dogs and also as hunting dogs (Owen 2009, 6, 15–16). The main wild animals included in the tractate are hawks and falcons and bees (Owen 2009, 13–14; see also Charles-Edwards and Kelly 1983), though the section on bees is not always included within all manuscript variants of The Value of Wild and Tame.

Hunting

Hunting is the closest we get to the wild animals in the laws – although there are references to squirrels, badgers, foxes, and otter – since the focus is always on animals which were used in one way or another. In the Iorwerth texts, hunting animals are included with the Value of Wild and Tame, but in other redactions there is a separate section on hunting, both with dogs and also with hawks and falcons. Dafydd Jenkins noted that the laws show more preoccupation with hunting wild animals than with matters relating to farm animals (Jenkins 1993, 2); but this may reflect the relative risks of hunting, and its greater potential for legal claims. The king had priority in hunting, and the hunting section in some Cyfnerth manuscripts is part of the Laws of Court. The Laws of Court, giving details of the royal court and its organisation, were obsolete by the date of the earliest extant lawbooks, and the hunting section suggests an earlier social setup than that of the twelfth or thirteenth century: it reflects an itinerant court and a ruler (called a king rather than the better-known prince, which appears to reflect an earlier period than the thirteenth century when *tywysog* or *princeps* was the term in common usage; Stephenson 2000, 400) possessed of ample leisure for hunting (Jenkins 1993, 2). The twenty-four officers of the court include several officers linked to the royal hunt: the chief falconer, the chief groom, and the chief huntsman (Charles-Edwards, Owen and Russell 2000, 19). Each of the three was very high ranking, in the top ten of the royal officers, and had special rights. They would have been expected to travel with the court as it went on circuit, and the details of their roles tell us about the practicalities of hunting and controlling the royal hunt. The hunting officers had special legal immunity at particular times, their horses had a larger share of feed, presumably as they were bigger hunting beasts and worked harder; and they were entitled to particular gifts such as skins, in order to make their equipment. The falconer had a limit on how much he could drink, since his main role was care of the valuable falcons.

> *Croen hyd a geif yr hebogyd yn hydref y gan y penkynyd y wneuthur tauylhualeu a menyc ida6. D6y ran a geif y varch o'r ebran. Nyd yf namyn teir dia6t yn y neuad rac bot g6all ar yr heboge6 dr6y veda6t. ... O ban dotto yr hebogyd y hebogeu yn y m6t hyt ban y tynho allan ny dyry atteb y'r neb a'e gofynnho. ... O pop taeoctref y kymmer pedeir keinhauc neu dauat hesb yn ymporth y'r hebogeu.*

The falconer shall have the skins of a stag in autumn from the chief houndsman to make jesses and gloves for himself. His horse shall have a double share of the fodder. He shall only take three drinks in the hall lest there be neglect of the hawks from drunkenness. ... From when the falconer shall place the hawks in the mew until he takes them out, he shall give no answer to anyone who makes a request of him. ... From every villain township he shall take four pence or a barren sheep as food for the hawks. (Owen 2000, 454–5; Cyfnerth)

While the context of the discussions in the laws on the royal hunt may have been obsolete by the time the surviving manuscripts were written, the details on the animals hunted most likely remained relevant. The lawbooks tell us that deer were hunted at specific times, hinds (female deer) in the spring, between 9 February and midsummer, and stags (harts) in summer and early autumn, from the day after St John's Day, 24 June, (or St Curig's Day on 16 June in some versions, see Wade-Evans 1909, 182) to 1 November (Jenkins 1993, 3–4; Jenkins 2000, 273–4). The king was allowed to hunt anything anywhere, and did not have to share any quarry taken with the landowner. There is also, in the Iorwerth redaction, mention of hunting wild boar: the wild boar hunting season ran from 9 November up to 10 December.

The details of the royal hunt – for instance the list of meat cuts in a stag or hart in the laws (Owen 2009, 18) – show that the king might sometimes have quite literally lived off the land when the Laws of Court were composed (Owen 2009, 18). They reflect an earlier period when the king would go on circuit around his kingdom twice a year (Charles-Edwards 2000, 320), taking with him his royal court and his officers and receiving food renders from the free townships in the winter, and from the bond townships in both winter and summer.

Food renders

The list of the renders owed is valuable evidence of food production in medieval Wales, and indicates a variety of foodstuffs. According to the laws, the king's villeins and the free subjects owed the royal court food-renders as well as money, and the renders are outlined in the texts (Charles-Edwards 2000, 320–1). *Gwestfa* ('hospitality', literally 'sleeping-place'; Charles-Edwards, Owen and Russell 2000, 567), is discussed in terms of money, '*gwestfa*-money', but the term shows clearly that it originated in a practical action of hosting the king and his household in a literal sense. This was payable by the king's free subjects, and the financial sum is also explained in commodities: *gwestfa* included wheat flour, an ox, oats, honey, and mead from a free township which had a *maer* or *cynghellor* (local officers of the king) or braggot (an alcoholic drink made from a blend of honey and malt) from a township which did not have the officers (Williams and Powell 1942, 67–8). Both mead and braggot were seen to be higher-status drinks, and the bondsmen owed ale which was lower in status (Charles-Edwards 2000, 321). In contrast, the unfree bondsmen owed renders called *dawnbwyd* (food-gift), which is detailed as being paid twice a year, and included a sow, high-quality bread, oats, ale, and cheese and butter. However, for both *gwestfa* and *dawnbwyd* the exact number and details vary across the redactions, which points to regional variations including differences in the size of townships in different areas. This is how the Iorwerth redaction describes the bondsmen's dawnbwyd:

> *O'r maenolyd caeth e deleyr deu daun buyt pob bluyden. Y gayaf, huch teyr bluyd,*
> *a llester emenyn try dernued hyt, try llet, a dogen keruen o uragaut nau dernued en*
> *e hyt en amryscoeu, a dreua o geyrch un ruym en ebran, a chue thorth arrugeynt o'r*

bara goreu a tyuo ar e tyr (o byd guenythtyr, chuech onadaunt en peyllyeyt; ony byd guenythtyr, chuech onadaunt en rennyon: pedeyr onadaunt parth a'r neuad a due parth a'r estauell; ac en gyulet ac o penelyn hyt ardurn ac en ken tewet ac na plyccoent er eu dale erbyn eu hemyl), a den a genewo tan e neuad e nos honno neu keynnyauc e'r nep a'e kynneuho trostau. Messur daun buyt er haf yu mollt teyr bluyd, a mannat emenyn kyulet a'r dyscel letaf a uo en e tref a chyn tewet ac y bo deu uoeldernued endau, a chue thorth ar ugeynt o ryu uara a dywespuyt uchot, a chynnullau a uo o luden blyth e perchennogyon e tref oll egyt ac eu godro un weyth en e dyd (ac na odroher namen er un weyth honno) a chossyn a wnelher o henne o laeth, hep urac, hep ebran, hep dym e kynneu tan. (Wiliam 1960, 64; Iorwerth)

From the bond maenolydd there is a right to two food-gifts every year. In winter, a three-year-old pig, and a vessel of butter three fistbreadths long and three wide, and a vat's quota of bragget (nine fistbreadths in length diagonally); and a thrave of single-bound oats as horse-fodder; and twenty-six loaves of the best bread that grows on the land: if it is wheat land, six of them of fine flour, and if it is not wheat land, six of them of groats (four of them for the hall and two for the chamber) – being as broad as from the elbow to the wrist, and so thick that they do not bend when held by the edges; with a person to light the fire in the hall that night, or a penny for him who lights it for him.

The measure of summer food-gift is a three-year-old wether; and a mass of butter as broad as the broadest dish in the townland and so thick that there are two bare fistbreadths in it; and twenty-six loaves of the kind of bread mentioned above, with all the milking beasts belonging to the owners in the town-land gathered together and milked save that once, so that a cheese be made from that milk; without brew, without horse-fodder, without anything to light a fire. (Jenkins 1986, 128–9)

The farming year

In the lawtexts, the bondsmen appear to live in hamlets, with some moving according to the season – there are references to their winter and summer dwellings, and details of their values and construction elements (see Comeau this volume).

Gwerth gayafty: o bop fforch a gynnhalyo y nenbrenn, vgeint yw; dros y nenbrenn, deugeint; y colofneu, meinkeu, ystyffyleu, amhinogeu, trothwyeu, gordrysseu, tubyst, doreu, pedeir keinnawc kyureith a tal pob vn o hynny; pollyon a gwyal, keinnawc kyureith; dorglwyt, dwy geinnawc kyureith; clwyt arall, keinnawc kyureith. Dros y gayafty oll, punt a telir a deudec mu y'r brenhinn.

Beuty gwarthec, dec ar hugeint a tal. Dros gynhaeafty, dec swllt. Dros hafty deugeint. Or noethir gayafty, trayann y werth a telir drostaw. Kynnhayafty, or byd twll taradyr yndaw, pedeir ar hugeint a tal; ony byd, deudec keinnawc kyureith; fforch kynnhayafty neu hafty, keinnawc kyureith. (Williams and Powell 1942, 95; Blegywryd)

The worth of a winter house: for every fork which supports the ridge-beam, forty; the pillars, benches, stanchions, door-posts, sills, lintels, side-posts, and doors, are each four legal pence in value; poles and rods, a legal penny; the door-hurdle,

two legal pence; other hurdle, a legal penny. For the whole winter-house, one
pound is to be paid and twelve cows to the king.

A cow-house is thirty pence in value. For an autumn-house, ten shillings. For a
summer-house, forty pence. If a winter-house be unroofed, the third of its value is
to be paid. An autumn-house, if there be auger-holes in it, is worth twenty-four;
if not, twelve legal pence; the fork of an autumn-house or of a summer-house, is
a legal penny in value. (Richards 1954, 92)

The descriptions are of wooden buildings on the whole although the winter
dwelling is of better quality; this is supported by the many references to burning
houses in the fire section of the laws. Other references to buildings provide
evidence of animal husbandry (Owen 2009, 6), and Butler notes there is a
large variety of farm buildings found in the laws (Butler 1987, 51). Apart from
the summer and winter houses, there is also the harvest house, *cynhaeafdy* (or
'autumn-house' in Richards 1954, 92), and barns for keeping grain. In the list
of values the laws also name a cattle yard, a lean-to, a pig-sty and a sheep fold,
all valued at thirty pence (Williams and Powell 1942, 96; Richards 1954, 93).
However, these were likely to belong to higher-status men, and the bondsmen
probably kept their animals in outhouses rather than in separate purpose-built
buildings; they were probably allowed to wander freely in the open air if the
evidence of the Corn Damage tractate is to be trusted (Butler 1987, 52).

The townships were organised communally, it seems, and this is true of the
farming activity as well. There are references in the laws to communal herdsmen
in bond hamlets – the 'hamlet herdsman' was one of the special witnesses
whose testimony would be believed, in a specific, specialist situation, above all
others: the list is called the 'Nine Tongued-Ones' and includes people such as
a donor on his own gift, a virgin on her own virginity, and a surety regarding
his suretyship (Jenkins 1986, 62 for the Iorwerth text, and Wade-Evans 1909,
41 for the Cyfnerth version). The hamlet's herdsman is the eighth in the list
and the section reveals some details on his work. If an animal is killed by an
animal belonging to another person, the herdsman's word is final on which
animal killed the other – and thus which owner has legal responsibility (Jenkins
1986, 62). This suggests that all, or many, of the animals owned by bondsmen
in one hamlet would be cared for communally, with one herdsman having
responsibility over a number of animals belonging to different people. This
evidence is supported by further references to the 'legal herd' of a township.
Within the Corn Damage section in the Cyfnerth and Blegywryd texts, the
obligation is to take a single animal from the 'legal herd'.

*O'r kadw kyfreith o'r deueit, dauat a geffir a phyrllig o pob pump llydyn hyt y kadw
kyfreith. Meint y kadw kyfreith o'r deueit, dec llydyn ar hugeint a hwrd. Meint y kadw
kyfreith o'r moch, deudec llydyn a baed.* (Williams and Powell 1942, 85; Blegywryd)

Out of the legal flock of sheep, a sheep is to be taken and a farthing for every
five head to the extent of a legal flock. The amount of the legal flock of sheep is
thirty animals and a ram. The amount of the legal herd of swine is twelve animals
and a boar. (Richards 1954, 85)

A legal herd of cattle is described as being twenty-four cows (Jenkins 1986, 178, taken from Cyfnerth). This is a large number of animals and with the reference to the hamlet herdsman it points to communal care for the animals. The animals would be taken out in the morning to graze and would be brought back in the evening to be kept in a safe place for the night, and the herdsman had the assistance of a herd-dog, which was as valuable as the most valuable animal in the herd it cared for (Jenkins 1986, 181–2). The legal herd had different statuses of animals within it – apart from the special status of the boar, needed in the legal herd, there were special animals which the owners of damaged corn were not permitted to take – these were known as the 'three special beasts'.

> *Tri ll6dyn vn 6erth yssyd yn y genuein pop amser; dec ar hugeint y6 g6werth pop vn ohonunt: baed kenuein, ac arbenhic y genuein, a h6ch a gat6er yg kyfeir yr argl6yd.*

There are three animals of the same value in the litter at all times; each of them is worth thirty [pence]: a herd pig, and the champion of the pigs, and a sow which is kept for the lord. (Roberts 2007, 146–7; Blegywryd).

The law itself also worked around the agricultural year: there was a specific season for hearing cases of land law, and that season was tied in with arable farming.

> *Am dadleu tyred yu henn. Deu amser e byd agoret keureyth am tyr a daear, a deu e byd kaeat: o nauuet dyd o kalan gayaf e byd agoret hyt nauuet dyd Chueuraur; o nauuet dyd Chueuraur e byd kaeat hyt nauuet dyd o Uey; o nauuet dyd o Uey e byd agoret keureyth hyt nauuet dyd guedy Aust; o nauuet dyd guedy Aust e byd kaeat keureyth hyt nauuet dyd guedy kalan gaeaf. A sef achaus e byd kayat keureyth e kenhayaf a'r guaeanhuen, urth dywyllyau e daear en e deu amser henne, rac llesteyryau eredyc e guaeanhuen a rac llesteyryau medy e kenhayaf.* (Wiliam 1960, 44; Iorwerth)

This is regarding actions for land. At two periods law is open for land and earth, and at two closed. From the ninth day from the Winter Kalends it is open until the ninth day of February; from the ninth day of February it is closed until the ninth day of May. From the ninth day of May law is open until the ninth day of August; from the ninth day of August law is closed until the ninth day after the Winter Kalends. And the reason that law is closed at Harvest and Springtime is that the earth is cultivated at those two periods, lest ploughing be hindered in Springtime and lest reaping be hindered at Harvest. (Jenkins 1986, 83)

Law was said to be 'open' for land cases at particular times of the year, periods which fitted around ploughing, reaping, and the ripening of crops in the land; and in the periods when law was 'closed', land cases could not be held at all (Wiliam 1960, 44; trans. Jenkins 1986, 83). This can be linked with practices for claiming land that involved the parties visiting the land and holding at least part of the case on the land under dispute, which would be problematic when land was in use for arable farming (Wiliam 1960, 45, trans. Jenkins 1986, 84).

Further detail on the timings of the agricultural year is found throughout the law (see Comeau this volume). There were specific times when grazing was permitted and also disallowed: grazing was not permitted on meadows from

17 March until the 'Winter Kalends' or 1 November (Jenkins 1986, 206–7, and 392), and on cornfields from 1 May according to Iorwerth (Jenkins 1986, 202); this points to the period the crops would be growing and ripening (Wiliam 1960, 101, trans. Jenkins 1986, 207). Prior to that, the land would be prepared and ploughing, according to the laws, started on St Bride's Day, 1 February (Wiliam 1960, 44, trans. Jenkins 1986, 83). Another regular activity involved burning scrub: 'muirburn fire' was allowed from mid-March until mid-April, but was otherwise illegal, again to protect the growing crops and presumably also to avoid fires getting out of control during drier weather (Roberts 2007, 106). In addition, livestock would be on the moor from late spring. The activities of pigs were also firmly seasonally regulated. While the laws have many references to the damage caused by pigs rooting on arable land, they were also valuable and useful animals, and pannage rights, allowing them to graze on acorns in the autumn, were important. The pannage season meant that pigs were permitted to wander in the woods from 29 August, the Feast of the Decapitation of St John the Baptist, known as *Gŵyl Ieuan y Moch* ('Feast of St John of the Pigs') in Welsh, up to 1 January (Wiliam 1960, 101, trans. Jenkins 1986, 206); they were also allowed on post-harvest corn fields during this period free of render. However, between Michaelmas, 29 September, and 1 January there was a render of 1 in 10 pigs, which meant that the owner of the woods was allowed to claim one pig from each ten in return for pannage access (Jenkins 1986, 179; Richards 1954, 83; this echoes medieval English pannage rights. With thanks to Rhiannon Comeau for her insights on this matter).

Corn Damage and *Cyfar*, co-tillage

While references to farming abound in the laws, there are two lengthy and important sections specifically dedicated to it: the sections on Corn Damage, covering animal damage to crops; and *Cyfar*, a tractate on joint-ploughing, called co-tillage by Jenkins (Jenkins 1993, 2). Both sections are discrete, titled, recognisable, and given some importance in the text, with Corn Damage occurring in all redactions. In the Iorwerth redaction both sections occur in the Test Book, in reworked, rewritten versions of the (sometimes very brief) material of other redactions (Charles-Edwards 1989, 29–30).

The Corn Damage section is a particular well-known element of the laws and occurs in the Cyfnerth, Blegywryd, and Iorwerth redactions, and in the Latin texts. While it is called *Llwgr Ŷd*, literally 'Corn Damage', the word '*ŷd*' can mean corn, grain, or cereal, and here it is a catch-all term referring to any crop, and may even refer to animal damage in general (Jenkins 1993, 3). The main focus of the section is on the consequences of animals wandering onto crops and eating or damaging them. Naturally, the owner of the crop would need to be compensated by the owner of the animal, and the solution was that the owner of the crop would catch and impound the animal. The animal's owner would then come to release his animal by paying the compensation for it. This is a self-help, self-contained action: the owner of the corn would receive compensation one way or another (if the animal's owner does not come to release the animal, then the crop owner would have an animal); and going to claim the animal would mean an admission of liability, which would require either the payment of compensation, or losing the animal. This sophisticated piece of law is not unique for Wales, and is found in other countries, primarily in medieval England; the Iorwerth rewriting seems to reflect more closely the English legal action of 'distress damage feasant', and is likely to have been developed through knowledge of it (Williams 1939).

In contrast, *Cyfar*, co-tillage, is only found as a sentence in the Cyfnerth texts of south Wales – 'No-one in a villein townland is entitled to plough until everyone in the townland has found a joint-ploughing' (Jenkins 1986, 199, and Wade-Evans 1909, 108) – but was developed into a full section in Iorwerth where it is presented as a neatly written contract, probably linked to Iorwerth ap Madog's editing work and therefore thirteenth century in date. The Iorwerth text explains in detail how to go about ploughing with other people – this was called 'voluntary co-operation among freemen' by Jenkins (Jenkins 1982, 3). For the bondsmen, however, nobody was allowed to start ploughing, according to the contract, before finding '*cyfar*', a partnership for doing so, which seems to imply that though the co-operation itself was compulsory, there was some freedom in the choice of partners (Jenkins 1982, 3). According to the contract, a group of occupiers were to plough a patch of land measuring twelve acres, with a wooden plough and an iron coulter and share. The work required a ploughman to guide the team of eight oxen which were under the control of a driver. The contract outlined the situation for twelve members, but some of the contractors could have more than one share, and the contract was fully adjustable according to the circumstances. Each of the contractors were to have one acre ploughed, and the order of ploughing is set out: the ploughman's acre was the first to be ploughed and the standard of the ploughing would be set from that acre (Jenkins 1982, 3). The section has wonderful detail on medieval ploughing technique – including care of the animals:

> *Guedy e del pob peth attadunt, er amaeth a'r geylwat byeu cadu en dywall e rey henne a guneythur udunt kystal ac e'r eydunt ehun. E geylwat a dele cauy arnadunt ual na bo ry geuyg arnadunt, ac eu galu mal na thorroent eu callon.* (Wiliam 1960, 97; Iorwerth)

> After everything has come to them, it is for the ploughman and the caller to keep everything faultless, and to do as well for them as for their own. It is right for the caller to close the oxen in so that it is not too confined for them, and to call them so that they do not break their heart. (Jenkins 1986, 200)

According to Jenkins *Cyfar* 'is perhaps the most interesting piece of material to be found anywhere in the corpus of Welsh law' (Jenkins 1982, 1). This is true on various levels, but for us '… its very existence … suggests the increasing importance of efficient arable farming in thirteenth-century Wales' (Jenkins 1982, 2). Although it is found as a concept in the Blegywryd, Cyfnerth and Latin texts it is not written out in full in these versions of the laws. This may imply that the content of *Cyfar* was commonly known but not committed to writing until the Iorwerth redaction. However, rewriting this section may have become necessary because of changes in ploughing and the adoption of a heavy plough with a team of eight oxen as opposed to the earlier plough (Comeau in this volume). The Corn Damage section, in contrast, existed in all of the lawtexts though was rewritten for the Iorwerth redaction. Jenkins described both the Corn Damage and *Cyfar* texts as 'significant', and noted that their inclusion in the Test Book 'is a sign that population was increasing, so that pressure on land was also increasing when the tractates were written' (Jenkins 1982, 2). When looking at living off the land in medieval Wales, the two rewritten texts – both the details they provide and the fact that they merited rewriting – are crucial evidence and emphasise the importance of the laws in considering society in medieval Wales.

These rewritten elements of the Iorwerth manuscripts show the importance of the land to everyday life in medieval Wales. Significantly, they are found in the Iorwerth Test Book of Gwynedd which is one of very few sections in the entire Welsh law tradition which can be dated and attributed. Equally significantly, much of the focus of the Test Book is on farming and agriculture, with the Test Book Appendix including heavily reworked or new sections – *Cyfar* and Corn Damage, as well as a list of equipment that may also have been written especially for this section. This legal focus on the very practical aspects of living off the land emphasises the all-pervading centrality of agriculture to the running of society.

Conclusion

There exists a wealth of material about animals and agriculture in the Welsh laws, reflecting a necessary preoccupation with a fundamental element of medieval life. The wellbeing of the populace rested on the success of crops and the good husbandry of livestock, and animals were likely to be the most valuable possession a person owned. Laws were therefore needed to safeguard property and crop production, and this factor explains the many references and sections of the Welsh laws which discuss agriculture, crops, and animals. The purpose of the Welsh law texts was not to explain contemporary farming practices but rather (as with all law in general) to regulate behaviour, exchanges, contracts, ensure fair deals, and provide a guide to punishment and retribution. In doing so, a great deal of information is included in passing which makes Welsh law an essential source of material on living off the land in medieval Wales.

References

Beverley Smith, J. (1998) *Llywelyn ap Gruffudd*. Cardiff, University of Wales Press.
Butler, L. A. S. (1987) Domestic Building in Wales and the Evidence of the Welsh Laws. *Medieval Archaeology* 31, 47–58.

Charles-Edwards, T. M. (1989) *The Welsh Laws: Writers of Wales*. Cardiff, University of Wales Press.

Charles-Edwards, T. M. (2000) Food, Drink and Clothing in the Laws of Court. In Charles-Edwards, Owen and Russell (eds) *The Welsh King and his Court*. Cardiff, University of Wales Press, 319–337.

Charles-Edwards, T. M. and Kelly, F. (1983) *Bechbretha*. Dublin, Dublin Institute for Advance Studies.

Charles-Edwards, T. M., Owen, M. E. and Russell, P. (eds) (2000) *The Welsh King and his Court*. Cardiff, University of Wales Press.

Davies, W. (1982) *Wales in the Early Middle Ages*. Leicester, Leicester University Press.

Emanuel, H. D. (1967) *The Latin Texts of the Welsh Laws*. Cardiff, University of Wales Press.

Emanuel, H. D. (1973) The Book of Blegywryd and Ms. Rawlinson 821. In D. Jenkins (ed.) *Celtic Law Papers: Introductory to Welsh Medieval Law and Government*. Brussels, International Council for Philosophy and Humanistic Studies with the Assistance of Unesco, 161–170.

Halloran, K. (2011) Welsh Kings at the English Court, 928–956. *Welsh History Review* 25(3), 297–313

James, C. (1993) Tradition and Innovation in Some Later Medieval Welsh Lawbooks. *Bulletin of the Board of Celtic Studies* 40, 148–156.

Jenkins, D. (2000) Hawk and Hound: Hunting in the Laws of Court. In T. M. Charles-Edwards, M. E. Owen and P. Russell (eds) *The Welsh King and his Court*. Cardiff, University of Wales Press, 255–280.

Jenkins, D. (1953) Iorwerth Ap Madog: Gŵr Cyfraith o'r Drydedd Ganrif Ar Ddeg. *National Library of Wales Journal* 8, 164–170.

Jenkins, D. (1977) The Significance of the Law of Hywel. *Transactions of the Honourable Society of the Cymmrodorion*, 54–76.

Jenkins, D. (1982) *Agricultural Co-Operation in Welsh Medieval Law*. Cardiff, National Museum of Wales.

Jenkins, D. (1986, 3rd Impression, 2000) *The Law of Hywel Dda: Law Texts from Medieval Wales*. Llandysul, Gomer Press.

Jenkins, D. (1993) *Hunting and Husbandry in Medieval Welsh Law*. Hallstatt Lecture, Machynlleth, Tabernacl Trust.

Owen, M. E. (2000) The Laws of Court from Cyfnerth. In T. M. Charles-Edwards, M. E. Owen and P. Russell (eds) *The Welsh King and his Court*. Cardiff, University of Wales Press, 425–477

Owen, M. E. (2009) The Animals of the Law of Hywel. *Carmarthenshire Antiquary* 45, 5–27.

Pryce, H. (1986) The Prologues to the Welsh Lawbooks. *Bulletin of the Board of Celtic Studies* 33, 151–182.

Pryce, H. (1993) *Native Law and the Church in Medieval Wales*. Oxford, Oxford University Press.

Richards, M. (1954) *The Laws of Hywel Dda (The Book of Blegywryd)*. Liverpool, Liverpool University Press.

Richards, M. (1990, 2nd Edition) *Cyfreithiau Hywel Dda Yn Ôl Llawysgrif Coleg Yr Iesu LVII*. Cardiff, University of Wales Press.

Roberts, S. E. (2007) *The Legal Triads of Medieval Wales*. Cardiff, University of Wales Press.

Roberts, S. E. (2011) *Llawysgrif Pomffred: An Edition and Study of Peniarth MS 259B*. Boston and Leiden, Brill.

Stephenson, D. (2000) The Laws of Court: Past Reality or Present Ideal? In T. M. Charles-Edwards, M. E. Owen and P. Russell (eds) *The Welsh King and his Court*. Cardiff, University of Wales Press, 400–414.

Wade-Evans, A. W. (1909, Reprinted 1979) *Welsh Medieval Law, Being a Text of the Laws of Howel the Good*. Oxford, Clarendon Press (repr. Darmstadt: Scientia Verlag Aalen, 1979).

Wiliam, A. Rh. (1960) *Llyfr Iorwerth: A Critical Text of the* Venedotian Code *of Medieval Welsh Law*. Cardiff, University of Wales Press.

Williams, G. (1939) *Liability for Animals: Distress Damage Feasant and the Duty to Fence*. Cambridge, Cambridge University Press.

Williams, S. J. and Powell, J. E. (1942) *Llyfr Blegywryd*. Cardiff, University of Wales Press.

CHAPTER SIX

Medieval field systems in north Wales

Bob Silvester

Almost fifty years ago Cambridge University Press published *Studies of Field Systems in the British Isles* (1973) edited by Alan Baker and Robin Butlin, a landmark publication which focused entirely on land use in the medieval and post-medieval centuries. Touted primarily as a set of studies in historical geography, it received favourable reviews and is still seen as a seminal work, not least because its fourteen chapters covered many though not all regions of Britain. Wales was allocated two chapters, that on north Wales prepared by Glanville Jones.

Given the regional approach envisioned by the editors the chapter by Jones, a Reader in Geography at Leeds University, could (and perhaps should) have laid firm foundations for subsequent research on the field patterns of the northern counties, and certainly over the next two decades at conferences on medieval settlement and their lands, it was Jones who was invited to contribute on the subject of fields (see Jones 1985; 1991). Yet on reflection his paper proves to be a conspicuous disappointment. It reiterated much that had already been delivered in print a year earlier in the *Agrarian History of England and Wales* volume devoted to the Roman and early medieval era (Jones 1972). At times other papers authored by him look to have been driven by a research agenda that was tangential to the avowed subject, and his stance on field systems based on statements in the Welsh law books testifies to this tendency (as for instance Jones 1965).

This becomes clear when one compares the contents pages of *Studies of Field Systems* where the editors unusually listed the various sections and sub-sections within each contribution. Virtually every one used the field system, its components, its tenure, its enclosure, and other attributes as a set of topic headings to be examined, or alternatively (as was the case with Margaret Davies' complementary paper on south Wales), approached field systems on a county by county basis. Glanville Jones alone headlined the written sources, identifying the origins and development of varying Welsh field systems through the medium of the law-books and later historical documents, embracing the conceptual and theoretical, and isolating field patterns in the landscape that exemplified his understanding of these sources. He had already written at length on Welsh sharelands (Jones 1959; 1964) but he openly eschewed anything that smacked of an Anglo-Norman or English origin, his focus being very much on Welsh Wales (1973, 477). Some recent commentators have commented sympathetically on Jones' field system assessment (*e.g.* Smith 2011, 15), but we might observe that his commentaries have been largely overlooked in more recent works on post-Roman Wales (Davies 1982; Charles-Edwards 2013), while Ian Jack in his contribution on Welsh field systems in the post-Conquest volume of the *Agrarian History of England and Wales* published some years later limited his comments on Jones's approach to two short paragraphs, whilst pointedly remarking on the tenurial differences that have 'so preoccupied Welsh historians' (1988, 428).

From the perspective of the landscape historian or archaeologist there were other academics who might have contributed a more germane paper to *Studies of Field Systems* to complement that by Margaret Davies on the south. Either Dorothy Sylvester in Manchester or Colin Thomas of the New University of Ulster would, I suspect, have produced assessments with broader and more informative foundations. Four years earlier, for instance, Sylvester had looked at field systems in eastern Wales in *The Rural Landscape of the Welsh Borderland* (1969). In fact the 1973 overview looks to have offered the first opportunity since the studies of Seebohm and Gray in the decades either side of 1900 to assess field systems across north Wales in any depth, and it is in many ways a dispiriting reflection that more than forty years on it remains the only one of any substance. Where medieval field analyses have appeared in published reports, they have tended to appear as localised and descriptive studies, and understandably the fields themselves as adjuncts to settlements.

What follows is an attempt to categorise various observations and reports, with the emphasis heavily on the field evidence coupled where relevant with data from historic cartography. It has been aided considerably by the fact that in recent years the Clwyd-Powys Archaeological Trust had the opportunity to examine medieval field systems in east and north-east Wales collectively, though rather superficially, in a grant-aided initiative by Cadw (Silvester and Hankinson 2013), this matched by an assessment by the Gwynedd Archaeological Trust for the north-west of Wales (Fig. 6.1; Kenney 2015).

Open fields of English type

The starting point for field systems in the north are the open fields that were influenced or inspired by agricultural practice in England, and which defined the core of the south Walian paper produced by Margaret Davies in 1973. Their origins, function and indeed even their nature have been the subjects of countless academic works (Rowley 1981; Astill 1988) and need no explanation here, other than to emphasise that those considered here generally appear in areas that saw early Anglo-Norman incursions or, in later centuries, purposeful English settlement. It is worth noting, too, that the term 'open field' is preferred here to the alternative 'common field'. Following Rippon (2008, 4) and others, the term 'common field' should be reserved for a specific type of open-field

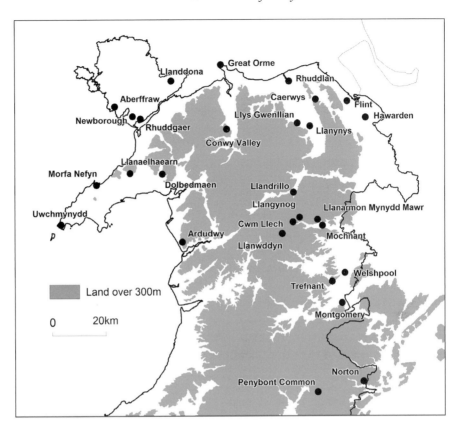

FIGURE 6.1. Field
systems in north
Wales: significant sites
mentioned in the text.

farming, commonplace in the English Midlands, where a two- or three-field
rotation system is well-evidenced in the historic record. This is not to deny the
presence of the three-field system in east Wales – Sylvester made a forceful case
for the presence of such practices further south in Breconshire (1969, 253) –
but is rather a reflection of the general lack of modern research into the nature
of the open fields, arguably a task for the historical geographer than for the
landscape historian.

Open fields survived as physical entities into the twentieth century in
south Wales though only rarely: Rhossili Vile on Gower is the survival that
immediately comes to mind, but there are none that remain, to the best of
our knowledge, in north Wales. It is other characteristics, and not restricted to
open fields of English type, that can signal their medieval presence: the survival
of strips on the ground today or their appearance on early maps revealing the
fossilisation of the ploughing units known as lands or selions (Adams 1976);
the shapes of fields exhibiting the distinctive aratral (reverse S) curve of the
medieval plough's course; the occurrence of specific field-name forms; and
the survival of earthwork ridge and furrow. For completeness, we can add the
written record of open fields in medieval deeds and manorial records (Bowen
1930; Owen in Miller 1991, 246), although these are less easy to locate in space
than in time.

Taking each of these characteristics in turn, strip fields defined by boundaries, whether banks, hedges, or even fences, are an increasingly fugitive element in the modern landscape as fields are amalgamated and rationalised, but are much more prevalent on tithe maps and earlier estate maps, the convention of a hatched line indicating a balk rather than a boundary division. Occasionally a series of dog-legged steps set within a single boundary may be the sole vestige of the terminals of fossilised strips that have been removed. A field boundary that mirrors the aratral curve of the medieval plough team as it was turned anti-clockwise onto a headland may be used as a guide, but is more compelling as evidence when a number occur together.

English field names incorporating such elements as 'furlong', 'selion', 'gore', or 'butt' may appear on relevant maps and their terriers but it is the Welsh equivalents deployed presumably by native farmers rather than their English landlords, which can be particularly informative. At the beginning of the twentieth century Alfred Palmer and Edward Owen (1910) and then Sir John Lloyd (1912) seem to have initiated this line of enquiry, followed in more recent times by Dorothy Sylvester (1954–1955) and Colin Thomas, the latter in several carefully researched and thorough assessments of available sources (1980). There is no universally accepted list of indicative field terms – *erw* (acre) for instance, espoused by Thomas and also by Adams (1976), is probably too general a field name to be usefully employed without support from other source material. Terms that do appear to have achieved general acceptance include *maes* (open field), *dryll* (strip or ridge), *llain/llein* (strip), *talar* (headland), and *cyfer* (a day's ploughing). Thomas (1980, 161) saw these as becoming prevalent in the fieldscape in the fifteenth century.

A further word commonly encountered is 'quillet'. Its origins are uncertain but appear to be English rather than Welsh, and its occurrence in Parliamentary Acts take its usage back into the sixteenth century, not that this is acknowledged in the Shorter Oxford Dictionary. Adams (1976, 88) defining it as 'a strip without any visible demarcation of different ownership in an enclosed field' revealed its early popularity across the western counties of England as well as Wales. Certainly it appears frequently in the mid-nineteenth century tithe surveys, and Palmer and Owen (1910, 1), Sylvester (1969, 513), Glanville Jones (1991), Longley (2001), and others have adopted it as a signifier of open-field agriculture. Palmer though was at pains to point out that he viewed it as a successor term to the Welsh and English terms listed above, being first encountered in the extensive open fields of the Wrexham region no earlier than 1602. Some recent commentators (as for instance Longley 2001) have preferred it to 'strip field' as a generic descriptor, while others including the present writer are more cautious, seeing it as a term which might be loosely applied to any narrow strip of land, regardless of whether that originated in the open fields. It is best treated like *erw* as a term that might indeed denote an open-field origin, but not exclusively so.

On the face of it, a close association with ridge and furrow ought to clinch the identification of a medieval open field, given our understanding of its evolution in the English midlands. In recent times, however, it has become apparent that other forms of cultivation ridging exist alongside medieval ridge and furrow, though all too often grouped together indiscriminately: the Historic Environment Record for east and north-east Wales carries over eleven hundred entries for ridge and furrow, and relatively few of them can realistically be allotted a medieval origin.

Dorothy Sylvester was the first and indeed the only researcher to publish a map of open-field systems in east Wales and the border counties (1969, 220), and though there has been some debate amongst historians as to whether two- or three-field methods were practiced (Jack 1988, 412) the overall picture seems not to be in doubt. Unsurprisingly on her distribution map the systems cluster along the eastern and northern fringes of the region, the lower lands which witnessed greater Anglo-Norman intrusion in the centuries after the Conquest. In Radnorshire, it was the lowlands bordering Herefordshire that generated examples with relict strip fields picked out on LiDAR around Norton and Presteigne (Silvester and Hankinson 2013, 20), even if the one area where open fields might have been anticipated – the Walton Basin also known as the Hindwell Valley – shows few characteristics and was dismissed in an earlier study (Rennell 1958, 160).

In lowland Montgomeryshire the wide vale around the River Severn displays both strip fields and occasional ridge and furrow, as for instance at Welshpool where seventeenth-century estate mapping shows the strips of Henfaes between the town and the river that gradually disappeared in subsequent centuries leaving only an area name today, around Montgomery where ridge and furrow was sealed by the creation of a park at Lymore, and at Hen Domen where earlier ridging was traced below the Conquest-era motte and bailey. Regarding the last of these, uncertainties as to whether these cultivation traces reflect open-field agriculture of late Saxon or Welsh origin and whether the faintly visible ridging around the castle is of the same or later date are addressed in a useful discussion of the wider landscape around Montgomery (Higham and Barker 2000, 141). Ridge and furrow appears, too, on the valley floor of the Severn-Vyrnwy confluence while Llinos Smith argued that there was no intrinsic difference between the medieval fields of Mochnant in the valley of the Rhaiadr and those of Ruyton further east into lowland Shropshire (quoted by Jack 1988, 414).

In the north it was the coastal strip through Denbighshire and Flintshire where Sylvester mapped extensive strip field fossilisation, at Rhuddlan, Flint and Hawarden and the settlements between them, leaving no doubt of their open-field origins. Typical is a mid-seventeenth-century estate map of Aston and Shotton townships in Hawarden which shows much of the area in strips, manorial documents taking the recording of selions back into the thirteenth century (Sylvester 1969, 245). These open-field systems extend too on to the limestone plateau inland, primarily and significantly around Caerwys, where the tithe survey reveals a continuing pattern of fragmented holdings in unbounded strips into the mid-nineteenth century, particularly to the north-west of the

FIGURE 6.2. Ridge and furrow cultivation near Pickhill Hall, Wrexham Maelor. © Clwyd-Powys Archaeological Trust (04-c-0055).

settlement which was an Edwardian plantation, the strong implication being that the open fields here were largely thirteenth-century creations dependent on the town. Neighbouring vills such as Whitford and Ysceifiog display comparatively few strip fields (Silvester forthcoming).

Of a visually divergent nature are the lowlands around Wrexham and particularly the Maelor, east of the River Dee. Topographically the region is obviously an extension of the Cheshire plain, resulting in similar patterns of land use. More widespread than anywhere in north Wales, broad ridge and furrow spreads over much of the area, extending west of the Dee but fading out closer to Wrexham itself (Fig. 6.2). Plots of its distribution exist only in manuscript, but a published plan of adjacent western Cheshire parishes reveals a picture comparable in the density of the ridging (Higham 2004, 57). Cheshire also provides a salutary warning that the ubiquity of ridge and furrow does not signal that the open fields were similarly extensive. Initial research suggested that the open fields (showing as town fields) were of limited extent especially where they related to townships dominated by dispersed settlements, that enclosure in severalty was initiated at an early date, and that the closes so created continued to be cultivated in ridges or were even ridged up anew to promote the drainage of dairy pasture (White 1995; Higham 2004, 56–78). More recently, detailed analysis of parishes south of Chester has generated a more nuanced view that sees most of the land surface ridged, but not necessarily cultivated every year, small parcels of strips or furlongs lying irregularly in unenclosed fields that were subsequently hedged, probably after the fourteenth century (Higham 2014, 141). These trends could probably be applied to Wrexham Maelor, and go a long way to explaining the sparsity of fossilised strip fields in the region, contradicting Sylvester's original contention that the Maelor open fields because of their limited spread, were expressions of Welsh influence (1969, 289).

West of the River Clwyd, open fields conforming to English norms largely disappear from the landscape. The recent Gwynedd Archaeological Trust survey (Kenney 2015) makes no distinctions in its consideration of open fields, while an earlier study postulating numerous upland settlements of medieval date accompanied by cultivation ridging (Longley 2006, 68) raises a suspicion that the field remains of structures and agriculture may not all be contemporary.

Welsh open fields and sharelands

Glanville Jones was not the first (in 1953) to propose that Welsh communities in the medieval era cultivated small open fields, otherwise termed sharelands (*rhandiroedd*, singular *rhandir*, appearing in the Laws of the twelfth century), but may have been responsible for articulating the view that they could have emerged in different ways: 'besides the open-field sharelands originally cultivated by bondmen, new sharelands were created and in due course, girdles of homesteads began to develop around these' (Jones 1964, 151), a concept which is occasionally useful now in identifying surviving remains. Subsequently, he elaborated his argument explaining that the Welsh 'sited [their] dwellings on the peripheries of arable sharelands so as to economise on increasing scarce resources of cropland' (1989, 183). One further point: Jones viewed sharelands as ubiquitous, associated with bond settlements which had been established at an early date in all areas of the country that were habitable.

Dorothy Sylvester (1954–1955, 13) too emphasised the role of the bond communities in the establishment of sharelands while Huw Owen (1991, 251) claimed that some might extend to several hundred acres. The former took it further, suggesting that '... a series of patterns evolved in the Welsh areas ... on a predominantly small square-field pattern ... and usually with some open arable strips either in small groups widely scattered or more concentrated in a number of larger open fields' (her 'nuclear small field types'). Barker and Lawson, basing their views on Glanville Jones and others, claimed that '... some form of open-field agriculture was widespread through the lowland regions of central Wales during the Middle Ages. Normally the infield-outfield system was followed, under which there was only one common field, permanently in cultivation, which was supplemented by outfields – temporary cultivations of the waste which were allowed to lapse after a few years' (1971, 68).

Jones (1973), Jacks (1988, 428), and Owen (1991, 250) have all cited historically documented Welsh open-field systems in the north, describing them on the page but avoiding their physical definition on the ground, something we now need to address. As with open-fields of English introduction, the most useful guides to the former presence of Welsh sharelands are the strips which though unlikely to survive today are occasionally detectable on historic mapping, together with a range of field-name elements, already noted above, to which can be added the term *rhandir* itself. Recognition is enhanced where settlement evidence can be linked to the fields, though it may be expedient to differentiate between manifestations in the lowlands and the uplands: with the former one might expect well-established communities practicing agriculture to leave diffuse traces across the landscape, the latter where communities spread as land became scarcer and which display higher levels of preservation. Secondly, it is worth stressing that small groups of lowland strips and girdles of settlements are not invariable bedfellows. Jones was keen to flag up a ring of dwellings around any shareland that he identified (see for instance 1991, 199), but such a consistent association has yet to be substantiated.

Jones identified some sharelands in the lowlands to support his classificatory system, though not many. Favourite were the quillets at Llanynys, a small settlement in the Vale of the Clwyd, hyped as 'the most perfect example of a surviving medieval pattern in North Wales' (1953, 63). Some of its strips survived well into the twentieth century and as an exemplar he returned to Llanynys several times after first publishing them in detail in 1964 (Jones 1972, 343; 1973, 472; 1991, 198). Convincing too are the small group of strips conjured from the tithe map of Cwm Pennant, Llandrillo in a valley on the western edge of the Berwyn mountains (1973, 457), but not so his attempt to conjure up a girdle pattern around open-field strips to the west of the Edwardian plantation of Caerwys (1985, 162). His depiction of the open fields around Llys Gwenllian immediately to the south of Denbigh is intuitive rather than deductive, arising from its documented inclusion in the Survey of Denbigh in 1334 (1991, 201). That the *maerdref* lay in the lee of the *llys* is logical, with its sharelands nearby also a logical assumption, except for the fact there is no cartographic or archaeological evidence to support what is at best supposition about the position of the *maerdref*; the tithe survey, normally the more useful indicator of open field information provides neither suggestive field morphology nor field names of any relevance.

Where others have been recognised, it is usually as a result of specific landscape research. Thus in Cwm Llech lying off another valley known as Cwm Pennant, this one in Pennant Melangell (Monts), a diminutive group of strips survived into the nineteenth century because of their varied ownerships; it is even possible that they functioned as meadows rather than arable (Jones and Silvester 2017, 66). The adjacent Tanat Valley had at least until recently similar survivals on a comparable scale, notably between Buarth-glas and Glan-yr-afon in Llangynog (Britnell and Martin 1999, 78). Further south in the valley of the upper Severn above Newtown traces of former open field arable farming, particularly to the west and south of Llanwnog village are suggested by reasonably distinct patterns of long, elongated strip-like patterns of fields, thought to be still associated with relict traces of broad ridge and furrow (Britnell 2007, 40).

It is however the north-west of Wales that provides altogether more emphatic examples, both in number and in scale (Fig. 6.3). Glanville Jones focused on the royal court site at Aberffraw on Anglesey with vestiges of its fields in the form of a few relict strips, and some minor names including Maes y Maerdref,

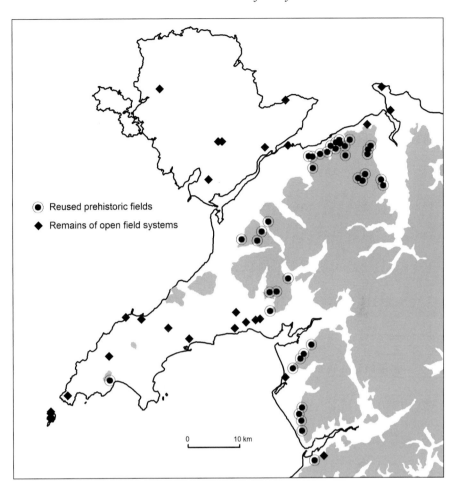

FIGURE 6.3. Distribution of Welsh open field cultivation and re-used prehistoric field systems in north-west Wales, after Kenney, 2015.

together suggesting the presence of open fields to the north and west of the settlement (Jones 1985, 161; Longley 2001, 52). Considerably more impressive, though, are the survivals along the northern mainland coast, collated by Jane Kenney in the GAT survey (2015, 10). Selecting just a sample of the more prominent examples, at Uwchmynydd near Aberdaron at the tip of the Llŷn peninsula, strip fields, some with distinctive curving boundaries, continued to fill the lower ground between the rocky coastal hills in the nineteenth century over an area of not much less than three square kilometres (Kenney 2015, 11, fig. 3); Morfa Nefyn overlooking Caernarfon Bay has similarly extensive strip fields covering a similar area, where Kenney has suggested that 'virtually all the present fields preserve, to some extent, the alignment of the open field system' (2015, 10, fig. 2). On Anglesey it is the enclosed strip fields at Newborough that are extensive (Longley 2001, 48; Kenney 2015, fig. 5). These, the three most impressive illustrations from a sizeable list of over twenty open-field systems presumably point to peculiar factors in location and tenure that have aided their survival. Many of the others are much more fragmentary (Kenney 2015,

FIGURE 6.4. Cultivation ridges on the Great Orme above Llandudno. © Gwynedd Archaeological Trust (VG009099).

10), while some areas of Gwynedd such as Arfon appear to be largely devoid of any visible traces as an earlier GAT survey revealed (Gwyn and Thompson 2000, 23). Yet there is little doubt that further survivals remain to be identified.

The fields at Uwchmynydd expose an issue requiring further consideration. While the strip fields are extensive, they give way to tracts of ridge and furrow spreading around the site of a former church on the unenclosed coastal promontory. Though there are other locales such as Llanfairfechan and the Aber valley (Kenney 2015, figs 15–17) where restricted patches of ridge and furrow might be loosely associated with relict field patterns that putatively could be medieval, Uwchmynydd is unusual in the apparent association of remains of different forms that are distinctively medieval. Newborough displays no such convincing traces of ridge and furrow, neither does Morfa Nefyn, nor a smaller coastal strip field system on Anglesey at Llanddona (Kenney 2015, fig. 7). On the other hand, there are places such as Cae Fadog Uchaf in Dolbenmaen (Kenney 2015, fig. 28), with good surviving ridge and furrow, and outstandingly so on the Great Orme above Llandudno, where cultivation ridges, some lying with fields defined by grassy baulks, coat the hill on which St Tudfil's church sits (Fig. 6.4; Aris 1996; Kenney 2015, 12 and pl. 9).

Several explanations might be invoked for this apparent dichotomy: that ridge and furrow simply hasn't survived the erosive effect of subsequent cultivation over more recent centuries; that the open fields that subsequently transmuted into enclosed strip fields in the lower lands were never ridged (for which see Comeau this volume); that in following Glanville Jones (1972, 351), we should see in the ridging the enhancement of outfield cultivation of temporary duration; or that the cultivation ridges are of an entirely different date from the sharelands. Any of these is possible, individually or perhaps in combination. And the topography of the relatively narrow coastal strip in north-west Wales adds the complication that the remains of multi-period activity may be intermingled in a compacted area. Much of the cultivation ridging recognised in the north-west does tend to favour upland margins where modern farming use is limited or non-existent. Uwchmynydd and Great Orme both exemplify this trend.

The majority of the few upland fields systems that have been identified in north-east and central Wales also exhibit ridging: Ty-uchaf, Llanwddyn (Monts), Penybont Common (Rads) above Builth Wells, and Y Gribin, Llangynog (Monts) are well-established examples (Silvester 2006, 24), although it might be remarked that at the last named the ridges are flat rather than mounded up and are defined by drainage slots. The medieval (or just possibly early post-medieval) date of each one of these is corroborated by the presence of adjacent rectangular house or platform sites, and Ty-uchaf is a prime manifestation of Jones' thesis of small shareland development surrounded by dwellings (Silvester 2006, fig. 2.4).

The field systems on Penybont Common and Aberedw Hill (Rads) combine ridging with more pronounced earthen banks acting as separators for the long strips. The difference between the two is that from the group of three or four platforms, Penybont functioned as a single farm, while on Cefn Wylfre, a part of Aberedw Hill, the cultivation ridges are so extensive that they surely represent the arable of several farms lower down the hillside (Silvester 2006, fig. 2.5).

Other upland areas, however, exhibit only the strip fields. Cwm Pennant, Llandrillo (Merioneths) displays an extensive expanse of narrow strips defined by stony banks which together with sporadic stone heaps are rather the product of clearance than of deliberate enclosure, extending over an area of 65 ha, with house platforms around the western and southern perimeter. Small surviving spreads of cultivation ridges close to these strips are likely to be of later date (Silvester 2000, 51). On the adjacent spur of Ffridd Camen an individual farm comprising a fine stone-walled long house accompanied by perhaps seven fields again defined by stony balks (Fig. 6.5; Silvester 1991) and further north the next tributary valley diving down the western flank of Y Berwyn to merge with the plain of the upper Dee retains fragmented field systems of similar appearance.

There are two points to emphasise. Regardless of the range of examples cited here, no specific research has focused on identifying Welsh open-field systems across north Wales. Those in the north-east have come to light primarily through the medium of aerial photography or occasionally through fieldwork focused on specific settlement sites, while in the north-west the more impressive number of field system remains highlighted in the GAT survey were sourced from the regional HER and by examining scheduled settlements and their immediate environs. A systematic search of tithe maps of the northern counties for distinctive field patterns, and the recognition of toponymic identifiers such as *maes* and *rhandir*, both now made much easier by the on-line access to the Cynefin project results, will inevitably produce additional examples.

FIGURE 6.5. Strip fields associated with a single house site on Ffridd Camen on the western edge of Y Berwyn. © Clwyd-Powys Archaeological Trust CPAT 86-MB-130.

An alternative approach – starting with known *maerdrefi* and examining the landscapes around them – would be too restricted methodologically and too dependent on a postulated historical model to be useful.

Secondly, the known examples display only limited uniformity in the design and layout of Welsh open fields. Kenney has pointed out that the field systems high up the Conwy valley identified in an earlier paper by Della Hooke (1997, 83) are hardly typical of the open fields found close to the coast, though the presence of Welsh field name indicators implies that they must have functioned in broadly similar fashion. Diversity is only to be anticipated – field patterns and our perception of them will be influenced by location, by local topography, and by varying degrees of survival, as well as by the nature of the communities that created them and the duration of the agricultural practices that adopted them. Each needs to be studied in its own right and perhaps 'deconstructed' before any meaningful classification can be attempted.

Nucleal fields

One of Glanville Jones' favoured field forms centred on what he termed 'nucleal land'. We should not read into this that it was clearly distinguished as such in historical documentation. Rather the law books referred to a form of tenure known as *tir corddlan* which 'may for convenience be translated as nucleal land' (Jones 1973, 435), and he interpreted the few relevant and in places contradictory observations in the lawbooks as evidence of gardens or enclosures radiating out from a single central core or nucleus, usually a graveyard boundary.

Not only, then, does nucleal land hinge on a correct interpretation of extremely limited documentary evidence, but it is clear too that such field layouts would have emerged at an early stage in the development of a local field sequence, and in consequence would have longer to undergo modification or obliteration by later land-use practice. As a result identifying traces that could still be recognised into the nineteenth century and perhaps more fundamentally validating the underlying thesis of their existence is extremely difficult.

Glanville Jones again cited Llanynys as a settlement with traces visible at the time of the tithe survey, basing his argument on an originally larger churchyard and just a couple of field divisions that ran out perpendicularly from it. Arguably there is an element of special pleading here. Analysed in detail by Jones (1972, 347), Llanynys is certainly amongst the more convincing east Walian examples of larger *clas* enclosures that over the centuries have been reduced in size (*cf.* Silvester and Evans 2009, 28); the boundaries running out from the enclosure are less convincing as remnants of a designed radiating system. Jones cited two further examples of nucleal land from his search of tithe maps, at Amlwch on Anglesey, and Llanfilo in Breconshire (1972, 349), neither of which stand up to close scrutiny. The present writer has been unable to pick out further examples in east Wales and is not aware of other commentators citing specific examples, but in south-west Wales Kissock has argued, and more persuasively, for nucleal systems in the Pembrokeshire parishes of Jeffreyston, Castlemartin, and Jameston (Kissock 1997, 132). Overall, confirming the integrity of nucleal field systems remains a significant challenge.

Re-used prehistoric fields

Archaeologists working in north-west Wales have long been conscious of the medieval re-use and modification of fields first created in the prehistoric and Romano-British eras (*e.g.* Musson 1994; Crew and Musson 1996; Longley 2006). As mapped by Jane Kenney in her detailed analysis these are concentrated, though apparently localised, west of the Conwy valley and in Ardudwy north of Barmouth, with a few other spreads scattered elsewhere in uplands that overlook the coastal plains (2015, fig. 1). Usefully this presents a rather different picture from the wider distribution of later prehistoric and Romano-British settlements for the region as illustrated by David Longley (2006, fig. 4.4), but it raises the issue of whether we are witnessing genuine lacunae in the medieval landscape or omissions that originate from other factors.

Critical to the recognition of fields that were used in either or both periods, are the presence of prehistoric and earlier first millennium AD settlement remains and medieval long huts; without them the unravelling of the complex landscapes would not be feasible. Re-use results in patterns of medieval fields that appear to be broadly more irregular than contemporary field systems newly created, and Kenney has argued that in Gwynedd 'extensive areas of current fields are probably also ancient in origin' but could not be included in her study because they did not coincide with scheduled medieval sites (2015, 13). Differentiating the medieval from the prehistoric demands closer analysis of surviving remains of multi-period activity, something that has yet to be undertaken on any scale.

The north-west though is remarkable in the quality of these multi-period remains. There is nothing at all comparable with them from the landscapes of north-east or mid-Wales, though we may suspect that the small fields remaining on the limestone plateau at Hen Caerwys were perhaps Romano-British in origin and were utilised by those who occupied the platform houses at the end of the Middle Ages (Davies and Silvester 2015).

Enclosures

Behind these self-defining classes lies the spectre of field enclosure. For the earlier open fields the evidence is incontrovertible: we witness the process at work in the transformation of the medieval strips to individual fields defined by stock-proof banks and hedges, a process that might occur at any time from the medieval period right up to the present. But the creation of entirely new systems of fields and enclosures is a rather different matter. In the context of this paper determining whether these new enclosures were cultivated or put down to permanent pasture is relatively inconsequential; more critical is the date at which new land was taken in. Differentiating sporadic enclosure of medieval origin from that of later centuries is not governed by fixed criteria. We have noted that Dorothy Sylvester argued for small square-shaped fields emerging around sharelands, and others have assumed development in a similar form, the implication being that by and large the field patterns that we observe today in the hills and valleys of Wales have been in existence since the Middle Ages (*e.g.* Pryce 1961). It is a reasonable argument and validation by specific examples has largely been avoided in the literature.

In fact, it is rather difficult to pinpoint specific instances that confirm the thesis of early enclosure. North Wales has little in the way of large-scale Tudor mapping, historical documentation tying enclosure to particular localities looks to be rare, and the scientific dating of boundaries through optically stimulated luminescence (OSL), still in its infancy, has been rarely tried out here. Again the examples cited here have emerged from landscape projects associated with medieval settlement. The township of Trefnant (in Castle Caereinion parish) in the hills of Montgomeryshire west of the Severn, contains a number of medieval platform house sites without any obvious associated fields, but also three farms that have similarly sized, sub-circular enclosures sub-divided into small fields as their cores. For one of them – Pant-yr-alarch – the inference from the documented history of ownership is that it might have been established around the beginning of the sixteenth century, perhaps a little earlier (Silvester 2000, 158). In the eastern foothills of the Berwyns at Llanarmon Mynydd Mawr north of the Rhaeadr valley, a regularly spaced group of longhouse platforms has one where the surviving building – Tŷ-draw – has been dendrochronologically attributed to the 1470s. The house was erected on an existing lynchet, one element it appears of an extremely irregular pattern of small fields which stretched down the slope to a small stream making its way to the Rhaeadr. The field layout was completely restructured in the nineteenth century, but the original pattern can dimly be made out on the ground and coincides with what is shown on an estate map of the mid-eighteenth century (Britnell *et al.* 2007, 184). There is no inherent reason why these two field systems should not be fairly typical of land intake practices across large parts of north Wales. Confirmation, however, may take a while. To these we might add the otherwise unparalleled patterning of field enclosures and cultivation ridging around the Hospitallers' grange above Lake Vyrnwy in western Montgomeryshire (Silvester 1997, 68) and possibly the terraced fields around the upland Cistercian grange at Cwm Cilio in Llanaelhaearn, in Caernarfonshire (Kenney 2015, 57), both atypical because of the nature of the medieval settlement.

Most recently, the publication of Rhuddgaer on the southern tip of Anglesey has, through geophysical survey and excavation, revealed a complex of irregular rectilinear fields of two phases seemingly centred on the later seventh to later eighth century; these were succeeded by ridge and furrow which from the apparent absence of associated field divisions might indicate shareland cultivation, and in turn the area was inundated by blown sand which on the basis of historical documentation might date from 1330 (Hopewell and Edwards 2017). Amongst the important implications of the Rhuddgaer investigations is the recognition of enclosed fields from the early medieval era, in itself not a surprise but probably the first time that they have been recognised in north Wales.

Conclusions

The study of medieval field systems in north Wales has generally, though not exclusively, tended to focus on historical models, usually employing selected exemplars derived from the modern landscape or from the cache of mid-nineteenth-century tithe surveys that exist for the country. Approaching the subject archaeologically offers an alternative perspective, yet one that is broadly comparable in its dependence on a relatively small corpus of examples drawn from various studies over a protracted period of time. Even the Gwynedd Archaeological Trust's field systems study of 2015 which can justifiably claim to be the most thorough assessment available requires qualification in that its momentum was driven by scheduled sites and existing HER entries.

Nevertheless, the difference between the north-west on the one hand, and the north-east and central regions of the country on the other is distinctively clear, most obviously so in the re-use of earlier field systems, but also so in other field system forms. This has nothing to do with the organisational division in archaeological research and recording through the Welsh Archaeological Trust system over the last forty years, but is a function of topography, geomorphology, and other allied factors. Yet the distinction between the north-east and the north-west also takes on a cultural dimension – shades of Seebohm in 1883, of Gray in 1915, and even of Dorothy Sylvester – with the extensive open fields of Anglo-Norman and subsequent English inspiration contrasting with the more limited Welsh sharelands. Yet we need to be cautious of pushing such a division too far. The open field indicators around Newborough and Morfa Nefyn are as extensive in areal terms as some of the putative open field tracts along the English border and Glanville Jones' citation (1991, 200) of a Welsh manor at Pickhill in the heart of Wrexham Saesneg on the edge of the Cheshire plain is warning enough against erecting hard and fast cultural divisions in the physical remains. Sylvester saw the interrelationship of Welsh and English systems as a core problem more than sixty years ago, although by the time of her Welsh Borderland volume she seems to have mitigated the doubts that she had (1954–1955, 16; 1969, 224). Whether we can be as adamant today is a moot point.

In the end the classification proposed here must be treated as no more than a provisional resting place on a long road. Examination of the field systems in north Wales in their own right is required and at a super-parochial scale, not simply as incidental adjuncts to other settlement forms that have been selected for their own intrinsic interest at a sub-parochial level. The recent work at Rhuddgaer confirms a fundamental archaeological truth: that the more information we accumulate, the more complex the situation that emerges.

Acknowledgements

My thanks are due to the Clwyd-Powys Archaeological Trust (CPAT) as an organisation and to my erstwhile colleagues who have been involved with me in various field projects over the years that have contributed information for this paper; to CPAT also for their permission to publish aerial photographs from their collection; and to Andrew Davidson and Jane Kenney for providing the images for north-west Wales and for facilitating Gwynedd Archaeological Trust's permission to reproduce them here.

References

Adams, I. H. (1976) *Agrarian Landscape Terms: a glossary for historical geography*. London, Institute of British Geographers.

Aris, M. (1996) *Historic Landscapes of the Great Orme*. Llanrwst, Gwasg Carreg Gwalch.

Astill, G. (1988) Fields. In G. Astill and A. Grant (eds) *The Countryside of Medieval England*. Oxford, Blackwell Publishers, 62–85.

Baker, A. R. H. and Butlin, R. A. (eds) (1973) *Studies of Field Systems in the British Isles*. Cambridge, Cambridge University Press.

Bowen, E. G. (1930) A Map of the Trehelig Common Fields. *Montgomeryshire Collections* 41, 163–8.

Britnell, W. J. (2007) *Caersws Basin Historic Landscape. Historic landscape characterization*. Unpublished report, Clwyd-Powys Archaeological Trust, Welshpool.

Britnell, W. J. and Martin, C. H. (1999) *Dyffryn Tanat Historic Landscape*. Unpublished report, Clwyd-Powys Archaeological Trust, Welshpool.

Britnell, W. J., Silvester, R. J., Suggett, R. and Wiliam, E. (2008) Tŷ-draw, Llanarmon Mynydd Mawr, Powys – a late-medieval cruck-framed hallhouse-longhouse. *Archaeologia Cambrensis* 157, 157–202.

Charles-Edwards, T. M. (2013) *Wales and the Britons 350–1064*. Oxford, Oxford University Press.

Crew, P. and Musson, C. (1996) *Snowdonia from the Air. Patterns in the landscape*. Penrhyndeudraeth, Snowdonia National Park Authority.

Davies, M. (1973) Field systems of south Wales. In A. R. H. Baker and R. A. Butlin (eds) *Studies of Field Systems in the British Isles*. Cambridge, Cambridge University Press, 480–529

Davies, W. (1982) *Wales in the Early Middle Ages*. Leicester, Leicester University Press.

Davies, W. R. and Silvester, R. J. (2015) Hen Caerwys: an historiography of the first fifty years. *Transactions Flintshire Historical Society* 40, 17–40.

Gray, H. L. (1915) *English Field Systems*. Cambridge (Massachusetts), Harvard University Press.

Gwyn, D. and Thompson, D. (2000). *Historic Landscape Characterisation: Ardal Arfon*. Unpublished report, Gwynedd Archaeological Trust, Bangor.

Higham, N. J. (2004) *A Frontier Landscape: The North West in the Middle Ages*. Macclesfield, Windgather Press.

Higham, N. J. (2014) The late Anglo-Saxon landscape of western Cheshire: open fields, ploughs and the manor within the Dykes. In G. R. Owen-Crocker and S. D. Thompson (eds) *Towns and Topography. Essays in memory of David Hill*. Oxford, Oxbow Books, 132–141.

Higham, R. and Barker, P. (2000) *Hen Domen, Montgomery. A timber castle on the English-Welsh border*. Exeter, University of Exeter Press.

Hopewell, D. and Edwards, N. (2017) Early medieval settlement and field systems at Rhuddgaer, Anglesey. *Archaeologia Cambrensis* 166, 213–242.

Jack, R. I. (1988) Wales and the Marches. In H. E. Hallam (ed.) *The Agrarian History of England and Wales, Vol II, 1042–1350*. Cambridge, Cambridge University Press, 260–271, 412–496.

Jones, G. R. J. (1953) Some Medieval Rural Settlements in North Wales. *Transactions and Papers Institute of British Geographers* 19, 51–72.

Jones, G. R. J. (1959) Medieval open fields and associated settlement patterns in north-west Wales. *Comptes Rendus de Colloque International de Geographie et Histoire Agraires, Annales de l'Est* 21, Nancy, 313–328.

Jones, G. R. J. (1964) The Llanynys Quillets: a measure of landscape transformation in north Wales. *Transactions Denbighshire Historical Society*. 13, 133–158.

Jones, G. R. J. (1965) Agriculture in north-west Wales during the later Middle Ages. In J. A. Taylor (ed.) *Climatic Change with Special Reference to Wales and its Agriculture*. Aberystwyth, University College of Wales, 47–53.

Jones, G. R. J. (1972) Post-Roman Wales. In H. P. R. Finberg (ed.) *The Agrarian History of England and Wales. Volume I, pt II, AD 43–1042*. Cambridge, Cambridge University Press, 281–382.

Jones, G. R. J. (1973) Field systems of north Wales. In A. R. H. Baker and R. A. Butlin (eds), *Studies of Field Systems in the British Isles*. Cambridge, Cambridge University Press, 430–479.

Jones, G. R. J. (1985) Forms and patterns of medieval settlement in Welsh Wales. In D. Hooke (ed.) *Medieval Villages: A review of current work*. Oxford, Oxford University Committee for Archaeology, 155–169.

Jones, G. R. J. (1989) The Dark Ages. In D. H. Owen (ed.) *Settlement and Society in Wales*. Cardiff, University of Wales Press, 177–198.

Jones, G. R. J. (1991) Medieval settlement. In J. Manley, S. Grenter and F. Gale (eds) *The Archaeology of Clwyd*. Mold, Clwyd County Council, 186–202.

Kenney, J. (2015) *Medieval Field Systems in North-west Wales Scheduling Enhancement, 2014–15*. Unpublished report, Bangor, Gwynedd Archaeological Trust.

Kissock, J. A. (1997) 'God made nature and men made towns': post-Conquest and pre-Conquest villages in Pembrokeshire. In N. Edwards (ed.) *Landscape and Settlement in Medieval Wales*. Oxford, Oxbow Books, 123–137.

Lloyd, J. E. (1911) *A History of Wales*. London, Longmans, Green and Co.

Longley, D. (2001) Medieval Settlement and Landscape Change on Anglesey. *Landscape History* 23, 39–59.

Longley, D. (2006) Deserted rural settlements in north-west Wales. In K. Roberts (ed.) *Lost Farmsteads. Deserted rural settlements in Wales*. York, Council for British Archaeology, 61–82.

Musson, C. (1994) *Wales from the Air*. Aberystwyth, Royal Commission on the Ancient and Historical Monuments of Wales.

Owen, D. H. (1991) The occupation of the land: Wales and the Marches. In E. Miller (ed.) *The Agrarian History of England and Wales. Volume III, 1348–1500*. Cambridge, Cambridge University Press, 92–106.

Palmer, A. N. and Owen, E. (1910) *A History of Ancient Tenures of Land in North Wales and the Marches*. Wrexham, privately published.

Pryce, W. T. R. (1961) Enclosure and Field Patterns in the Banwy Valley. *Montgomeryshire Collections* 57, 23–32.

Rennell, Lord (1958) *Valley on the March. A history of a group of manors in the Herefordshire March of Wales*. Oxford, Oxford University Press.

Rippon, S. (2008) *Beyond the Medieval Village. The diversification of landscape character in southern Britain*. Oxford, Oxford University Press.

Rowley, T. (ed.) (1981) *The Origins of Open Field Agriculture*. London, Croom Helm.

Silvester, R. J. (1991) Medieval Farming on the Berwyn. *Medieval Settlement Research Group Annual Report* 6, 12–14.

Silvester, R. J. (1997) The Llanwddyn Hospitium. *Montgomeryshire Collections* 85, 63–76.

Silvester, R. J. (2000) Medieval Upland Cultivation on the Berwyns in North Wales. *Landscape History* 22, 47–60.

Silvester, R. J. (2001) Ty Mawr and the Landscape of Trefnant Township. *Montgomeryshire Collections* 89, 147–162.

Silvester, R. J. (2006) Deserted rural settlements in central and north-east Wales. In K. Roberts (ed.) *Lost Farmsteads. Deserted rural settlements in Wales*. York, Council for British Archaeology, 13–39.

Silvester, R. J. and Evans, J. W. (2009) Identifying the mother churches of north-east Wales. In N. Edwards (ed.) *The Archaeology of the Early Medieval Celtic Churches*. Leeds, Maney Publishing, 21–40.

Silvester, R. J. and Hankinson, R. (2013) *Medieval and Early Post-Medieval Farms and Farming Scheduling Enhancement Programme*. Unpublished report, Welshpool, Clwyd-Powys Archaeological Trust.

Smith, J. B. (2011) Glanville Jones: an appreciation. In P. S. Barnwell and B. K. Roberts (eds) *Britons, Saxons and Scandinavians. The historical geography of Glanville R. J. Jones*. Turnhout, Brepols Publishers, 9–23.

Sylvester, D. (1954/55) Settlement Patterns in Rural Flintshire. *Publications Flintshire Historical Society* 15, 6–42.

Sylvester, D. (1955) The Rural Landscape of Eastern Montgomeryshire. *Montgomeryshire Collections* 54, 14–26.

Sylvester, D. (1969) *The Rural Landscape of the Welsh Borderland*. London, Macmillan.

Thomas, C. (1980) Place-name Studies and Agrarian Colonisation in North Wales. *Welsh History Review* 10, 155–171.

White, G. (1995) Open fields and rural settlement in medieval west Cheshire. In T. Scott and P. Starkey (eds) *The Middle Ages in the North-West*. Oxford, Leopard's Head Press, 15–35.

CHAPTER SEVEN

Y Filltir Sgwâr: mapping the history of local land in a Welsh heartland

David Austin

Y Filltir Sgwâr ('the Square Mile') is a popular phrase in Welsh which signifies the small locality in which one grew up and lived and from which a core identity and belonging is drawn. It bespeaks a close-knit community of mutual support, kinship, and neighbourliness. As such it is an emotional and perhaps romantic response to the space around people, but it can nonetheless be drawn on a map. It is, therefore, a way into a landscape for an historian such as myself from both an individual and a collective perspective. It can be expressed, if inadequately, as conventional map graphics and, by introducing also the sense of time passing into the narrative which attends the drawings, there can be written a direct relationship with the nostalgia which lies within the phrase. This also links to the feeling of *hiraeth*, a longing for a place and its lost people which is a powerful sentiment in the Welsh diaspora viewing the homeland from distance and through the refracting lens of memory (Austin 2013).

You should know too that the square mile I am going to narrate is one I have adopted and within whose bounds I plan to be buried along with my Welsh-born and Welsh-speaking wife, Gaenor. *Deo volente* this is some time off, but I need to declare that this piece of ground is important to us both and that the people who live there are more than acquaintances. We have, in the fabric of our own lives, appropriated this square mile as an adoptive identity. I am also wedded to the notion that we can best contribute to our understanding of how land was used and landscapes made by researching and narrating holistic localities (Austin 2006, 205). This is something I did first in Wales in the parish of Cellan, Ceredigion which I studied for nearly 30 years before publishing (Austin 2016).

The land depicted in the maps is not far north of Cellan, in Ceredigion in west Wales in the upper valley of the Afon Teifi (Plate 7.1). This river flows westwards through *y filltir sgwâr* and is joined from the south by the tributary waters of the Afon Glasffrwd (Plate 7.2). They come together on the flat floor of a narrow glaciated valley set more or less at right-angles to the main course of the Teifi which turns southwards into Cors Caron (Tregaron Bog). This little side valley is surrounded on three sides, north, south, and east, by the smoothed ridges of the Cambrian Mountains, which are a broad expanse of upland serving as the spine of Wales and, as such, in the *longue durée*, a barrier to communications over thousands of years. It is a significant watershed as well as a political and cultural divide.

The choice of frame for the maps of *y filltir sgwâr* (Plates 7.2–7.6) is determined by the presence at its centre of the remains of the former Cistercian Abbey of Strata Florida, or Ystrad Fflur in Welsh, on which I have been working for nearly 20 years. This Abbey was first founded by a Norman knight in 1164 (Robinson 2007) on a site probably located a couple of miles to the south at Henfynachlog ('Old Abbey'). It was then effectively re-founded in 1184 by the great Lord Rhys of Deheubarth to be, I would argue, the national church of an independent *Pura Wallia*. The outer edges of *y filltir sgwâr* are set by wanting to have the village of Pontrhydfendigaid ('The bridge at the blessed ford') at top left and the appearance of a *hafod* ('summer house') at bottom right, to allow me to talk about the relationship with the uplands. This is more than the metaphoric square mile (nearly four in fact), but it is the circuit of a daily working world of inter-relationship for those who lived in this place.

At Strata Florida there is both a long-term research programme and a major heritage initiative centred on a complex of buildings (Mynachlog Fawr or 'Great Abbey' farm) lying immediately south of the consolidated remains of the Abbey church and part of its cloister. Both elements of this project are closely inter-linked and run under the auspices of the Strata Florida Trust (Austin 2018; SFT 2017).

Plate 7.2 shows that *y filltir sgwâr* consisted of four micro-topographies:

1. Village lands: at the north-western corner of the map is the village of Pontrhydfendigaid, a place which can be traced back to the earliest extant documents of the twelfth century. Around it, north of the river are well-drained lands which were probably ancient open fields supporting the village.

2. Wetlands: to the south and west of the village are the outer (eastern) margins of Cors Caron, an extensive area of raised bog in the main valley of the Afon Teifi and the source of many important palynological studies (Godwin and Mitchell 1938; Turner 1964; Morriss 2001) giving us a complete ecological sequence for the last 12,000 years.

3. Upland *ffridd* as part of the *mynydd*: to the east, south and north are the slopes and thin, acid soils of the Cambrian Mountains (see Plate 7.1 also) which are identified as *mynydd* in Welsh, usually translated into English as 'mountain', but with more embedded cultural meaning related to its ancient use as common pastures and refuge. Another and more nuanced Welsh word to be applied here is *ffridd,* a word borrowed from Middle English (RSPB 2017). In English the word is associated with upland moors or woodlands where there is clearance and use for pasture or, indeed, hunting lodges and breeding places for game in designated forests or chases. In Welsh it comes specifically to mean the land which is on the junction between the open upland pastures and the enclosed ploughed fields of the lower slopes and

valley floors. In this transitional zone were to be found, in the Middle Ages, the majority of the *hafodydd* ('summer houses') where the short-distance transhumant cattle and sheep were managed, serving as temporary shelter and dairying locations (see Hooke this volume). It is worth noting also that the majority of late Bronze Age and Iron Age hill-forts (see Plate 7.1) were situated on these zones and probably originated for similar reasons with enclosures for corralling beasts and huts for seasonal use. It was on the *ffridd* that, in the modern era, permanent intakes were created, sometimes as successors of *hafodydd*, as Welsh custom broke down in the context of the imposition of English land and inheritance law when many were dispossessed of their rights of access to, and use of, land based formerly on extended kinship. The complex and fluid relationship between *ffridd* and *mynydd* has been explored more fully in this project by Fleming and Barker (2008).

4. Teifi lowlands: on the flat valley floor of the Teifi east of the village were the best of the agricultural lands with richer and deeper soils, but occasionally still badly drained, on the gentle slopes and abundant meadows along the flood plain of the river itself. Only Abbey Wood of these lands was not used for arable or meadow.

The nineteenth century (Plate 7.3)

The primary methodology in this exercise is traditional map regression, combined with a myriad of other sources, documentary and oral, as well as field survey and reconnaissance. So I begin with the first edition Ordnance Survey 25-inch-to-the-mile maps which for this area were surveyed in 1886 and published in 1888–1889. By chance this is also precisely the moment when Stephen Williams, a railway engineer and architect as well as antiquarian scholar, excavated the church and cloister remains at Strata Florida (Williams 1889).

In 1886 most of the land within *y filltir sgwâr* was owned by the Lisburne (Vaughan) estate of Trawscoed who had acquired it in 1878 when it was part of an exchange with the Powells of Nanteos who themselves had acquired it in 1745 from the Stedman family. The Powells and Vaughans, who could trace their lineages back to later medieval Welsh lords and princes, were major regional, economic, and social players with considerable interests not just in agriculture, but also in metal mining (Morgan 1997; 2001). They held extensive lands, many of which could be traced back to the holdings of Strata Florida released at the Dissolution first to the Devereux family (the later Earls of Essex). Slowly this massive portfolio of landholding was broken up and sold on to the Vaughans, Powells, Stedmans, and other gentry families who by these means radically changed their status and prospects. In these processes of freehold transfer, the arrangements for farm leasehold tenancy and management seem to have remained largely untouched and may have done so from the later Middle Ages onwards. The tenant farmers worked closely with their estate managers and owners and those who held the major farms were considerable social agents in their localities, employing work forces housed among their home buildings and scattered in the small cottages of the rural poor (Howell 2000; Wiliam 2010), often in liminal or marginal points of the landscape.

The first analytical map (Plate 7.3) depicts the landscape of the 25-inch map. At the heart was the tenant farm of Mynachlog Fawr (Great Abbey). At this point the land itself was farmed by Mary Jones, while the main house was occupied by Thomas Arch who had been put there by the Powell estate in 1871, probably to act as agent for their holdings in the upper Teifi valley (Arch 2005). The Arches still farm this land today and part of their holding, apart from the bottom land around the old Abbey, consists of enclosed grazing on the *mynydd*. This had been added to the farm when traditional common grazing on the open uplands was transformed through enclosure (largely undocumented) into individual ownership blocks and assigned to the leasehold properties which had held the ancient rights from time immemorial. When precisely this happened is uncertain, but is likely to be at some point in the eighteenth century, perhaps not long after the acquisition by the Powells, who were also locked into disputes with Crown agents about mineral rights and mining throughout the Cambrian Mountain region (Lewis 1998, 163–4).

Around the Abbey farm were neighbours, also tenants, some in similar valley-floor locations and others eking out tougher livings on the intakes which had reached their zenith on the surrounding slopes and hill-tops. Of the former, all lay to the north on the other side of the Teifi on south-facing slopes largely below the 700 ft/210 m contour. Out to the west, around the edges of Cors Caron were other small farms which most likely began as cottage holdings on the edge of the upland or on the low, dry ridges perched just above the wetlands. Some never became more than that. Morphologically the 25-inch map shows the rigid straight-line patterns of late enclosure boundaries, often ditches draining the wetlands and patches of boggy peat. These enclosures were only completed in the years between the Tithe map of 1840 and 1886.

On the lower, steeper slopes of the upland edge were surviving broadleaf woodlands, some of which, by 1886, had been reduced to scrubland by felling. These woods are now almost entirely restricted to sessile oak regenerated after clear felling in the First World War. However, they had once been much more diverse and had long been managed resources for local farms for grazing and various types of timber and underwood.

On the higher land of the *ffridd* the intake farms were of varying sizes and viability, most having been created over many centuries completely *de novo*, while some were on, or close to, earlier *hafodydd* sites as their names suggest (*e.g.* Hafod-newydd). By the mid-twentieth century the majority of these intakes were gone, swept away by the protracted agricultural recession of recent times, and their lands either absorbed into other properties or bought by the Forestry Commission and planted with conifers.

Thus it is that the 1886 map is dominated by land cleared for cultivation either as ancient fields or as intakes (both left uncoloured on Plate 7.3). At that time these were still mixed farms, albeit with a tendency towards stock management, both cattle and sheep, and there was a strong tradition of self-sufficiency going back centuries (Jenkins 1998a). Market activity was largely local, although another tradition of droving to distant markets using the great transmontane routes passing through Strata Florida had only recently been replaced by the arrival of the railway across Cors Caron (opened in 1867).

Also on the map are very evident traces of industrial activity, both the dominant, but already declining woollen mills (Jenkins 1998b) and large-scale mining. The greatest industrial presence, however, was Abbey Consol Mine begun in 1859, but finished before the Second World War when it failed to compete with other lead producers across the globe (Lewis 1998, 162). The brief success of this mine led to a rapid expansion of Pontrhydfendigaid on the south side of the Afon Teifi when terraces of workers cottages and overseer houses were built and to the north, in the old village, two large chapels appeared. The houses remain, but the mine and its workers are gone. Together with the loss of the mountain farms and cottages, this creates a strong sense of *hiraeth* for a time early in the twentieth century when *y filltir sgwâr* flourished and community was strong and vibrant around its Welsh culture and ancestry. This is now passing out of living memory as people can only just recall what their parents and grandparents told them of the past. This sense of a 'golden age' of community, albeit in reality bitterly hard and poor for most people, is still also an invisible yard-stick for what government policy, private enterprise, and third-sector activity is being asked to achieve in regenerating the life of the place and protecting its Welsh values and language.

The late seventeenth and early eighteenth centuries (Plate 7.4)

By 1886 this seemingly stable life was already beginning to crumble as economic and social change began to overwhelm it and populations started to drift away. Substantially the later nineteenth-century map is actually the reflection and product of the preceding two centuries. This was the heyday of the Great Estates. During this time the gradual encroachment onto the upland and the upgrading of farms was encouraged not just by English land law and tenant succession, but also by an agrarian boom coupled with the first waves of industrialisation, all of which gave the owners large wealth and the tenants the confidence to continue expanding their cultivation and investing in farm buildings (Moore-Colyer 1998a). Most of these late nineteenth-century dispersed farms had their dwelling houses built or rebuilt in the previous century as small, two-storey broadly Georgian structures with, often, their single-storey predecessors left among the buildings of the farmyards. The ideological impulse to all of this was the universal aspiration to Improvement and Progress. Some landowners embraced these concepts along with the aesthetics of the Picturesque, like Thomas Johnes of Hafod further to the north but still on former Strata Florida lands, who greatly 'beautified' his core demesnes (MacVe 2004). In the case of

Johnes this led to almost immediate bankruptcy, but even where the expenditure was more circumspect, the gentry of upland Wales were doomed once the cold winds of the world system began to blow at the end of the nineteenth century.

Some members of the gentry, however, had over-stretched themselves long before that and in *y filltir sgwâr* the major casualty was the Stedmans of Strata Florida. By the time Richard Stedman died in 1745 he was already deep in debt to his brother-in-law, Thomas Powell of Nanteos (Morgan 2001, 27–8). Richard had married Anne Powell in 1723, but had lost both his daughters in childhood and their heart-wrenching memorial can still be read in Strata Florida parish church. On his death without any direct Stedman heir Thomas Powell seems to have taken the Strata Florida lands as repayment of his brother-in-law's debts.

In terms of *y filltir sgwâr*, the property later called Mynachlog-fawr (Great Abbey), as shown on Plate 7.4, had probably been assembled by the mid-sixteenth century if not before, at first as a leasehold. It included the former Abbey itself and its precincts and adjacent pieces of land which seem, by the Dissolution, to have formed essential elements of the Abbey's home farm, such as Abbey Wood and curvilinear meadow enclosures on the north side of the Teifi. The farm itself was a mixture of pasture, meadow, arable, and woodland (Fig. 7.1). This was all surveyed in 1765 by John Davies for the Powell estate some 20 years after its acquisition from the Stedmans (NLW Map 302). What it shows are, at its core, the remains of the gentry-designed landscape within which had been incorporated certain surviving elements of the medieval buildings and layout (Fig. 7.2).

Mynachlog-fawr and all the farms and cottages shown on Plate 7.4 were, by 1765, in the freehold of the Powells with leases held by a variety of tenants. By this date the house of Mynachlog-fawr or Strata Florida had ceased to be a gentry mansion and its tenure separated from the land around it. These lands were extensive and stretched to the north of the Teifi, to the west onto the hill of Pen-lan, to the south onto the *ffridd* including a cottage at Waun-wen and to the east almost to the margins of Pontrhydfendigaid. This was a major farm in the Powell estate and may actually have been run from the remains of the old Abbey Gatehouse at Penny-porth (*Pen-y-porth* in Welsh – 'the Head Gate'). It is clear, however, that there were at least four cottage holdings within the Strata Florida curtilage, including Cornwall-fawr and Cornwall-fach each of which carried in their names (*Cornel-y-wal*) the fact that they were at the corners of the former Abbey precinct wall and had originally been the north and south gates.

The other five leasehold farms on the Teifi valley floor were smaller than Mynachlog-fawr, but were still in command of the better, often south-facing land, and were significant mixed farms with stock wintered on the arable stubble and meadows around them and in the summer pastured on the upland commons where grazing rights can be tracked back into the Middle Ages, indeed to the first documented land grants of the twelfth century.

Plate 7.4 also gives a snap-shot of the upland intakes and enclosures we know to have occurred by the later seventeenth or earlier eighteenth century.

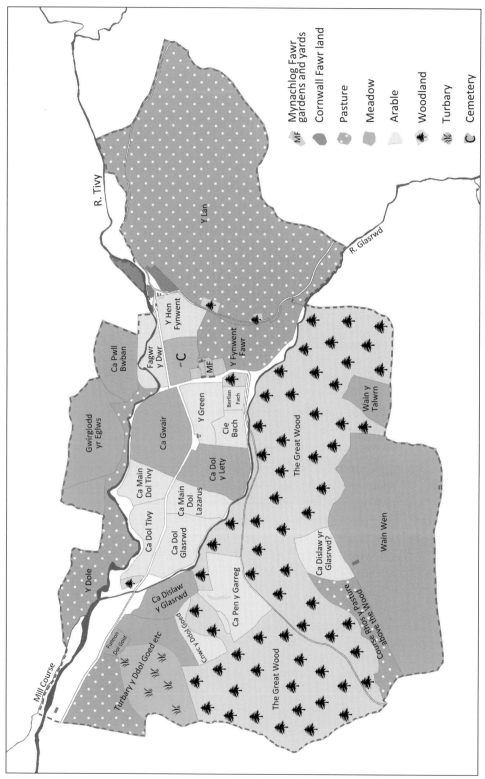

FIGURE 7.1. The layout and land-use of the farm in 1765.

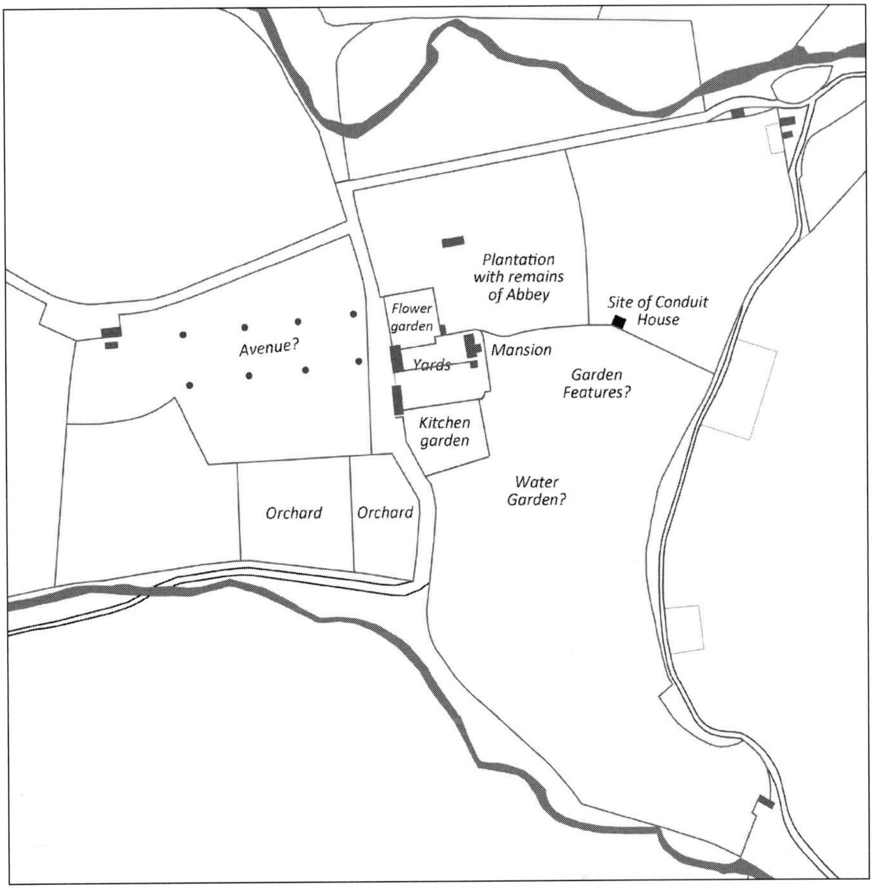

FIGURE 7.2. The gentry arrangements from the 1765 map.

These bit into the *ffridd* particularly along the deeply incised valley of the Afon Glasffrwd. Some of these, such as Talwrn, Crofftau, Cil-garn, and Gargoed seem to have begun in the later Middle Ages, but had relatively restricted areas of cleared land around them even by the mid-eighteenth century. Essentially they were self-sufficient but relatively poor units with dependency on patches of the still-uncleared uplands incorporated into their curtilages to support small flocks of sheep and a few cattle (Moore-Colyer 1998b).

At this time too the wetlands to the west were in the process of being drained and enclosed within rigidly rectilinear fields with a few holdings emerging into the same category as the farms on the upland and the Teifi lowland. Although it is difficult to date such enclosures (Moore-Colyer 1998b, 19–20), the consistent patterns of the fields and the resources required to do these works strongly suggest they were part of an estate management intent on improvement. If this is the case, it is most likely that this reflects the hand of the Powells rather than the Stedmans who were probably not, in the later seventeenth and early eighteenth centuries, in any financial position to fund such ventures.

Also notable is the evidence not just of intake farms, but also tiny smallholdings or cottages (*tyddyn* and *bwthyn*) scattered around the countryside, often in liminal situations on the edges of wood or bog, but also on farms. Here was the rural underclass, bobbing and weaving, doing anything to prevent starvation. These are the people most often to be found in the returns of the Poor Law inscribed into the parish Vestry Books. We also find *tyddyn* names in the surviving indentures of some of the estates in the region, as landowners struggled to control small-scale encroachment which was often silently sanctioned by local land agents. The map shows that one area subject to the creation of these holdings was the margins of the wetlands where the shapes of small, often curvilinear, curtilages around the cottage yards can be traced on estate, tithe, and early OS maps, as at Tŷ'n-y-coed, Cnwch, or Cefn-llwyd.

On the map too are various aspects of what we must regard as the first post-medieval industrial phase of the valley. This includes not just the medieval demesne corn mill on the eastern side of Pontrhydfendigaid, but also a small mine close to Bron-y-berllan which we know was being worked in the seventeenth century as well as earlier. Traditional mining, although using hydraulic techniques imported from elsewhere, was largely undertaken by seasonal labour and perhaps quite intermittently (Bick 1976). Many of those working the shafts and stopes were almost certainly drawn from the local community, although increasing numbers of professionals, both engineers and miners were being imported through the eighteenth century when exploitation was at its most intense. Nevertheless this industrial population was lost among the farms and the existing buildings of the village and it was not until a century later that special housing was constructed on the southern side of Pontrhydfendigaid.

Another key industry was cloth production, again perhaps with its roots in the later Middle Ages, although there is no specific evidence for this at Strata Florida. In *y filltir sgwâr* its presence was to be found again to the east of the village, in the form of fulling and weaving complexes exploiting water drawn in leats from the Afon Teifi and from the mountain tributary of Nant Mawr. Unlike the mining population, there are signs, certainly in the case of the mill on the Teifi, that some specific housing was made available close to the centre of production.

From the gentry to the poorest, all living in the same *milltir sgwâr*, this was a time of some optimism, but one too of deprivation and risk from high to low. Perhaps the most secure were the tenant farmers in the middle with their long leases and rising productivity serving growing markets both regionally and nationally.

The sixteenth century (Plate 7.5)

This century saw massive changes, not least the dissolution of the Abbey by the Act of 1539 when its former site and lands were appropriated, first as lease and then as freehold, by Richard Devereux in his role as its Receiver General. It is possible that the first John Stedman came from a gentry family in Staffordshire as the Devereux agent, and by the 1560s he was said to be 'of Strata Florida' and living in a substantial house on the site, with significant leases of former Abbey land in the area. In 1571 he bought the freehold of the Abbey and its 'demesne' which can be documented in a Devereux rental of 1577 (Green 1927, I, 75). This document also shows that John Stedman was leasing other former Abbey lands, but the original description of the core demesne is in 1546:

> ... the site of the late monastery aforesaid with the demesne lands [which included] the house and site of the late monastery ... and all houses, edifices, barns, stables, dovecots, pleasure grounds, orchards, gardens, and all our land whatsoever within the fences, walks, circuits, and precincts to the site of the said late monastery belonging ... (Green 1927, 1, 4)

This demesne included the remains of the Abbey, even by then in use as a house, and further detail in both 1546 and 1577 shows that it included the Orchard Cottage (Tyddyn-berllan), meadow enclosures, lands, sundry other cottages, and Rhydfendiagaid corn mill, all on both sides of the river Teifi. In many ways this was essentially the same as the farm surveyed in 1765.

John Stedman and his son, another John (Moel), built up a significant estate, part freehold and part leasehold, and by the time he died in 1607, they were prominent in Cardiganshire, marrying into major gentry families and holding high office in the county. All these tenures seem to have been consolidated into one freehold in 1636–1637 when the Vaughans of Trawscoed in a complex series of land exchanges and purchases bought the Devereux holdings, re-selling parts onto various prominent families including the Stedmans (NLW Crosswood 2, I, 262). The first half of the seventeenth century, however, saw the zenith of the Stedman family fortunes and slow decline followed until the end in 1745.

Prior to the Dissolution it is clear that the Abbey, to meet growing pressures from the Crown for money, had issued a large number of long-term leases in return for cash payments. These are recorded in the first rent rolls and it is not until all these lapsed in the 1630s that the Devereux were able to sell. To what extent this practice of leasehold was actually a feature of earlier centuries, as we might expect, will never be known as the Abbey muniments vanished after the Dissolution. Whatever the tenure, however, the land use and structure of the landscape can be recovered by regression analysis and this produces Plate 7.5 with some degree of confidence.

Part of the steady acquisition process of former Abbey land by prominent local families can be seen on Plate 7.5 which uses the two Devereux rentals of 1546 (Green 1927, I, 4) and 1577 (Green 1927, I, 75). In the 1546 record, all of *y filltir sgwâr* was being held by lease from the Crown with most of the individual tenures still governed by the long-term Abbey leases. Almost all the tenements named in this document can still be identified apart from a few small cottages and fields. In 1564 Walter Devereux acquired the freehold from the Crown (NLW Crosswood 1, II, 1566) and was then in a position to start issuing new leases as the old ones expired. By 1577, John Stedman was also able to add to the extent of the core Strata Florida 'demesne' by leasing two upland farms to the south, Cilgarn and Crofftau.

What is striking is the extent to which the upland *ffridd* had been colonised by farms by the time the Abbey was in its last days. This, and the work at Troed-y-rhiw (Fleming and Barker 2008), runs counter to the usually held view that this was a phenomenon of modernity (Moore-Colyer 1998b, 20). It is even possible, by examining the morphology of fields, to identify the first land clearances around the farm garths. These were relatively modest and even as late as the Tithe map, some of these clearances had extensive areas of unenclosed rough pasture attached to them within the circuit of an outer curtilage hedgerow. This gives some clue to the remaining dependence on stock within the farm economies. The name of one of these farms, Hafod-newydd, may also be a clue that their origins may have lain in the consolidation of *hafodydd* sites into permanent habitations during the later Middle Ages as the Abbey allowed the conversion of upland commons into ring-fenced farms. This progression to consolidation and permanency is generally reflected in the archaeology of the upland in Wales (Roberts 2006) and at Hafod-newydd it is possible to see the morphology of the old site on the 1886 map.

Less certain is what was happening to the wetlands in the south-west corner of *y filltir sgwâr* on the edge of Cors Caron. On the two later maps already considered (Plates 7.3 and 7.4) a large amount of the clearance and drainage can be attributed to rectilinear enclosures we can assign to the modern era by comparison with similar morphologies in the region. This suggests that farm sites named in the 1546 rental were quite modest with small infield curtilages still visible in the farm layouts on the first maps. It is these nodes which in some cases became larger farms as a result of enclosure perhaps under the impetus of the Powell management after 1746. The origins of the farms may be suggested by their names: Cnwch, 'nook' or 'corner'; Gilfach, 'nook', 'niche' or 'lodge'; Bryn-y-Gors, 'bog-hill'. They all seem to have been named when they were in very restricted locations or micro-environments between larger elements of the landscape, *cors/gors* ('bog'), *mynydd* ('mountain'), and *coed* ('wood').

It is also possible to see, although not date precisely, that many of these farms, especially those on the upland, were beginning to cut into, not only the common pastures, but also the ancient woodlands along the steep sides of the Afon Glasffrwd. Here there are a number of piecemeal enclosures strongly suggesting individual acts of clearance. On Plate 7.5 some of these have been shown as being there by the sixteenth century, as at Crofftau and Crofftau Ddryssiog (later Pantyfedwen). Indeed the latter, with its name meaning the 'brambly crofts or crevices', had all its best cleared land below it in what must previously have been woodland. It is entirely possible that an impetus to this clearance may have been the well-known instruction by Edward I shortly after the Conquest for the Abbey to clear the woodland which could harbour the Crown's enemies (Linnard 2000, 32). When Leland came in 1536 or thereabouts he noted that:

Strateflure is set around about with montanes not far distant ... Many hilles
therabout hath been well woddid, as evidently by old rotes apperith, but now
in them is [almost no woode.] The causes be these; first the wood cut doun was
never copisid, and this hath beene a great cause of destruction of wood throrough
Wales. Secondly after cutting down of wooddys the gottys hath so bytten the
young spring that it never grew but like shrubbes. Thirddely men for the nonys
destroyed the great woddis that thei shuld not harborrow theves. (Toulmin-Smith
1906, 118)

That he could see tree stumps in abundance does suggest he was looking not
at the great open pastures, clear since the later Bronze Age, but rather at newer
clearances along the routeways rising up the river valleys, such as the Glasffrwd,
which Leland would have passed along as he went up into the mountains.

The reconstruction of this sixteenth-century landscape probably leaves us
looking also at the later medieval life spaces of the Abbey and its people. By
the fifteenth century two Abbots, Rhys and Morgan, had tried hard to revive
the fortunes and reputation of Strata Florida (Robinson 2007, 15). It had been
brought to its knees both physically and politically during the period at the
beginning of the fifteenth century when Owain Glyndŵr had been raising
the flag of Welsh independence. The Abbey seems to have come out in full
support of the Welsh dream and on three occasions English armies encamped
at Strata Florida and took it over (Riley 2015). The result was devastation and
the appropriation for a time of the Abbey's estates by the English Crown.
Despite the best efforts of Rhys and Morgan the place never really recovered.
When Leland saw the place just before the Dissolution only four buildings were
identified as being part of the Abbey, that is the church, cloister, refectory, and
infirmary, the last three of which were 'in ruins' (Toulmin-Smith 1906, 118). This
rump of monastic architecture probably existed in a precinct much reduced in
size from its original extent.

The thirteenth century (Plate 7.6)

Plate 7.6 shows the layout of the Abbey as effectively re-founded in 1184 and
consecrated in 1201. The figure also shows a reconstruction of the farmlands
which we can recover from regression analysis and fleeting references in the
documents. The map, however, makes an important assumption which runs
contrary to the understanding that Strata Florida, as a Cistercian house,
organised and operated its landholdings as granges organised on broadly the
same principle as English and French feudal manors – a premise that lies at
the heart of an important article by David Williams (2010) on the history of
Strata Florida. This understanding is drawn largely, as we shall see, from early
post-Dissolution rentals.

Plate 7.6 embodies the idea, by contrast, that this may not have been the case
and I argue that the running of the monastic lands was much more akin to the
organisation to be found in the Welsh law codes which have been studied and
mapped extensively in Wales (Pierce 1959; 1972; Jones 1972; Johnstone and Riley
1995; Johnstone 2000). Overlaid onto this, however, in the area immediately

around the Abbey, was an inner demesne of specialist farms, transforming the previous arrangements of the *llys* and *maerdref* of a former Welsh royal estate.

Hard evidence is not easy to find given the dearth of documents. We are only on secure ground in the rentals of the immediately post-Dissolution period when land-holdings, mostly at will or leasehold, are listed within different granges. The grange as a unit of space can, in fact, only be recovered by mapping the places listed in those post-medieval documents and from the attribution to it of certain renders, seemingly given within the framework of the grange, such as *commorth*, an ancient grazing tribute. It is clear that the administrators of the later sixteenth and subsequent centuries knew exactly the geographical limits of these granges as mapped by David Williams (Williams 1990). Yet the earliest specific reference we have to granges before that time is in a plea to the king in 1428–1429 after a serious invasion of Strata Florida property by the Abbot of Conway (Williams 1889, xxxix–xli). This is not, it should be pointed out, evidence of their absence before that. Indeed in a papal bull of 1181 which confirms the first grant of land to the Abbey, there is reference to '*Stratflur cum omnibus grangis et impendiciis [sic] suis*' (Davies 1946, 200). However, this is somewhat formulaic and, given the normal pattern of Cistercian land administration the papal office may just have assumed, rather than known, that this was the actual arrangement at Strata Florida (see also Bezant 2014).

One set of documents we do have at Strata Florida is the original grants of land in the later twelfth and early thirteenth centuries together with some references to land disputes (Pryce 2005). These have come down to us largely as a result of *inspeximi* retained in the English royal records as Strata Florida sought validation for its holdings in the years after the Edwardian annexation of Wales. These documents refer to places and situations as they were before the Abbey took over administration and jurisdiction and are, essentially, tenures and tenements of a pre-manorial kind. The question is, to what extent did the Abbey, in following Cistercian practice, establish the 'grange economy' from the start or was it a much later creation?

Between the two temporal poles of the twelfth and the later fifteenth centuries, however, lies a black hole of specific knowledge and thus a range of possibilities, and to recover the foundation landscape we must perforce begin with the early grants as they survive to us. The first to be considered, in this regressive analysis, is the comprehensive charter of 1184 by which the Lord Rhys effectively re-founded the Abbey and gave massive landholdings stretching right across the Cambrian Mountains and over to the Irish Sea (Pryce 2005, no. 28, 172–5). Others of his family followed suit and the lands were defined by bounds as in the standard European charter format. Unusually, however, the 1184 charter also included a list of what the charter writers (probably the Strata Florida scribes themselves) called *loci excellentiores*, 'the more excellent places'.

Plate 7.7 widens out from *y filltir sgwâr* to show the location of all these more excellent places. There are two identifiable components to this mapping: 1. a group of places (which I would call 'ancient farms') which can be located from modern place-names (shown as green circles on Plate 7.7), which largely lay to the west of *y filltir sgwâr*; 2. another group of ancient farms whose names cannot be identified from modern or medieval sources, probably because, I would argue, they were replaced and re-named after 1184 as part of a 'demesne' of specialist farms (red circles on Plate 7.7). I have mapped also a third component of ancient farms (grey circles on Plate 7.7) which appear in other documents (including the first charter of 1165), but which were not counted among the 'more excellent places'. Most of this third component can be traced also from modern names. A notable feature of all three of these categories of ancient farm is that they are on what was, and still is, the very best agricultural land in the area, *i.e.* on the valley floor, but above the boggy flood plains. They occupied, therefore, favourable niches in the landscape and reflect an agrarian world view expressed in the 1184 identification of three main elements: *terram campestram et agriculturam et montuosam ad animalium pasturam.*

Terra campestra was meadow and valley pasture ground including bogs and flood areas (notably Cors Caron) from which a host of food resources for animals and humans alike could be won, with fish, fowl, hay, and winter grazing being prominent. *Terra agricultura* was ploughed and improved land. These two elements appear to have been farmed within discrete ancient farm units and later estate maps show that these units lay within fixed outer boundaries but with little internal sub-division, often only with small enclosures around the homesteads. Land was ploughed within these curtilages as rotated patches in cycles dictated by the farm-holders themselves. The internal enclosures of these farm units are, therefore, almost entirely post-medieval and often quite late into modernity. The third element, *terra montuosa*, mountain pasture or *mynydd*, was an important right for these prominent farms and used by short-distance transhumance through the *hafodydd* dairies on the *ffridd*.

In tenurial terms, however, these farms had different relationships with the Abbey, all set by Welsh law and customary practice which seems to have survived throughout the whole life of the institution. This is a matter for another article, but most of the places identified in Plate 7.7 were probably held by Welsh custom, except the ones (in red) directly run from a Home Farm perhaps within the outer precinct of the Abbey itself. This latter group were converted into specialist farms, with their uses still betrayed by their modern place-names and include, within *y filltir sgwâr*, Dôl-ebolion (horses: 'Meadow of the foals'), Bron-y-berllan (fruit trees: 'Hillside of the orchard'), Cae-Madog and Cae-mawr (arable fields: 'Madog's field' and 'Great field'), Pen-ddôl-fawr (meadow: 'Head of the great meadow') and further west there are Dôl-yr-ychain (draught animals: 'Meadow of the Oxen'), Dôl-beidiau (dairy: 'Meadow of the cow-byres') and Brynhope (pigs: 'Hill of the pigs'). These farms would have produced the full array of agrarian commodities needed for the running of a major abbey such as Strata Florida was designed to be. This arrangement is reminiscent of one to be found in the earlier and Carolingian Middle Ages with *mansum dominicatum* near to the manorial centre (Verhulst 2002, 38). Echoes of this can also be found in Anglo-Saxon estates with place-names such as Butterwick, Herdwick, or Barton. Although reminiscent, we should see these changes as transformations of an existing pattern of landholding and not a colonial replacement.

A clue to this may come from the consideration and mapping (Plate 7.8) of one other document, the Lord Rhys' confirmation of the first foundation grant in 1164–1165 (Pryce 2005, no. 25, 167–8). It has no boundary clauses, just a list of names, most of which we can identify, but some not. There is some overlap with the 1184 charter, but not as much as one might expect. The map shows that the places are limited, for the most part, to the narrow band of 'good' lands, around Cors Caron as in 1184. However we should remember that these places, in all probability, had rights of access to *cors*, *ffridd*, and *mynydd*. We should also remember that these places were granted within the customs of practice covered by Welsh law and we should read them with this in mind. To this end one of the few places which cannot be identified in 1164–1165 is *lispennard* which can readily be rendered as Llys Pennardd or the royal centre of the commote of Penardd within which Strata Florida Abbey stood. Pryce (2005, 168) has already speculated that

> … Llys Pennardd was probably the site to which the Abbey was moved from its original location at Ystrad-fflur, also granted by Rhys, i.e. Henfynachlog …

I am inclined to agree and this would place this secular site somewhere under the present remains of the re-founded Abbey. If this is the case, then close together would be the three-fold arrangement noted by Jones Pierce (1959, 271)

> One of the most ancient institutions of the soil in medieval Wales was the tripartite unit (there was normally one in every commote) consisting of a local hall (*llys*), a demesne or home-farm (*tir-bwrdd*), and a *maerdref* – a village occupied by a community of bondmen (*taeogion*) who carried out menial tasks in and about the courts. Down to the time of the conquest, these estates, although showing signs of decreasing vigour, were a prominent feature in the economy of commotes all over north Wales, being actively exploited by native lords and princes who, for cultivating the demesne, continued to draw on a not inconsiderable labour force, over and above the resources of the *maerdrefs*, from groups of bond communities settled nearby.

It is most likely that the *maerdref* was at Pontrhydfendigaid with its demesne mill and small nucleated settlement. Adjacent too is the modern Tŷ-mawr which I would suggest was once Tŷ-maer or the house of the royal official who ran the estate and the *tir-bwrdd*.

This all suggests that the re-located Abbey took over an agricultural and administrative set-up already deeply embedded in the Welsh landscape. The main change in 1184 would then have been the extension of the demesne on a Carolingian model of specialist producers and the appropriation of royal status and rights, perhaps within the bounds of the original *llys* and *maerdref*. Out around Cors Caron we must then consider that the freemen (*breyr* or *bonheddig*) in their *loci excellentiores* were organised in *gwelyau* or kin-based groupings as could be found elsewhere in medieval Ceredigion (Dodgshon 1994, 350; Bezant 2009, 34). Their tribute of *gwestfa* or food-rents to the royal steward (*rhingyll*) would simply have been transferred to the Abbey and perhaps commuted into rents quite early on.

Once, however, the Abbey was up and running, land use consisted of an Inner Precinct of major buildings, an Outer Precinct housing a Home Farm and specialist closes, a Demesne of specialist farms, a new woodland, a variety of other holdings from which renders and service dues were taken, and a range of access rights, especially those onto the mountain pastures. Within *y filltir sgwâr* and out into the Upper Teifi Valley much functioned according to Welsh law and custom and probably not as granges as mapped by David Williams (1990, figs 12 and 15). Socially and culturally this would have played to the Abbey's aspirations to be a centre of continuing Welsh identity, instead of creating an act of Cistercian colonialism. How this evolved into the tenurial situation of the later middle ages will be hard to discover, given the dearth of documents. However, it is clear that the functioning places of land exploitation remained remarkably stable throughout this time with the major changes being in tenure, status, and the growing encroachment onto the traditional pastures on the *ffridd* and *mynydd*, with the consequent break-down of the *hafodydd* system.

Much still needs to be done to map this early agrarian world in detail, but living off the land in an upland context was always a precarious business relying on bonds of kinship and mutual assistance to produce subsistence and tributes from small niches of arable land and rights of access to extensive but poor grazing. This was the essence of *y filltir sgwâr*. It was a long-term Welsh society with deeply-laid attitudes to land, its meaning and use. The regression promoted in this article seems to demonstrate long continuity of place as well, but I must be clear that, at the moment this is a proposition which can only be tested by archaeological fieldwork. In particular we must test the longevity of the core ancient farms in the *loci excellentiores*, but if the reconstruction is right it was probably these farms which survived through long periods of social, environmental, institutional, and economic change, perhaps deep back into prehistory.

Acknowledgements

This article is produced as part of the AHRC-funded project 005842: *The Sacred Landscapes of Medieval Monasteries*.

References

Arch, C. (2005) *Byw dan y Bwa*. Caernarfon, Gwasg Gwynedd.

Austin, D. (2006) The future: discourse, objectives and directions. In K. Roberts (ed.) *Lost Farmsteads: deserted rural settlements in Wales, CBA Report 148*. York, Council for British Archaeology, 193–205.

Austin, D. (2013) An aura of *hiraeth* – Strata Florida. In H. Bowen (ed.) *Buildings and Places in Welsh History*. Llandysul, Gomer Press, 51–8.

Austin, D. (2016) Reconstructing the Upland Landscapes of Medieval Wales. *Archaeologia Cambrensis*, 165, 1–20.

Austin, D. (2018) Strata Florida: a former Welsh Cistercian Abbey and its future. In E. Jamroziak, J. Kerr and K. Stober (eds) *Monastic Life in the Medieval British Isles: Essays in Honour of Janet Burton*. Cardiff, University of Wales Press, 53–68.

Bezant, J. (2009) *Medieval Welsh Settlement and Territory: archaeological evidence from a Teifi valley landscape. BAR British Series 487*. Oxford, British Archaeological Reports.

Bezant, J. (2014) Revising the monastic 'grange': problems at the edge of the Cistercian world. *Journal of Medieval Monastic Studies* 3, 51–70.

Bick, D. E. (1976) *The Old Metal Mines of Mid-Wales: Part one, Cardiganshire south of Devil's Bridge*. Newent, The Pound House.

Davies, J. C. (1946) A Papal Bull of Privileges to the Abbey of Ystrad Flur. *National Library of Wales Journal* 4, 197–203.

Dodgshon, R. A. (1994) Early society and economy. In J. L. Davies and D. P. Kirby (eds) *Cardiganshire County History: volume 1, From the earliest times to the coming of the Normans*. Cardiff, Royal Commission on the Ancient and Historical Monuments of Wales, 342–364.

Fleming, A. and Barker, L. (2008) Monks and Local Communities: the late medieval landscape at Troed-y-rhiw, Caron Uwch Clawdd, Ceredigion. *Medieval Archaeology* 52, 261–288.

Godwin, H. & Mitchell, G. F. (1938) Stratigraphy and Development of Two Raised Bogs Near Tregaron, Cardiganshire. *New Phytologist* 37(5), 427–454.

Green, F. (1927) *Calendar of Deeds and Documents, Vol. II The Crosswood Deeds*. Aberystwyth, National Library of Wales.

Howell, D. W. (2000) *The Rural Poor in Eighteenth-century Wales*. Cardiff, University of Wales Press.

Jenkins, D. (1998a) Land and community around the close of the nineteenth century. In G. H Jenkins and I. G. Jones (eds) *Cardiganshire County History: Volume 3, Cardiganshire in modern times*. Cardiff, Royal Commission on the Ancient and Historical Monuments of Wales, 94–112.

Jenkins, J. G. (1998b) Rural industries in Cardiganshire. In G. H Jenkins and I. G. Jones (eds) *Cardiganshire County History: Volume 3, Cardiganshire in modern times*. Cardiff, Royal Commission on the Ancient and Historical Monuments of Wales, 135–159.

Johnstone, N. (2000) Llys and Maerdref: the royal courts of the Princes of Gwynedd: a study of their location and selective trial excavation. *Studia Celtica* 34, 167–210.

Johnstone, N. and Riley, H. (1995) *Llys and Maerdref: an investigation into the location of the royal courts of the Princes of Gwynedd*. Unpublished Report. Bangor, Gwynedd Archaeological Trust Report 167.

Jones, G. R. J. (1972) Post-Roman Wales. In H. P. R. Finberg (ed.) *The Agrarian History of England and Wales. Vol. 1(ii), AD 43–1042*. Cambridge, Cambridge University Press, 281–382.

Lewis, W. J. (1998) Lead mining in Cardiganshire. In G. H. Jenkins and I. G. Jones (eds) *Cardiganshire County History: Volume 3, Cardiganshire in modern times*. Cardiff, Royal Commission on the Ancient and Historical Monuments of Wales, 160–181.

Linnard, W. (2000) *Welsh Woods and Forests, 2nd ed.* Llandyssul, Gomer.

MacVe, J. (2004) *The Hafod Landscape*. Pontrhydygroes, The Hafod Trust.

Moore-Colyer, R. J. (1998a) The landed gentry of Cardiganshire. In G. H. Jenkins and I. G. Jones (eds) *Cardiganshire County History: Volume 3, Cardiganshire in modern times*. Cardiff, Royal Commission on the Ancient and Historical Monuments of Wales, 51–75.

Moore-Colyer, R. J. (1998b) Agriculture and land occupation in eighteenth and nineteenth century Cardiganshire. In G. H. Jenkins and I. G. Jones (eds) *Cardiganshire County History: Volume 3, Cardiganshire in modern times*. Cardiff, Royal Commission on the Ancient and Historical Monuments of Wales, 19–50.

Morgan, G. (1997) *A Welsh House and its Family: the Vaughans of Trawsgoed*. Llandyssul, Gomer.

Morgan, G. (ed.) (2001) *Nanteos: a Welsh house and its families*. Llandyssul, Gomer.

Morriss, S. H. (2001) *Recent Human Impact and Land Use Change in Britain and Ireland: a Pollen Analytical and Geochemical Study*. Unpublished PhD thesis, University of Southampton, Department of Geography.

Pierce, T. Jones (1959) Medieval Cardiganshire; a study in social origins. *Ceredigion* 3, 265–283.

Pierce, T. Jones (1972) Some Tendencies in the Agrarian History of Caernarvonshire during the Later Middle Ages. In J. Beverly-Smith (ed.) *Medieval Welsh Society. Selected Essays by T. Jones Pierce*. Cardiff, University of Wales Press, 39–60.

Pryce, H. (2005) *The Acts of the Welsh Rulers,* Cardiff, University of Wales Press.

Riley, J. (2015) The Military Garrisons of Henry IV and Henry V at Strata Florida, 1407 and 1415–16. *Welsh History Review* 27(4), 645–71.

Roberts, K (ed.) (2006) *Lost Farmsteads: deserted rural settlements in Wales, CBA Report 148*. York, Council for British Archaeology.

Robinson, D. (2007) *Strata Florida Abbey; Talley Abbey: the guidebook* (3rd edition). Cardiff, Cadw.

RSPB (2017) *Ffridd – a habitat on the edge*. http://ww2.rspb.org.uk/Images/ffridd_tcm9–384432.pdf (accessed 15.09.17).

SFT, Strata Florida Trust and Project http://www.strataflorida.org.uk (accessed 03.09.18).

Toulmin-Smith, L. (1906) *The Itinerary in Wales of John Leland*. London, G. Bell. [incorporated as part 6 into the publication of the whole itinerary by Toulmin Smith 1907–11]

Turner, J. (1964) The Anthropogenic Factor in Vegetational History. I. Tregaron and Whixall Mosses. *New Phytologist* 63, 73–90.

Verhulst, A. (2002) *The Carolingian Economy*. Cambridge, Cambridge University Press.

Wiliam, E. (2010) *The Welsh Cottage: building traditions of the rural poor, 1750–1900*. Aberystwyth, Royal Commission on the Ancient and Historical Monuments of Wales.

Williams, D. H. (1990) *Atlas of the Cistercian Lands in Wales*. Cardiff, University of Wales Press.

Williams, D. H. (2010) The Cistercians in West Wales II: Ceredigion. *Archaeologia Cambrensis* 159, 241–286.

Williams, S. W. (1889) *The Cistercian Abbey of Strata Florida: its history, and an account of the recent excavations made on its site*. London, Whiting.

Unpublished sources

NLW Crosswood, National Library of Wales, Deeds and Documents of the Crosswood Estate, Cardiganshire.

NLW Map 302, National Library of Wales, John Davies plan Nanteos Deposit Map 302, 66 'A survey of the Abbey Farm in the Parish of Carron within the county of Cardigan Taken & delineated 1765'.

CHAPTER EIGHT

The practice of 'in rodwallis': medieval Welsh agriculture in north Pembrokeshire

Rhiannon Comeau

In rodwallis is a thirteenth-century term for the medieval agriculture of Welsh Pembrokeshire that, as will be seen, encapsulates a set of interrelated practices of pre-Conquest origin. It comes not from the much-discussed 'Little England Beyond Wales' of Flemish colonists, but from the Welshry lands north of the Preseli hills where there was a little English settlement beyond the Anglo-Norman plantation town of Newport/Trefdraeth (Owen 1994, 41, 64, 170, 175; Kissock 1997; Austin 2005; Rippon 2008, 227–248). Here manorial records and medieval ridge and furrow – the staples of English medieval landscape research – are rare. This is a common situation in the Welshries of south and west Wales and explains the research emphasis, visible in the Welsh sections of Baker and Butlin's *Field Systems in the British Isles* (1973), on two particular and very different areas: the early-conquered, colonised and manorialised lowlands of south Wales, and late-conquered north Wales with its detailed Edwardian records.

How, therefore, should we approach poorly recorded areas like north Pembrokeshire? This paper will present one possibility: a multidisciplinary investigation that combines regressive analysis of maps, place-names, and soil types to provide a context for sixteenth-century descriptions of local farming practice, references to agriculture in twelfth- and thirteenth-century Welsh law, and archaeological excavation. Three locales will be examined in the north Pembrokeshire *cantref* and lordship of Cemais that are representative of *hendrefi* (permanent arable settlements) and *hafodau* (seasonal pasture with its temporary settlements): the coastal parish of Dinas, occupied by the tenants of aristocratic Welsh freemen; the Lord of Cemais' demesne manor of Bayvil in the Nevern valley; and an area of the Preseli hills at Carn Goedog (Fig. 8.1).

As well as illustrating the seasonal patterns of use of this landscape, four key points will be made. Firstly, local sixteenth-century Welsh agricultural practices indicate the operation of an infield-outfield system similar to other areas of northern Britain and Ireland, a suggestion first made in 1956 by Howells (1956, 325–6) but since largely ignored; and secondly, these practices, together with newly identified evidence for transhumance, closely mirror those defined in pre-Conquest Welsh law. Thirdly, it will argue that these practices (which focus

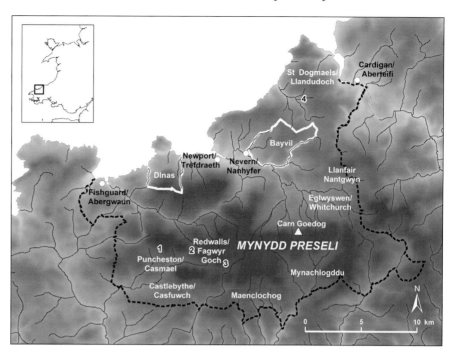

FIGURE 8.1. The medieval *cantref* and lordship of Cemais, showing case study areas and key locations mentioned in text. (Map contains OS data © Crown copyright and database right 2018.)

on spring-sown crops) can be linked with the regional medieval use of a light plough, and with the minimal presence of medieval ridge and furrow. And last but not least it will suggest that (as in medieval Scotland and early Anglo-Saxon England) we should regard the shared seasonal pastures of the outfield not as marginal zones but as central both to agrarian economy and to social identity (*cf.* Hooke this volume).

Hamlets, open fields and ploughs

The landscape to be considered, of coastal plain and hills, is (beyond Anglo-Norman Newport) one of dispersed settlement with no large villages in the medieval period. In the sixteenth century, when detailed records first become available, most people lived in hamlets which were commonly located at the junction of free-draining arable-quality soils and poorer seasonally waterlogged soils (Plate 8.1; Comeau 2019, 161). Most of these hamlets (86% or 50/58) contained between 3 and 6 dwellings, a similar size range to the bond townships of pre-Conquest south Wales law (Wade-Evans 1909, 205, 347; Comeau 2019, 171–4, 642–3). The majority of landholders were tenants, either of freeholders of mostly aristocratic Welsh lineage (66% of all Welsh Cemais landholdings in 1594: 331/504) or of the Anglo-Norman Lord of Cemais whose lands derived from the pre-Conquest Welsh prince (14% of all Welsh Cemais landholdings in 1594: 69/504; Comeau 2019, 123–5, 637). Bondmen origins are likely in both cases.[1]

Open fields are associated with these hamlets, mentioned in passing in medieval records (*e.g.* Charles 1971, 117–8), and visible as areas of intermingled strips on first edition 6-inch Ordnance Survey maps of the 1880s and tithe maps of the 1840s, the earliest detailed maps for much of the region (Plates 8.2A, B, C). On the southern foothills of the Preselis these residual open fields are found in parishes like Puncheston/Casmael and Castlebythe/Casfuwch, which were held in the thirteenth and fourteenth centuries as Anglo-Norman manors of mixed Welsh, English, and Flemish settlement (*e.g.* Owen 1862, 57–60, 88–9), and could therefore be argued to represent agricultural methods introduced by incomers. Intermingled strips can however also be seen north of the Preselis in areas (like Dinas, Llanfair Nantgwyn, and Eglwyswen/Whitchurch) held by medieval Welsh freeholders, and here they probably represent the small permanently cultivated open fields of Welsh law agriculture (Howells 1956, 324–6; Jones 1973, 435). One of these, at Llanfair Nantgwyn (Plate 8.2c), is ringed by tenanted dwellings, which suggests that Glanville Jones' association of such 'girdle' patterns with freeholder settlement may reflect particular north Wales social conditions, and indeed some English girdle patterns are also linked to tenants (Jones 1973, 455, 458–9; Atkin 1985, 173–182; Roberts and Wrathmell 2002, 102–3).

The presence of open fields means that the evidence (or lack of it) for medieval ridge and furrow must be addressed. Ridge and furrow is indeed present, but is found almost exclusively on moors and hillsides where it usually takes the form of close-set narrow cultivation ridges resembling the 'cord rig' of north Britain (*e.g.* Fagwr Fran NPRN 276051 and Mynydd Morvil HER 14344: (1) and (2) on Fig. 8.1; Fowler 2002, 156; Driver 2008, figs 208 and 209). There are a few hillside instances of broader ridging, some of which may be lazy beds used in post-medieval potato cultivation. Both the narrow cultivation ridges and lazy beds may in principle be of any date from late prehistory onwards, and could be created by ards, simple ploughs, spades, or people-powered breast-ploughs which were used locally in the temporary cultivation of rough pasture (Fussell 1933; Morris 1991, 31; Fowler 2002, 149–151, 156–8). The two most likely instances of broad medieval-type ridge and furrow, one on a hillside (Banc Du NPRN 114214: (3) on Fig. 8.1; Driver 2008, figs 195 and 196) and the other in the lowlands (Pant Saeson NPRN 265253: (4) on Fig. 8.1), are associated with Anglo-Norman manorial centres.

The absence elsewhere of broad medieval ridge and furrow is probably attributable to the widely used Pembrokeshire plough, a much lighter implement than the heavy mouldboard plough associated with classic ridge and furrow (Payne 1957, 81–2). Also known as the Cardiganshire, Breconshire, Glamorgan, Cornish, or Devon plough, its area of use coincides with records of open fields where arable strips were separated by flat turf baulks ('landshares') rather than by furrows (Davies 1956, 94–6; 1973, 491, 528). This light plough had only a minimal mouldboard, and none is shown in the earliest drawing of it in a fifteenth-century Cardiganshire manuscript of Welsh law (Llanstephan MS 116 [National Library of Wales], discussed and reproduced in Payne 1947, 152–3). A report of 1794 describes it witheringly as

> not calculated to cut a furrow but to tear it open by main force ... the earth
> board is a thing never thought of, but [is] a stick ... [that] extends to the hind

part of the plough … a field ploughed with this machine looks as if a drove of swine had been moiling it. (Hassall 1794, 18)

In the medieval period it was commonly pulled by teams of four oxen which are also recorded in early medieval Ireland (Payne 1947, 52; Thorpe 1978, 252; Owen 1994, 66; Kelly 2000, 474–6). Oxen were valuable beasts (Banham and Faith 2014, 86), and both Welsh law and analyses of thirteenth-century north Wales records make it clear that plough teams were necessarily co-operative ventures: although most families owned one or two oxen, some owned none and would presumably have been among those who contributed plough parts or their own skills as caller or ploughman to the joint ploughing arrangements specified by north Wales law (Thomas 1968, 4–6, 8; Roberts this volume). The smaller south Wales plough teams would have required fewer ox-owners and less co-operation than the eight-oxen heavy plough whose organisational needs underlie the detailed north Wales arrangements, and signal differences in agricultural development between south and north Wales that reflect, perhaps, greater pressure for intensification in the latter area.

Dinas

Ploughs and open fields were part of a broader system of agriculture whose landscape footprint can be identified from nineteenth-century field patterns and names. These are clearly visible in Dinas where nineteenth-century maps show areas of strip fields indicative of medieval open fields, and large rectangular fields that represent the early modern enclosure of both open fields and seasonal pasture (Comeau 2012, 32–7). In tithe records the former open fields show as concentrations of intermingled landholdings (of both strip and irregularly shaped fields) next to small hamlets (Plates 8.2B, 8.3). The same hamlets, occupied largely by tenants of non-resident aristocratic Welsh freemen, appear in sixteenth-century records (Comeau 2009, 229). Three open fields are mentioned: a *carrucata* of 1331 at Brynhenllan, and two ploughlands or *tir arad* at Trevawr (1519) and Hescwm (1594) (NLW Bronwydd 1170 of 1519; Owen 1862, 31; Howells 1977, 30). Pre-enclosure, these open fields and hamlets encircled an area of common grazing, some of it surviving as nineteenth-century common land. Place- and field-names identify it as shared or undivided pasture (*cytir*), or as land types indicative of rough grazing: moor and hill (*rhos, garw, gwaun, cors, mynydd*), gorse and ferns (*eithin, drysi, gwryg, rhedyn, ysgall*), and woodland, some of it rather damp (*allt, coed, helyg, perth, gwern, llwyn*) (for interpretations see Glossary and http://welsh-dictionary. ac.uk/gpc/gpc.html).

This medieval and sixteenth-century patterning takes advantage of soil conditions, with arable open fields on the better soils, and shared grazing on the poorer, wetter lands; a stock-proof bank and ditch called a *gorchlawdd* or *penclawdd* – the equivalent of the English and Scottish head dyke, corn ditch and ring garth – separated them (Comeau 2012, 37). One *penclawdd* is still visible on Dinas mountain, on the moorland edge of the fields at SN00183716.

The physical pattern suggests medieval mixed farming with a substantial pastoral component, and this is also indicated by the food renders or tributes that pre-Conquest Welsh princes required from their bond tenants and freeholders. Bond tenants had to provide bread (preferably wheat), ale, a three-year-old wether (castrated ram) and sow, bacon, cheese, butter, and oats for horse fodder; much the same was required of freeholders, apart from the substitution of wheat flour for bread, the carcass of an ox for sheep and honey for cheese (Wade-Evans 1909, 206–8; Richards, 1954, 72–3; Davies 1982, 46; Jenkins 1990, 128–9; Charles-Edwards 2013, 280–2; Roberts this volume). A food rent was still being paid by a Dinas tenant to his freeholder landlord in 1611, when the Cemais Hundred court roll recorded an annual obligation of '6 pecks of barley, 6 pecks of ground oats, 1 peck of peas, 1 peck of wheat, and 2½ stone of cheese and 2 gallons of butter for each cow [there were six of them on the farm] and two calves every Michaelmas' (Charles 1951, 44).

Bayvil

A similar medieval arrangement of fields and hamlets around a central pasture area can be identified at Bayvil from documentary records, place- and field-names (Plate 8.4), though it is much less readily apparent from nineteenth-century maps: Bayvil was home to several Welsh gentry families and, unlike Dinas, most of this area was extensively reorganised in the later sixteenth and seventeenth centuries (Charles 1973, 35–39). It is however relatively well documented (by Welsh standards) as a demesne manor of Welsh bondsmen held by the Lord of Cemais, with several resident medieval freeholders and place-name evidence of a pre-Conquest royal court or *llys*, used by the Welsh prince for periodic visits (*Henles, Henllis, Henllys*: 'old/former court', 1345, Charles 1992, 140; Howells 1977, 41–53). Its sixteenth-century hamlets are distinctive for their number (ten, assuming a hamlet to have at least three dwellings) and their size: Bayvil, an eleven-dwelling hamlet, was one of the largest in Welsh Cemais (Comeau 2019, 163–6, 172). Twelve ploughlands or open fields (nine bond and three free) are recorded in 1594, most of which are mentioned in fourteenth- and fifteenth-century documents of the Bronwydd Archive (Howells 1977, 49). Records suggest that most of the open fields were adjacent to medieval hamlets though detailed reconstruction of medieval field patterns is not possible. There are also numerous references to areas of shared grazing, much of it focused on one central area (NLW Bronwydd 7010 of 1349; 950 & 952 of 1508; 1045 of 1515; 1031 of 1517; 1037 of 1520), although unlike Dinas, no common land survived enclosure. Nonetheless the fundamental medieval pattern is similar, with shared grazing corresponding to place- and field-names for moor and rough ground, uncultivated land, thistles and gorse, and occasionally cultivated outfield (see below). Its use of soils is, though, somewhat different to Dinas, with some of the outfield pasture using good light free-draining soils for premium quality grazing – which fits with the area's high status.

George Owen

Much of the information about Bayvil derives from the records of the Elizabethan antiquary George Owen (d. 1613) who lived at Henllys. His writings, most notably his 1603 book, the 'Description of Pembrokeshire', include details of traditional agricultural practices, and distinguish carefully between local Welsh practice – in other words, how his Bayvil neighbours are managing things – and the practices of English south Pembrokeshire (Owen 1994, 62–77, 170, 175). These longstanding Welsh practices include the *in rodwallis* practice of this paper's title. References to land (usually specified as arable) lying '*in rodwallis/radivallis/rudivallis*' are found in Bayvil and St Dogmaels Latin charters of the thirteenth and fourteenth centuries; in the sixteenth century the term appears as *rudwall* (NLW Bronwydd 7010 of 1349; 7014 of 1355; 1348 of 1369/70; Owen 1862, 55–6). It refers both to the intermingled lands of open fields and more generally to shared land subject to seasonal grazing rights – the local open fields being customarily grazed in common after harvest until mid-March. Similar post-harvest grazing practices are recorded in fifteenth-century Lancashire ('half year lands') and in the Lake District and Scottish Borders (Winchester 2000, 55–8; Hall 2014, 79, 84). The *rodwallis* term is also found in the place-name Redwalls (*Redwalles* 1293) in the south Preseli parish of Morvil whose 1555 'Vagwr Goch' form (modern Fagwyr Goch) is a literal (and late) translation of 'Redwalls' (see Charles 1992, 114 for details of instances). Varied explanations for its derivation have been offered in the past, involving red-coloured walls or the Welsh place-name elements *rhyd* ('ford') or *rhydd* ('free'), and another interpretation will be offered here. The term and place-name first appear in the medieval records of the Lord of Cemais, suggesting (given Owen's observation that *rodwallis* was a Welsh practice) that the 'wallis' element is a term for Welsh land used by Anglo-Norman clerks: *walais/waleis* and *wallus* are Anglo-Norman and medieval Latin terms for 'Welsh' (Anglo-Norman dictionary – http://www.anglo-norman.net/gate/; Owen 1892, 179, note 7; Fenton 1903, 190; Baxter and Johnson 1934, 461). 'Red' or 'rod' probably indicates the rod or rood used to measure acreage, Welsh and English rod and acre measures being different with numerous regional variations: there are nineteenth-century references to the use of the 'Welsh rod' in mid, north-east and south Wales and in border areas of England to measure areas of upland cultivated by beat-burning (see below) (Palmer 1896, 10–11; Jones-Pierce 1943; Adams 1976, 2). A meaning akin to 'Welsh acre' or 'Welsh land' can therefore be identified for both the name 'Redwalls' and the charter term *radivallis/rudivallis/rodwallis*.

The scattered seasonally grazed lands of the *in rodwallis* landholdings formed part of a tripartite structure of land use, described by Owen in 1603, and broadly matched by nineteenth-century field-name elements (Table 8.1, Fig. 8.2 which also shows the *rhandir*/shareland arrangements of south Wales law, discussed by Seaman in this volume). There were, first of all, small open fields that were ploughed annually. Unlike the Midlands common fields these had no rotation or fallow period and fertility was maintained by the manure of the livestock that grazed them after harvest (Jones 1973, 435). These permanently cultivated areas or infields (*cf.* the *rhandiroedd*/sharelands of medieval Welsh law) are often represented by field name elements like *maes* ('open field'), *llain* ('strip'), and *gardd* ('strip, quillet'). The second element was good pasture land that was periodically used as arable after improving it by keeping animals on it overnight, that is to say, by 'folding', while the third element was much poorer land, rough (often upland) pasture, which was very occasionally used for the short-term growing of crops by the removal and burning of turf. This latter practice, called beat burning (Owen 1994, 66–7), is identified by field name elements like *bietyn* ('pared and burnt turf or hillside'), *brith* ('chequered, pied, partly'; *cf. braenar brith,* 'partially pared burnt fallow'), and *poeth* ('burnt'). *Terra montana* – the Latin equivalent of *tir mynythe* – is recorded as a name for outfield in early fourteenth-century north Wales (Jones 1973, 444). Owen says that mountain land prepared by beat burning can only be used to grow crops for a very few years, and afterwards has to rest for many years to regain its fertility (see Table 8.1).

Essentially, Owen is describing an infield-outfield system, familiar in other areas of western and northern Britain (Buchanan 1973, 586, 617; Whittington 1973, 532–4; Kelly 2000, 46, 370; Hall 2014, 87). The periodic cultivation of outfield pastures – a practice called convertible or long-ley husbandry, or Devonshiring – and occasional cultivation of moorland areas offers a flexible means of increasing arable production and was a feature of other areas of western Britain and Scotland (Rippon 2008, 130–6; Hall 2014, 86–94; Dodgshon 2015, 107–8, 133–8). In the south-west of England pollen evidence indicates its use during the eighth to tenth centuries AD (Fyfe and Rippon 2004, 38–9), and it appears to have been a Roman practice (Kron 2000). The associated practice of beat burning (*ad baticium*) on moorland areas was a deeply rooted, integral part of the convertible husbandry practices of medieval Cornwall and Devon from at least the thirteenth century; it is also found in post-medieval Scotland and thirteenth-century Ireland (Whittington 1973, 534; Fox 1991, 309–310, 315; Kelly 2000, 230). The improving of land through overnight folding of livestock is similarly widespread, and is recorded across much of southern and eastern England from the thirteenth century onwards with a variety of field systems, and was used in Ireland and Scotland to create arable plots around summer dwellings (Bil 1989, 160; Hall 2014, 53–60, 69–73; Costello 2015, 52).

There are also close parallels between George Owen's description and the agricultural practices to which twelfth- and thirteenth-century Welsh law refers (Tables 8.1, 8.2; for a discussion of the Welsh law practices see Jones 1973). These suggest that (as the name itself hints) the north Pembrokeshire *in rodwallis* practice of post-harvest grazing was originally regulated by Welsh law. Similar crops were grown – barley, oats, and wheat. Little or no rye was grown by the north Pembrokeshire Welsh and its cultivation is not mentioned in south Wales law (Wade Evans 1909, 206–7, 219; Richards 1954, 72–3, 88; Jones 1973, 438; Jenkins 1990, 128–9, 176; Owen 1994, 63–4, 66). Welsh law also

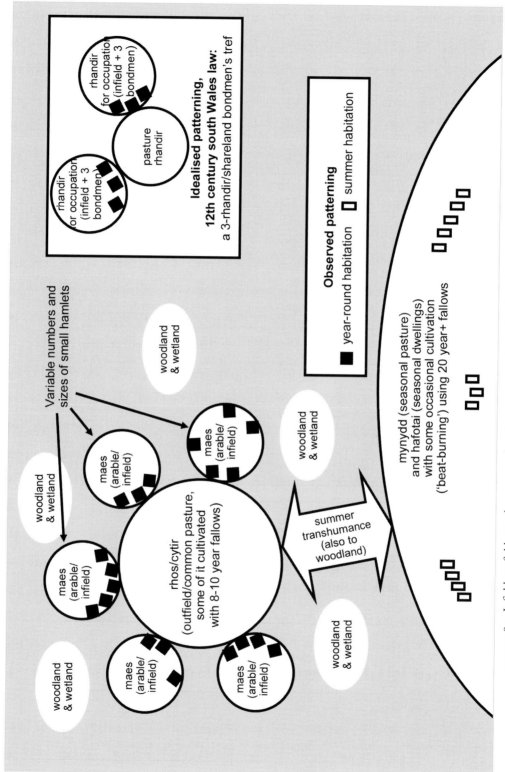

FIGURE 8.2. Infield-outfield, transhumance and settlement patterns in medieval south Wales. (Drawing: R. Comeau.)

assumes that spring ploughing was the norm, which fits with the growing of spring-sown oats and barley, though some winter ploughing is also mentioned, presumably on (perhaps temporarily) enclosed outfield areas. Given the frequent identification in early medieval and medieval excavations of winter-sown free-threshing bread wheat (*triticum aestivum L.*), this pattern raises questions about wheat cultivation, particularly given the requirement for wheat bread and flour in Welsh law food rents (Moffett 2011, 349–350; Banham and Faith 2014, 28–9, 58). Was wheat only grown on areas of enclosed, folded outfield? Or – as recent English bioarchaeological research asks – was spring sowing of wheat more common than current models acknowledge? McKerracher, who poses this question, notes that Bede describes the routine spring sowing of wheat in seventh-century Northumbria (Colgrave 1940, 221; McKerracher 2014, 274–5). In south Pembrokeshire, at the South Hook excavation, spring-sown club wheat (*Triticum aestivum* subsp. *Compactum)* rather than bread wheat is present in the site's pre-tenth-century samples, together with ample evidence of oats and barley (Carruthers 2010, 172–180).

Little light is shed by the only confirmed medieval archaeobotanical sample from north Pembrokeshire, which comes from the southern Preseli Anglo-Norman settlement of Maenclochog. It has a radiocarbon date of 980–1160 cal AD (95.4% confidence, Beta 240209, 990±40 BP[2]), and consists mainly of oats and rye, with a very small amount of barley and bread wheat, though poor preservation may restrict evidence of the latter (Carruthers 2007). The unusually high levels of rye are more typical of continental rather than of English or Welsh samples and its coincidence with an area of twelfth-century Flemish settlement is striking.

More illuminating is an undated but rich assemblage from a corn dryer at Bayvil Farm, in the heart of the study area. This is described as 'medieval' from context and make-up (Simmons 2018, 132), and contained large quantities of hulled barley and oat, as well as small amounts of spelt wheat and other grains. The latter exhibited 'characteristics intermediate between spelt wheat and free-threshing wheat (*Triticum spelta/nudum*) although no free-threshing wheat grains were positively identified'. Weed taxa were also illuminating: some indicated spring-sown crops, and others were associated with manuring and with both grassland as well as cultivated soils.

This is interesting evidence, albeit in need of better dating, in light of local medieval husbandry practices and George Owen's mention of a spring-sown wheat cultivated by the north Pembrokeshire and Cardiganshire Welsh. This spring-sown wheat was favoured because the winter grazing of animals on cornfields prevented the growing of winter-sown bread-wheat, and it was very productive though it did not like cold conditions and had a long growing season. Owen describes it in these terms:

> There is a ... kind of wheat, not well known in other counties, which is called holy wheat, or summer wheat. This is used most in the Welsh parts of this shire, as also in Cardiganshire, and is sowed in the latter end of March and beginning

of April, and is a dainty grain like the barley and cannot endure to be pinched with cold. It is a very profitable grain and yields more increase than the winter wheat. It bears a greater ear and stalk … The only discommodity of this corn is, it is long a-ripening, so that if the harvest be not very timely and the weather warm, it will hardly be saved. The bread of this wheat is said to be somewhat more brown in colour than the winter wheat. (Owen, 1994/1603, 63–4)

The identity of this wheat variety is uncertain, but it may, perhaps, be rivet wheat (*triticum turgidum* L.), a free-threshing frost-sensitive relative of emmer and durum that can be sown in spring (Percival 1921, 243; Moffet 1991, 234–6; 2011, 350–1; I am indebted to Wendy Carruthers for the suggestion). Rivet wheat is known from Neolithic central Europe and classical Mediterranean contexts, and there is archaeobotanical evidence for it in pre-Conquest and medieval England but not as yet in Wales, where research is limited. Identification in samples is often difficult, since it can be hard to differentiate from bread-type wheat; club wheat presents similar problems (Carruthers 2010, 172, 180; McKerracher 2016, 92).

These identification issues are significant. Both rivet wheat and club wheat have characteristics that might, independently of their spring-sown status, confer advantages over bread wheat in some circumstances: club wheat is better suited than bread wheat to poor soils and copes well with rain and delayed harvesting, while rivet wheat is rust-resistant and unattractive to birds (Carruthers 2010, 180; Percival 1921, 242). Both, therefore, were useful varieties that fitted into the annual cycles implied by Welsh law and by infield-outfield systems, and the limited evidence for them in Welsh contexts highlights the need for more archaeobotanical research.

Livestock and the hills

It will be apparent from the information presented so far that crop growing and animal husbandry in medieval Wales were interdependent. The fertility of arable land relied on animal manure, whether over the autumn and winter (in the case of the permanent infield) or over the summer, prior to ploughing and cultivation, in the case of temporarily cultivated areas of outfield. In summer, while wheat, oats, and barley ripened, livestock fattened on the fresh grass of summer pastures that were the focus of (highly seasonal) milk and cheese production.

Livestock were therefore, in different ways, fundamental to the payment of food rents. As in Anglo-Saxon England, cattle represented wealth: the word *praidd*, which Welsh law uses for a Welsh prince's or freeman's herd of cattle, is also used for plunder and figuratively denotes treasure or riches (Williams and Powell 1961, 107; Davies 1982, 39, 53, 130; Owen 2009, 6; Banham and Faith 2014, 86–7, 160). Cattle could be substituted for some elements of food rents, and were used to quantify compensation payments in Welsh law and as units of valuation in the Llandaff and Llancarfan charters (Wade Evans 1909, 147, 152, 206–7; Richards 1954, 24–5, 29, 72–3; Charles-Edwards 1993, 377–8, 385, 390–2; 2013, 286–7). Rents of cows and sheep continue under the Normans in twelfth- to fourteenth-century south Wales, and livestock fairs were the principal means of raising cash and settling debts in the seventeenth century (Davies 1978, 134, 141; Owen 1994, 142).

The movement of cattle to seasonal pastures was accordingly an essential component of the seasonal patterning of medieval Welsh life. Welsh law expected animals to be removed from arable land around the winter dwelling or *hendref* by May 1st, and not to return until after the harvest, specified as August in north Wales though it may have been later, perhaps September, in south Wales (Table 8.2, see Roberts this volume). In sixteenth-century Pembrokeshire, the move to seasonal pasture was earlier, in mid-March. This drift to earlier dates is also noted in the Lake District and Scottish Borders where it is suggested that it may reflect increasing enclosure of open fields (and easier associated livestock management) and the Julian calendar's growing disjuncture between calendrical dates and the natural seasons (Winchester 2000, 55–8).

Some of the seasonal grazing would have been near the *hendref*, on the local rough pasture seen at Dinas and Bayvil. Some of it though was further away: pollen samples indicate that the Preseli hills were heavily grazed from the late prehistoric period onwards, and twelfth- to sixteenth-century sources indicate extensive seasonal pasturage here, linked with coastal and other lowland areas by a complex mosaic of rights (Fig. 8.3; Seymour 1985, 340–1, 346; Comeau 2019, chapter 5). There was a cattle ranch or grange at Mynachlogddu on the southern Preseli slopes, granted in 1121 to the northern coastal abbey of St Dogmaels (Llandudoch), at the time of the abbey's Norman re-founding (Pritchard 1907, 46–8; Davies 1948, 242; Lewis 1969, 30; 1972, 33). Pasture rights at Mynachlogddu were also claimed by post-medieval inhabitants of the parish and manor of Monington (Eglwys Wythwr), which borders St Dogmaels (Lewis 1969, 36). The Mynachlogddu pastures were separated from St Dogmaels and Monington by the seasonal grazing of the north Preseli moors, held by descendants of the pre-Conquest *maer* (pre-Conquest *cantref* governor) under the thirteenth-century Charter of Preseli (Owen 1862, 48; Jones 1979, 29). The simplest interpretation of these various rights and grants is that they perpetuate pre-Conquest arrangements, involving local *uchelwyr* (aristocratic freemen) and the Welsh church, though whether this indicates early medieval cattle granges at Mynachlogddu is an open question. Similar long-term seasonal arrangements are probably indicated by the sole rights of the Lord of Cemais to summer pasture at Redwalls in Morvil, where he kept 120 horses, mares, oxen, kine, and young cattle, and about 300 sheep and lambs in 1594 (Howells 1977, 39–40). A deserted medieval hamlet here (unexcavated, but with enclosures suggestive of stockyards) may be associated (HER 1560; Fenton 1903, 191).

A picture emerges of some intensified medieval exploitation of the hills for cattle ranching, superimposed on patterns of local transhumance; the overall impression is that the Preselis were an important central resource for the pre-Conquest *cantref* (*cf.* Barrow 1973, 52; see Hooke this volume). Local transhumance focused on rough pastures adjacent to local communities, whose connection with their users was shown by the place-name format '*mynydd/*

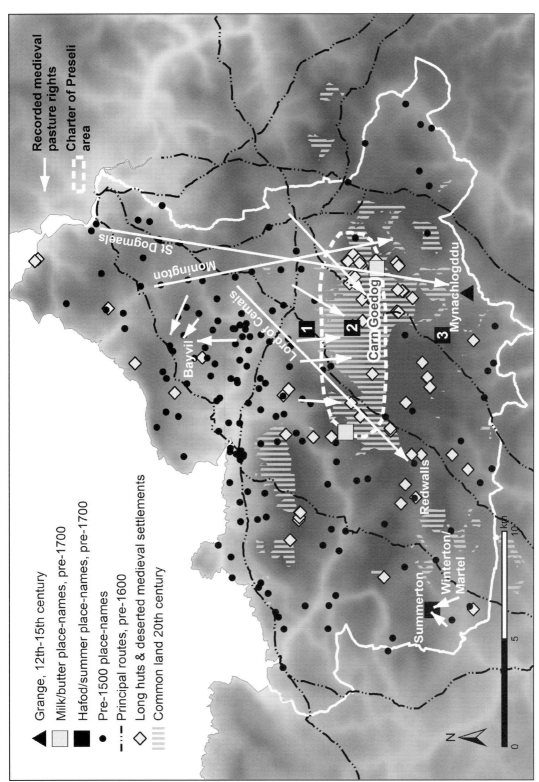

FIGURE 8.3. Patterns of pasture rights in medieval Cemais. The numbered *hafod* sites are named in the text. (Map contains OS data © Crown copyright and database right 2018.)

rhos + community name' (*cf.* the *ffridd* name element of north Wales). Some Preseli summer pastures were designated by *hafod* place-names, as at Hafod Madog (1538, SN112293), Hafod Tydfil (1585, SN115337), and Hafod Wnnog (1598, SN115358) (locations (1), (2) and (3) on Fig. 8.3; Fig. 8.4; Charles 1992, 84, 105, 196). The term *hafod* (the equivalent of the Scottish shieling and Irish booley) denotes unenclosed summer pasture in its earliest thirteenth-century usages, and is applied to the summer dwelling after the sixteenth century; in twelfth- and thirteenth-century sources this dwelling is a *hafdy* (Davies 1980, 4–7; Jenkins 1990, 353). South of the Preselis, similar seasonal arrangements are indicated by matching 'Summerton' (Somerton 1458, SM984298) and 'Winterton' (Wynterton 1521, SM990287) settlements: everyone with a messuage on Summerton mountain (there were seven of them) also had one at Little Newcastle or Martel, which was also known as Winterton (Charles 1992, 67, 176; NLW Bronwydd 931 of 1595; 763 of 1595; 1278 of 1596/7). Summerton and Hafod Tydfil survived into the modern period as single farms, but the earlier forms of these settlements can be seen in small groups of structures, some rectangular and others ovoid, near transmontane tracks on the upper slopes of the Preseli pastures (Fig. 8.3; *cf.* Locock 2006, 45; Silvester 2006, 33–4). Since they are not mentioned by George Owen, their seasonal usage may have largely ceased by the sixteenth century.

Exactly who occupied them is an interesting question. Although there are eighteenth- and nineteenth-century references to the seasonal movement of whole households in north Wales, early modern records in Ireland and northern Britain indicate that it was more usual for young women – dairymaids – to accompany the summer herds with some help from male herders, while others stayed in the winter settlements to tend crops and harvest the hay (Sayce 1955–6, 132–3; Davies 1984, 88; Fox 1996, 12–14). In Cornwall, similar early medieval practices may explain the small huts on Bodmin moor (Herring 2012, 94, 97).

FIGURE 8.4. The northern Preseli hills seen from the Nevern valley. The farmland of Eglwyswen/Whitchurch and Llanfair Nantgwyn is to the left. Hafod Tydfil is the small tree-lined area on the moorland to the right of centre; Carn Goedog is above it. (Photograph: R. Comeau.)

FIGURE 8.5. Remains of hafotai at Carn Goedog, looking north over the Nevern valley. (Photograph: R. Comeau.)

In the study area the only documentary possibility is offered by George Owen's reference to young male herdsmen whose cattle wandered freely across the unenclosed landscape, though there is no mention of their habitations (Owen 1994, 45). There is however archaeological evidence at one site, Carn Goedog, that indicates the twelfth-century presence of women, and it is to this that we turn next.

Carn Goedog

Carn Goedog lies on the northern Preseli slopes where patterns of medieval summer pasturage, represented by Hafod Tydfil and the thirteenth-century Charter of Preseli, are especially clear and rights to seasonal grazing survive to the present day (Fig. 8.4). The bogginess of its moorland is a late medieval or early modern development, and numerous small abandoned enclosures, some perhaps representing permanent settlement, show its use in earlier periods (DAT HLC Preseli; Seymour 1985, 363–5). The names of two rock outcrops, Carn Goedog (*Carn Goediog* 1888 Ordnance Survey: 'wooded cairn/rock') and Carn Menyn/Meini (*Garn y Menyn* 1573: 'butter cairn/rock') suggest that the area's open moorland character is a relatively recent phenomenon, and that it was associated with (seasonal) dairying (Charles 1992, 125). A transmontane track, shown on the first map of Pembrokeshire of 1602, crosses this moorland, connecting it with the arable hamlets of the coast and the Nevern valley (NLW Map 5359). At Carn Goedog it passes a line of nine sub-rectangular structures set at right angles to the contours, with pre-excavation lengths of 4 to 7 m (Fig. 8.5; Schlee *et al.* 2018). Both location and pattern are typical of medieval Welsh summer settlements (Silvester 2006, supra; Hooke this volume).

Excavation of one of these structures, House C, in 2015 revealed a small rectangular building with rounded corners measuring 6×4 m externally. It had a centrally placed entrance on its long side, with perhaps another facing it in the opposite site, a central hearth, and walls probably made of turf on top of stone footings. Finds included medieval pottery of Dyfed gravel-tempered type and a spindle whorl. Dating is provided by the pottery, which is of probable late twelfth- to thirteenth-century date, and a sample of carbonised hazel from the hearth, which was radiocarbon-dated to cal AD 1030–1200 at 95.4% confidence (SUERC-68382; 917±34 BP). It is therefore likely that it was occupied at some stage between the mid-eleventh to early thirteenth century AD, and its occupants were probably tenants of the aristocratic Welsh freeholders who held rights to the north Preseli pastures. The spindle whorl suggests the presence of women, though not necessarily whole families: spinning by milkmaids (usually of flax; wool spinning was a winter activity) is recorded on nineteenth-century Scottish shielings (Sayce 1957, 70), and dairying activities are likely, given the adjacent Carn Menyn place-name and the butter and cheese elements of bond tenant rents. The accompanying of these milkmaids by the township herdsman or *bugail* (who dealt primarily with cattle rather than sheep and was the predecessor of Owen's young male herdsmen) is suggested by Welsh law's requirement that both milkmaid and *bugail* swear to the wellbeing of a cow (Jenkins 1990, 62, 176, 321).

At the time of writing this site is the earliest firmly dated seasonal settlement in Wales (*cf.* Roberts 2006). Excavated sites that have produced dateable material are however scarce – this is, for instance, the only excavation of a seasonal settlement in the Preseli hills – so we should be wary of inferring too much from its evidence. The indications are that seasonal pasturing is a practice of much older vintage: Gildas refers in the fifth century to 'mountains especially suited to varying the pasture for animals', and the early medieval use of central shared pasture resources is thought to be fundamental to the development of social and territorial identities (Winterbottom 1978, 17; Banham and Faith 2014, 157; Hooke this volume). These practices are closely linked to the seasonal gatherings used for early medieval governance, celebration, and trade, and connections can be identified between the spatial and seasonal patterning of the agricultural-pastoral landscape and times and places of assembly (Comeau 2019). Carn Goedog is therefore particularly significant. In combination with Dinas and Bayvil, it allows us to see the settings of long-lasting interrelated agricultural practices that are also characteristic of other areas of western and northern Britain and Ireland: practices that produced and sustained wealth, linked upland and lowland, summer pasture and spring-ploughed arable, and shaped the lives of local communities.

TABLE 8.1. Agricultural practice compared: sixteenth-century Welsh north Pembrokeshire and twelfth/thirteenth-century Welsh law.

Owen describes	Agricultural element	Preparation technique – sixteenth century (Owen 1994, 65–77)	Preparation technique – twelfth- and thirteenth-century Welsh law (J: Jenkins 1990; R: Richards 1954; WE: Wade-Evans 1909)	Typical place-name elements
Arable areas that are cropped continuously (100 years +) and maintained by dunging during winter months (Owen 1994, 74)	INFIELD – permanently cultivated arable inner core	• Lime, marl (glacial till), sand, seaweed. • Carting of dung not favoured. • No rotations like English common fields.	• Manured annually (J113)	• *maes* – open field • *llain* – strip • *(g)ardd* – strip, quillet
Good pasture land that is periodically used as arable after improving by keeping animals on it overnight ('folding') (7–10 years arable, then 8–10 ley/fallow) (Owen 1994, 65)	OUTFIELD – areas of good pasture periodically used as arable to supplement infield – 'flexible convertible husbandry'	• Folding – animals folded overnight mid-March to mid-November. • Folded land crops: summer wheat grown in first year; oats then grown for 7–10 years; then 8–10 years ley/fallow.	Cultivation time allowed on land prepared using: • Fallow – 2–3 years (J113; WE211) • Folding – 3 years (J113; WE211) • Carted dung – 4 years (J113; WE211) • Manured fallow – 4 years (WE211)	• *cytir* – common land • *gwndwn* – unploughed/ uncultivated land, ley-land
Poorer land (mountain typically) that is very occasionally cultivated through beat-burning (2–6 years arable, 20–24 years ley/ fallow) (Owen 1994, 66–7)	OUTFIELD/MOORLAND – unenclosed rough pasture	• Beat-burning on hills/ moors – removing and burning turf; scattering ashes on land. • Beat-burning land crops – oats, rye and barley grown for 2–6 years, then 20–24 years ley/fallow.	Cultivation time allowed for: • Former scrub land – 2 years (J113, WE211) • Former wooded land – 4–6 years (J113, WE211) • Beat-burning practice not specifically mentioned	• *mynydd* – mountain, common, unenclosed land *rhos* – (upland) moor, heath *gwaun* – moorland, heath *bating, beting, bieting, batin, bietyn* – pared and burnt turf or hillside • *brith* – chequered/ pied/ partially deturfed beatland • *poeth* - hot, burnt

TABLE 8.2. The agricultural year according to George Owen and Welsh law, showing seasonal divisions defined by Welsh law.

Season (Roberts 2011, 218–9)		Sixteenth-century north Pembrokeshire (Howells 1977, 39–40; Owen 1994, 63–5, 175; cf. Davies 1973, 521–2)	Twelfth- and thirteenth-century Welsh law (J: Jenkins 1990; R: Richards 1954; Rus: Russell 2000; WE: Wade-Evans 1909)	Dominant seasonal activity
Winter	January	• Livestock grazing on arable open fields until mid-March	• Pigs excluded from corn land; pannage in woods ends (R83; J178, 206, WE254)	
Spring	February		• Main ploughing period begins: ploughing and sowing from 1 February–30 April (J202; R88; WE 219, 282)	Ploughing and sowing
	March	• Sowing oats; ploughing for barley • Livestock moved to outfield (mid-March in sixteenth century; 25 March/Lady Day in eighteenth century)	• Meadows closed to grazing (17 March) (J206) • Heath-burning – March (J170) or mid-March to mid-April (R106, WE 274)	
	April	• Sowing summer ('holy') wheat (late March–early April) • Sowing barley (late April–early May)		
Summer	May	• Seasonal pastures (agistement/herbage) open (1 May)	• Animals excluded from arable open fields of the hendref (1 May) (J40, 236; Rus 513) • Summer dwelling occupation begins (1 May) (J40, 236; Rus 513)	Seasonal pasture
	June			
	July	• Harvest – barley (July and August)		

TABLE 8.2. (*Continued*)

Autumn	August	• (Time of oat harvest, though not specifically mentioned by Owen)	Harvest
		• Harvest period: 1 August–31 October (J83, WE298–9, 317)	
		• North Wales: bondsmen's summer dwelling period ends (J40, 236)	
		• North Wales: animals allowed on arable open fields from now (J40). Pigs on corn land and in woods from 29 August (J178, J206; *cf.* R91, W222)	
	September	• Harvest of summer wheat	• South Wales: bondsmen's summer dwelling period ends after reaping/harvest (*medi*; also the name for September); animals allowed on arable open fields from then (WE265)
		• Seasonal pastures (agistement/herbage) close (29 September)	
	October	• Open arable fields grazed in common after harvest to mid-March	• Animals on arable open fields (see above)
Winter	November	• Return of stock from outfield areas (mid-November)	• Harvest in, barns closed (1 November) (J204, R93, WE246)	Animals on arable
	December	• Ploughing for oats (on folded land)	• Some winter ploughing, presumably on enclosed/ folded outfield (J195, 202; R58; WE174, 319)	

Not shown: animal mating times in summer and autumn, given by Welsh law, and George Owen's timings for preparing land by beat-burning (Jenkins 1990, 206; Owen 1994, 66–7).

Notes

1   This is a different pattern to that found in north Wales, where medieval dependent tenants developed into small freeholders (Davies 1991, 120–1; Davies 2004, 212). Calculations are based on, firstly, the 1594 Extent of Cemais (Howells 1977), which lists both the Lord of Cemais' landholdings and those who were liable to pay him Rent of Extent, a charge of Welsh law origin; and secondly, on records of landholdings of some prominent Welsh freeholders (all descended from the pre-Conquest *maer*) which are not listed in the Extent and appear to have been exempted from the Rent of Extent (Comeau 2019). Calculations do not include landholdings in Newport or of Anglo-Norman knights.
2   Radiocarbon dates quoted have been calibrated using the INTCAL13 calibration curve (Reimer *et al.* 2013) and OxCal v4.3.2 (http://c14.arch.ox.ac.uk/; Bronk Ramsey 2009).

Acknowledgements

I am grateful to Peter Fowler and Bob Silvester for their thoughts on earlier versions of this paper and to the Arts and Humanities Research Council for funding the PhD research on which this paper draws.

Abbreviations

HER: Historic Environment Record, Dyfed Archaeological Trust, Llandeilo.
NPRN: National Primary Record Number, Royal Commission on the Ancient and Historical Monuments of Wales, Aberystwyth.

References

Adams, I. H. (1976) *Agrarian Landscape Terms*. London, Institute of British Geographers.
Atkin, M. A. (1985) Some settlement patterns in Lancashire. In D. Hooke (ed.) *Medieval Villages: a review of current work*. Oxford, Oxford University Committee for Archaeology, 171–185.
Austin, D. (2005) Little England Beyond Wales: Re-defining the Myth. *Landscapes* 6(2), 30–62.
Baker, A. R. H. and Butlin, R. A. (eds) (1973) *Studies of Field Systems in the British Isles*. Cambridge, Cambridge University Press.
Banham, D. and Faith, R. (2014) *Anglo-Saxon Farms and Farming*. Oxford, Oxford University Press.
Barrow, G. W. S. (1973) *The Kingdom of the Scots*. London, Edward Arnold.
Baxter, J. H. and Johnson, C. (1934) *Medieval Latin Word-List*. Oxford, Oxford University Press.
Bil, A. (1989) Transhumance Economy, Setting and Settlement in Highland Perthshire. *Scottish Geographical Magazine* 105(3), 158–167.
Bronk Ramsey, C. (2009) Bayesian Analysis of Radiocarbon Dates. *Radiocarbon*, 51(1), 337–360.
Buchanan, R. H. (1973) Field systems of Ireland. In A. R. H. Baker and R. A. Butlin (eds) *Studies of Field Systems in the British Isles*. Cambridge, Cambridge University Press, 580–618.

Carruthers, W. (2007) Maenclochog Excavation Report Appendix 2: Assessment of the charred plant remains. Report 2008/ 27. In D. Schlee, *The Maenclochog Community Excavation September 2007: Discovering the Origins of Maenclochog. Report No. 2008/ 27.* Unpublished report. Llandeilo, Dyfed Archaeological Trust.

Carruthers, W. (2010) Charred Plant Remains. In P. Crane and K. Murphy, An Early Medieval Settlement, Iron Smelting Site and Crop-processing Complex at South Hook, Herbranston, Pembrokeshire. *Archaeologia Cambrensis* 159, 117–196 at 164–181.

Charles, B. G. (1951) The Records of the Borough of Newport in Pembrokeshire. *National Library of Wales Journal* 7(1), 33–45.

Charles, B. G. (1973) *George Owen of Henllys: A Welsh Elizabethan.* Aberystwyth, National Library of Wales Press.

Charles, B. G. (1971) Early Ancestors of the Owen of Henllys Family. *National Library of Wales Journal* 17, 115–9.

Charles, B. G. (1992) *The Place-Names of Pembrokeshire.* Aberystwyth, National Library of Wales.

Charles-Edwards, T. M. (1993) *Early Irish and Welsh Kinship.* Oxford, Clarendon Press.

Charles-Edwards, T. M. (2013) *Wales and the Britons 350–1064.* Oxford, Oxford University Press.

Colgrave, B. M. N. (1940) *Two Lives of Saint Cuthbert.* Cambridge, Cambridge University Press.

Comeau, R. (2009) Cytir and Crosses: the archaeological landscape of the Parish of Dinas. *Archaeologia Cambrensis* 158, 225–53.

Comeau, R. (2012) From Tref(gordd) to Tithe: Identifying Settlement Patterns in a North Pembrokeshire Parish. *Landscape History* 33(1), 29–44.

Comeau, R. (2019) Land, people and power in early medieval Wales: the cantref of Cemais in comparative perspective. Unpublished PhD thesis, University College London Institute of Archaeology.

Costello, E. (2015) Post-medieval Upland Settlement and the Decline of Transhumance: a case-study from the Galtee Mountains, Ireland. *Landscape History* 36(1), 47–69.

DAT HLC Preseli: Dyfed Archaeological Trust Historic Landscape Characterisation for Preseli area – www.dyfedarchaeology.org.uk/HLC/Preseli/area/area281.htm (accessed 04.01.2019).

Davies, E. (1980) Hafod, Hafoty and Lluest: their distribution, features, and purpose. *Ceredigion* 9(1), 1–41.

Davies, E. (1984) Hafod and Lluest: The Summering of Cattle and Upland Settlement in Wales. *Folk Life* 23(1), 76–96.

Davies, J. C. (ed.) (1948) *Episcopal Acts and Cognate Documents relating to the Welsh Dioceses 1066–1272, Volume II.* Cardiff, Historical Society of the Church in Wales.

Davies, M. (1956) Rhosili Open Field and Related South Wales Field Patterns. *The Agricultural History Review* 4(2), 80–96.

Davies, M. (1973) Field Systems of South Wales: Pembrokeshire. In A. R. H. Baker and R. A. Butlin (eds) *Studies of Field Systems in the British Isles.* Cambridge, Cambridge University Press, 515–522.

Davies, R. R. (1978) *Lordship and Society in the March of Wales, 1282–1400.* Oxford, Oxford University Press.

Davies, R. R. (1991) *Age of Conquest.* Oxford, Oxford University Press.

Davies, W. (1982) *Wales in the Early Middle Ages.* Leicester, Leicester University Press.

Davies, W. (2004) Looking Backwards to the Early Medieval Past: Wales and England, a contrast in approaches. *Welsh History Review* 22(2), 197–221.

Dodgshon, R. (2015) *No Stone Unturned: A History of Farming, Landscape and Environment in the Scottish Highlands and Islands.* Edinburgh, Edinburgh University Press.

Driver, T. (2008) *Pembrokeshire: historic landscapes from the air.* Aberystwyth, Royal Commission on the Ancient and Historical Monuments of Wales.

Fenton, R. (1903) *Historical Tour Through Pembrokeshire (1811)* (2nd edition, with Additional Notes and Biography by Richard and John Fenton). Brecknock, Davies and Co.

Fowler, P. (2002) *Farming in the First Millennium AD.* Cambridge, Cambridge University Press.

Fox, H. S. A. (1991) Devon and Cornwall. In E. Miller (ed.) *The Agrarian History of England and Wales, Vol III, 1348–1500.* Cambridge, Cambridge University Press, 152–174, 303–323, 722–743.

Fox, H. S. A. (1996) Introduction: transhumance and seasonal settlement. In H. S. A. Fox (ed.) *Seasonal Settlement.* Leicester, University of Leicester Department of Adult Education, 1–23.

Fussell, G. E. (1933) The Breast Plough. *Man* 33, 109–114.

Fyfe, R. and Rippon, S. (2004) A landscape in transition? Palaeoenvironmental evidence for the end of the 'Romano-British' period in southwest England. In R. Collins and J. Gerrard (eds) *Debating Late Antiquity in Britain, AD 300–700.* BAR British Series 365. Oxford, British Archaeological Reports, 33–42.

Hall, D. (2014) *The Open Fields of England.* Oxford, Oxford University Press.

Hassall, C. (1794) *A General View of the Agriculture of the County of Pembroke.* London, Board of Agriculture and Internal Improvement.

Herring, P. (2012) Shadows of Ghosts: Early Medieval Transhumants in Cornwall. In S. Turner and B. Silvester (eds) *Life in Medieval Landscapes: People and Places in the Middle Ages.* Oxford, Windgather Press, 89–105.

Howells, B. E. (1956) Pembrokeshire Farming circa 1580–1620. *National Library of Wales Journal* 9(3), 313–333.

Howells, B. E. and K. A. (eds) (1977) *The Extent of Cemais, 1594.* Haverfordwest, Pembrokeshire Record Society.

Jenkins, D. (ed.) (1990) *The Law of Hywel Dda.* Llandysul, Gomer Press.

Jones, F. (1979) Bowen of Pentre Ifan and Llwyngwair. *Pembrokeshire Historian* 5, 25–57.

Jones, G. R. J. (1973) Field Systems of North Wales. In A. R. H. Baker and R. A. Butlin (eds) *Studies of Field Systems in the British Isles.* Cambridge, Cambridge University Press, 430–479.

Jones Pierce, T. (1943) Ancient Welsh Measures of Land. *Archaeologia Cambrensis* 97, 195–204.

Kelly, F. (2000) *Early Irish Farming.* Dublin, Dublin Institute for Advanced Studies.

Kissock, J. (1997) God Made Nature and Men Made Towns: Post-Conquest and Pre-Conquest Villages in Pembrokeshire. In N. Edwards (ed.) *Landscape and Settlement in Medieval Wales.* Oxford, Oxbow Books, 123–138.

Kron, G. (2000) Roman Ley-farming. *Journal of Roman Archaeology,* 13, 277–297.

Lewis, E. T. (1969) *Mynachlog-ddu – a Historical Survey.* Haverfordwest, C. I. Thomas.

Locock, M. (2006) Deserted rural settlements in south-east Wales. In K. Roberts (ed.) *Lost Farmsteads: Deserted Rural Settlements in Wales. CBA Research Report 148.* York, Council for British Archaeology, 41–60.

McKerracher, M. J. (2014) Agricultural Development in Mid Saxon England. Unpublished PhD thesis, University of Oxford.

McKerracher, M. (2016) Bread and Surpluses: the Anglo-Saxon 'bread wheat thesis' reconsidered. *Environmental Archaeology* 21, 88–102.

Meredith Morris, W. (1991) *A Glossary of the Demetian Dialect of North Pembrokeshire.* Felinfach, Llanerch Publications.

Moffett, L. (1991) The archaeobotanical evidence for free threshing tetraploid wheat in Britain. In E. Hajnalovd (ed.) *Palaeoethnobotany and Archaeology*, Acta Interdisciplinaria Archaeologica, 7. Nitra, Slovac Academy of Sciences.

Moffett, L. (2011) Food plants on archaeological sites. In H. Hamerow, D. A. Hinton and S. Crawford (eds) *Oxford Handbook of Anglo-Saxon Archaeology.* Oxford, Oxford University Press, 346–60.

Owen, G. (1862) *Baronia de Kemeys.* London, Cambrian Archaeological Association.

Owen, G. (1892) *The Description of Penbrokshire (sic) Part I*, ed. H. Owen. London, Cymmrodorion Society.

Owen, G. (1994) *The Description of Pembrokeshire (1603).* Llandysul, Gomer Press.

Owen, M. E. (2009) The Animals of the Law of Hywel. *Carmarthenshire Antiquary* 45, 5–27.

Palmer, A. N. (1896) Notes on Ancient Welsh Measures of Land. *Archaeologia Cambrensis* 49, 1–19.

Payne, F. G. (1947) An Old Cornish Plough, And Others. *Antiquity* 21, 151–5.

Payne, F. G. (1957) The British Plough: Some Stages in its Development. *British Agricultural History Review* 5(2), 74–84.

Percival, J. (1921) *The Wheat Plant.* London, Duckworth.

Pritchard, E. M. (1907) *The History of St Dogmael's Abbey.* London, Blades, East and Blades.

Reimer, P. J., Bard, E., Bayliss, A., Beck, J. W., Blackwell, P. G., Ramsey, C. B., Buck, C. E., Cheng, H., Edwards, R. L., Friedrich, M., Grootes, P. M., Guilderson, T. P., Haflidason, H., Hajdas, I., Hatté, C., Heaton, T. J., Hoffmann, D. L., Hogg, A. G., Hughen, K. A., Kaiser, K. F., Kromer, B., Manning, S. W., Niu, M., Reimer, R. W., Richards, D. A., Scott, E. M., Southon, J. R., Staff, R. A., Turney, C. S. M. and van der Plicht, J. (2013) IntCal13 and Marine13 Radiocarbon Age Calibration Curves 0–50,000 Years cal BP, *Radiocarbon*, 55(4), 1869–1887.

Richards, M. (ed.) (1954) *The Laws of Hywel Dda (The Book of Blegywryd)*, translated by Melville Richards. Liverpool, Liverpool University Press.

Rippon, S. (2008) *Beyond the Medieval Village.* Oxford, Oxford University Press.

Roberts, B. K. and Wrathmell, S. (2002) *Region and Place.* London, English Heritage.

Roberts, K. (ed.) (2006) *Lost Farmsteads: Deserted Rural Settlements in Wales.* CBA Research Report 148. York, Council for British Archaeology.

Roberts, S. E. (2011) *Llawysgrif Pomffred: an edition and study.* Leiden, Brill.

Russell, P. (2000) The Laws of Court from Latin B. In T. M. Charles-Edwards, M. E. Owen, and P. Russell (eds) *The Welsh King and his Court.* Cardiff, University of Wales Press, 478–530.

Sayce, R. U. (1955–1956) The Old Summer Pastures, part I. *Montgomeryshire Collections*, 54, 117–145.

Sayce, R. U. (1957) The Old Summer Pastures, part II: Life at the Hafodydd. *Montgomeryshire Collections*, 55(1), 37–86.

Schlee, D., Comeau, R., Parker Pearson M. and Welham, K. (2018) Carn Goedog Medieval House and Settlement, Pembrokeshire. *Archaeologia Cambrensis* 167, 245–255.

Seymour, W. P. (1985) The environmental history of the Preseli region of South-West Wales over the past 12,000 years. Unpublished PhD thesis, Aberystwyth University.

Silvester, R. (2006) Deserted rural settlements in central and north-east Wales. In K. Roberts (ed.) *Lost Farmsteads: Deserted Rural Settlements in Wales.* CBA Research Report 148. York, Council for British Archaeology, 13–40.

Simmons, E. (2018) Charred Plant Macrofossils and Charcoal. In M. Parker Pearson *et al.* 2018, A Late Bronze Age Ring-fort at Bayvil Farm, Pembrokeshire. *Archaeologia Cambrensis,* 167, 126–135.

Thomas, C. (1968) Thirteenth Century Farm Economies in North Wales. *Agricultural History Review* 16(1), 1–14

Thorpe, L. (1978) *Giraldus Cambrensis: The Journey through Wales and The Description of Wales.* Harmondsworth, Penguin.

Wade-Evans, A. W. (1909) *Welsh Medieval Law.* Oxford, Oxford University Press.

Whittington, G. (1973) Field Systems of Scotland. In A. R. H. Baker and R. A. Butler (eds) *Studies of Field Systems in the British Isles.* Cambridge, Cambridge University Press, 530–579.

Williams, S. J. and Powell, J. E. (1961) *Llyfr Blegygywryd.* Cardiff, University of Wales Press.

Winchester, A. J. L. (2000) *The Harvest of the Hills: Rural Life in Northern England and the Borders 1400–1700.* Edinburgh, Edinburgh University Press.

Winterbottom, M. E. T. (1978) *Gildas: The Ruin of Britain and other works.* London, Phillimore.

Unpublished sources at National Library of Wales (NLW)

NLW Bronwydd 763 of 1595: messuages *etc.* in vills of Newcastle and Somerton

NLW Bronwydd 931 of 1595: lands *etc.* in Newcastle and Somerton

NLW Bronwydd 950, 952 of 1508: messuages *etc.* in Crugie Vcha and elsewhere

NLW Bronwydd 1031 of 1517: lands *etc.* at the vill of Crugie and elsewhere

NLW Bronwydd 1037 of 1520: lands *etc.* at vill of Crugieuchaf and elsewhere

NLW Bronwydd 1045 of 1515: messuage *etc.* in vill of Crugie and elsewhere

NLW Bronwydd 1170 of 1519: messuages *etc.* in ploughland of Trefvawr, Dinas

NLW Bronwydd 1278 of 1596/7: messuages in vills of Newcastle and Somerton

NLW Bronwydd 1348 of 1369/70: two acres of arable land *in rodivall'* within carucate of Trefginwran in fee of Bayuill

NLW Bronwydd 7010 of 1349: messuages, tenements, land, meadow, wood and rights *in rodwallis* in fee of Bayuil

NLW Bronwydd 7014 of 1355: land and rights in fee of Cassia Abbatis Sancti Dogmaelis *in rudivall'.*

NLW Map 5359, George Owen map *'Penbrochiae* comitatus olim Demetiae regionis descriptio 1602'

Landscape, settlement and agriculture in early medieval Brycheiniog: the evidence from the Llandaff Charters

Andy Seaman

Charters, together with the Welsh lawbooks (see Roberts this volume), provide the principal written evidence for early medieval Welsh society (Charles-Edwards 2013, 274). The corpus of early medieval charters from Wales totals around 170, and is therefore considerably smaller than that available for Anglo-Saxon England where over a thousand exist. The Welsh charters rarely refer explicitly to settlement and agriculture, but since farming was central to early medieval life and household and community organisation they provide us with much important information whose value is enhanced by the evidence of the lawbooks, archaeology, place-names, and the fabric of the landscape itself. The charters are found in three principal sources: the Book of Llandaff (Evans and Rhys 1979), The Life of Saint Cadog (Wade-Evans 2013), and the Lichfield Gospels (Evans and Rhys 1979). In this chapter I will consider primarily the evidence from the largest group, the 149 charters in the Book of Llandaff, although constraints of space permit examination of only two in detail. The Llandaff charters, as they are known, are complex documents, and prior to their rehabilitation by Wendy Davies in the 1970s (see below) had been both uncritically accepted and dismissed as valid sources for the early medieval period (compare, for example, Lloyd 1911, 273, n. 253 with Brooke 1958). Davies' seminal study of the charters formed the basis of a detailed study of early medieval south-east Wales that is yet to be surpassed (Davies 1978a). However, Brycheiniog was on the periphery of her main focus on Gwent and Glamorgan, where the majority of the charters record grants of estates. Moreover, her analysis focused on broad comparisons, rather than case studies of individual estates. Thus, my intention here is to complement Davies' work by considering two of the Brycheiniog charters in detail: Llan-gors (charter 146) and Llandeilo'r-fân (charter 154). It will be argued that while the estates recorded in these particular charters are not typical of the wider corpus in certain respects, a great deal can be learnt about how they operated as part of the early medieval agrarian landscape. First, however, it is necessary to introduce the study area and consider the evidence from the Llandaff charters more generally.

Brycheiniog

Brycheiniog was probably recognised as a distinct region within south-east Wales throughout the early medieval period, but its existence as an independent kingdom can only be seen intermittently within the sources. The earliest reliable reference is in *Annales Cambriae*, where in the entry for 848 the 'men of Brycheiniog' are recorded as killing King Ithael of Gwent (Morris 1980, 48). However, the first unambiguous reference to a king of Brycheiniog is not until the late ninth century when Bishop Asser's *Life of Alfred the Great* recounts that 'Elise ap Tewdwr, king of Brycheiniog, being driven by the might of the same sons of Rhodri, sought of his own accord the lordship of King Alfred' (Keynes and Lapidge 1983, 96). As we will see, the Llandaff charters suggest that kings had been active within Brycheiniog several centuries earlier, but it is not known if these were rulers of Brycheiniog or of some other area (Davies 1978a, 18–20). No kings of Brycheiniog are recorded after 934, and their genealogy comes to an end with the grandson of Elise ap Tewdwr (Bartrum 1966, 45). Thus, the kingdom appears to have been subsumed by one of its neighbours sometime in the mid- or late tenth century. The boundaries of Brycheiniog are hard to define, but at its core lay the fertile lowlands of the upper Usk and middle Wye valleys. This lowland core was encircled by the Brecon Beacons to the south, the Black Mountains to the east, the Epynt to the north and west, and the River Wye to the north-east. Yet as its history attests, Brycheiniog was not isolated from external influences, and the valleys of the Usk and Wye served as important channels of communication (see Fig. 9.1).

Despite being surrounded by extensive areas of the upland, the comparative productivity of the lowland core of Brycheiniog has long been acknowledged. For instance, Gerald of Wales, writing in the late twelfth century, stated that the 'region produces a great amount of corn … There is ample pasture and plenty of woodland, the first full of cattle, the second teeming with wild animals' (Thorpe 1978, 93). Similarly, in his *Itinerary*, written in the mid-sixteenth century, John Leland observed 'valleys fruitful of corn, and especially pastures' (Toulmin Smith 1906, 104). Thus, the medieval economy of Brycheiniog focused on mixed agriculture, with the lowland providing land for arable, pasture, and meadow, and woods and upland providing summer grazing and resources such as timber (Owen 1991, 239). As we shall see, integration of upland and lowland through systems of transhumance was an essential feature of this system (see also Hooke and Comeau this volume). The palaeoenvironmental evidence is scant, but pollen evidence from high-altitude blanket peat suggests woodland clearance started in the mid-Bronze Age and that in broad terms the mixed farming landscape of the Middle Ages was well established by the Iron Age (Chambers 1982). Patterns of land-use did not remain fixed however; the pollen evidence

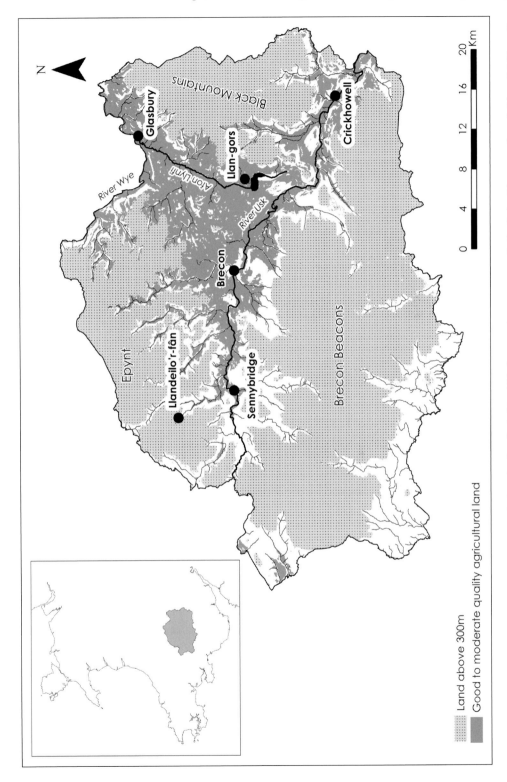

FIGURE 9.1. The historic county of Brecknock (not including the *hundred* of Builth) showing the comparatively fertile land between Sennybridge, Crickhowell and Glasbury that is likely to have formed the core of early medieval Brycheiniog. Soil data from http://lle.gov.wales/map/alc.

suggests woodland regeneration in the early Iron Age and possibly post-Roman period (see Davies this volume), whilst the record of sedimentation observed in a core taken from Llan-gors Lake suggests that increased woodland clearance and arable activity coincided with the onset of the Roman period (Jones *et al.* 1985, 229, 234; Chambers 1999, 354–5).

The Llandaff charters

Liber Landavensis (the Book of Llandaff) is a twelfth-century collection of documents relating to the purported early history of the episcopal see at Llandaff, its bishops and alleged sixth-century founding saints. It includes a corpus of 158 charters that claim to record grants of property made in favour of the bishops of Llandaff between the sixth and the eleventh centuries. The Book of Llandaff was compiled between 1119 and 1134 under the influence of Urban, the first bishop of Llandaff appointed under Norman rule, who was at the time of its compilation pursuing a series of disputes over diocesan boundaries and episcopal properties with the bishops of Hereford and St Davids. The book sets out to show that the see had been archiepiscopal in the sixth century and ruled by Saint Dyfrig, Saint Teilo and Saint Euddogwy and a single line of bishops to the eleventh century (Davies 1979a, 2; Davies 2003, 17–26). The charters were compiled as part of Urban's legal campaign and are clearly fraudulent within this twelfth-century context. Nevertheless, Wendy Davies has demonstrated, through careful examination of the charter formulae and witness lists, that a considerable number of original records lie behind the layers of later editing and interpolation, and are likely to have been contemporary with the events they describe. The reliability of the Llandaff charter material has been challenged by some scholars but Davies' main arguments for the time depth of the charter material appear robust. Sims-Williams and Guy queried the attribution of the earliest charters to the sixth century but have cited convincing evidence from orthography and witness lists that most charters are genuine, that some of the vernacular estate boundaries are linguistically Late Old Welsh, and that the earliest charters can be dated first half of the seventh century (Sims-Williams 1982; 1991; Guy 2018). Maund has suggested that the narratives associated with some of the charters, particularly ones with a high proportion of interpolated formulae, are highly formulaic and consequently of little historical value (Maund 1991, 183–206). However, Davies herself identified standard formulae but argued that some narrations were original although they were embellished in the twelfth century (Davies 1979a, 21–3). Davies argued that whilst there is no reliable evidence that Llandaff was a major ecclesiastical centre prior to the eleventh century, the charters within the Book of Llandaff were derived from genuine records that were originally compiled at, and related to, other genuine monastic houses in south-east Wales. Charles-Edwards' recent discussion of the charters lends support to Davies' arguments, and he concludes that 'As documents claiming that Llandaff was the beneficiary of the grants, the charters are admittedly forgeries; but the argument that genuine grants to churches other than Llandaff underlie most texts is persuasive' (Charles-Edwards 2013; 267). Nevertheless, he notes that whilst the cores of many of the charter texts are trustworthy, they were fluid texts and should not be understood as 'fixed title deeds' (2013; 266). Thus, whilst the quality of the individual charters varies, the corpus provides valuable and otherwise unique evidence for the Welsh landscape between the seventh and eleventh centuries.

Now that we have established that the charters contain material pertinent to the early medieval period, we can consider what they represent in terms of land units and what these can tell us about settlement, landscape, and agriculture. With one or two exceptions the charters record donations of land and the food renders and labour dues owed by the occupiers of that land (Charles-Edwards 2013, 274–283). The majority of the land granted in the charters took the form of pre-existing estates, measured in either *modii* or *unciae*, with their appurtenant estate-centres, usually a church and/or settlement (Charles-Edwards 2013, 284–5). Nevertheless, some, such as 169a and 257, record grants of parts of estates, and 171a records land *in deserto* (the wilderness) that was presumably uncultivated and not therefore part of an existing estate. Prior to the ninth century most estates are measured in units recorded as *uncia* of *c.* 500 acres. These early estates are described as *agri* (*ager*: a generic term meaning 'estate' or 'land' that is used at different scales in the charters), and are often between one or three *unciae* in extent (Charles-Edwards 284–8). They are large in comparison to the later estates and are likely to have included several settlements and a variety of land-use zones. Davies argued that *uncia* originally meant a 'hereditary portion', and suggested that the terminology represented the survival of certain conceptual approaches to property rights, and possibly actual estates, from the Romano-British period (Davies 1973, 119; 1979b, 160–1). Identifying direct continuity at the level of individual estates is difficult, but it is reasonable to suggest that the early Llandaff estates were broadly comparable to the rural estates focused on the late Roman villa-farmsteads that have been found along the coastal strip of south-east Wales. Nevertheless, continuity of concepts of landholding and territorial units should not be conflated with continuity of the agricultural systems operating within them. Excavated villas such as Whitton in the Vale of Glamorgan, with its evidence for granaries, barns, and a mechanical mill, point towards the existence of an arable-orientated surplus-producing economy in the more Romanised parts of western Britain (Jarrett and Wrathmell 1981). However, comparable levels of agricultural intensity are difficult to identify in the post-Roman period, where the evidence points towards a period of 'abatement' in which pastoralism played a more important role and surplus extracted from estates was defined in terms of food renders that were not overly onerous (Faith 2009; Seaman 2018; Davies this volume). The distribution of these early *agri* is focused on Gwent and Ergyng/ Archenfield (Herefordshire) (Davies 1973, Map 1), and they seem to have been absent from lowland Glamorgan, where it is possible that estates were smaller.

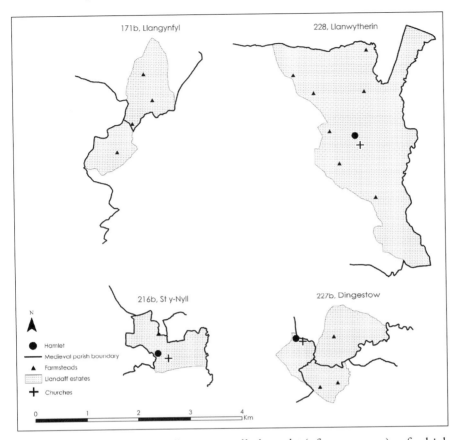

FIGURE 9.2.
Reconstruction of four
uillae/trefi recorded in
the Llandaff charters.
Translations of the
bounds are taken from
Coe (2001).

Estates measured in smaller units called *modii* (of *c*. 40 acres), of which there were twelve in an *uncia*, are found throughout the corpus, but apart from one isolated tenth-century instance no estates are measured in *uncia* after the eighth century, implying changes in the organisation of estates at this time (Davies 1973, 112). The later estates were described as *uillae* (the equivalent of the Welsh *trefi*). They were generally smaller than the earlier *agri*, and were granted by non-royal members of the laity as well as kings (Davies 1978a, 50). Davies also noted that the later estates are easier to locate on the ground and relate more closely to later medieval settlement patterns; usually encompassing a main settlement and outlying farms (see Fig. 9.2). These later estates are comparable with the *trefi* of the Welsh lawbooks and the *vills* of the Domesday survey, both in terms of their size and the way they were grouped into larger units (Davies 1978a, 38–40). These changes come in the wake of a shift in high status settlement away from defended hilltop locations, an increase in the intensity of arable cultivation in the pollen record, as well as changes in burial practices and funerary monuments (Seaman 2014; 2016; see also Davies and Rippon this volume). Thus, the charters provide further evidence on how the Welsh landscape was transformed by the socio-political and economic changes of the 'long eighth century' (Davies 1978b, 10–14).

Estates described as *uillae* are typically recorded as being of three *modii* or multiples thereof, although there are some exceptions (Davies 1978a, 33). Charles-Edwards has argued that the *modius* was primarily a unit of grain and by extension ale, and he sees the three *modii* estate as the area of land that would produce a render of three *modii* of ale, this being a key element of food renders in Wales with a standard vat of ale containing 3 *modii* (Charles-Edwards 2013, 276–8). As a unit of land the *modii* appear to be equivalent to what the Welsh lawbooks called *rhandiroedd* (arable sharelands broadly comparable to English ploughlands) (Jones 1989, 179). According to the south Wales lawbooks the sharelands consisted of arable open fields (the word *maes* is used), pasture, and woodland, and they envisage a system whereby one of the sharelands in a *tref* would be used as pasture whilst the others were used for cultivation and habitation (Wade-Evans 1909, 55, 204–5; 346–7). Within the inhabited sharelands there are likely to have been discrete areas of permanently cultivated 'inland' arranged in stripfields, supplemented by temporarily enclosed and cultivated areas of 'outfield' in the pasture shareland or on the shared rough pasture that lay beyond the bounds of the *uilla/tref* (see Comeau 2012; this volume). The precise boundaries of the estates are difficult to trace on the ground, but enough features can usually be identified to allow us to reconstruct their broad extent (see Fig. 9.2). What we see are comparatively small units that, in the nineteenth century when good mapping is available, included a main settlement/church and a number of outlying farms. These estates often share a portion of the medieval parish boundaries, but are generally somewhat smaller in extent. Thus, the estates appear to have been defined by the extent of the cultivated sharelands (Davies 1978b, 34), and the ditches and dykes that are frequently mentioned in the boundary clauses may be examples of the *penclawdd* (head-dyke or corn-ditch) (Austin 2016, 11). Outside the *uillae/trefi* estates were larger areas containing what later medieval documents describe as 'appurtenances', areas of rough pasture and grazing, woodland, meadow, and waste, which were held through use-rights and very possibly in shared rather than exclusive ownership.

As we saw in chapter 5 (Roberts), the lawbooks distinguished between free and bond *trefi*, and Glanville Jones suggested that the three *modii* estates in the Llandaff charters represented bond *trefi*, since the southern Welsh *Cyfnerth* redaction of the lawbooks recorded that there were three sharelands in a bond *trefi* as opposed to four in a free *trefi* (Jones 1989, 179). The lawbooks also envisage groups of *trefi* forming a higher order unit known as a *mainaur/ maenor*, and the south Welsh Cyfnerth redaction records seven *trefi* in a bond *mainaur* and thirteenth *trefi* in a free *mainaur* (Wade-Evans 1909, 205). The *mainaur* formed the basis of Glanville Jones' influential 'multiple estate model' (Jones 1972; 1976). The multiple estate model has much to commend it as a way of conceptualising the early medieval landscape, but has been criticised for being too static and over-schematic (Seaman 2012). There is certainly evidence from the Llandaff charters as well as the Domesday entries for Gwent that suggests *uillae/trefi* could be grouped into higher order units focused on estate centres (Charles-Edwards 2013, 284–6). In charter 235a an estate is described as being a *membrum de territorio Merthir Teudiric* ('part of the territory of *Merthir Teudiric*'). In early twelfth-century papal bulls *Merthir Teudiric* (mod. Mathern) is listed 'together with [its] churches', implying that it was a principal church with other churches dependent on it, and Charles-Edwards (2013, 284) interprets this as suggesting that *Merthir Teudiric* was the centre of a multiple estate. Similarly, the Domesday Book for Gwent records five groups of *vills* (two groups of thirteen, two of fourteen, and one of seven) held by Welsh reeves, and notes that they paid food renders similar to those described in the lawbooks (Moore 1982, 162a–b). Several *mainaur* place-names also appear in the Llandaff charters, although generally in the later rubrics (for example charters 125a, 72a, 263, and 127b). It is difficult, however, to reconstruct these *mainaur*-level units with any certainly, and we have little evidence to show how they operated. It is clear from the boundary clauses that some neighbouring estates were contiguous, but the *uilla/tref* estate granted in charter 235a is unlikely to have been adjacent to Merthir Teuderic/Mathern, the principal church of its *territorium,* and may have been over 13 kilometres to the west at Bishton (Coe 2001, 868–9). Moreover, the Domesday Book also records single *vills* that co-existed with the larger multiple estates. Thus, we should not assume that the entire landscape was divided up into a coherent patchwork of contiguous *mainaurau* (Jones 1998; Seaman 2012, 171).

The charters themselves provide little direct evidence on the nature of the agricultural landscape, but incidental references, particularly in boundary clauses, provide us with important, albeit limited, evidence. As would be expected the estates, or at least their centres, appear to be located on what is classified today as good quality agricultural land and they generally lie below the 150 m contour, and springs/wells and streams are very frequently mentioned in boundary clauses (Davies 1978a, 26). Several charters, including 125a, 146 and 204a, specify weirs and fishing rights, whilst charter 180b (Bishton) includes shore rights on the Severn Estuary. Woods and woodlands feature in about a third of boundaries or the grants themselves, and several charters, including 171b, 228, and 257, record grants of estates with their woods. Marsh, meadow, pasture, pannage, and arable are also recorded (Davies 1978a, 35). For example, the late ninth-century charter 216b records the grant of *Uilla Penn Onn* (St-y-Nyll) with three *modii* of land and six *modii* of wheat, whilst pannage and hawking rights are recorded in charter 187, an early eighth-century grant of a church and estate at Llansoy. For a more comprehensive understanding of how the *uillae/trefi* recorded in the Llandaff charters fitted into the agricultural landscape, we must attempt to reconstruct them on the ground and draw upon a range of complementary evidence, including place-names and archaeology. In the following section I will focus on two estates in particular, Llan-gors (146) and Llandeilo'r-fân (154), both of which were located in Brycheiniog.

Two Brycheiniog estates: Llan-gors and Llandeilo'r-fân

Charters 146 and 154 record grants by King Awst and his sons Eiludd and Rhiwallon in favour of Bishop Euddogwy of Llandaff. Charter 146 records the donation of 'their bodies for burial and *Lann Cors*', whilst 154 records their return of *Lannguruaet* with its *territorium*. Both charters are complex records that contain a high proportion of interpolated formulae and neither are likely to have been based upon surviving genuine detailed charters. Nevertheless, there is sufficient evidence to suggest they were compiled at Llandaff from early records that did relate to Brycheiniog, and their boundary clauses are genuine and pre-date the compilation of the Book of Llandaff (Davies 1979a, 98, 101; Sims-Williams 1993, 61; Coe 2004; Seaman forthcoming A; for translations of the boundary clauses see Coe 2001, 975–6 and 977–8). We do not know the full content of these early records, but Awst does appear to have been a king of the early eighth century who was active in the Brycheiniog region, although the reference to Bishop Euddogwy is unlikely to been part of an original early record (Davies 1979a, 81, 98). The absence of genuine witness lists prevents these charters from being fitted into Davies' dated charter sequences, but she has argued that Awst and his sons should date to the early to mid-eighth century (Davies 1979a, 76).

Lann Cors, the subject of 146, can be identified as Llan-gors on the basis of both the place-name and the features in the boundary clause that can be reconstructed with some certainty (Fig. 9.3) (Coe 2001, 519–520; Seaman forthcoming A). The estate is comparatively large (*c.* 1200 hectares/2965 acres), and encompasses much of the medieval parish of Llan-gors and around half of the adjoining parish of Llanfihangel Tal-y-llyn, the remainder of which appears to have formed a smaller estate of *c.* 240 hectares/600 acres that was granted by a King Tewdwr of Brycheiniog in charter 167 (mid-eighth century) and later re-granted by a King Tewdwr ap Elisedd in charter 237b (*c.* 935) (Seaman forthcoming A). These two adjacent royal estates both focused on Llangorse Lake, which was also bounded to the south and south-east by a further two parishes, Cathedine and Llangasty Tal-y-llyn. It is possible that together these units formed an early royal territory focused on Llangorse Lake, and in this regard it is interesting to note that the lake has long been noted as lying at the centre of a network of early route ways (Camden 1587, 357).

The Llan-gors estate stretched from the shores of the lake (*c.* 150 m OD) up to the edge of the post-medieval enclosure (*c.* 350 m OD) and included a range of resource zones. The lake would have provided fish and wild fowl. Indeed, Gerald of Wales noted that it 'supplies plenty of pike, perch, excellent trout, tench and mud-loving eels for the local inhabitant' (Thorpe 1978, 93–5), whilst fish-traps are portrayed on an estate map of 1584 (see Plate 9.1; TNA MPF 1/12). The seasonally waterlogged land immediately surrounding and to the north-west of the lake is unsuitable for arable cultivation, but provides excellent meadows and pasture. The loamy Milford soils on the sloping ground between 160 m OD and 270 m OD are classified as 'good' or 'good to moderate' by

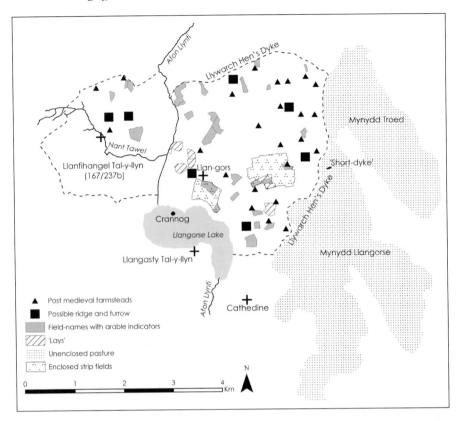

FIGURE 9.3. The early medieval estate at Llangors recorded in charter 146.

the Predictive Agricultural Land Classification map and would have been the focus for arable cultivation, particularly areas with a south-facing aspect (http://lle.gov.wales/map/alc). These soils have low natural fertility, and the region as a whole suffers from high rainfall and a comparatively short growing season with late frosts (NSRI 2018; Coppock 1971, 29–53). Nevertheless, drainage is very good and fertility could have been maintained through the folding of sheep (Williamson 2013, 48). The eastern and north-eastern boundary of the estate was defined by a feature described in the charter as *claud Lyuarch hen* (Llywarch Hen's dyke). This place-name incorporates a reference to Llywarch Hen, a legendary Brittonic ruler who featured prominently in medieval Welsh tradition, including a substantial body of poetry that survives in documents of the thirteenth century and later (Sims-Williams 1993). On the ground the dyke appears to be represented by a substantial hollow-way and field-bank that defines a large stretch of the parish boundary and runs along the upper limit of the post-medieval enclosure (see Fig. 9.4) (Seaman forthcoming B). It is therefore likely to represent a *penclawdd* that separated cultivated land from unenclosed mountain pasture. It would have originally been topped by a hedge, and its primary function was to keep grazing livestock on the commons of Mynydd Llangorse and Mynydd Troed and prevent them from damaging crops and pasture. A possible 'cross-ridge' dyke that cuts off the northern tip of

FIGURE 9.4. Section of Llywarch Hen's Dyke, looking north. The open pastures of Mynydd Llangorse are to the right. (Photograph: Peter Seaman.)

Mynydd Llangorse may have been associated with controlling the movement of livestock on and off of the common pasture (RCAHMW 1986, 96).

In terms of settlement, the estate today encompasses the small nucleated settlement at Llan-gors and its medieval church that is thought to lie on the location of an early medieval monastery (Redknap and Lewis 2007, 560–1), as well as 24 outlying farms, the majority of which are located to the east and north of Llan-gors on the lower south-facing slopes of Mynydd Llangorse and Mynydd Troed. Not all of the farmsteads are likely to be medieval in origin, particularly those on 'moderate to poor' soils above 270 m OD (Silvester 2006,

25), but the 1584 estate map shows that some farmsteads are at least late medieval in origin (Plate 9.1). This map is highly schematic and clearly inaccurate in places, but it provides important evidence at a crucial time in the development of this landscape. Unfortunately, it only depicts part of the Llan-gors estate, but it does show the adjacent parishes of Llanfihangel Tal-y-llyn, Cathedine, and Llangasty Tal-y-llyn. The settlement pattern is depicted as small nucleations focused on parish churches, with outlying farms arranged in 'girdle patterns' around open areas that may originally have been commons or areas of infield. The former is particularly clear at Llanfihangel Tal-y-llyn, where a funnel-shaped track leads into an unenclosed area surrounded by dwellings. This narrowing entrance is a distinctive feature of common pasture and would have made it easier to manage livestock as they were herded out of the common and on to the track (Oosthuizen 2013, 25). This area is now partly developed and divided into fields, but several are named as 'common' on the Tithe apportionment. The 1584 estate map depicts a network of rectilinear and curvilinear boundaries that are far larger than the individual fields of the nineteenth-century tithe maps. These boundaries are difficult to interpret since the corresponding field-book is missing, but the rectilinear boundaries could represent consolidated holdings of the late medieval/sixteenth-century enclosure period, whilst the curvilinear boundaries, which tend to be located on wetter ground at the western end of the lake may represent meadow, pasture, or former woodland. Interestingly, the land immediately surrounding Cathedine appears not to have been enclosed, perhaps indicating an area of surviving open field or common. Within Llangors the presence of former open fields may also be traced through tithe map field-names incorporating elements such as *maes*, *erw*, and *cyfer*, some of which correspond with blocks of what appear to be enclosed strip-fields to the south and west of the church. Possible ridge and furrow has also been identified through aerial photography, but the interpretation and date of this is not fully understood (see Fig. 9.3). In addition to what were probably quite discrete areas of permanent arable, there appear to have been areas of 'outfield' pasture brought into cultivation through a 'long ley' system of convertible husbandry (Hall 2013, 84–6). Such areas are represented by field-names incorporating the element *lay/layer*, with the contiguity of such field names to areas of arable representing the footprint of former areas of long ley husbandry management.

Uniquely for a Llandaff estate Llan-gors is able to boast good quality archaeological evidence in the form of the Llan-gors crannog, a late ninth to early tenth-century residence on an artificial island constructed *c.* 30 m from the northern shore of the lake (Lane and Redknap forthcoming). Crannogs are most commonly associated with early medieval Ireland and it is unlikely to be a coincidence that the kingdom of Brycheiniog had strong Irish connections (Charles-Edwards 2013, 20). It is quite possible that an Irish dynasty or a dynasty with close connections to Ireland was responsible for the construction of the crannog. The crannog was partially excavated by Alan Lane and Mark Redknap between 1989 and 1994. Unfortunately, the occupation levels had eroded prior to excavation, but sampling of the silts around the crannog's edges have revealed evidence for high status occupation, including part of a small portable reliquary, an elaborately decorated textile, part of a pseudo-penannular brooch, a copper alloy drinking-horn end, and a section of a copper alloy bracelet or torc. The excavators interpret the crannog as a royal centre of the kingdom of Brycheiniog, and they associate its abandonment with a Mercian raid on *Brecenan mere* recorded in the Anglo-Saxon Chronicles for 916. Since the site may only have been occupied for as little as twenty years the substantial animal bone and plant macrofossil assemblages recovered during the excavation provide us with valuable evidence about how a royal community were living off the land in the late eighth and early ninth centuries.

The plant macrofossil remains includes substantial quantities of free-threshing naked wheat, the majority of which is of bread wheat type. Thus, the crannog's residents were probably eating white bread, an essential sign of status in the early medieval world (Hoffmann 2014, 115; see also McClatchie this volume). Barley was present, most likely as hulled barley, as well as oats, and possibly rye. These could have been consumed in ale, pottage, oatcakes, and lower quality bread, and may also have provided animal feed. Cultivated flax may be represented, possibly for the production of linen given the size of the seeds (Caseldine and Griffiths forthcoming). Barley, oats, and rye would have grown well on the light well-drained but comparatively unfertile soils of the estate and surrounding areas, and would also have been able to tolerate the high rainfall and comparatively short growing season. The area is less conducive to growing bread wheat, but spelt, club, and emmer may have been tolerant (Moffett 2011, 350–1). The lawbooks acknowledge that 'wheat land' was not ubiquitous (Jenkins 1986, 128), and the local climate has been identified as an important factor behind the low wheat acreages reported during the early modern period (Thomas 1963, 63). Nevertheless, since it was only a small elite who consumed wheat, low wheat acreages may not have been an issue in the early medieval period. At Llan-gors it has been suggested that the mixing of different cereal grains within the assemblage could indicate that wheat was grown together with rye or barley, in case one crop failed (Caseldine and Griffiths forthcoming; *cf.* Pretty 1990). Alternatively, the wheat from the crannog could have arrived as part of food renders from areas more suited to its cultivation, such as the Usk Valley. This interpretation could be supported by the limited occurrences of chaff and weed seeds, suggesting that the grain was largely processed before arriving at the crannog (Caseldine and Griffiths forthcoming).

The main domestic mammals represented in the animal bone assemblage were cattle, sheep/goat, and pigs. Where sheep and goats could be speciated, sheep were more frequent, but pig was the most predominant species and would have contributed most to the meat consumed on the site, followed by cattle and then sheep/goats. However, wild mammals, including red deer, roe deer and wild fowl, made an unusually large contribution, and it is clear that hunting, a major high-status activity, was important (Mullville and Powell forthcoming). This pattern is in keeping with the evidence from broadly contemporary high-status settlements in Anglo-Saxon England (Sykes 2011, 338–9). It is however noticeable that, in contrast to the English sites where whole carcasses are generally represented in the late Anglo-Saxon period, the bones deriving from the head and extremities of deer are underrepresented at Llan-gors. This suggests that deer carcasses were processed at the site of the kill with only selected elements brought back to the crannog. It is possible that the remainder of the carcass was given to the owner of the land, as specified in the lawbooks, and/or symbolically distributed amongst the hunting party as has been argued for in middle Anglo-Saxon contexts (*cf.* Roberts this volume; Jenkins 2000, 275; Marvin 2006, 32–4). The mortality profiles of the domestic mammals, which show a preponderance of older specimens, also do not reflect the economy of a self-sufficient producer site (Mulville and Powell forthcoming). The age-profile of the cattle suggests that they were bred primarily for dairying and traction, as is implied in the lawbooks where female cattle are said to be in their prime until the ninth calf and males until their sixth season of ploughing (Wade-Evans 1909, 220). A meat steer is included in the *gwestfa* payment, but cattle and sheep could also be paid in lieu of food renders (Davies 1978, 134). Taken together the animal bone assemblage from the crannog resonates well with what we would expect from a high-status early medieval settlement: feasting on pigs, hunting of deer, and the collection of food renders. Perhaps surprisingly, however, there is little evidence for the consumption of wild fowl (Mulville and Powell forthcoming). The comparatively large quantities of pig bones and deer suggest that use of the crannog may have focused upon the period between midsummer and winter, since the lawbooks state that the winter food render paid by bondsmen included a sow (as opposed to dairy products in the summer), and that the hunting of stags began at midsummer and ended in November (Wade-Evans 1907, 182, 207; Jenkins 1986, 22, 128; 2000, 273). It may not be coincidence therefore that the feast of the sixth-century saint Paulinus, to whom the church at Llan-gors with its early medieval documentary evidence and stone sculpture appears to have been dedicated, was celebrated on 22nd November (Baring-Gould and Fisher 1913, 72–5; Redknap and Lewis 2007, 560–1). Since many early Christian saints' festivals were associated with times of seasonal gathering at cross-quarter days and midsummer with the November gatherings marking the payment of food renders and the end of the stag hunting season (Comeau 2019), it is not unreasonable to suggest that the feasting evidence from the crannog was linked with these events.

Lannguruaet, the subject of 154, can be identified as Llandeilo'r-fân on the basis of features named in its boundary clause that can again be reconstructed with some certainly (Fig. 9.5) (Coe 2001, 429). This estate is one of the largest within the corpus (*c.* 2500 hectares/6000 acres), and lies on the very edge of Brycheiniog at much higher altitude (200 to 440 m OD) than the majority of the Llandaff estates. Indeed, the focus of the estate, if this can be taken to

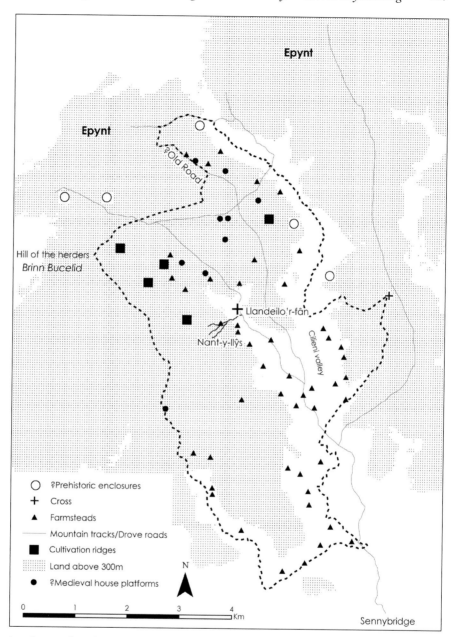

FIGURE 9.5. The early medieval estate at Llandeilo'r-fân recorded in charter 154.

be the medieval parish church of St Teilo, lies at 260 m OD, above the usual limit of permanent settlement in upland Wales (*cf.* Austin 2016, 7). Llandeilo'r-fân is not, therefore, a typical rural community of the period. Unfortunately, Llandeilo'r-fân lacks the comparatively rich historical, archaeological, and cartographical evidence afforded at Llan-gors, and neither does the Tithe apportionment provide us with many field-names. Nevertheless, we are able to reconstruct something of the estate's agricultural context by considering the archaeological evidence and its position within the landscape. The estate encompasses land in the parishes of Llandeilo'r-fân and Llywel, with sections of their boundaries being contiguous with those of the Llandaff estate. The majority of the land within the estate is classified as 'poor' or 'very poor', with limited patches of 'moderate quality agricultural land' in the Cilieni valley to the south-east. The estate broadly divides into two zones, the smaller of these being unenclosed *mynydd* above *c.* 400 m OD to the north. This includes land on what has been known since at least the twelfth century as the Epynt ('mountain crossed by a horse-path': Wyn Owen and Morgan 2007, 333). The other zone, the lower land to south, consists largely of enclosed fields with patches of woodland on often quite steep slopes of the Cillieni, Mawan, Eithrim, and Clydach valleys (see Fig. 9.5). The estate centre is likely to have focused on what is now the hamlet of Llandeilo'r-fân. The medieval church here was heavily restored in 1873, but its Teilo dedication and curvilinear churchyard suggest, albeit tentatively, earlier origins. A stream that runs into the Eithrim immediately to the south of the church is called Nant-y-llŷs (stream of the court). This place-name might suggest the presence of a royal court but being attested only from the seventeenth century, not too much significance should be attributed to it. In the nineteenth century the settlement pattern included forty-nine isolated farmsteads all lying below 370 m OD. None are of proven medieval date, and many may be post-medieval in origin (*cf.* Griffiths 1989, 233), but their distribution probably reflects something of the medieval settlement pattern. At least ten deserted enclosures, farmsteads, and house-platforms have been identified on the *mynydd*. None have been excavated and many are likely to have been comparatively late encroachments that were abandoned in the nineteenth century, but some may represent medieval *hafodydd* associated with seasonal transhumance (Silvester 2006).

Given the soils and topography, the agricultural potential of this estate must have been limited, although the presence of relict cultivation ridges (of probable late or post-medieval date) associated with house-platforms as high as 400 m OD demonstrates that even the *mynydd* could be brought into cultivation under the right conditions (see Comeau this volume). We may ask ourselves, therefore, why an estate that appears to have included a church and *llys* was located in such a remote and marginal location, particularly since there appears to have been little population pressure and no shortage of better quality land in the valley floors (Austin 2016, 8). The answer may lie in the agricultural importance of upland pasture. The Epynt was celebrated as a breeding ground for Brecknockshire cattle and sheep in the nineteenth century (Moore-Colyer 2001, 119), and a track (now an unclassified road running between Llandeilo'r-fân and Sennybridge) which linked the Epynt with the core areas of lowland settlement in the Usk valley via the Brecon to Llandovery Roman road ran through the middle of the estate and immediately around the churchyard. This road is marked by a deep hollow-way in places and is associated with a number of enclosures of presumed prehistoric date. It was used as a drove road in the early modern period (Godwin and Toulson 1977), and may be of considerable antiquity. Interestingly, a cross appears to have been located on the boundary of the estate at the closest point to another track that ran from the Epynt towards Sennybridge (Coe 2001, 193; see Fig. 9.4). The significance of the seasonal pastoral economy is also attested by a reference to the *Brinn Bucelid* ('hill of the herders') in the charter's boundary clause (Davies 1978a, 36; Coe 2001, 96). During the summer months animals could have been driven from settlements in the Usk valley up to Llandeilo'r-fân, from which they could have been easily moved onto the *mynydd*. It is possible, therefore, that the estate was, initially at least, seasonally occupied, although the place-name *Lannguruaet*, which implies the presence of a church and cemetery, indicates a more permanent arrangement by the date of the charter. Such a high altitude permanent settlement is unusual in this period, but this may be explained by the fact that it appears, like Llan-gors, to have been part of a royal estate held, initially at least, by King Awst and his sons. This is significant since later Welsh kings are known to have maintained extensive upland areas as year-round horse/cattle ranches that included permanently occupied habitations (Smith 1998, 231–4). Perhaps, therefore, Llandeilo'r-fân represents an example of *hafotir*, upland pasture held by the king, or maybe the church, and maintained by an official (Jenkins 1986, 121; Jones 1989, 178). It may also be relevant to note that Llandeilo'r-fân lies on what would have been the very edge of the kingdom of Brycheiniog, close to the major watershed which marks the border with Ystrad Twyi and adjacent to the confluence of two transmontane horse roads on the Epynt, one which ran north-east towards a small kingdom/territory focused on Builth Wells. Indeed, the charter states that the estate's boundary follows an 'old road' for some distance on its north-east side, and it has recently been suggested that the Epynt was used as an upland route in the Roman period (Moore-Colyer 2001, 119; Wyn Owen and Morgan 2007, 333; Musson and Driver 2015). Such horse roads are unlikely to have been mere tracks however, and probably played an important role in exercising and displaying elite power (Fleming 2011). Thus, it is possible that the estate's unusual location also owed something to its strategic position within the early medieval political landscape.

Conclusions

The Llandaff charters contain much important evidence about the early medieval landscape of south Wales, but they are complex sources that must be used with caution. On the macro-scale they provide evidence for an agricultural landscape that contrasts markedly with the nineteenth- and early twentieth-century characterisation of the 'wandering pastoralist' (Parain 1966, 171). The charters also provide opportunities for detailed local studies which hitherto have not featured prominently in the historiography of medieval Wales. The limited range of complementary documentary sources, dearth of early place-name records, and the nature of the Welsh archaeological record have in large part precluded us from implementing the techniques and methods that have been central to the rapid advances in understanding of the medieval landscapes of England since the 1970s (*e.g.* Aston and Rowley 1974). These techniques – field-walking, test pitting, aerial photography, and earthwork survey – have much to contribute but are of limited efficacy for much of Wales. The examples of Llan-gors and Llandeilo'r-fân demonstrate that there are other ways to develop valuable insights.

References

Aston, M. and Rowley, T. (1974) *Landscape Archaeology: An Introduction to fieldwork techniques on Post-Roman landscapes*. Newton Abbot, David and Charles.

Austin, D. (2016) Reconstructing the Upland Landscapes of Medieval Wales. *Archaeologia Cambrensis* 165, 1–20.

Baring-Gould, S. and Fisher, J. (1913) *The Lives of the British Saints, Volume IV*. London, The Honourable Society for the Cymmrodorion.

Bartrum, P. (1966) *Early Welsh Genealogical Tracts*. Cardiff, University of Wales Press.

Brooke, C. (1986) *The Church and the Welsh Border in the Central Middle Ages*. Woodbridge, Boydell.

Camden, W. (1587) *Britannia siue Florentissimorum regnorum, Angliae, Scotiae, Hiberniae, et insularum adiacentium ex intima antiquitate chorographica descriptio*. London.

Caseldine, A. and Griffiths, C. (forthcoming) The plant remains. In A. Lane and M. Redknap (ed.) *Llangorse Crannog: The Excavation of an Early Medieval Royal Site in the Kingdom of Brycheiniog*. Oxford, Oxbow Books.

Chambers, F. (1982) Two Radiocarbon-dated Pollen Diagrams from High-altitude Blanket Peats in South Wales. *Journal of Ecology* 70, 445–459.

Chambers, F. (1999) The Quaternary History of Llangorse Lake: implications for conservation. *Aquatic Conservation: Marine and Freshwater Ecosystems* 9, 343–359.

Charles-Edwards, T. (2013) *Wales and the Britons 350–1064*. Oxford, Oxford University Press.

Coe, J. (2001) The Place-Names of the Book of Llandaf. Unpublished PhD thesis, University of Wales Aberystwyth.

Coe, J. (2004) Dating the Boundary Clauses in the Book of Llandaff. *Cambrian Medieval Celtic Studies* 48, 1–43.

Comeau, R. (2012) From Tref(gordd) to Tithe: identifying settlement patterns in a north Pembrokeshire parish. *Landscape History* 33(1), 29–44.

Comeau, R. (2019) Land, people and power in early medieval Wales: the cantref of Cemais in comparative perspective. Unpublished PhD thesis, University College London, Institute of Archaeology.

Coppock, J. (1971) *An Agricultural Geography of Great Britain*. London, G. Bell and Sons.

Davies, J. (2003) *The Book of Llandaff and the Norman Church*. Woodbridge, Boydell.

Davies, R. R. (1978) *Lordship and Society in March of Wales 1282–1400*. Oxford, Oxford University Press.

Davies, W. (1973) Liber Landavensis: its Construction and Credibility. *English Historical Review* 88, 335–351.

Davies, W. (1978a) *An Early Welsh Microcosm*. London, Royal Historical Society.

Davies, W. (1978b) Land and Power in Early Medieval Wales. *Past and Present* 81, 3–23.

Davies, W. (1979a) *The Llandaff Charters*. Aberystwyth, The National Library of Wales.

Davies, W. (1979b) Roman Settlements and Post-Roman Estates in South-East Wales. In P. Casey (ed.) *The End of Roman Britain*. BAR British Series 71. Oxford, British Archaeological Reports, 153–173.

Evans, J. G. and Rhys, J. (1979) *The Text of the Book of Llan Dâv*. Aberystwyth, National Library of Wales.

Faith, R. (2009) Forces and Relations of Production in Early Medieval England. *Journal of Agrarian Change* 9(1), 23–41.

Fleming, A. (2011) Horses, Elites … and Long-distance Road. *Landscapes* 2, 1–20.

Godwin, F. and Toulson, S. (1977) *The Drovers' Roads of Wales*. London, Wildwood House.

Griffiths, M. (1989) The Emergence of the Modern Settlement Pattern, 1450–1700. In D. H. Owen (ed.) *Settlement and Society in Wales*. Cardiff, University of Wales Press, 225–248.

Guy, B. (2018) The Life of St Dyfrig and the Lost Charters of Moccas (Mochros), Herefordshire. *Cambrian Medieval Celtic Studies* 75, 1–37.

Hall, D. (2013) *The Open Fields of England*. Oxford, Oxford University Press.

Hoffmann, R. (2014) *An Environmental History of Medieval Europe*. Cambridge, Cambridge University Press.

Jarrett, M. and Wrathmell, S. (1981) *Whitton: An Iron Age and Roman Farmstead in South Glamorgan*. Cardiff, University of Wales Press.

Jenkins, D. (1986) *The Law of Hywel Dda*. Llandysul, Gomer.

Jenkins, D. (2000) Hawk and Hound: Hunting in the Laws of Court. In T. Charles-Edwards, M. Owen, and P. Russell (eds) *The Welsh King and His Court*. Cardiff, University of Wales Press, 255–280.

Jones, G. (1972) Post-Roman Wales. In H. P. R. Finburg (ed.) *The Agrarian History of England and Wales: Volume I.ii, Prehistory to AD 1042*. Cambridge, Cambridge University Press, 218–382.

Jones, G. (1976) Multiple Estates and Early Settlement. In P. H. Sawyer (ed.) *Medieval Settlement: Continuity and Change*. London, Edward Arnold, 9–34.

Jones, G. (1989) The Dark Ages. In D. H. Owen (ed.) *Settlement and Society in Wales*. Cardiff, University of Wales Press, 177–198.

Jones, R. (1998) Problems with Medieval Welsh Local Administration – The Case of the Maenor and Maenol. *Journal of Historical Geography* 24(2), 135–146.

Jones, R., Benson-Evans, K. and Chambers, F. (1985) Human influence upon sedimentation in Llangorse Lake, Wales. *Earth Surface Processes and Landforms* 10, 1377–1382.

Keynes, S. and Lapidge, M. (1983) *Alfred the Great: Asser's Life of King Alfred and other contemporary sources*. London, Penguin.

Lane, A. and Redknap, M. (eds) (forthcoming) *Llangorse Crannog: The Excavation of an Early Medieval Royal Site in the Kingdom of Brycheiniog*. Oxford, Oxbow Books.

Lloyd, J. E. (1911) *A History of Wales from the Earliest Times to the Edwardian Conquest, Volume 1*. London, Longmans, Green, and Co.

Marvin, W. (2006) *Hunting Law and Ritual in Medieval English Literature*. Cambridge, Brewer.

Maund, K. (1997) Fact and Narrative Fiction in the Llandaff Charters. *Studia Celtica* 31, 173–193.

Moffett, L. (2011) Food Plants on Archaeological Sites: The Nature of the Archaeobotanical Record. In H. Hamerow, D. Hinton, and S. Crawford (eds) *The Oxford Handbook of Anglo-Saxon Archaeology*. Oxford, Oxford University Press, 346–360.

Moore, J. (ed. and trans.) (1982) *Domesday Book: Gloucestershire*. Chichester, Phillimore.

Moore-Colyer, R. (2001) *Roads and Trackways of Wales*. Ashbourne, Landmark.

Morris, J. (1980) *Nennius: British History and the Welsh Annals*. London, Phillimore.

Mulville, J. and Powell, A. (forthcoming) The Animal Bone. In A. Lane and M. Redknap (eds) *Llangorse Crannog: The Excavation of an Early Medieval Royal Site in the Kingdom of Brycheiniog*. Oxford, Oxbow Books.

Musson, C. and Driver, T. (2015) *Above Brecknock: An historic county from the air*. Welshpool and Aberystwyth, The Brecknock Society & Museum Friends and The Clwyd-Powys Archaeological Trust.

National Soil Resources Institute (2018) Soil Site Report for location 313652E, 227554N, 5km x 5km, National Soil Resources Institute, Cranfield University. Accessed via http://www.landis.org.uk/sitereporter/.

Oosthuizen S. (2013) *Tradition and Transformation in Anglo-Saxon England: Archaeology, Common Rights and Landscape*. London, Bloomsbury Academic.

Owen, H. (1991) Wales and the Marches. In E. Miller (ed.) *The Agrarian History of England and Wales: Volume III, 1348–1500*. Cambridge, Cambridge University Press, 92–105.

Parain, C. (1966) The Evolution of Agricultural Technique. In M. M. Postan (ed.) *The Cambridge Economic History of Europe: Volume I: The Agrarian Life of the Middle Ages*. Cambridge, Cambridge University Press, 126–179.

Pretty, N. (1990) Sustainable agriculture in the Middle Ages: The English manor. *Agricultural History Review* 38, 1–19.

RCAHMW (1986) *An Inventory of the Ancient Monuments in Brecknock (Bryncheiniog): The Prehistoric and Roman Monuments Part ii: Hill-forts and Roman Remains*. London, HMSO.

Redknap, M. and Lewis, J. (2008) *A Corpus of Early Medieval Inscribed Stones and Stone Sculpture in Wales: Volume I*. Cardiff, University of Wales Press.

Seaman, A. (forthcoming A) The Llangorse Charter Material. In A. Lane and M. Redknap (eds) *Llangorse Crannog: The Excavation of an Early Medieval Royal Site in the Kingdom of Brycheiniog*. Oxford, Oxbow Books.

Seaman, A (forthcoming B) The Dyke of Llywarch Hen at Llan-gors. *Offa's Dyke Journal*.

Seaman, A. (2012) The Multiple Estate Model Re-Considered: Power and Territory in Early Medieval Wales. *Welsh History Review* 26, 163–185.

Seaman, A. (2014) Tempora Christiana? Conversion and Christianization in Western Britain AD 300–700. *Church Archaeology* 16, 1–22.

Seaman, A. (2016) Defended Settlement in Early Medieval Wales: Problems of Presence, Absence and Interpretation. In N. Christie and H. Herold (eds) *Fortified Settlements in Early Medieval Europe: Defended Communities of the 8th–10th Centuries*. Oxford, Oxbow, 37–50.

Seaman, A. (2018) Landscape, Economy and Society in Late and Post Roman Wales. In N. Christie and P. Diarte Blasco (eds) *Interpreting Transformations of People and Landscapes in Late Antiquity and the Early Middle Ages*. Oxford, Oxbow Books, 123–136.

Silvester, R. (2006) Deserted rural settlements in central and north-east Wales. In K. Roberts (ed.) *Lost Farmsteads: Deserted Rural Settlements in Wales*. York, Council for British Archaeology, 13–40.

Sims-Williams, P. (1982) Review of Davies, W. (1979a & 1978). *Journal of Ecclesiastical History* 33, 124–9.

Sims-Williams, P. (1991) The Emergence of Old Welsh, Cornish and Breton Orthography, 600–800: The Evidence of Archaic Old Welsh. *Bulletin of the Board of Celtic Studies* 38, 20–86.

Sims-Williams, P. (1993) The Provenance of the Llywarch Hen Poems: A Case for Llangors, Brycheiniog. *Cambrian Medieval Celtic Studies* 26, 27–63.

Smith, J. B. (1998) *Llywelyn ap Gruffudd: Prince of Wales*. Cardiff, University of Wales Press.

Sykes, N. (2011) Woods and the Wild. In H. Hamerow, D. Hinton, and S. Crawford (eds) *The Oxford Handbook of Anglo-Saxon Archaeology*. Oxford, Oxford University Press, 327–345.

Thomas, D. (1963) *Agriculture in Wales during the Napoleonic War*. Cardiff, University of Wales Press.

Thorpe, L. (1978) *The Journey Through Wales; and The Description of Wales, by Gerald of Wales*. London, Penguin.

Toulmin Smith, L. (ed.) (1906) *The Itinerary in Wales of John Leland in or about the years 1536–1539, Vol. 3 Containing Part 6 (The Itinerary in Wales)*. London, George Bell and Sons.

Wade-Evans, A. (1909) *Welsh Medieval Law*. Oxford, Clarendon Press.

Wade-Evans, A. (2013) *Vitae Sanctorum Britanniae et Genealogiae: The Lives and Genealogies of the Welsh Saints*, ed. S. Lloyd. Cardiff, Welsh Academic Press.

Williamson, T. (2013) *Environment, Society and Landscape in Early Medieval England*. Woodbridge, Boydell and Brewer.

Wyn Owen, H. and Morgan R. (2007) *Dictionary of the Place-Names of Wales*. Llandysul, Gomer.

Unpublished Sources

TNA MPF 1/12, The National Archives (TNA), Brecknockshire Llangorse '*Plott describing the poole called Brecknock Poole 1584*'

CHAPTER TEN

Culture, climate, coulter and conflict: pollen studies from early medieval Wales

Tudur Davies

Studies of the early medieval economy in Wales commonly suffer from a lack of available source material. Archaeological settlement sites with identifiable material culture are scarce and documents of early medieval date relating to Wales are 'few, fragmentary and difficult to use' (Davies 1982, 198). Many sites were excavated prior to the development of modern excavation techniques and their standard of recording and the quality of the archive do not meet modern standards. Site-based environmental analysis capable of examining aspects of the early medieval economy has been especially problematic, as few sites have been systematically sampled for archaeobotanical remains or smaller sized animal bone. Some aspects of the Welsh environment and economy are, however, described in medieval texts. The most detailed of these are the Laws of Hywel Dda (see Roberts this volume) and Gerald of Wales' *Journey through Wales* and *Description of Wales* (Thorpe 1978). The relevance of these sources to the early medieval period is uncertain, since Gerald's accounts were written in the late twelfth century, whilst the laws of Hywel Dda, although of supposed early tenth-century origin, only survive as texts of twelfth- and thirteenth-century composition. Therefore while it is probable that the information within these documents reflects conditions in Wales at the end of the early medieval period, their relevance to the earlier parts of the period is less certain, especially as there may have been changes in land use and settlement practices following Anglo-Norman campaigns that began in the late eleventh century AD.

Activities relating to the early medieval economy have, however, left a record elsewhere in the landscape. Where conditions favour palaeoenvironmental preservation it is possible to study the environment of the past without the need for archaeological deposits. When the archaeological record is limited or not forthcoming, 'off-site' samples from lake sediments, peat bogs, river systems, or coastal wetlands can significantly contribute to our understanding of changes in past environments, climate, land use, and, more indirectly, human social developments (*e.g.* work by Fyfe and Rippon 2004 in Exmoor). By examining fluctuations in different pollen taxa at different depths within a core sample (a long vertical sample of peat or other sediment obtained using a hollow corer), we can use changes in the environment to infer human activity in the surrounding landscape over time. Decreases in woodland cover could indicate clearance episodes for settlement or farming, while fluctuations in certain herb types can indicate changes in land use; for example, an increase in cereal-type pollen or other arable weeds could reflect intensification of arable practices. An 'age-depth' model for these sampling sites can be formed through scientific dating techniques (*e.g.* radiocarbon, optically stimulated luminescence, tephra, or geosecular magnetic variation dating), enabling us to place the environmental record within a cultural context.

This paper undertakes a review of palaeoenvironmental studies undertaken across Wales, seeking to examine the development of the Welsh landscape and its economy during the early medieval period. Other researchers have attempted similar syntheses that compare the early medieval palynological record for Wales with changes elsewhere in Britain, most notably Petra Dark (2000), and more recently Rippon *et al.* (2013, 2015, see also Rippon this volume) whose analysis was undertaken concurrently with the research undertaken for this paper. Dark's conclusions in relation to Wales were limited by the scarcity of relevant studies identified at that time – a total of six pollen sampling sites, all in upland contexts, only one of which she considered relevant for the later part of the period (Dark 2000, 165). Dark's work indicates a varied picture of vegetation change in Wales at the end of the Romano-British period, with mixed evidence for clearance activity, woodland regeneration and continuity in woodland levels. These changes conform with her tentative conclusions for Britain as a whole, with woodland regeneration at higher altitudes, possibly the result of climatic deterioration leading to the abandonment of areas that were 'already marginal for agriculture' (Dark 2000, 153). Despite a scarcity of pollen sampling sites to confirm these conclusions, their validity is supported by the similar conclusions drawn by Rippon *et al.* (2013, 2015) who drew on a much larger dataset. In broad terms, Rippon *et al.* (2015) identified increasing woodland percentages throughout the early medieval period and a decrease in arable land from the Roman to early medieval period. The current study has undertaken an updated review of suitable pollen studies covering the early medieval period in Wales and provides an analysis of changes in their environmental record.

Methodology

Potentially relevant studies were identified through a review of grey literature and published sources, the majority identified in Astrid Caseldine's seminal *Environmental Archaeology in Wales* (1990), the *Radiocarbon Dates from Great Britain and Ireland* (CBA 2000), and the *Wales and Borders Radiocarbon Database* (Burrow and Williams 2010).

The original radiocarbon dates from each sampling site were re-calibrated using the IntCal13 (Reimer *et al.* 2013) calibration curve with Clam 2.2 (Blaauw 2010). The pollen data from these studies were subsequently examined in association with revised age-depth models, to assess their viability in contributing to relevant environmental data relating to the early medieval period. Sites without horizons directly dated to the early medieval period were not discounted out of hand if they contained radiometric dates either side of the early medieval period and demonstrated constant accumulation rates. In fact, given the wide date range of calibrated radiocarbon during some intervals in the early medieval period, radiocarbon dates outside the period of interest in a number of cases were considered to be more reliable for the construction of depth models.

In addition to a relevant chronological range, sampling sites selected for the current paper required a sufficiently high pollen sample frequency to provide detailed examination of environmental changes. Unfortunately, however, many palaeoenvironmental studies do not focus on the historical period and their sampling frequencies are often very low, sometimes limited to single samples for the entirety of the early medieval period. Whilst these low frequency samples showed interesting environmental characteristics for a given time, they often missed key episodes of environmental change seen elsewhere across Wales and could not, therefore, be used in direct comparison with other sites. Where sampling frequencies and dating evidence were of sufficient quality for only parts of a core, those sections have been included within the current analysis.

Results

The literature review identified a total of 38 relevant sampling sites, though not all sites contained suitable data for the entirety of the early medieval period (Table 10.1, Fig. 10.1). These were all located in peat bogs and lake sediments – such contexts provide excellent conditions for pollen preservation, often have sequential sealed deposits and contain organic material suitable for radiocarbon dating. Pollen studies on archaeological sites were also examined, but were found to have limited capacity to examine changes in the environment over time. For example, pollen analysis has been undertaken at the early medieval sites of Dinas Emrys (Carn) (Seddon 1961), Rhuddlan (Flints) (Tomlinson 1987), and Arddleen (Mont) (Grant and Shimwell 2004), but inclusion within the current study was precluded by limitations in datasets – lack of time-depth at Rhuddlan, preservation bias of the pollen assemblages at Arddleen, and poor dating clarity at Dinas Emrys.

A similar dataset to those used by the current study is identified by Rippon *et al.* (2015) in their *Fields of Britannia* study. Their conclusions relating to the Welsh lowlands were limited by low numbers of sampling sites, but their conclusions for upland Wales, that woodland levels increase with almost no variability in arable levels throughout the period, do not match those of the current study (especially for the period covering *c.* 600–800 AD, discussed below). This difference is likely to derive from the methodological differences between the two studies. There are slight differences in geographical coverage,

TABLE 10.1. Palynological studies with detailed, well dated early medieval environmental sequences.

Site ID	Site Name	Reference
1	Migneint 1	Blackford 1990
2	Llyn Goddionduon	Bloemendal 1982
3	Llyn Geirionydd	Bloemendal 1982; Snowball and Thompson 1992
4	Cors Gyfelog – peripheral	Botterill 1988
5	Cas Troggy, Wentwood	Brown 2010, 2013
6	Llyn Morwynion	Caseldine *et al.* 2001
7	Erglodd Trench 5	Caseldine *et al.* 2012
8	Erglodd Trench 6	Caseldine *et al.* 2012
9	Moel y Gerddi	Chambers and Price 1988
10	Brecon Beacons	Chambers 1982
11	Cefn Ffordd	Chambers 1982
12	Cefn Gwernffrwd A	Chambers 1983
13	Cefn Gwernffrwd B	Chambers 1983
14	Drygarn Fawr	Chambers *et al.* 2007
15	Afon Dwy	Davies 2015
16	Coed Bryn Bras 1	Davies 2015
17	Coed Bryn Bras 2	Davies 2015
18	Merddwr y Graig	Davies 2015
19	Ty Cerrig 1	Davies 2015
20	Llyn Tegid 1	Davies 2015
21	Llyn Padarn	Elner *et al.* 1980
22	Moel Llys y Coed	Grant 2009
23	Rhos Goch Common	Hughes *et al.* 2007
24	Crymlyn Bog	Hughes *et al.* 2002
25	Bryn y Castell 2	Mighal and Chambers 1995
26	Borth Bog	Mighall, unpublished
27	Tregaron – West Bog	Morriss 2001
28	Tregaron – Southeast bog	Morriss 2001
29	Waun Fach South	Price and Moore 1984
30	Waun-Fignen-Felen (B46.5N)	Smith and Cloutman 1988
31	Waun-Fignen-Felen (D7E)	Smith and Cloutman 1988
32	Waun-Fignen-Felen (E13N)	Smith and Cloutman 1988
33	Tregaron	Turner 1964
34	Melynllyn	Walker 1979
35	Llyn Cororion	Watkins *et al.* 2007
36	Aber Valley 8.1	Woodbridge *et al.* 2012
37	Aber Valley 9.1	Woodbridge *et al.* 2012
38	Aber Valley 10.1	Woodbridge *et al.* 2012

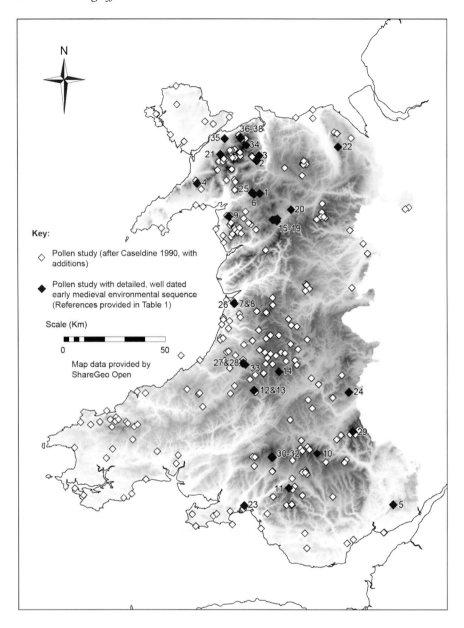

FIGURE 10.1. Distribution map of pollen studies with detailed, well dated early medieval environmental sequences.

period coverage classification, as well as some of the sampling sites examined, but there are also differences in how the data was analysed and quantified. Rippon *et al.* (2015) calculated the total percentages of pollen taxa indicative of woodland, arable, improved and unimproved pasture, which may be problematic when comparing sites with varying pollen catchments on an equal basis. For example, a large increase in woodland pollen types on a site with a largely local pollen catchment may skew the results for a given region if all other sites show either no change or reduced woodland pollen percentages. In such a scenario, a sampling site with a largely regional pollen catchment showing a slight reduction in woodland pollen taxa may be more representative of actual environmental changes for that period, but would be masked when calculating the total change in woodland percentages in comparison with a site with more dramatic changes occurring on a local scale. In an attempt to avoid such potential problems, the current study presents the results as distribution maps showing the location and nature of habitat changes rather than graphs showing the total percentage difference of pollen taxa indicative of habitat types (Figs 10.2–10.4). While it is acknowledged that this method of presenting the data does not account for potential misrepresentation based on pollen catchment types, the overall results should not be excessively skewed based on changes in land use local to individual sites.

A re-assessment has been undertaken of the relevant pollen studies identified by the literature review, looking in specific detail at proportions of pollen taxa indicative of woodland, pastoral, and arable land use. The assessment of relevant habitat types and land use indicators is based on the observations of Behre (1981), Turner (1964), Clapham *et al.* (1987), Grime *et al.* (2007), and Stace (2010). It should be noted that where distribution maps show that no arable indicators are present, this reflects an absence of both cereal-type pollen and other arable weeds (*e.g. Chenopodiaceae* – Goosefoot family, *Achillea*-type – Yarrow, *Plantago major/ media* – hoary/broadleaf plantain). In some instances, the absence of cereal-type pollen reflects the fact that the original author did not differentiate between wild grass-type pollen and cereal-type pollen. However, the absence of arable weeds in association with cereal-type pollen should always be interpreted with caution, since some wild grass pollen types have similar dimensions to cultivated variants (*e.g. Glyceria* – sweet-grass – a wetland grass species – *cf.* Andersen 1978).

There may, however, be geographical biases to these results that have led to an under-representation of arable activity across Wales. The majority of sites are located within upland contexts (Fig. 10.1), corresponding with the distribution of peat deposits traditionally used in palaeoenvironmental research. Elsewhere in Britain, developer-funded and research-driven projects provide an increased proportion of lowland pollen studies (Rippon *et al.* 2015, 57), but this is not the case in Wales. Although there are also some lower-lying lake sediment studies, as well as lower-lying peat sites, these are comparatively few in number and are lacking from the areas of the country more suitable for arable activities, for example, Anglesey, south-east and south-west Wales. The lack of any pollen studies covering the medieval period from Anglesey is especially disappointing given the extensive arable lands that Gerald of Wales notes (Thorpe 1978, 230). The lack of sampling sites from lower-lying areas of south Wales may also hide patterns relating to Roman influences in those areas. This unrepresentative distribution may, however, be addressed in the near future by the *Manifestations of Empire* project (Davies *et al.* 2018), which aims to examine land use and cultural transformations in south-east Wales during the late Roman and early medieval periods through detailed pollen analysis of multiple sampling sites from core areas of settlement.

In general terms, there is evidence for both arable and pastoral farming activities at the majority of sampling sites examined by this study. Research undertaken in Penllyn, north Wales, examining multiple coring sites from the upland to lowland zones, suggests spatially distinct zones for farming practices during the early medieval period (Davies 2015). The cores from lowland sampling sites in Penllyn had higher percentages of cereal-type pollen and other arable indicators than upland cores, whilst the upland cores had a higher proportion of pastoral indicators. Microcharcoal evidence, present from *c.* 2000 BC to *c.* 1300 AD, also suggests the control of heathland in the uplands of Penllyn by burning, a practice that maintains pasture. These spatial differences in pollen distribution are what one would expect with the transhumance practices described in Welsh law texts (*cf.* Jenkins 1986 and Roberts, Hooke, Comeau this volume) and possibly also by Gildas (Higham 1991, 369–370). Other studies in Wales have also been undertaken in close proximity to one another, but have not crossed between landscape zones in a similar manner. Spatial patterns can, however, be discerned in pollen trends seen across Wales for the early medieval period. Three distinct periods of development can be identified that are consistent across the country.

These three periods range from:

1. *c.* 400–600 AD (the immediate post-Roman period)
2. *c.* 600–800 AD
3. *c.* 800–1050 AD

The palynological changes observed in these three periods are discussed below. The reader should be reminded, however, that the timing of some changes may be affected slightly by known variations in the radiocarbon calibration curves. For example, some of the developments attributed to the fifth century may actually have occurred in the late fourth century. In most cases, however, any variance caused by radiocarbon calibration ranges only affects the dating of one pollen sample at each site. This study also examined the environmental conditions for each sub-period as a whole in comparison with the preceding centuries. Therefore, although the onset of some environmental changes may be questionable, the broad changes observed for each sub-period should reflect an accurate assessment of the pollen record for that time frame.

c. 400–600 AD

In the immediate centuries following the Romano-British period in Wales, numerous sampling sites exhibit increased heath and woodland pollen, possibly indicative of the abandonment of settlements or reduction in areas managed for farming practices. However, there are also a small number of sites that show no change in the percentage of woodland or heath pollen, whilst in north Wales there are also instances of decreased woodland percentages, suggesting possible woodland clearance. Wetland indicators for this time, for the most part, indicate an increase in wetland habitats: only six sampling sites across Wales suggest a decrease in wetland habitat and five show no change in wetland pollen or spore taxa. Arable and pastoral indicators for this time almost uniformly exhibit either a decrease or no perceptible change.

As noted earlier, traditional interpretations of environmental change at the start of the early medieval period propose that climate deterioration caused the abandonment of upland and coastal wetland areas, regarded as 'marginal' for agriculture (Dark 2000, 153). The wetland indicators for the first two centuries of the early medieval period conform to the model for climatic deterioration, as demonstrated by numerous sites with increased wetland pollen taxa (Fig. 10.2a), but the pattern of woodland and heathland regeneration does not support specific abandonment of 'marginal' upland areas. Leaving aside the question of whether early medieval people regarded upland and coastal wetland areas as 'marginal' (*cf.* Brown *et al.* 1998), the heath and woodland pollen evidence from Wales suggests that upland and lowland areas were abandoned in equal measure. Also, the locations of sites showing woodland decline in north Wales at this time raise the possibility that deforestation indicates increased settlement in both upland and lowland settings. It is noteworthy that this evidence for deforestation is limited to north-west Wales, an area associated with early medieval references to migration from Ireland and northern Britain (Charles Edwards 2013, 190; Edwards 2013, 7). Whilst it is not advocated that the pollen trend substantiates these shadowy and uncertain events, the evidence for clearance activity supports the possibility of an increased population in north-west Wales that may correlate with migration from Ireland or from elsewhere in Britain. Alternative explanations, like an attempt to increase farming production to counter the possible effects of climatic downturn may also be possible, though this is not reflected in the levels of pastoral or arable indicators. It should also be noted, however, that there are far more pollen sampling sites here with early medieval environmental sequences than in any other parts of the country. It is possible that similar patterns of deforestation might be observed elsewhere in Wales with better sampling site distribution.

Despite these suggestions of increased colonisation of woodland areas in north Wales, the anthropogenic indicators of pastoral and arable activities suggest widespread decline in the farming economy (Fig. 10.2b). Three sampling sites are, however, exceptions to this. Two of them, Llyn Tegid (Mer) (Davies 2015) and Borth Bog (Cards) (Mighall n.d.) show an increased percentage of arable indicators, but this increase is caused by a spike in cereal-type pollen within single samples in each case, rather than a sustained increase throughout the period. The third site with increased farming indicators is the peripheral core collected from Cors Gyfelog (Carn), at the east end of the Lleyn peninsula (*cf.* Botterill 1988). At Cors Gyfelog, an increase in *Plantago lanceolata* pollen (Ribwort plantain – a typical pastoral indicator – Behre 1981) is observed which, although corresponding with slight reduction in woodland taxa, might not be directly related to an increase in pollen catchment. The level of the increase in

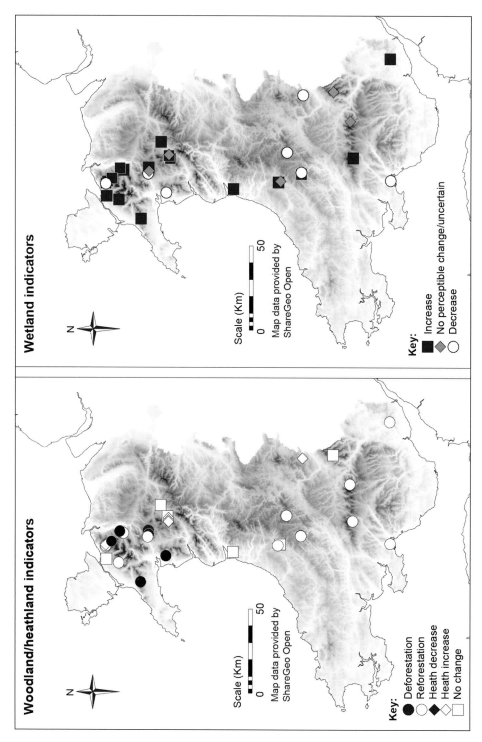

FIGURE 10.2a. Palynological changes in Wales – *c.* 400–600 AD (woodland and wetland).

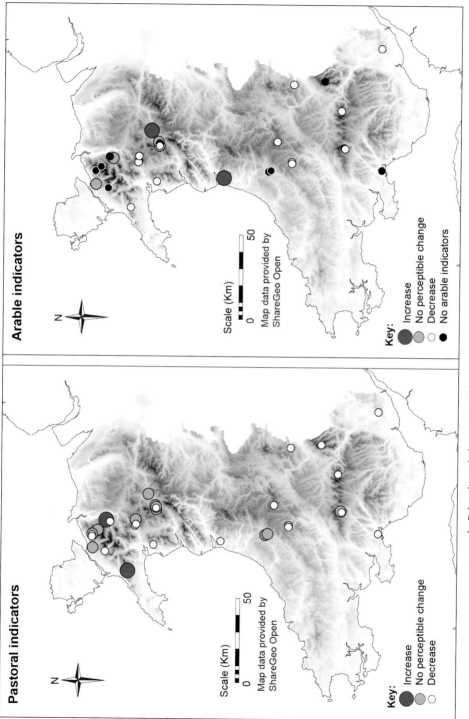

FIGURE 10.2b. Palynological changes in Wales – *c.* 400–600 AD (pastoral and arable indicators).

Plantago lanceolata appears to be relatively high in proportion to the increase in other open habitat taxa, and may therefore represent a genuine increase in pastoral activities. This apparent increase in pastoral activity may be related to the potentially high density of settlement in the neighbouring area, which has several possible early medieval settlement sites (Cefn Graeanog II – Mason and Fasham 1988, Cefn Graeanog Quarry – Kenney and Roberts 2008, Graeanog – Kelly 1998 and Pen Llystyn – Hogg 1969).

It is possible that the decline in farming indicators observed in the Welsh pollen record is related to climate change. Evidence of climate deterioration at this time, including increased precipitation and cooler temperatures, has been noted by a number of studies (Rippon 1997; Charman *et al.* 2006; Büntgen *et al.* 2011; Barber *et al.* 2013); this is also supported in the Welsh pollen record by increased pollen taxa indicative of wetland habitats (see above and Fig. 10.2b). Correlations between wetter climate conditions with reduced crop yields and increased livestock mortality in medieval England have been made by Parry (1978, 136–143). With this in mind, the wetter conditions indicated by the pollen record across Wales at this time (Fig. 10.2b) are likely to have severely reduced the growing season and crop yields in many areas. The reduced growing season would also have limited the ability to provide fodder for animals through the winter months, diminishing flocks and reducing indicators of grazing activity within the pollen record.

Whilst the coincidence of a decline in farming indicators with climate change is provocative, it is possible that socio-economic factors associated with the end of Roman administration in Britain may have been more influential on farming intensity. The demise of Roman administrative structures, and with them taxes dependent on the production of increased agricultural surplus, may have been at least as significant for farming in Wales as the deteriorating climate. The extent to which Roman administrative systems continued into the post-Roman period has been the subject of some debate (*cf.* Esmonde Cleary 1989, Dark 1994, White 2007). On face value, the downturn in the farming economy suggested by the pollen data would support arguments championed by Esmonde Cleary (1989) for a rapid end to Roman ways of life. However, if we follow the view expressed by Ken Dark (1994) and Roger White (2007), that taxation, increasingly paid in kind in the late Roman period, survived in Wales beyond the withdrawal of the Roman army from Britain, we must ask how the reduced farming indicators respond to the end of Roman rule. It is after all unlikely that fifth- or sixth-century taxation levels would have been on a similar scale to the Roman period, given differences in scale and complexity between early Welsh kingdoms and the Roman Empire – estimates suggest that Roman peasants paid half their produce in taxation and rent (Esmonde Cleary 1989, 7). Whichever scenario is advocated, however, the pollen evidence in Wales infers a dramatic fall in the farming economy in the fifth and sixth century AD compared to the Romano-British period, suggesting either reduced demand or capacity, or possibly a mixture of the two.

c. 600–800 AD

The pollen record for the seventh and eighth century AD in Wales displays a reversal of the changes observed in the previous two centuries. The majority of pollen sampling sites have either decreased woodland or heath pollen, possibly indicative of increased deforestation for farming or settlement, or no change in woodland and heath levels (Fig. 10.3a). With the exception of the site of Cas Troggy in south-east Wales (*cf.* Brown 2010, 2013), all sampling sites display either an increase or no perceptible change in pastoral and arable pollen indicators (Fig. 10.3b). On the whole, there are higher numbers of sites suggesting decreased wetland habitats, but not significantly higher than sites showing no perceptible change or increased wetland pollen and spore taxa.

European climate evidence reconstructed from tree ring data by Büntgen *et al.* (2011) suggests a more stable climate from around 600 AD that was both wetter and warmer than the preceding century and a half. They also note that this more stable climate marked the onset of medieval prosperity in Europe. However, since Charman *et al.* (2006) have demonstrated regional variability in the effects, persistence, and extent of environmental change attributable to climate fluctuation, it is difficult to assess the applicability of the data of Büntgen *et al.* (2011), especially since the latter study did not include British data. In Wales, Blackford and Chambers' study of peat humification at Migneint (Snowdonia) and the Brecon Beacons had previously proposed that increased peat bog surface wetness in the mid-seventh century AD marked the start of an episode of climatic downturn (Blackford 1990; Blackford and Chambers 1991). This identification of increased surface wetness is not incompatible with the results of Büntgen *et al.* (2011), which recognises increased precipitation. Otherwise, however, the pollen evidence for Wales is rather inconclusive in regard to either climatic improvement or downturn. Whilst marginally increased numbers of sites show reduced wetland habitats, the evidence for an improved climate across the country is not overwhelmingly convincing, and there is no discernible pattern to the distribution of reduced or increased wetland indicators. The evidence for increased arable activity would, however, suggest better growing conditions related to a warmer climate, but could conversely be the result of an expansion of arable activity to compensate for reduced crop yields. It is also possible that the increased arable indicators seen in Wales at this time may be inflated by increased cereal-type pollen, which could include wild grass pollen from wetland habitats (*e.g. Glyceria*). Nevertheless, a genuine increase in arable activity is supported by increased numbers of other arable indicators like *Brassicaceae* (Cabbage family – Llyn Goddionduon, Carns – Bloemendal 1982), *Cannabaceae* (Hop family – Moel y Gerddi, Mer – Chambers and Price 1988), *Chenopodiaceae* (Goosefoot family – Bryn y Castell 2, Mer – Mighall and Chambers 1995; Cefn Gwernffrwd B, Carms – Chambers 1983; Llyn Goddionduon, Carns – Bloaemendal 1982; Tregaron West Bog, Cards – Morriss 2001) and *Leguminosae* (Pea family – Bryn y Castell 2, Mer – Mighall and Chambers 1995).

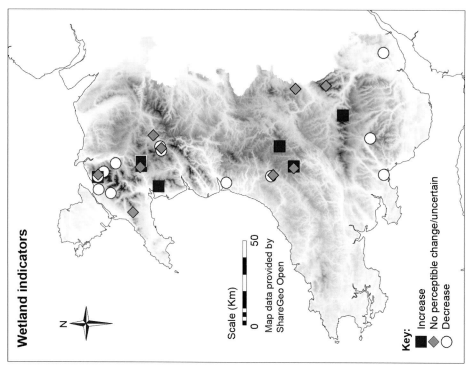

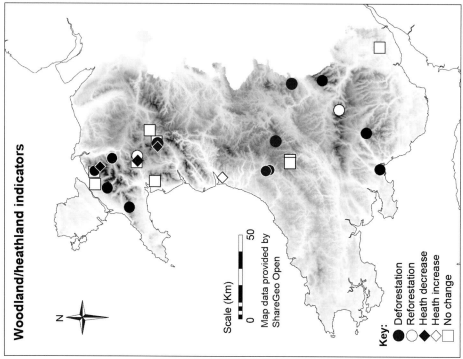

FIGURE 10.3a. Palynological changes in Wales – *c.* 600–800 AD (woodland and wetland).

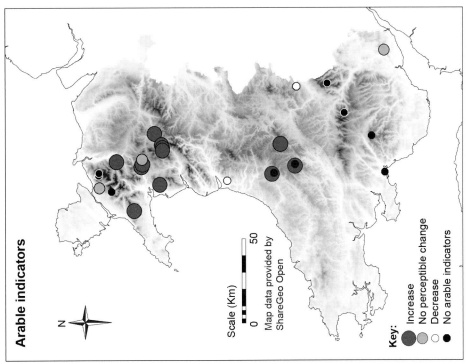

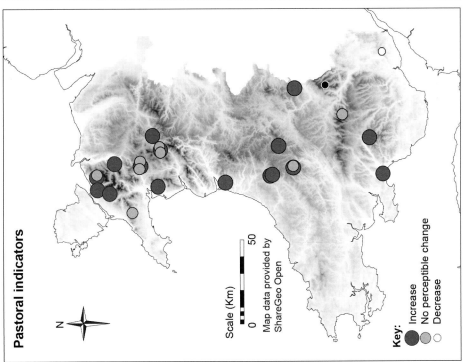

FIGURE 10.3b. Palynological changes in Wales – *c.* 600–800 AD (pastoral and arable indicators).

The evidence for climate change affecting the farming economy in Wales is therefore uncertain for this period. There is however evidence for dramatic socio-political and economic changes that may have influenced land use. A possible shift in settlement patterns is intimated by the disappearance of material culture post-dating the seventh or eighth centuries from high status defended hillfort sites, suggesting widespread abandonment (Seaman 2016, 43), though the picture is complicated by poor preservation of the aceramic material culture of subsequent centuries. At the same time the power of the church appears to have increased substantially, with a growth in church landholdings and evidence of greater ecclesiastical intervention in burial practices reflected in the development of enclosed cemeteries, the latter sometimes associated with cross-inscribed stone monuments (Davies 1978, 13; Petts 2009, 122–9). Wendy Davies' review of charter evidence from south-east Wales, supplemented by Ben Guy's recent identification of the early seventh-century commencement of these charters, shows that the majority of land transfers to the church date to the late seventh or eighth century AD (Davies 1978, 6–13; Guy 2018). It is likely that these changes in settlement, burial practice, and landholding were linked to alterations in land use and environment, and are reflected in transformations in the palynological record of the seventh and eighth centuries AD. The widespread nature of these changes suggests that they may have been as revolutionary and significant, if not more so, as the social transformations following the withdrawal of the Roman Empire from Britain.

Beyond the abandonment of hillfort sites, the exact nature of the changes in settlement in Wales is uncertain as few sites definitively dated to the seventh century AD or later have been identified. One such exception is the recently discovered site of Rhuddgaer (Anglesey), consisting of a group of rectangular buildings and an associated field system of approximately seventh- to eighth-century date (Hopewell and Edwards 2017). This site type is currently unique for Wales but may well be representative of the landscape changes at this time that lead to evidence for increased farming activity in the pollen record.

Contemporary landscape and social transformations have been widely noted elsewhere in neighbouring regions of Britain and across mainland Europe at this time, during what has been referred to as the 'long eighth century', typified by an intensification of farming practices and changes in settlement patterns (Hansen and Wickham 2000). This intensification of farming practices in England is indicated by the recovery of a coulter (a metal blade used in a mouldboard plough) from excavations at the ecclesiastical site of Lyminge (Kent) which suggests the use of mouldboard ploughs here as early as the seventh century AD (Thomas *et al.* 2014). Elsewhere, in Whithorn Priory in south-western Scotland, Hill and Kucharski (1990) have identified linear cultivation ridges dating to the sixth or seventh century AD, which they speculatively attribute to mouldboard ploughing, and associated 'plough pebbles' interpreted as objects 'used to protect the wooden parts of ploughs from erosion' (Hill and Kucharski 1990, 73). It should be noted, however, that Topping (1989) has shown that in the Scottish borders, late prehistoric linear cultivation ridges ('cord rig') could have been formed using an ard or a precursor of the mouldboard plough (Topping 1989, 166). In Wales, although currently no linear cultivation ridges are firmly dated to the early medieval period, archaeobotanical evidence from Melin y Plas (Angl) (Ciaraldi 2012), Newton (Pembs) (Griffiths 2004), and South Hook (Pembs) (Carruthers 2011) has identified arable weeds suggestive of cultivation on damp, heavy soils from features radiocarbon dated from the mid-seventh to early eleventh century AD. Mouldboard ploughs facilitate cultivation of heavy, wetter soils and their possible introduction could account for both the increase in arable indicators and the reduced wetland taxa, when arable land may have replaced formerly inaccessible wetlands. Alternatively, these changes could also be explained by improved climate conditions, possibly augmented by an intensification of existing practices (*e.g.* convertible husbandry – Rippon, Fyfe and Brown 2006; Comeau this volume).

The ecclesiastical context for the plough ridges at Whithorn Priory and also for the plough pebbles identified there and elsewhere led Hill and Kucharski to suggest that the church had a role in the dissemination of ploughing technology (1990, 82). This argument is consistent with the work of other scholars who have highlighted the increased power of the church in both England and Wales during the 'long eighth century' (Davies 1978; Moreland 2000; Petts 2009; Rippon 2010). The consequent impact on the organisation of the contemporary landscape could well account for some of the changes observed in the Welsh pollen and archaeological record. The environmental changes observed in Wales are, therefore, likely to relate to transformations observed on a wider scale over much of mainland Europe at this time.

c. 800–1050 AD

In contrast to the previous two periods, there do not appear to be any uniform environmental changes within the pollen record in Wales at this time (Figures 10.4a and 10.4b). Both woodland clearance and regeneration appear across the country, though there is perhaps a greater degree of woodland clearance rather than regeneration. The majority of pollen studies display no significant changes in wetland indicators, with fluctuations – both increases and decreases – at a smaller number of sites. Arable and pastoral indicators also fluctuate across the country, with instances of reduced and increased arable indicators occurring in similar numbers. Pastoral indicators also show a mixture of increase and decrease, though increased or continued high levels of pastoral indicators are present at a much higher number of sites. Only five sites show decreasing pastoral indicators, four of which may be related to changing pollen catchment conditions rather than farming activity as these sites also show evidence of woodland regeneration.

Given the scarcity of pollen sampling sites in south Wales, it is difficult to see any specific geographical trends in the pollen record for sites in that region.

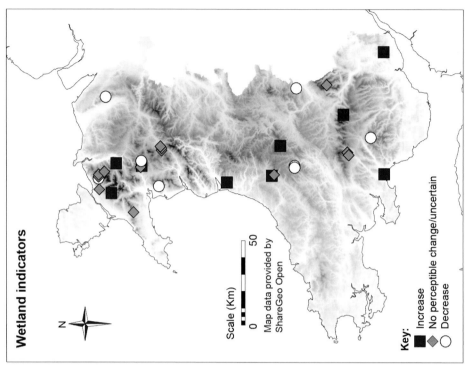

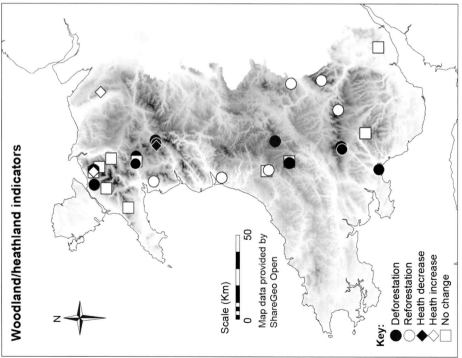

FIGURE 10.4a. Palynological changes in Wales – *c.* 800–1050 AD (woodland and wetland).

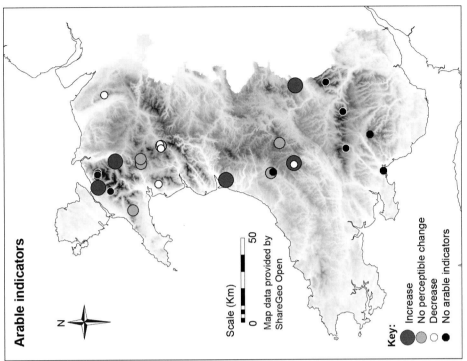

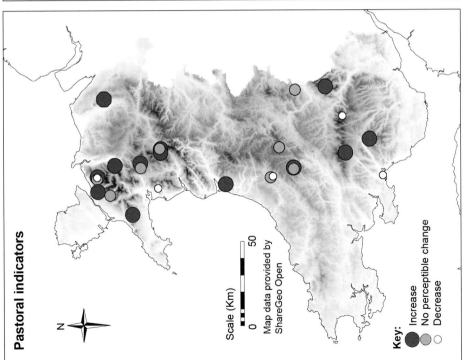

FIGURE 10.4b. Palynological changes in Wales – *c.* 800–1050 AD (pastoral and arable indicators).

Some inferences can however be made from evidence from north Wales where there is a higher concentration of pollen studies. With the exception of two sampling sites where woodland regeneration may account for decreased pastoral indicators, all other sites display either continued high percentages or an increase in pastoral pollen indicators across north Wales. Towards the southern and eastern outskirts of the medieval kingdom of Gwynedd, at sampling sites such as Moel Llys y Coed (Grant 2009), Merddwr y Graig and Tŷ Cerrig (Davies 2015), there is a decrease in arable indicators in the pollen record, whilst sampling sites further north-west, towards the inner core of the kingdom, either show no change or an increase in arable indicators. Although there are not sufficient relevant sampling sites to positively confirm spatial patterns in the pollen record, the manner whereby arable farming indicators respect the boundary of the kingdom of Gwynedd may reflect changes or even deliberate intervention in farming practices during the ninth and tenth centuries AD. This could be a response to the documented increase in raiding and warfare, both between Gwynedd and other Welsh kingdoms and between Gwynedd and foreign powers. In the ninth and tenth centuries AD it is likely that the border areas of the kingdom of Gwynedd became subject to increased conflict with other Welsh kingdoms. Inter-kingdom dispute, warfare, and raiding are common before this, but Wendy Davies proposes that they intensify during the tenth century AD (Davies 1990, 45, 85; 2002, 163). During the power struggles of the mid-ninth century onward, the kingdom of Gwynedd under Rhodri Mawr and his descendants expanded and contracted from one generation to the next, with recorded battles focusing on border locations. Documentary and archaeological evidence also notes an increased threat from Hiberno-Scandinavians and Anglo-Saxon kingdoms during the ninth and tenth centuries AD, notably the destruction of Llan-gors crannog, Brycheiniog, in 916 AD by the army of Aethelflaed (Campbell and Lane 1989, 678–9), the establishing of the Anglo-Saxon burgh of *Cledemutha* at Rhuddlan in 921 AD (Manley 1987), and Viking incursions into Wales that include the killing of Cyngen of Powys in 852 AD (Redknap 2000, 29).

This background of conflict contributes to a twofold explanation for the spatial variation in both arable and pastoral indicators in Gwynedd at this time. Away from the core of the kingdom, where increased arable activity is inferred from the pollen record, the rulers of Gwynedd may have required a reliable food supply less susceptible to devastation by raiding activities, which could be moved at times of need to more secure locations. It is also possible that the pattern observed in the pollen record for Gwynedd reflects the impact of a tribute system of the kind described by Charles-Edwards (1989). Within a kingdom, tribute paid to a ruler may have been more varied in nature towards its core, where regular visits by the king are expected as part of the royal circuit. Towards the outskirts of that kingdom, however, where royal visits may have been infrequent, perishable arable goods could not be efficiently transported as tribute. Tribute from such areas may therefore have been extracted as livestock

(Charles-Edwards 1989, 28–33). Furthermore, at a time when tribute, involving large numbers of cattle, seems to have been increasingly demanded from kingdoms as an expression of a clientship relationship (typically from Welsh kingdoms by Anglo-Saxon kings: Davies 1990, 73–7), an increased demand for livestock may have stimulated pastoral activity. The deforestation observed here in upland areas such as Migneint (Blackford 1990), Bryn y Castell (Mighall and Chambers 1995) and Cwm Lliw (Davies 2015) may reflect the creation of specialist upland pastures, similar to the Snowdonian vaccaries that supplied cattle to Llywelyn ap Gruffudd in the thirteenth century (*cf.* Smith 2014, 232–3).

A further interpretation is also possible, given the observation that evidence for deforestation is restricted to lower-lying sampling sites in mid- and north Wales. It is therefore possible that deforestation in upland areas of north Wales may represent settlement relocation to sites that are more defensible. This may also be reflected in the archaeological record of this time by a move towards more defensive settlement types, demonstrated in the ninth century AD by the rebuilding of the boundary of the settlement at Llanbedrgoch (Angl) in stone (Redknap 2007, 62), and by the palisaded crannog at Llan-gors, established *c.* 890 AD (Redknap and Lane 1999).

It is also possible that the strategic control of farming produce is symptomatic of wider administrative systems, put in place by the kingdom of Gwynedd at this time. Jones (1998) has argued that the subdivision of Wales into *cantrefi* dates to this period, as part of an attempt by either Rhodri Mawr, or one of his descendants, to formulate a coherent administrative framework for the collection of tribute from territories incorporated into the expanding political unit of Gwynedd. Given the uneven distribution of pollen sampling sites across the country, it is not possible to see if similar processes occurred elsewhere across Wales, and how they might relate to the known territorial boundaries of the ninth and tenth centuries AD. In the event of future pollen studies having suitably dated environmental sequences elsewhere in Wales, it might be possible to see if spatial differences in farming practices can be discerned within the other kingdoms of early medieval Wales.

Conclusion

Despite some of the biases seen in the pollen record for Wales (especially in the geographical distribution of suitable sampling sites), the number of studies with relevant data relating to the early medieval period now greatly outnumber the contemporary settlement sites identified through archaeological investigation. Their examination enables a broad understanding of environmental change throughout the period and identifies relationships to cultural changes observed in the limited archaeological and documentary record. The fluctuations observed in the farming economy provide material for wider debates relating to the cessation of Roman rule in Britain, the 'long eighth century' and interaction between the emergent kingdoms of the early medieval period. The limitations of this dataset should, however, be noted, particularly the sparse distribution of sampling sites in some areas of the country. Some of the interpretations should therefore be considered as tentative, and revised as additional information emerges in future.

References

Andersen, S. T. (1979) Identification of Wild Grass and Cereal Pollen. *Danmarks Geologiske Undersoegelse Aarbog 1979*, 69–92.

Barber, K., Brown, A., Langdon, P. and Hughes, P. (2013) Comparing and Cross-validating Lake and Bog Palaeoclimatic Records: a review and a new 5,000 year chironomid-inferred temperature record from northern England. *Journal of Paleolimnology* 49(3), 497–512.

Behre, K. (1981) The Interpretation of Anthropogenic Indicators in Pollen Diagrams. *Pollen et Spores* 23(2), 225–245.

Blaauw, M. (2010) Methods and Code for 'Classical' Age-modelling of Radiocarbon Sequences. *Quaternary Geochronology* 5, 512–8.

Blackford, J. (1990) *Blanket mires and climatic change; a palaeoecological study based on peat humification and microfossil analyses.* Unpublished PhD thesis, University of Keele.

Blackford, J. J. and Chambers F. M. (1991) Proxy Records of Climate from Blanket Mires: evidence for a Dark Age (1400 BP) climatic deterioration in the British Isles. *The Holocene* 1, 63–7.

Bloemendal, J. (1982) *The quantification of rates of total sediment influx to Llyn Goddionduon, Gwynedd.* Unpublished PhD thesis, University of Liverpool.

Botterill, E. M. (1988) *A palaeoecological study of Cors Gyfelog and Tre'r Gof: Lowland Mires in North West Wales.* Unpublished PhD thesis, University of Keele.

Brown, A. (2010) Pollen Analysis and Planted Ancient Woodland Restoration Strategies: a case study from the Wentwood, southeast Wales, UK. *Vegetation History and Archaeobotany* 19, 79–90.

Brown, A. (2013) From Iron Age to Early Medieval: Detecting the Ecological Impact of the Romans on the Landscape of South-East Wales. *Britannia* 44, 4–11.

Brown, A. G., Crane, S., O'Sullivan, D., Walsh, K. and Young, R. (1998) Marginality, multiple estates and environmental change: the case of Lindisfarne. In C. M. Mills and G. Coles (eds) *Life on the Edge: human settlement and marginality.* Oxford, Oxbow Books, 139–148.

Büntgen, U., Tegel, W., Nicolussi, K., McCormick, M., Frank, D., Trouet, V., Kaplan, J. O., Herzig, F., Heussner, K. U., Wanner, H. and Luterbacher, J. (2011) 2500 Years of European Climate Variability and Human Susceptibility. *Science* 331 (6017), 578–582.

Burrow, S. and Williams, S. (2010) *Wales and Borders Radiocarbon Database.* Cardiff, National Museums and Galleries of Wales. (Available by request: accessed 22.03.13)

Campbell, E. and Lane A. (1989) Llangorse: a 10th Century Royal Crannog in Wales. *Antiquity* 63, 675–681.

Carruthers, W. (2011) Charred plant remains. In P. Crane and K. Murphy, An Early Medieval Settlement, Iron Smelting Site and Crop-processing Complex at South Hook, Herbrandston, Pembrokeshire. *Archaeologia Cambrensis* 159, 163–181.

Caseldine, A. (1990) *Environmental Archaeology in Wales.* Lampeter, St David's University College, University of Wales.

Caseldine, A., Griffiths, C., and Crowther, J. (2012) Palaeoenvironmental investigations. In N. Page, G. Hughes, R. Jones and K. Murphy, Excavations at Erglodd, Llangynfelyn, Ceredigion: prehistoric/Roman lead smelting site and medieval trackway. *Archaeologia Cambrensis* 161, 313–334.

Caseldine, A., Smith, G. and Griffiths, C. (2001) Vegetation History and Upland Settlement at Llyn Morwynion, Ffestiniog, Meirionnydd. *Archaeology in Wales* 41, 21–33.

CBA (2000) *Archaeological Site Index to Radiocarbon Dates from Great Britain and Ireland* (updated 2012). York, Council for British Archaeology (accessed 11.05.13)

Chambers, F. M. (1982) Two Radiocarbon-Dated Pollen Diagrams from High-Altitude Blanket Peats in South Wales. *Journal of Ecology* 70(2), 445–459.

Chambers, F. M. (1983) The Palaeoecological setting of Cefn Gwernffrwd – a prehistoric complex in mid-Wales. *Proceedings of the Prehistoric Society* 49, 303–316.

Chambers, F. M. and Price, S. M. (1988) The Environmental Setting of Erw-wen and Moel y Gerddi: Prehistoric Enclosures in Upland Ardudwy, North Wales. *Proceedings of the Prehistoric Society* 54, 93–100.

Chambers, F. M., Moquoy, D., Cloutman, E. W., Daniell, J. R. G., and Jones, P. S. (2007) Recent Vegetation History of Drygarn Fawr (Elenydd SSSI), Cambrian Mountains, Wales: implications for conservation management of degraded blanket mires. *Biodiversity and Conservation* 16(10), 2821–2846.

Charles-Edwards, T. M. (1989) Early Medieval Kingships in the British Isles. In S. Bassett (ed.) *The Origins of the Anglo-Saxon Kingdoms.* Leicester, Leicester University Press

Charles-Edwards, T. M. (2013) *Wales and the Britons 350–1064.* Oxford, Oxford University Press.

Charman, D. J., Blundell, A., Chiverrell, R., Hendon, D. and Langdon, P. G. (2006) Compilation of Non-annually Resolved Holocene Proxy Climate Records: stacked Holocene peatland palaeo-water table reconstructions from northern Britain. *Quaternary Science Reviews* 25, 336–350.

Ciaraldi, M. (2012) Charred plan remains. In R. Cutler, A. Davidson and G. Hughes (eds) *A Corridor Through Time: The Archaeology of the A55 Anglesey Road Scheme.* Oxford, Oxbow Books, 222–242.

Clapham, A., Tutin, T. and Moore, D. (1987) *Flora of the British Isles. 3rd edition.* Cambridge, Cambridge University Press.

Dark, K. R. (1994) *Civitas to Kingdom: British Political Continuity 300–800.* Leicester, Leicester University Press.

Dark, P. (2000) *The Environment of Britain in the First Millennium AD.* London, Duckworth.

Davies, T. (2015) *Early Medieval Llyn Tegid: An environmental landscape study.* Unpublished PhD thesis, University of Sheffield.

Davies, T., Rippon, S., and Seaman A. (2018) Manifestations of Empire: palaeoenvironmental analysis and the end of Roman Britain. *Medieval Settlement Research* 33, 92–3.

Davies, W. (1978) Land and Power in Early Medieval Wales. *The Past and Present Society* 81, 3–23.

Davies, W. (1982) *Wales in the Early Middle Ages.* London, Leicester University Press.

Davies, W. (1990) *Patterns of Power in Early Wales.* Oxford, Clarendon Press.

Davies, W. (2002) Adding insult to injury. In W. Davies and P. Fouracre (eds) *Property and Power in the Early Middle Ages.* Cambridge, Cambridge University Press, 137–164.

Edwards, N. (2013) *A Corpus of Early Medieval Inscribed Stones and Stone Sculpture in Wales. Volume III: North Wales.* Cardiff, University of Wales Press.

Elner, J. K., Happey-Wood, C. M. and Wood, D. G. E. (1980) The History of Two Linked but Contrasting Lakes in North Wales from a Study of Pollen, Diatoms and Chemistry in Sediment Cores. *The Journal of Ecology* 68, 95–121.

Esmonde-Cleary, A. S. (1989) *The Ending of Roman Britain.* London, Routledge.

Fyfe, R. and Rippon, S., (2004) A landscape in transition? Palaeoenvironmental evidence for the end of the 'Romano-British' period in South West England. In R. Collins and J. Gerrard (eds) *Debating Late Antiquity in Britain AD 300–700.* BAR British Series 365. Oxford, British Archaeological Reports, 33–42.

Grant, F. (2009) *Analysis of a peat core from the Clwydian Hills, North Wales.* Report No. 209. Aberystwyth, Royal Commission on the Ancient and Historical Monuments of Wales (unpublished report).

Grant, F. and Shimwell, D. (2004) Plant remains. In I. Grant, The excavation of a double-ditched enclosure at Arddleen, Powys, 2002–3. *The Montgomeryshire Collections* 92, 21–4.

Griffiths, C. (2004) Macrofossils. In P. Crane, Excavations at Newton, Llandstadwell, Pembrokeshire. *Archaeology in Wales* 44, 3–32.

Grime, J. P., Hodgson, J. G. and Hunt, R. (2007) *Comparative Plant Ecology: a functional approach to common British species.* 2nd edition. Colvend, Castlepoint Press.

Guy, B. (2018) The *Life* of St Dyfrig and the Lost Charters of Moccas (Mochros), Herefordshire. *Cambrian Medieval Celtic Studies* 75, 1–37.

Hansen, I. L. and Wickham, C. (eds) (2000) *The Long Eighth Century: Production, Distribution and Demand.* Leiden, Brill.

Higham, N. J. (1991) Old Light on the Dark Age Landscape: the description of Britain in the De Exidio Britanniae of Gildas. *Journal of Historical Geography* 17(4), 363–372.

Hill, P. and Kucharski, K. (1990) Early Medieval Ploughing at Whithorn and the Chronology of Plough Pebbles. *Transactions of the Dumfrieshire and Galloway Natural History and Antiquaries Society* 65, 73–83.

Hogg, A. H. A. (1969) Pen Llystyn: A Roman fort and other remains. *Archaeological Journal* 125, 101–191.

Hopewell, D. and Edwards, N. (2017) Early Medieval Settlement and Field Systems at Rhuddgaer, Anglesey. *Archaeologia Cambrensis* 166, 213–242.

Hughes, P. D. M., and Dumayne-Peaty, L. (2002) Testing Theories of Mire Development Using Multiple Successions at Crymlyn Bog, West Glamorgan, South Wales, UK. *Journal of Ecology* 90, 456–471.

Hughes, P. D. M., Lomas-Clarke, S. H., Schulz, J. and Jones, P. (2007) The Declining Quality of Late-Holocene Ombrotrophic Communities and the Loss of Sphagnum Austinii (Sull. ex Aust.) on Raised Bogs in Wales. *The Holocene* 17(5), 613–625.

Jenkins, D. (ed.) (1986) *Hywel Dda, The Law.* Llandysul, Gomer Press.

Jones, R. (1998) The Formation of the Cantref and the Commote in Medieval Gwynedd. *Studia Celtica* 32, 169–177.

Kelly, R. (1998) The excavation of an enclosed hut group at Graeanog, Clynog, Gwynedd 1985, 1987, 1988. In P. J. Fasham, R. S. Kelly, M. A. Mason and R. B. White (eds) *The Graeanog Ridge, Evolution of a Farming Landscape and its Settlements in North-West Wales. Cambrian Archaeological Monographs* 6. Cardiff, Cambrian Archaeological Association, 113–157.

Kenney, J. and Roberts, J. (2008) Cefn Graianog Quarry. *Archaeology in Wales* 48, 134.

Manley, J. (1987) Cledemutha: A Late Saxon Burh in North Wales. *Medieval Archaeology* 31, 13–46.

Mason, M. A. and Fasham, P. J. (1988) The report on R. B. White's excavations at Cefn Greanog II, 1977–9. In P. J. Fasham, R. S. Kelly, M. A. Mason and R. B. White (eds) *The Graeanog Ridge: The evolution of a farming landscape and its settlement in north-west Wales. Cambrian Archaeological Monographs 6.* Cardiff, Cambrian Archaeological Association, 2–112.

Mighall, T. (n.d.) *Pollen Analysis at Borth Bog.* Unpublished report.

Mighall, T. M. and Chambers, F. M. (1995) Holocene Vegetation History and Human Impact at Bryn y Castell, Snowdonia, North Wales. *New Phytologist* 130(2), 299–321.

Moreland, J. (2000) The significance of production in eighth-century England. In I. L. Hansen and C. Wickham (eds) *The Long Eighth Century: Production, Distribution and Demand,* 69–104. Leiden, Brill.

Morriss, S. H. M. (2001) *Recent human impact and land use change in Britain and Ireland: a pollen analytical and geochemical study.* Unpublished PhD thesis, University of Southampton.

Parry, M. L. (1978) *Climate Change, Agriculture and Settlement.* Folkestone, Dawson.

Petts, D. (2009) *The Early Medieval Church in Wales.* Stroud, The History Press.

Price, M. D. R. and Moore, P. D. (1984) Pollen Dispersion in the Hills of Wales: a pollen shed hypothesis. *Pollen et Spores* 26, 127–136.

Redknap, M. (2000) *Vikings in Wales: An Archaeological Quest.* Cardiff, National Museums and Galleries of Wales.

Redknap, M. (2007) Llanbedrgoch: An early medieval settlement and its significance. *Transactions of the Anglesey Antiquarian Society and Field Club* 47, 53–72.

Redknap, M. and Lane, A. (1999) The Archaeological Importance of Llangorse Lake: an environmental perspective. *Aquatic Conservation: Marine and Freshwater Ecosystems* 9, 377–390.

Reimer, P. J., Bard, E., Bayliss, A., Beck, J. W., Blackwell, P. G., Ramsey, C. B., Buck, C. E., Cheng, H., Edwards, R. L., Friedrich, M. and Grootes, P. M. (2013) IntCal13 and Marine13 Radiocarbon Age Calibration Curves 0–50,000 years cal BP. *Radiocarbon* 55(4), 1869–1887.

Rippon, S. (1997) *The Severn Estuary. Landscape Evolution and Wetland Reclamation.* London, Leicester University Press.

Rippon, S. (2010) Landscape change during the long eighth century in southern England. In N. Higham and M. Ryan (eds) *Landscape Archaeology of Anglo-Saxon England.* Woodbridge, Boydell Press, 39–64.

Rippon, S., Fyfe, R. and Brown, A. (2006) Beyond Villages and Open Fields: the origins and development of a historic landscape characterised by dispersed settlement in South-West England. *Medieval Archaeology* 50, 31–70.

Rippon, S., Smart, C. and Pears, B. (2015) *The Fields of Britannia.* Oxford, Oxford University Press.

Rippon, S., Smart, C., Pears, B. and Fleming, F. (2013) The Fields of Britannia: Continuity and Discontinuity in the Pays and Regions of Roman Britain. *Landscapes* 14(1), 33–53.

Seaman, A. (2016) Defended Settlement in Early Medieval Wales: Problems of Presence, Absence and Interpretation. In N. Christie and H. Herold (eds) *Fortified Settlements in Early Medieval Europe: Defended Communities of the 8th–10th Centuries,* 37–50. Oxford, Oxbow Books.

Seddon, B. (1961) Report on the Organic Deposits in the Pool at Dinas Emrys. In H. N. Savory, Excavations at Dinas Emrys, Beddgelert (Carn.), 1954–56. *Archaeologia Cambrensis* 109, 72–77.

Smith, A. G. and Cloutman, E. W. (1988) Reconstruction of Holocene Vegetation History in Three Dimensions at Waun-Fignen-Felen, an Upland Site in South Wales. *Philosophical Transactions of The Royal Society of London,* B 322(1209), 159–219.

Smith, J. B. (2014) *Llywelyn ap Gruffudd: Prince of Wales.* Cardiff, University of Wales Press.

Snowball, I. and Thompson, R. (1992) A Mineral Magnetic Study of Holocene Sediment Yields and Deposition Patterns in the Llyn Geirionydd Catchment, North Wales. *The Holocene* 2(3), 238–248.

Stace, C. (2010) *New Flora of the British Isles. 3rd edition.* Cambridge, Cambridge University Press.

Thomas, G., McDonnell, G., Merkel, J. and Marshall, P. (2014) Technology, Ritual and Anglo-Saxon Agriculture: the biography of a plough coulter from Lyminge, Kent. *Antiquity* 90(351), 742–758.

Thorpe, L. (1978) *Gerald of Wales: The Journey through Wales and the Description of Wales.* London, Penguin Books.

Tomlinson, P. (1987) Pollen. In J. Manley, Cledemutha: A Late Saxon Burh in North Wales. *Medieval Archaeology* 31, 41.

Topping, P., Halliday, S. and Welfare, A. (1989) Early Cultivation in Northumberland and the Borders. *Proceedings of the Prehistoric Society* 55, 161–179.

Turner, J. (1964) The Anthropogenic Factor in Vegetational History. I. Tregaron and Whixall Mosses. *New Phytologist* 63(1), 73–90.

Walker, R. (1979) Diatom and Pollen studies of a Sediment Profile of Melynllyn, a Mountain Tarn in Snowdonia, North Wales. *New Phytologist*, 81(3), 791–804

Watkins, R., Scourse, J. D. and Allen, J. R. M. (2007) The Holocene Vegetation History of the Arfon Platform, North Wales, UK. *Boreas* 36, 170–181.

White, R. (2007) *Britannia Prima: Britain's Last Roman Province.* Stroud, Tempus.

Woodbridge, J., Fyfe, R., Law, B. and Haworth-Jones, A. (2012) A Spatial Approach to Upland Vegetation Change and Human Impact: the Aber Valley, Snowdonia. *Environmental Archaeology* 17(1), 80–94.

CHAPTER ELEVEN

Welsh landscape history:
notes from the edge

Andrew Fleming

I spent fifteen enjoyable years (1994–2009) living and working in south-west Wales. As a landscape historian, I sometimes found myself wondering why there was no Welsh version of (or antidote to?) W. G. Hoskins' *The Making of the English Landscape* (1955). (This would have made a good student essay question, I suppose, though I never tried it on my students at Lampeter.) Not that a Welsh Hoskins would have helped much in my attempts to 'read' the unfamiliar landscapes of Ceredigion. Practical field archaeology wasn't W. G's strong suit; his appeal lies in his love of cultural landscapes deeply marinated in history – *English* history. His writing was elegiac as well as pastoral in tone (it is well that he did not live to see the invasion of the enormous sheds). The ancestry of Hoskins' nostalgia has been critically located in the English Romantic movement and accordingly disdained (Bender 1998; Johnson 2006); but perhaps it is not far from the seemingly more demotic Welsh *hiraeth*, which conveys the sense of an exile 'longing for the land'. *Hiraeth* would surely have helped a Welsh Hoskins to find his or her voice. So too would the urge to reconstruct, or rediscover, a cultural heritage much affected by the hegemony of England. A Hoskins-style narrative for Wales would surely need to develop its own distinctive themes.

A notable feature of Hoskins' account of English landscape history was his celebration of Anglo-Saxon land-taking after the demise of Roman *Britannia* – the clearing of woodland, the breaking of new (and 'virgin') land, the establishment of the villages and open fields which set the pattern for much of the later landscape. This story was soon shown to be historically inaccurate. Nor was it new; a nation which had set a planetary record for dispossessing other peoples of their land had already made such activities a key feature of their own origin myth. Legitimation involved an appeal to the woodcutter's axe rather than the warrior's sword. Understandably in terms of his own life experience (he had lived through two world wars before the age of forty), Hoskins liked to celebrate the achievements of the Anglo-Saxons as peaceful settlers rather than warlike invaders and colonists. His essentially self-regarding portrayal of the origins of the English nation, written at a time of national insecurity and frantic nuclear armament, doubtless helped to generate the acclaim which greeted his most celebrated book.

Narratives of the origins of the Welsh landscape have to deal with a different kind of land-taking, carried out in the late Middle Ages by people memorably described by the late Rhys Jones (the archaeologist) as 'some alien hotchpotch of *nouveaux arrivistes*'. In his 'British aboriginal's claim to Stonehenge', Jones noted how the 'British' past as presented by Geoffrey of Monmouth (for example), then the mythic past of a beleaguered people, was appropriated by Camden and others to form the master narrative for the prehistory of the 'British Isles' as a whole (1990, 72–3). He did not comment on the role of 'the Celts' in the writings of those mid-twentieth century scholars, such as H. J. Fleure, Jacquetta Hawkes, and Hoskins himself, who did not altogether embrace the mind-numbing cultural sequences which often constituted prehistorians' narratives at that time. Such scholars preferred culture in a broader sense, borne by named peoples. For them, individuals displaying the 'Celtic' racial characteristics could still be identified, especially in Wales, perhaps stacking sheaves of corn, or waiting in line at the pithead (see Fleming 2007). When Hoskins wrote about south-west England, Celts were there too, lurking in the background, reminiscent of the ghostly figures walking through the trees in one of Heywood Sumner's most memorable drawings (Cunliffe 1985, 142). Although recruited as models for the people of the 'Iron Age', 'the Celts' were more frequently the epitome of Otherness in the British historical literature. In the mid-twentieth century, archaeology was still in the process of establishing its core task as the representation of human history in the long term and in the absence of written records. From the perspective of cultural nationalism, Iorwerth Peate tended to perceive the science of archaeology, as promoted by Sir Cyril Fox (Director of the National Museum of Wales from 1926 to 1948), as a form of hegemonic discourse (Fleming 2007). For Peate, Fox's artefact distribution maps were anathema; what Fox termed 'bygones' were not merely sources of 'ethnographic parallels' for prehistorians, but rather Folk Culture, representing the past of a colonised nation. The Welsh house constituted much more than 'vernacular architecture'; it was an expression of Welsh life (1944, 1–4). At St Fagans, Peate aimed not to preserve 'the dead past under glass' but to link the past with the present 'to provide a strong foundation and a healthy environment for the future of the people' (1948).

One answer to my hypothetical essay question might be that Hoskins was a man of his place and time, and that the Hoskins moment has now passed. Nevertheless, Hoskins' archetypal yeoman has retained an important role in the discourse of landscape history in England. And the spirit of Cyril Fox is very much alive (rather like Elvis, as claimed on a celebrated painted inscription on a rock beside the A44 on the way to Aberystwyth). We have sought the 'personality' of medieval England in terms of the diversity of regional rural landscapes. A central zone of 'planned' or 'champion' countryside is flanked to east and west by 'ancient' or 'woodland' countryside (Rackham 1976, fig. 1;

Williamson 2013, chapter 6). In eastern England, smaller zones have been recognised, defined by open field types reflecting variable agrarian practice responding to local geographical factors (*e.g.* Williamson 2003; 2013). For earlier times, regional diversity in the development of field systems has been documented by Stephen Rippon and his co-authors in *The Fields of Britannia*. They have divided England and Wales into eight regions on the basis of physiography, degree of 'Romanisation', extent of 'Germanic' influence, and historic landscape character (2015, chapter 2); Rippon has updated the Welsh section of the book for *Living off the Land*. For England, Roberts and Wrathmell (2000) have out-foxed Fox, producing a series of distribution maps which pose intriguing questions about the origins of patterning and diversity in regional landscapes. The medieval landscapes of England have been frameworked, overviewed, paysified. The discipline of landscape history has tended to plod on, like the medieval yeoman at the plough, pursuing a traditional agenda within an established research paradigm.

In the twelfth century, it was not long since the English people had come under the Norman yoke; figuratively speaking, they had been 'subjugated'; for a man of mixed Norman and Welsh descent such as Gerald de Barri ('of Wales') they could be the object of mild scorn. The conquest of Wales was then of course a work in progress. Nowadays the preferred historical themes in Wales, in the popular imagination at least, involve heroic resistance and the glories of a more ancient, autochthonous 'Celtic' past. If the beauty of the Welsh landscape is widely acknowledged, its 'making' is not a concept which has achieved much historical salience. The labours of the medieval ploughman tend to have little traction, so to speak; as the editors of *Living off the Land* point out, historical narratives of rural Wales traditionally placed the emphasis on pastoralism, not always presented in a very favourable light. The theme runs from Stuart Piggott's 'footloose Celtic cowboys' through medieval cattle raiders to post-medieval stereotypes created in England (Leland's 'consuete idilness') and finally the drovers, whose activities linked the people of rural Wales with the wider world in various ways. The drovers still fire the popular imagination; when a group of us in Lampeter set up a celebration of local artistic and cultural activity (short-lived, alas), 'The Drovers' Festival' was the most obvious name for it.

Traditionally, then, Wales has been England's Other not just ethnically, but also in terms of agrarian and landscape history. These research areas seem relatively under-developed and under-resourced in comparison with their English equivalents. Furthermore, Wales tends to provide fewer development-led opportunities for rescue archaeology than many areas of England, reducing the chances of those serendipitous discoveries which may transform our understanding almost overnight. Of the nine contributions to *Living off the Land*, one comes from Ireland, and in two others Wales appears as an outlier of research developed in and for England – although of course wider perspectives should always find a welcome in the hillsides. In this book, Bob Silvester's useful survey of medieval field systems in Wales shows how far we need to travel to arrive at the stage reached in eastern England, whilst Tudur Davies's review of the pollen evidence notes the uneven areal distribution of the 38 pollen sites relevant to the Middle Ages; evidently there is a need for more lowland work of the kind undertaken in, for example, Devon.

However, invidious comparisons with England are unhelpful. The 're-boot' represented by *Living off the Land* is timely and welcome – especially if there is a prospect for the creation of Welsh narratives refreshingly different from those developed on the other side of Offa's Dyke. Those who fear that Wales may be the Cinderella of British landscape and agrarian history should perhaps be reminded of how that particular story ended. Wales has suffered somewhat for being lumped into Fox's Highland Zone. However, we have understood for a long time that her geographical 'personality' is a good deal more complex and nuanced than that. There is, for example, the question of the Atlantic seaways, Wales's maritime connections, her position on the shores of the British Mediterranean (which to be fair, Fox did not ignore). At Lampeter I was privileged to supervise Toby Driver's doctoral research as he demonstrated the importance of display in the siting and construction of the hillforts of Ceredigion (2013; 2016). The coastal sites were evidently of crucial regional importance. Ceredigion has long stretches of steep and rocky coastline, offshore reefs, and sandbars. However, 'where there are good inlets, gravel beaches or river mouths suitable for pulling up small sea-going craft, then there are often found hillforts nearby' (Driver 2016, 54). Coastal 'gateways' were evidently important. The well-known hillfort at Pen Dinas (Aberystwyth) is the archetypal coastal gateway site; further south two routeways led from the Llanrhystud/Llansantffraed portal to the hillforts of the interior (Driver 2013).

In *Living off the Land*, the influence of Welsh geography on Welsh agrarian history is far from insignificant. In her discussion of cereal crops in south-west Wales, Rhiannon Comeau notes the advantages of club wheat on poor soils and in rainy conditions with delayed harvests, and also rivet wheat's resistance to rust and its unattractiveness to birds; both, she points out, sown in the springtime, would have fitted into the annual cycles implied both by Welsh law and infield-outfield systems. In the climatic conditions of Wales, the qualities of specific varieties of cereals, and perhaps also those which have been selected (or evolved) for properties such as short stalks, could be critical. Comeau also notes the increased bogginess of Carn Goedog (Preseli) during the Little Ice Age – a finding which chimes with my own observations of the western part of the Monks' Trod, the much-engineered road which linked the Cistercian monasteries of Ystrad Fflur (Strata Florida) with Abbey Cwmhir, and probably Ystrad Marchell (Strata Marcella) too (Fleming 2009). For the period around the 'long eighth century', Tudur Davies asks whether the pollen evidence for increased arable activity is due to better growing conditions relating to a warmer climate or whether, on the contrary, it was stimulated by reduced crop yields. (I can't help being reminded here that the density of mole-hills is inversely related to the density of the mole population; moles have to work much harder in poorer soils containing fewer earthworms). It is evidently not clear how far, and in what ways, generalisations about the changing climate affected Wales (not to mention her different regions, and the microclimates of particular places). To address such conundrums, the carefully-focused work of an older generation of climate geographers such as James Taylor, Peter Moore, and Martin Parry (*e.g.* respectively 1967, 1974, 1978) might well be worth revisiting. In this volume, the contribution from Ireland by McClatchie and her colleagues also reminds us of the importance of collective facilities such as corn-drying kilns and mills. Although the latter tend to present as single sites posing technical questions, we also need to ask whether they are also components of recognisable 'toolkit horizons'. As ever, uncertainties bedevil our understanding of the history of the plough, and as Bob Silvester's contribution makes plain, much the same can be said about the dating of various horizons of 'ridge and furrow' in Wales.

It once seemed that in regions like Wales questions about 'marginality' were hard to ignore almost by definition. For myself, I have generally found the concept unhelpful – and, as applied to the pre-modern era, anachronistic. It is better in my view to regard the presence of diverse environments and a relatively sharp gradation of physiographic and climatic conditions as providing excellent opportunities for studying versatility, flexibility, and resilience in past agrarian and economic strategies – opportunities perhaps better than those presented by regions with (apparently) more subtle or nuanced ecotones. It is refreshing to see that the contributors to *Living off the Land* are not much concerned with the concept of 'marginality'. In terms of agrarian strategy and the socio-agrarian calendar, which were closely linked, access to the shared resources of *mynydd* and *ffridd* was evidently just as vital as access to sharelands. This emerges very clearly from Comeau's general model of the infield/outfield pattern of resource exploitation in early Wales. In this book, Andy Seaman ponders the role of the 2500-hectare early medieval estate of Llandeilo'r-fân, at the edge of Brycheiniog, high among the hills of the Mynydd Epynt. Why should such a 'marginal' location have been chosen for such a large royal estate, given that there was much better agricultural land on the valley floor to the south, and no apparent 'population pressure'? Seaman interprets Llandeilo'r-fân as an early example of a summer ranch for cattle and horses, probably run by an official, and he notes the presence of 'horse roads'; the very name of the district means 'upland grazing crossed by a horse-path'. This estate may have been a vital resource for the summering of the Welsh equivalent of the Irish *creaght*, the vast herd owned by the ruler – essentially the medieval equivalent of a very large savings account paying a very good rate of interest, and a major element, perhaps *the* major element, in his exercise of patronage and power (note Comeau's passing reference to the lord of Cemais's 120 horses).

Given the ruler's role in the articulation of the economy, zones like the Epynt were far from 'marginal'. And their marginality may have been less than obvious to the medieval 'tax-payer', owing tribute in the form of honey, accustomed to taking bee-skeps onto the hills for the heather season. An area used *extensively* may be just as critical, in economic terms, as one used *in*tensively. In this book, Della Hooke notes the value of the *ffridd*, the zone on the edge of the *mynydd*, as an 'intermediate resource', a diverse and versatile ecotone whose scattered trees and zone of undergrowth could provide shelter and a bite for livestock if the weather behaved badly in spring or autumn. The *ffridd* must have been a form of wood-pasture, the kind of bosky landscape depicted by the Dutch master Frans Vera (2000) and now productively embraced by many historical ecologists. Before the hardening of the *penclawdd*, the 'head dyke', as a concept and as a physical barrier, the *ffridd* may well have served as 'buffer zone' in a more long-term sense, absorbing fluctuations in population numbers and fiscal demands over the centuries. David Austin regards the *ffridd* at Strata Florida as a critical zone, where upland summer grazing was managed from the *hafodydd*, the summer houses – in his model not only in the early Middle Ages but in late prehistory too. For the purposes of his discussion, Austin focuses on the four square miles of his *milltir sgwâr*, an area which may be readily categorised in terms of zones of agrarian potential. It seems that the Cistercians also came to see their estate in these terms, developing 'an inner demesne of specialist farms, transforming the previous arrangements of the *llys* and *maerdref* of a former Welsh royal estate'. Thus there emerges a multiple estate in all but name, with farm names 'ticking the boxes' almost too neatly, documenting the meadows of the foals, the oxen and the cow-byres, the hills of the orchard and of the pigs, and so on. Austin suggests that 'grange' was a scribe's formulaic term, and that rather than imposing a new 'colonial' system the Cistercians transformed the existing pattern of landholding. Of course, the lordly overview of an estate's land, infrastructure and potential (no doubt provided by local informants) was not a Cistercian monopoly. In the case of the Monks' Trod, it is a moot point whether the engineered roadbed seen along most of those sections which do not run along fairly level ground was created at the behest of the Cistercians or of the powerful ruler Rhys ap Gruffydd. Either party would have had the motive and the opportunity to improve long-distance communications; perhaps they acted together in terms of realising a key civil engineering project (Fleming 2009). The same kind of question must surely apply to the Strata Florida estate as a whole. It's interesting how documentary terminology shapes discussion; whatever its actual origins, if a place is *recorded* as a vaccary, bercary or a grange it takes on a much more monastic persona, as I noticed in Swaledale (Fleming 1998). When Louise Barker and I wrote our piece about a fragment of this landscape (2008) we didn't assume that it was shaped anew by the Cistercians.

It's hard to mention horses, engineered roads and the Epynt without thinking of the *rhiwiau* – those 'cut and filled' road-beds, running diagonally across the contour, which traverse the steep slopes of the Black Mountains of south-east Wales. They are numerous, variable in character and apparent function, and hard to date (Eddie Procter pers. comm.). However, one of them, Rhiw Arw, still part of the footpath between Longtown and Llanthony, is mentioned in an eighth-century charter (Coplestone-Crow 2009, 67). I have seen *rhiwiau* on the edge of Mynydd Epynt, from a distance, and there is certainly one on the island of Skomer, where it is interpreted as a necessary facility, a ramp for moving livestock onto and off the island (Toby Driver and Louise Barker pers. comm.). The construction of such roads, whether cut along the contour or at 45° to it, would make all the difference to the speed and safety of travellers on horseback (even those mounted on resilient Welsh cobs) (Fleming 2010) and would also have helped considerably with movement of transhumant livestock. Study of such engineered roads is in its infancy; in due course these interesting phenomena may illuminate our understanding far beyond Offa's Dyke.

Reading this book, I am struck by familiar areas of tension and dialogue – the value of the in-depth case study compared with that of the overview, the challenge of understanding both continuity and change, and the differences between sustainable ways of making a living on the ground, and 'the economy' as orchestrated – or predated upon – by elites – those who lived off the people who 'lived off the land'. (We need to talk of kings as well as cabbages. It's hard to avoid recalling the close relationship between cattle and money in European languages (as in *pecuniary*); in this volume Comeau reminds us that *praidd* can mean 'booty' as well as 'flock'.) Of the first, landscape history in Wales, just like anywhere else, needs Rosetta stones. The Bayvil area is clearly a very good one (see Comeau this volume, and her other referenced work) and it may be that Strata Florida will turn out to be another. Of the second, it seems to me that the *phenotypes* of apparent or possible continuity – the Anglo-Saxon farm which once had a Celtic name, for example, or the hillfort overlooking the former *llys* – no longer excite landscape historians as they did Hoskins. Nowadays we are more interested in the *genotypes*, the *anatomy* of continuity and change, and the first question is, continuity of what exactly? In this volume, a perceptive comment by Seaman reminds us of the complexity of these issues: 'continuity of landholding and territorial units' he notes, 'should not be conflated with continuity of the agricultural systems operating within them'. In *Fields of Britannia*, Stephen Rippon and his team have made great progress in addressing questions of continuity and change in the use of Romano-British field systems after the legions left – a study which is particularly valuable given its attempt to transcend the diverse disciplinary concerns of prehistorians, Romanists and medievalists, not to mention the dilemmas of landscape historians when documents become thin on the ground. In my own review of *Fields* (Fleming 2016), I suggested that we now need to bridge earlier gaps by developing a 'Fields of the Pretani' project. At this stage some bridges may be constructed by argument as much as from evidence. Susan Oosthuizen has argued for deep continuities in the management of common property regimes, structured 'to ensure the long-term sustainability of a resource, the maximisation of its output, and its equitable distribution among those with a right to its exploitation' (2013, 1 and *passim*). She also suggests (2013, xi) that the landscape re-organisations of mid-Saxon times 'might constitute a negotiated compromise between traditional forms of collective governance and new systems of lordly management'.

Personally, I have become accustomed to this way of thinking, having spent time in recent years considering three topics where long-term investment and multiple stakeholding feature heavily in the maintenance of continuity – that is to say, transhumance (Fleming in press), wood-pasture (Fleming 2011a, and see Hooke this volume) and early long-distance roads (Fleming 2009; 2010; 2011b; 2011c; 2012). Some institutions appear so 'locked in' to social organisation, economic expectations and the annual calendar as to make change seem harder to explain than continuity.

Although some may question the foundations of Oosthuizen's bridge, for me her argument is achieving increasing salience. A Welsh historian once called a book *When was Wales?* (Williams 1985). It would perhaps be a brave author who chose *When was there no such thing as Wales?* as a title; nevertheless, the tentative formulations of landscape historians around the early post-Roman centuries, variously encompassing Wales, other 'Celtic' countries and also the land which became England, are becoming very interesting. Glanville Jones discerned multiple estates in deepest England (*e.g.* 1976, 26–35). He may have gone too far; nevertheless I cannot help noticing how the horizon of significant change associated with 'the long eighth century' now seems to encompass Wales as well as England (see Davies, Seaman and Rippon this volume). We evidently need to think more about the mode of land occupation (in the fullest sense) which obtained *before* the long eighth century. In this volume, Comeau has carefully delineated for the Preseli area the differential survival of the main elements of the 'infield/outfield system' in the cultural landscape; some of these find good parallels in Devon and Cornwall, and there are broad similarities with Scotland and Ireland too.

For some scholars, the 'infield/outfield system' now seems to underlie the medieval pattern in Britain as a whole. To knock Piers the Ploughman off his perch may be unthinkable. It seems to me, however, that if we are trying to understand and represent the 'pre-medieval' mode of living off (and in) the land, we need a terminology and a way of thinking which no longer privileges the evolution and mode of operation of fallow systems (or, for that matter, field systems). Somehow, we need to develop a more holistic model, and one which also acknowledges the built-in entropy associated with many institutions and practices. This is not simply a matter of the 'conservatism' of people dependent on the land for their livelihoods, people who need to have risk-buffering agrarian strategies in place. It is about multiple stakeholding, investment in the productivity of the land, the intricacies of socio-political relationships, and the relentless imperatives and annual rhythms of the agrarian calendar. The reader who wishes to understand something of what I am driving at here could do worse than read Nerys Patterson's *Cattle-lords and Clansmen*, especially chapter five on the seasonal rhythms of social life – which, Patterson notes, are closely integrated with the rhythms of economic, political, military, and reproductive cycles (human and animal). Patterson's perspective is Irish-centred but ultimately pan-Celtic, perhaps one might say north-west European. As the earth circles the sun, and whether we appeal to Pete Seeger or the Book of Ecclesiastes, there are times of plenty and times of dearth, times for hard work and times for rest and recuperation, times for courting and times for marriage, times for initiating cattle-raids and times for disbanding the retinue – even an 'assassination season'. All this implies a continuously maintained physical infrastructure – tracts of wood-pasture, routeways, and so on – and the maintenance of conventional rules of engagement, whether facilitating the sharing of resources or establishing the ground-rules for their contestation. In this volume, Austin's phrase – 'a long-term Welsh society with *deeply-laid* attitudes to land, its meaning and use' [my italics] is applied to his *milltir sgwâr*; actually it has much wider application.

It is not that change does not occur. Of course it does, at various chronological and spatial scales; archaeologists and historians are trained to spot it and make it the driving force of much historical narrative. My point is that, against the background which I have sketched, we need more holistic ways of thinking – both about continuity and about change. We need to do more than toggle between these concepts, so to speak, or to think of each as a kind of historical default setting. In landscape and agrarian history, we are addressing nuanced and multi-dimensional questions operating at several scales – which is an absorbing project. Looking at my ancient, rather worn first edition of *The Making of the English Landscape*, I remember reading Hoskins's text for the first time, not long after it was published – lying in a field of long grass, struck by the curious fragrance of its paper. I really ought to take it to the bookbinder. But that would be for strictly sentimental reasons; as *Living off the Land* demonstrates, we have moved on since those days.

References

Bender, B. (1998) *Stonehenge: making space.* Oxford and New York, Berg.

Coplestone-Crow, B. (2009) *Herefordshire Place-names.* Almeley, Logaston Press.

Cunliffe, B. (ed.) (1985) *Heywood Sumner's Wessex.* Wimborne, Roy Gasson Associates.

Driver, T. (2013) *Architecture, Regional Identity and Power in the Iron Age Landscapes of Mid Wales: the Hillforts of North Ceredigion.* BAR British Series 583. Oxford, British Archaeological Reports.

Driver, T. (2016) *The Hillforts of Cardigan Bay.* Almeley, Logaston Press.

Fleming, A. (1998) *Swaledale: Valley of the Wild River.* Edinburgh, University Press.

Fleming, A. (2007) 1955 and all that: prehistoric landscapes in the *Making.* In A. Fleming and R. Hingley (eds) *Landscape History after Hoskins. Volume 1: Prehistoric and Roman Landscapes.* Oxford, Windgather Press, 1–15.

Fleming, A. (2009) The Making of a Medieval Road: the Monks' Trod routeway, Mid Wales. *Landscapes* 10(1), 77–100.

Fleming, A. (2010) Horses, Elites…and Long-distance Roads. *Landscapes* 11(2), 1–20.

Fleming, A. (2011a) Working with wood-pasture. In S. Turner and R. Silvester (eds) *Life in Medieval Landscapes: people and places in medieval England*, 15–31. Oxford, Windgather Press.

Fleming, A. (2011b) The Crossing of Dartmoor. *Landscape History* 32(1), 27–45.

Fleming, A. (2011c) The Lich Way: a path for all seasons. *Transactions of the Devonshire Association* 143, 91–103.

Fleming, A. (2012) Devon's Early Roads: Devon Archaeological Society Presidential Lecture 2011. *Proceedings of the Devon Archaeological Society* 70, 1–23.

Fleming, A. (2016) Review of Rippon, Pears and Smart, *Fields of Britannia. Antiquity* 90, 826–7.

Fleming, A. and Barker, L. (2008) Monks and local communities: the late medieval landscape at Troed y Rhiw, Caron Uwch Clawdd, Ceredigion. *Medieval Archaeology* 52, 261–90.

Fleming, A. (forthcoming) Exploring the origins and character of transhumance in England. In W. Morrison (ed.) *Challenging Preconceptions*. Oxford, Archaeopress.

Hoskins, W. G. (1955) *The Making of the English Landscape*. London, Hodder and Stoughton.

Johnson, M. (2006) *Ideas of Landscape*. Oxford, Blackwell.

Jones, G. R. J. (1976) Multiple estates and early settlement. In P. Sawyer (ed.) *Medieval Settlement: continuity and change*. London, Edward Arnold, 15–40.

Jones, R. (1990) Sylwadau cynfrodor ar Gôr y Cewri, or a British Aboriginal's land claim to Stonehenge. In C. Chippindale, P. Devereux, P. Fowler, R. Jones, R and T. Sebastian (eds) *Who Owns Stonehenge?* London, Batsford, 62–87.

Moore, P. D. and Bellamy, D. (1974) *Peatlands*. New York, Springer.

Oosthuizen, S. (2013) *Tradition and Transformation in Anglo-Saxon England: Archaeology, Common Rights and Landscape*. London, Bloomsbury.

Parry, M. (1978) *Climatic Change, Agriculture and Settlement (Studies in Historical Geography)*. Folkestone, Dawson/Archon.

Paterson, N. (1994) *Cattle-lords and Clansmen: The Social Structure of Early Ireland*. Notre Dame (Indiana), University of Notre Dame Press.

Peate, I. (1944) *The Welsh House: A Study in Folk Culture* (second, revised, edition; first published in 1940). Liverpool, Hugh Evans & Sons, The Brython Press.

Peate, I. (1948) quoted in https://museum.wales/stfagans/stfagans-history/ (accessed 06.02.19)

Rackham, O. (1976) *Trees and Woodland in the British Landscape*. London, Dent.

Rippon, S., Smart, C. and Pears, B. (2015) *The Fields of Britannia: Continuity and Change in the Late Roman and Early Medieval Landscape*. Oxford, Oxford University Press.

Roberts, B. and Wrathmell, S. (2000) *An Atlas of Rural Settlement in England*. London, English Heritage.

Taylor, J. A. (ed.) (1967) *Weather and Agriculture*. Oxford, Pergamon Press.

Vera, F. (2000) *Grazing Ecology and Forest History*. Wallingford, CABI Publishing.

Williams, G. (1985) *When Was Wales? A History of the Welsh*. Harmondsworth, Penguin Books.

Williamson, T. (2003) *Shaping Medieval Landscapes: Settlement, Society, Environment*. Macclesfield, Windgather Press.

Williamson, T. (2013) *Environment, Landscape and Society in Early Medieval England*. Woodbridge, Boydell.

Glossary

This list comprises terms used in this volume, with Welsh words italicised. Unless otherwise indicated, definitions are based on those of *Geiriadur Prifysgol Cymru* (*The University of Wales Dictionary*, published by University of Wales Press and available online at http://welsh-dictionary.ac.uk/gpc/gpc.html), the *Oxford English Dictionary*, and *Agrarian Landscape Terms: a glossary for historical geography* (Adams 1976). Useful glossaries will also be found in Butlin 1961, Jenkins 1990, Charles-Edwards, Owen and Russell 2000, Coredon and Williams 2004, and the index of Rackham 1986. Comprehensive information about English field-names is provided by Cavill 2018. Details of these and other sources will be found in the References section of the Introduction.

ager (pl. **agri**): Latin term used in Llandaff Charters to mean either 'estate' or 'land' (Charles-Edwards 2013, 284–7)

aillt: unfree subject, villein bondman, serf, slave, foreigner. See also *bilain*, *taeog*, **bond(s)man**

allt, *gallt*: hill(side), (steep) slope, steep road or path, woods, wooded slope

arad, *aradr*: a plough; *tir arad*: ploughland. See also **carucate**

aratral: pertaining to ploughing

barlys: barley (also *haidd*)

beat burning ('**ad baticium**'): paring and burning of rough moorland sod to prepare such land for occasional cultivation

bietyn, *bating*, *beting*: pared and burnt hillside; pared turf used as fuel; soil ashes

bilain: villein, serf, labourer, farmer, husbandman, peasant. See also *aillt*, **bond(s)man**, *taeog*

bond(s)man: a person of hereditary unfree status, legally dependent on their lord and tied to the land. Broadly equivalent to a medieval villein (Davies 1987, 117–9). See also *aillt*, *bilain*, *taeog*

bonheddig: noble, aristocrat

brith: variegated; chequered, pied, speckled, brindled, grey; half-, partly. In field names it may refer to partially deturfed beat-burning land ('pied beatland': Owen 1994, 66).

butt: a piece of land in or deriving from an open field. Shorter than a full length **land/selion** and often abutting other lands/selions at right angles.

bwthyn: cottage, hut

cae: hedge or (small) enclosed field. See also *parc*

cantref: a hundred, province or district

carucate: literally, a **ploughland**, the area capable of being tilled by one plough-team of eight oxen in the year. Commonly consisted of eight oxlands or bovates, though there are regional variations (Howells 1967). Equivalent to a **modius** or 'Welsh hide' of *c.* 60 acres in south-east Wales (Domesday: Jones 1989, 192)

ceirch, *cerch*, *cyrch*: oats

Central Province: the central zone of England, focusing on the east Midlands, which is characterised after the mid-/late Anglo-Saxon period by nucleated settlements and **common fields** (Roberts & Wrathmell 2002, 10, 124, 144)

clawdd: soil thrown up from digging a pit or trench; dyke, earthwork; hedge, fence

clun: meadow, moor

coed: forest, wood, trees, timber

common field: (sometimes referred to as a 'Midland' common field) – an **open field** with a communally regulated crop rotation and fallowing. See **open field**

common land: land (belonging to one person) where another person holds **rights of common** whether arising from a grant or from the custom of the manor (Bird 1983, 80)

common, right of: the right to use the land or waters of another for pasture, piscary (fishing), estover (cutting wood, gorse or furze), or turbary (cutting turves) (Bird 1983, 80)

commote, *cwmwd*: a territorial and administrative subdivision (often a half or a third) of a *cantref*

convertible husbandry: the periodic cultivation of an area of **outfield**, possibly in conjunction with the use of an **infield**. Cultivation intervals varied considerably: forty-year intervals are recorded on poorer land (Hall 2014, 86–94)

corn ditch: see **head dyke**

cors (gors): swamp, bog, fen, marsh

cyfar: co-tilling, joint-ploughing; also a measure of land in an open field cultivated under such agreements, either equivalent to or a subdivision of an *erw* (Jones Pierce 1943)

cyfer, *cyfair*: a day's ploughing, an acre or *erw*

cynghellor: chancellor, principal steward of king

cynhaeafdy: harvest-house, autumn-house

cytir: literally 'joint land' (*cyd+tir*); refers to shared or common pasture

dawnbwyd: food rent paid by **bondman**

demesne: land possessed or occupied by an owner, including (in its widest sense) lands held of him by villeins/**bondmen** or copyhold tenure. It might or might not be intermingled with the holdings of others

den(e): swine-pasture in forest or marsh, used seasonally. Term used mainly in Kent

dôl: meadow, dale, field, pasture, valley. The **dole** was a portion or strip in a common meadow

dryll: strip or ridge

erw: an acre – a medieval measure of land in an open field, whose size varied in different areas of Wales (Jones Pierce 1943; Jones 1972, 368–9). See also **land**

Extent: a survey recording an estate's lands and other properties and the charges/rents due from them

ffridd, ffrith: see *hafod*

furlong: (a) a standard measure of length of 40 perches/rods/poles or 220 statute yards, from 'furrow-long' and possibly indicating the distance that a team of oxen could plough in a day, and therefore dependent on plough-type, soil, terrain, etc. Also (b) an area of strips (perhaps of 10 acres) in an open field, held by different owners and typically running in the same direction

gallt: see *allt*

gardd (pl. *gerddi*): literally 'garden'. Refers to strips in open fields

garw: rough, rugged, craggy, uncultivated

gorchlawdd: bank, wall, ditch

gore: a triangular plot left in the corner of an open field and often cultivated with a spade

grange: an ecclesiastical manor, typically created from wasteland, set at some distance for the parent monastery. Frequently used for sheep and cattle farming in Wales

gwaun: high and wet level ground, moorland, heath OR low-lying marshy ground, meadow

gwely: bed OR (medieval Wales) group of descendants of common ancestor who jointly occupy land; or the land that they hold in joint ownership

gwenith: wheat

gwestfa: food-rent or render paid by a freeman

gwndwn: unploughed or uncultivated land

hafod (pl. *hafodau*/*hafodydd*): an area of summer pasture, usually rough moorland, which might also (in north/mid-Wales) be termed *ffridd* or *ffrith*. The term is transferred in the early modern period to the dairies and dwellings on these pastures (Davies 1980, 4–7)

hafotir: the land of the summer grazing area (*hafod+tir*)

hafdy (pl. *hafdai*), *hafoty* (pl. *hafotai*): *hafdy* (*haf+tŷ*: 'summer house') is used for seasonal summer dwellings in medieval Welsh law, *hafoty* (*hafod+tŷ*: 'dwelling on the hafod') appears from the sixteenth century, with a secondary meaning of 'dairy house' (Davies 1980, 7–9)

haidd: barley (also *barlys*)

hamlet: a group of houses, possibly quite scattered. Smaller than a village. See *trefgordd*

head-dyke: a stock-proof bank and ditch that separated the arable land of a township from the rough grazing beyond it; also called a corn ditch or, in Wales, a *penclawdd* (Fleming and Ralph 1982, 105; Austin 2016)

hendre(f): winter (permanent) settlement or township; literally 'old township'

infield, inland: arable land under permanent cultivation, often held in common as an open field. (NB – 'inland' is also used to refer to the core areas of Anglo-Saxon estates – see Faith 1997)

land: A strip of arable land in an open field, sometimes ridged, sometimes flat and separated by a turf baulk. Also called a **selion** or an **erw.** The **dole** was a portion or strip in a common meadow. See also **butt**

lathe: an administrative unit in early medieval Kent, comprising several hundreds

ley: fallow, unploughed land; periodically-cultivated arable land laid down for pasture for a number of years: *e.g.* 'long ley'

llain (pl. **lleiniau**): a strip or quillet in an open field

lluest, llety: temporary dwelling, especially of soldiers or shepherds; upland summer dwelling; shieling

llwyn: bush, shrub, thicket, copse, woods

llys: court/high status dwelling; habitation (periodically occupied) and entourage of a pre-Conquest prince

maenor, maenol, mainaur: early medieval administrative unit comprising a number of townships, with *maenor* and *maenol* being, respectively, south and north Wales variants. *Mainaur* is the early medieval manuscript form

maer: a steward; in medieval Welsh Law, an administrative officer of the pre-Conquest prince who is responsible for land supervision and the collection of dues

maerdref: land (and settlement) adjacent to a prince's court (*llys*) worked by unfree tenants

maes: see **open field**

modius: a measure of grain, in early medieval Latin sources referring to the tribute or food-rent (**gwestfa/dawnbwyd**) that arable land produced (Charles-Edwards 2013, 277). Used as a measure of land. Alternative terms as land unit: **rhandir** and **shareland**. See *rhandir*

mynydd: literally 'mountain', but in medieval sources refers to upland rough grazing, usually grazed in common, and occasionally cultivated using convertible husbandry techniques

nucleal land: see *tir corddlan*

odyn: kiln (for drying grain)

open field: sometimes called a subdivided field or a townfield: a field composed of unenclosed strips, usually appearing either as ridge and furrow or (in south Wales and south-west England) as flat strips separated by turf balks that are called landshares (Davies 1956, 94–6; Butlin and Baker 1976, 622–4; Roberts and Wrathmell 2002, 2; Oosthuizen 2011; Hall 2014, 2–5). In Wales often termed a *maes*. See also **common field**

outfield: an area of shared, periodically cultivated pasture associated with an **infield** (see **convertible husbandry**)

pannage: The right of tenants to pasture pigs (or other animals) in the lord's woods, waste or demesne during a certain specified period; the payment, sometimes in kind (*i.e.* pigs), made to the owner of the land for this right

pant: hollow, valley

parc: park or (small) enclosed field. See also *cae*

pastoralism: the keeping or grazing of sheep or cattle

pays: a naturally-defined cantref-scale resource zone, typically comprising a river valley and adjacent woodland/resources (Ford 1976; Everitt 1977; Hooke 1982; Williamson 2013).

pen: head, top, source

penclawdd: see **head-dyke** and **corn ditch**

perth: hedge, (thorn) bush, thicket, copse

ploughland: see **carucate**

poeth: hot, burning (associated with beat burning)

quillet: a small plot or narrow strip of land, often but not always of open field origin

rhandir: Welsh term for **modius** or **shareland**. Its size and relationship with townships differs in north and south Wales law

rhiw (pl. *rhiwiau*): (steep) gradient or slope, hill(side); road or footpath on a slope or hillside

rhos: (upland) moor, heath(land)

rhyg: rye

selion: see **land**

shareland: alternative term for **modius** or *rhandir*

shiel, **shieling**: a temporary building; a shepherd's summer hut; summer pasturage. See also *hafod, hafdy, hafoty*

taeog: serf, **bondman**, or villein. See also *aillt, bilain*

talar: headland or cross-boundary at the end of a ploughed strip

tir corddlan: a term used in north Wales law to refer to an **infield** composed of arable strips, which Glanville Jones linked with the small nucleated settlements of dependent tenants or bondmen – hence his term **nucleal land** (Jones 1973,

435, 471–6). One translator uses the term 'hamlet land' for it (Jenkins 1990, 113, 328)

transhumance: the seasonal use of pastures, involving the movement of livestock from a permanent winter base to a temporary summer base some distance away. May be short or long distance, and can vary in scale

tref: in medieval sources this usually refers to a hamlet-scale township rather than a town (the modern meaning). Its size varies between north and south Wales law

trefgordd: a **hamlet**. According to a fifteenth-century Welsh law source it might typically comprise 9 houses, 1 plough, 1 corn kiln and 1 herdsman, implying communal organisation (Jones 1973, 437)

tyddyn: homestead or smallholding. In thirteenth-century north Wales law consisted of 4 *erwau*

uchelwr (pl. **uchelwyr**): land-holding freeholder. Pre-Conquest freeholders were *de facto* noble (Davies 1982, 62–3)

uncia (pl. **unciae**): Latin term used in Llandaff Charters for a unit of (essentially arable) land of around 500 acres, made up of 12 modii (sharelands) (Davies 1978, 33–4, 57; Charles-Edwards 2013, 275–6, 279)

vill, villa, uilla: Latin term for a township/*tref*

wood-pasture: an area of woodland or mixed grassland and scattered trees here animals are pastured

ŷd: corn, grain, cereal

A general bibliography of key work on Wales

....

This bibliography is intended to provide researchers who are new to the field with a starting point from which to navigate the literature relating to agriculture in medieval Wales. It is not exhaustive, and researchers can also consult the expanding range of resources that are freely available online. Regional 'Historic Environment Records' can be accessed via an internet search for *Archwilio*, whilst *Coflein*, the online database for the National Monuments Record of Wales (NMRW) held by the Royal Commission on the Ancient and Historical Monuments of Wales (RCAHMW), is also freely accessible. Many of the out-of-print county inventories of sites and monuments produced by RCAHMW in the twentieth century are available as free downloads: search for 'RCAHMW Inventory'. RCAHMW also hosts an online *List of Historic Place Names*, compiled from nineteenth-century Ordnance Survey maps and Tithe maps. The webpages of the *Research Framework for the Archaeology of Wales*, the *Cymdeithas Enwau Lleoedd Cymru* (*Welsh Place-Name Society*), and the *National Library of Wales* contain much valuable information and links to further resources: the last-named hosts both *Welsh Journals*, an online repository of county and national periodicals, and *Welsh Tithe Maps*, an online repository of tithe maps and schedules. A considerable amount of published literature can also be accessed through the *Archaeological Data Service*, and many doctoral theses can be downloaded free of charge through the British Library's EthOS service.

General works on medieval Welsh society

Arnold, C. J. and Davies, J. (2000) *Roman and Early Medieval Wales*. Stroud, Sutton.

Charles-Edwards, T. M. (2013) *Wales and the Britons 350–1064*. Oxford, Oxford University Press.

Davies, R. R. (2000) *The Age of Conquest, Wales 1063–1415*. Oxford, Oxford University Press. (Originally published in 1987 as *Conquest, Co-existence and Change: Wales 1063–1415*)

Davies, W. (1982) *Wales in the Early Middle Ages*. London, Leicester University Press.

Jack, R. I. (1972) *Medieval Wales*. Cambridge, Cambridge University Press.

Walker, D. (1990) *Medieval Wales*. Cambridge, Cambridge University Press.

Major journals

Agricultural History Review, Archaeologia Cambrensis, Archaeology in Wales, Welsh History Review, Landscape History, Landscapes, Medieval Archaeology, Medieval Settlement Research.

General works on medieval agriculture in Wales

Adams, I. H. (1976) *Agrarian Landscape Terms: A Glossary for Historical Geography.* London, Institute of British Geographers.

Aris, M. (1996) *Historic Landscapes of the Great Orme.* Llanrwst, Gwasg Carreg Gwalch.

Austin, D. (2005) Little England Beyond Wales: Re-defining the Myth. *Landscapes* 6(2), 30–62.

Austin, D. (2006) The future: discourse, objectives and directions. In K. Roberts (ed.) *Lost Farmsteads: Deserted Rural Settlements in Wales.* CBA Research Report 148. York, Council for British Archaeology, 193–206.

Barker, P. A. and Lawson, J. (1971) A Pre-Norman Field System at Hen Domen, Montgomery. *Medieval Archaeology* 15, 58–72.

Beverley Smith, J. (1998) *Llywelyn Ap Gruffudd: Prince of Wales.* Cardiff, University of Wales Press. (See especially Chapter 5: Lord of Snowdon)

Bezant, J. (2009) *Medieval Welsh Settlement and Territory: Archaeological Evidence from a Teifi Valley Landscape. BAR British Series 487.* Oxford, British Archaeological Reports.

Carr, A. D. H. (2011) *Medieval Anglesey (second edition).* Llangefni, Anglesey Antiquarian Society.

Colyer, R. J. (1983) Crop Husbandry in Wales Before the Onset of Mechanisation. *Folk Life* 21, 49–70

Comeau, R. (2009) Cytir and Crosses: the archaeological landscape of the Parish of Dinas. *Archaeologia Cambrensis* 158, 225–25.

Comeau, R. (2012) From Tref(gordd) to Tithe: Identifying Settlement Patterns in a North Pembrokeshire Parish. *Landscape History* 33(1), 29–44.

Courtney, P. (1983) *The Rural Landscape of Eastern and Lower Gwent c. A.D. 1070–1750.* Unpublished PhD thesis, University College, Cardiff.

Davies, M. (1956) Rhosili Open Field and Related South Wales Field Patterns. *The Agricultural History Review* 4(2), 80–96.

Davies, M. (1973) Field Systems of South Wales. In A. R. H. Baker and R. A. Butlin (eds) *Studies of Field Systems in the British Isles.* Cambridge, Cambridge University Press, 480–529.

Davies, T. (2006) Llanfor and the Upper Dee Valley: an early medieval landscape study. *Medieval Settlement Research Group Annual Report* 21, 29–33

Davies, W. (1978) *An Early Welsh Microcosm: Studies in the Llandaff Charters.* London, Royal Historical Society.

Davies, W. (1978) Land and Power in Early Medieval Wales. *Past and Present* 81, 3–23.

Davies, W. (2001) Thinking about the Welsh environment a thousand years ago. In G. Jenkins (ed.) *Cymru a'r Cymry 2000. Wales and the Welsh 2000.* Aberystwyth, Centre for Advanced Welsh and Celtic Studies, 1–18.

Davies, W. (2004) Looking Backwards to the Early Medieval Past: Wales and England, a contrast in approaches. *Welsh History Review* 22, 197–221

Dodgshon, R. A. (1980) *The Origin of British Field Systems: An Interpretation.* London, Academic Press.

Dodgshon, R. A. (1994) Early Society and Economy. In J. L. Davies and D. P. Kirby (eds) *Cardiganshire County History.* Cardiff, University of Wales Press, 343–364.

Edwards, N. (1997) Landscape and Settlement in Medieval Wales: an Introduction. In N. Edwards (ed.) *Landscape and Settlement in Medieval Wales.* Oxford, Oxbow Books, 1–12.

Fisher, J. L. (1968) *A Medieval Farming Glossary: Latin and English.* London, National Council of Social Service.

Fleming, A. (2007) 1955 and All That: Prehistoric Landscapes in The Making. In A. Fleming and R. Hingley (eds) *Prehistoric and Roman Landscapes.* Macclesfield, Windgather, 1–15.

Fleming, A. (2012) Working with wood pasture. In S. Turner and B. Silvester (eds) *Life in Medieval Landscapes. People and places in the Middle Ages.* Oxford, Windgather Press, 15–31.

Fowler, P. (2002) *Farming in the First Millennium AD.* Cambridge, Cambridge University Press.

Gresham, C. (1950–1951) A Further Note on Ancient Welsh Measurements of Land. *Archaeologia Cambrensis* 101, 118–122.

Gresham, C. A. (1973) *Eifionydd: A Study in Landownership from the Medieval Period to the Present Day.* Cardiff, University of Wales Press.

Hooke, D. (1975) Llanaber: a study in landscape development. *Journal of the Merioneth Historical and Record Society* 7, 221–230.

Hooke, D. (1983) The Ardudwy Landscape: Fieldwork in Western Merioneth, 1979–81. *Journal of the Merioneth Historical and Record Society* 9(3), 245–260.

Howells, B. (1955–1956) Pembrokeshire Farming circa 1580–1620. *National Library of Wales Journal* 9, 239–250, 313–333, 413–439.

Howells, B. (1964) Medieval Settlement in Dyfed. In D. Moore (ed.) *The Land of Dyfed in Early Times.* Cardiff, Cambrian Archaeological Association, 36–9.

Howells, B. (1967) The Distribution of Customary Acres in South Wales. *National Library of Wales Journal* 15(2), 226–233.

Howells, B. (1971) Open Fields and Farmsteads in Pembrokeshire. *The Pembrokeshire Historian* 3, 7–27.

Jackson, V. and Kissock, J. (2013) A Medieval Landscape: Llanelen, Abergavenny. *Monmouthshire Antiquary* 29, 3–8.

Johnson, N. (1978) The Location of Pre-Medieval Fields in Caernarvonshire. In H. C. Bowen and P. J. Fowler (eds) *Early Land Allotment in the British Isles.* BAR British Series 48. Oxford, British Archaeological Reports, 127–132.

Jones, G. R. J. (1955) The Distribution of Medieval Settlement in Anglesey. *Transactions of the Anglesey Antiquarian Society* (1955), 27–96.

Jones, G. R. J. (1961) The Tribal System in Wales. *Welsh History Review* 1(2), 111–132.

Jones, G. R. J. (1964) The Distribution of Bond Settlements in North-west Wales. *Welsh History Review* 11, 19–36.

Jones, G. R. J. (1972) Post-Roman Wales. In H. P. R. Finberg (ed.) *The Agrarian History of England and Wales Volume 1(2).* Cambridge, Cambridge University Press, 281–382.

Jones, G. R. J. (1973) Field Systems of North Wales. In A. R. H. Baker and R. A. Butlin (eds) *Studies of Field Systems in the British Isles.* Cambridge, Cambridge University Press, 430–479.

Jones, G. R. J. (1976) Multiple Estates and Early Settlement. In P. H. Sawyer (ed.) *Medieval Settlement: Continuity and Change.* London, Edward Arnold, 15–40.

Jones, G. R. J. (1985) Forms and Patterns of Medieval Settlements in Welsh Wales. In D. Hooke (ed.) *Medieval Villages: a review of current work.* Oxford, Oxford University Committee for Archaeology, 155–170.

Jones, G. R. J. (1989) The Dark Ages. In D. Huw Owen (ed.) *Settlement and Society in Wales.* Cardiff, University of Wales Press, 177–197.

Jones, G. R. J. (1992) The Models for Organisation in Llyfr Iorwerth and Llyfr Cyfnerth. *Bulletin of the Board of Celtic Studies* 39, 95–118.

Jones, G. R. J. (1994) Tir Telych, the gwestfâu of Cynwyl Gaeo and Cymwd Caeo [Memorandum, Lichfield Gospels, AD 830–50]. *Studia Celtica* 28, 81–95.

Jones, G. R. J. (1996) The "Gwely" as a Tenurial Institution. *Studia Celtica* 30, 167–188.

Jones, G. R. J. (2000) Llys and maerdref. In T. Charles-Edwards, M. E. Owen and P. Russell (eds) *The Welsh King and his Court.* Cardiff, University of Wales Press, 296–318.

A collection of Glanville Jones' papers were republished together with an introductory essay as: P. S. Barnwell and B. Roberts (2012) *Britons, Saxons, and Scandinavians: The Historical Geography of Glanville R. J. Jones.* Turnhout, Brepols.

Jones Pierce, T. (1943) Ancient Welsh Measures of Land. *Archaeologia Cambrensis* 97, 195–204.

Jones Pierce, T. (1972) *Medieval Welsh society: Selected essays.* Cardiff, University of Wales Press. See especially the papers for 1940 (Ch IV), 1942 (Ch VII), 1951 (Ch IX), 1959 (Ch XII), and 1961 (Ch XIII).

Kenney, J. (2015) *Medieval Field Systems in North-West Wales Scheduling Enhancement 2014–2015, Part 1: Report and Gazetteer. Report no. 1236.* Bangor, Gwynedd Archaeological Trust (unpublished report).

Kissock, J. (1991) Pre-conquest Village Origins in South East Wales: a conjectural model. *Morgannwg* 35, 31–46.

Kissock, J. (1991) Farms, Fields and Hedges: aspects of the rural economy of north-east Gower, c. 1300 to c. 1650. *Archaeologia Cambrensis* 140, 130–147.

Kissock, J. (1993) Some Examples of Co-axial Field Systems in Pembrokeshire. *Bulletin of the Board of Celtic Studies* 40, 190–198.

Kissock, J. (1997) God Made Nature and Men Made Towns: Post-Conquest and Pre-Conquest Villages in Pembrokeshire. In N. Edwards (ed.) *Landscape and Settlement in Medieval Wales.* Oxford, Oxbow Books, 123–138.

Kissock, J. (2001) The Upland Dimension: further conjectures on early medieval settlement in Gower. *Morgannwg* 45, 55–68

Kissock, J. (2008) Settlement and society. In R. A. Griffiths, T. Hopkins and R. Howell (eds) *Gwent County History, Volume 2: The Age of the Marcher Lords, 1070–1536.* Cardiff, University of Wales Press, 70–88.

Kissock, J. (2014) Llanau, Llysoedd, and Llociau: identifying the early medieval landscape of Gower. *Landscape History* 35(2), 5–20.

Linnard, W. (2000) *Welsh Woods and Forests.* Llandysul, Gomer Press.

Longley, D. (2001) Medieval Settlement and Landscape Change on Anglesey. *Landscape History* 23, 39–59.

Owen, D. H. (1989) *Settlement and Society in Wales.* Cardiff, University of Wales Press.

Owen, G. (1897) *The Description of Penbrokshire (sic) Part II.* London, Cymmrodorion Society.

Palmer, A. N. (1896) Notes on Ancient Welsh Measures of Land. *Archaeologia Cambrensis* 49, 1–19.

Payne, F. G. (1947) An Old Cornish Plough, And Others. *Antiquity* 21, 151–5.

Payne, F. G. (1957) The British Plough: Some Stages in its Development. *British Agricultural History Review* 5(2), 74–84.

Richards, M. (1969) *Welsh Administrative and Territorial Units: Medieval and Modern.* Cardiff, University of Wales Press.

Rippon, S. (1996) *The Gwent Levels: the Evolution of a Wetland Landscape.* CBA Research Report 105. York, Council for British Archaeology.

Rippon, S. (2008) *Beyond the Medieval Village.* Oxford, Oxford University Press.

Rippon, S., Smart, C. and Pears, B. (2015) *The Fields of Britannia: Continuity and Change in the Late Roman and Early Medieval Landscape.* Oxford, Oxford University Press.

Roberts, J. and Thompson, D. (2002) *Field Boundaries in Wales – Pilot Project (Part II) (Gl677) Gwynedd Archaeological Trust Report no. 467.* Bangor, Gwynedd Archaeological Trust (unpublished report).

Seaman, A. (2010) Towards a Predictive Model of Early Medieval Settlement Location: A Case Study from the Vale of Glamorgan. *Medieval Settlement Research* 25, 12–22.

Seaman, A. (2017) Further Research on a Predictive Model of Early Medieval Settlement Location in South Wales: Exploring the Use of Field-Names as Proxy Data. *Medieval Settlement Research* 32, 27–34.

Silvester, R. J. (1991) Medieval Farming on the Berwyn, North Wales. *Medieval Settlement Research Group Annual Report* 6, 12–14.

Silvester, R. J. (2000) Deserted rural settlements of medieval or later date in north-east and central Wales. In J. A. Atkinson, I. Banks and G. MacGregor (eds) *Township to Farmsteads: Rural Settlement Studies in Scotland, England and Wales.* BAR British Series 293. Oxford, British Archaeological Reports, 100–8.

Silvester, R. J. (2001) The Landscape and Settlement of Trefnant. *Montgomeryshire Collections* 89, 147–162.

Silvester, R. J. (2004) The commons and the waste: use and misuse in central Wales. In I. D. Whyte and A. J. L. Winchester (eds) *Society, Landscape and Environment in Upland Britain.* Birmingham, Society for Landscape Studies Supplementary Series 2, 53–66.

Silvester, R. J. (2005) The historic landscape. In R. Farmer (ed.) *Lake Vyrnwy Farming and Conservation, a Case Study.* Cardiff, Royal Society for the Protection of Birds, 12–14.

Silvester, R. J. (2006) Open-field agriculture in the central Welsh borderland. In M. Meek (ed.) *The Modern Traveller of our Past. Festschrift in honour of Ann Hamlin.* Dublin, DPK, 252–8.

Silvester, R. J. (2010) Historical concept to physical reality; forests in the landscape of the Welsh borderlands. In J. Langton and G. Jones (eds) *Forests and Chases of Medieval England and Wales c. 1100-c. 1500.* Oxford, St John's College Research Centre, 141–54.

Silvester, R. J. (2011) *Mynydd Hiraethog. The Denbigh Moors.* Aberystwyth, RCAHMW.

Silvester, R. J. and Kissock, J. (2012) Wales: Medieval Settlements, Nucleated and Dispersed, Permanent and Seasonal. In N. Christie and P. Stamper (eds) *Medieval Rural Settlement: Britain and Ireland, AD 800–1600.* Oxford, Windgather Press, 151–171.

Silvester, R. J. and Hankinson, R. (2013) *Farms and Farming SEP.* CPAT report no. 1199. Welshpool, Clwyd-Powys Archaeological Trust (unpublished report).

Smith, G. R. (2011) The 1284 Extent of Anglesey revisited: some facts and figures. *Studia Celtica* 45, 83–104.

Smith, G., Caseldine, A. E., Hopewell, D. and McPhail, R. (2011) *The North-West Wales Early Fields Project*. Gwynedd Archaeological Trust report no. 933. Bangor, Gwynedd Archaeological Trust (unpublished report).

Sylvester, D. (1969) *The Rural Landscape of the Welsh Borderland: a study in historical geography*. London, MacMillan.

Thomas, C. (1962) Thirteenth-century Farm Economies in North Wales. *Agricultural History Review* 16(1), 1–14.

Thomas, C. (1975) Peasant Agriculture in Medieval Gwynedd: An Interpretation of the Documentary Evidence. *Folk Life* 13(1), 24–37.

Thomas, C. (2001) Rural society, settlement, economy and landscape. In J. Beverley Smith and L. Beverley Smith (eds) *History of Merioneth Volume 2: The Middle Ages*. Cardiff, University of Wales Press, 168–224.

Environmental: pollen, cereal and bio-archaeological

Excavations carried out in advance of the 317 km South Wales Gas Pipeline (completed 2007) identified a number of medieval sites from which palaeoenvironmental assemblages were recovered. Final publication and synthesis of this data is awaited, but unpublished 'grey literature' reports with assessments of the palaeoenvironmental material can be accessed through the website of Cotswold Archaeology.

Brassil, K. S. (1987) Mollusca. *Medieval Archaeology* 31, 40.

Brown, A. (2010) Pollen Analysis and Planted Ancient Woodland Restoration Strategies: a case study from the Wentwood, southeast Wales, UK. *Vegetation History and Archaeobotany* 19, 79–90.

Brown, A. (2013) Iron Age to Early Medieval: Detecting the Ecological Impact of the Romans on the Landscape of South-East Wales. *Britannia* 44, 250–257.

Carruthers, W. (2007) Appendix 2: Assessment of the Charred Plant Remains. In D. Schlee, *Maenclochog Excavation Report. Report 2008/27*. Llandeilo, Dyfed Archaeological Trust (unpublished report).

Carruthers, W. (2010) Charred Plant Remains. In P. Crane and K. Murphy, An Early Medieval Settlement, Iron Smelting Site and Crop-processing Complex at South Hook, Herbranston, Pembrokeshire. *Archaeologia Cambrensis* 159, 117–196 at 164–181.

Caseldine, A. (2006) The environment and deserted rural settlements in Wales. In K. Roberts (ed.) *Lost Farmsteads: Deserted Rural Settlements in Wales*. CBA Research Report 148. York, Council for British Archaeology, 171–186.

Caseldine, A. E. (2013) Pollen Analysis at Craig y Dullfan and Banc Wernwgan and Other Recent Palaeoenvironmental Studies in Wales. *Archaeologia Cambrensis*, 162, 275–307.

Caseldine, A. E. (2015) Environmental Change and Archaeology – a retrospective view. *Archaeology in Wales* 54, 3–14.

Caseldine, A. E. and Evans, J. G. (1990) *Environmental Archaeology in Wales*. Lampeter, Department of Archaeology, Saint David's University College.

Caseldine, A. E. and Griffiths, C. J. (2004) Paleo-environmental evidence from the corn-drying kilns. In P. Crane, Excavations at Newton, Llanstadwell, Pembrokeshire. *Archaeology in Wales* 44, 3–31 at 14–17.

Caseldine, A. E. and Griffiths, C. J. (2012) Charred plant remains and charcoal from West Angle Bay. In P. Groom, D. Schlee, G. Hughes, P. Crane, N. Ludlow and K.

Murphy, Two early medieval cemeteries in Pembrokeshire: Brownslade Barrow and West Angle Bay. *Archaeologia Cambrensis* 160, 133–203 at 177–82.

Caseldine, A. E., Griffiths, C. J. and Crowther, J. (2012) Palaeoenvironmental investigations. In N. Page, G. Hughes, R. Jones and K. Murphy, Excavations at Erglodd, Llangynfelyn, Ceredigion: prehistoric/Roman lead smelting site and medieval trackway. *Archaeologia Cambrensis* 161, 313–34.

Challinor, D. (2010) Wood charcoal. In P. Crane and K. Murphy, Early Medieval Settlement, Iron Smelting and Crop Processing at South Hook, Herbranston, Pembrokeshire, 2004–05. *Archaeologia Cambrensis* 159, 117–195, at 181–5.

Chambers, F. M. (1983) Three Radiocarbon-dated Pollen Diagrams from Upland Peats North-west of Merthyr Tydfil, South Wales. *The Journal of Ecology* 71, 475–487.

Chambers, F. M. and Price, S.-M. (1988) The Environmental Setting of Erw-wen and Moel y Gerddi: Prehistoric Enclosures in Upland Ardudwy, North Wales. *Proceedings of the Prehistoric Society* 54, 93–100.

Chambers, F. M., Kelly, R. S. and Price, S.-M. (1988) Development of the late-prehistoric cultural landscape in upland Ardudwy, north-west Wales. In H. H. Birks, H. J. B. Birks, P. E. Kaland and D. Moe (eds) *The Cultural Landscape – Past, Present and Future.* Cambridge, Cambridge University Press, 333–348.

Ciaraldi, M. (2012) Charred plant remains. In R. Cuttler, A. Davidson and G. Hughes (eds) *A Corridor Through Time. The Archaeology of the A55 Road Scheme.* Oxford, Oxbow Books, 222–242.

Crampton, C. B. and Webley, D. (1960) The Correlation of Prehistoric Settlement and Soils in the Vale of Glamorgan. *Bulletin of the Board of Celtic Studies* 18(4), 387–396.

Crampton, C. B. (1966) Analysis of Pollen in Soils on the Peaks of South Wales. *The Scottish Geographical Magazine* 82, 46–52.

Dark, P. (2000) *The Environment of Britain in the First Millennium A.D.* London, Duckworth.

Davies, T. L. (2015) *Early Medieval Llyn Tegid: an Environmental Landscape Study.* Unpublished PhD thesis, University of Sheffield.

Dorling, P. and Chambers F. M. (1990) Field survey, excavation and pollen analysis at Mynydd y Drum, Ystradgynlais, Powys, 1983 and 1987. *Bulletin of the Board of Celtic Studies* 37, 215–246.

Gilchrist, R. (1988) A Reappraisal of Dinas Powys: local exchange and specialised livestock in fifth-seventh century Wales. *Medieval Archaeology* 32, 50–62.

Grant, F. and Shimwell, D. (2004) Plant remains. In I. Grant, The Excavation of a Double-ditched Enclosure at Arddleen, Powys, 2002–03. *Montgomeryshire Collections* 92, 21–4.

Grant, F. R. (2008) Human Impact and Landscape Change at Moel Llys y Coedin the Clwydian Hills, North Wales: the Mesolithic – present day. *Archaeology in Wales* 48, 3–15.

Hammon, A. (2011) Understanding the Romano-British–Early Medieval Transition: a zooarchaeological perspective from Wroxeter. *Britannia* 42, 275–305.

Hemer, K. A., Lamb, A., Chenery, C. A. and Evans, J. A. (2017) A Multi-isotope Investigation of Diet and Subsistence Amongst Island and Mainland Populations from Early Medieval Western Britain. *American Journal of Physical Anthropology* 162(3), 423–440.

Hughes, P. D. M., Morriss, S. H., Schulz, J. and Barber, K. E. (2001) Mire development and human impact in the Teifi valley: evidence from the Tregaron (Cors Caron) peatlands. In M. J. C. Walker and D. McCarroll (eds) *The Quaternary of West Wales: Field Guide.* London, Quaternary Research Association, 76–92.

Kenney, J. and Roberts, J. (2008) Cefn Graianog Quarry. *Archaeology in Wales* 48, 134.

Levitan, B. (1994) The vertebrate remains. In H. Quinnell, M. Blockley and P. Berridge, *Excavations at Rhuddlan, Clwyd: 1969–73 Mesolithic to Medieval*. CBA Research Report 95. York, Council for British Archaeology, 147–159.

Mann, A. and Hurst, D. (2014) Buttington Cross, Powys: a Bronze Age barrow and post-Roman grain processing site. *Archaeology in Wales* 53, 130–8.

Mighall, T. M. and Chambers, F. M. (1989) The Environmental Impact of Iron-working at Bryn y Castell Hillfort, Merioneth. *Archaeology in Wales* 29, 17–21.

Mighall, T. M. and Chambers, F. M. (1995) Holocene Vegetation History and Human Impact at Bryn y Castell, Snowdonia, North Wales. *New Phytologist* 130(2), 299–321.

Morriss, S. H. (2001) *Recent human impact and land use change in Britain and Ireland: a pollen analytical and geochemical study*. Unpublished PhD thesis, University of Southampton

Rippon, S., Smart, C. and Pears, B. (2015) *The Fields of Britannia*. Oxford, Oxford University Press.

Rudeforth, C. C., Hartnup, R., Lea, J. W., Thompson, T. R. E. and Wright, P. S. (1984) *Soils and Their Uses in Wales*. Harpenden, Soil Survey of England and Wales.

Seymour, W. P. (1985) *The environmental history of the Preseli region of South-West Wales over the past 12,000 years*. Unpublished PhD thesis, Aberystwyth University.

Taylor, P. and Lewin, J. (1996) Non-synchronous Response of Adjacent Upland Floodplain Systems to Environmental Change. *Geomorphology* 18, 251–264.

Tomlinson, P. (1987) Pollen. In J. Manley, *Cledemutha*: A Late Saxon Burh in North Wales. *Medieval Archaeology* 31, 41.

Turner, J. (1964) The Anthropogenic Factor in Vegetational History. I. Tregaron and Whixall Mosses. *New Phytologist* 63, 73–90.

Van der Veen, M., Hill, A. and Livarda, A. (2013) The Archaeobotany of Medieval Britain (c. AD 450–1500): identifying research priorities for the 21st century. *Medieval Archaeology* 57, 151–182.

Woodbridge, J., Fyfe, R., Law, B. and Haworth-Johns, A. (2012) A Spatial Approach to Upland Vegetation Change and Human Impact: the Aber Valley, Snowdonia. *Environmental Archaeology* 17(1), 80–94.

Transhumance and uplands

Austin, D. (2016) Reconstructing the Upland Landscapes of Medieval Wales. *Archaeologia Cambrensis* 165, 1–19.

Davies, E. (1973) Hendre and Hafod in Merioneth. *Journal of the Merioneth Historical and Record Society* 7, 13–27.

Davies, E. (1977) Hendre and Hafod in Denbighshire. *Transactions of the Denbighshire Historical Society* 26, 49–72.

Davies, E. (1979) Hendre and Hafod in Caernarvonshire. *Transactions of the Caernarvonshire Historical Society* 40, 17–46.

Davies, E. (1980) Hafod, Hafoty and Lluest. *Ceredigion: Journal of the Cardiganshire Antiquarian Society* 9(1), 1–41.

Davies, E. (1984): Hafod and Lluest: The Summering of Cattle and Upland Settlement in Wales. *Folk Life* 23(1), 76–96.

Driver, T. and Silvester, R. J. (2003) Mynydd Epynt: rediscovering an abandoned farming landscape. In D. Browne and S. Hughes (eds) *The Archaeology of the Welsh Uplands*. Aberystwyth, RCAHMW, 87–98.

Fleming, A. and Barker, L. (2008) Monks and Local Communities: the late-medieval landscape of Troed y Rhiw, Caron Uwch Clawdd, Ceredigion. *Medieval Archaeology* 52, 261–290.

Leighton, D. (2012) *The Western Brecon Beacons: the archaeology of Mynydd Du and Fforest Fawr*. Aberystwyth, RCAHMW.

Locock, M. (2006) Deserted rural settlements in south-east Wales. In K. Roberts (ed.) *Lost Farmsteads: Deserted Rural Settlements in Wales*. CBA Research Report 148. York, Council for British Archaeology, 41–60.

Longley, D. (2006) Deserted rural settlements in north-west Wales. In K. Roberts (ed.) *Lost Farmsteads: Deserted Rural Settlements in Wales*. CBA Research Report 148. York, Council for British Archaeology, 61–82.

Roberts, K. (ed.) (2006) *Lost Farmsteads: Deserted Rural Settlements in Wales*. CBA Research Report 148. York, Council for British Archaeology.

Sambrook, P. (2006) Deserted rural settlements in south-west Wales. In K. Roberts (ed.) *Lost Farmsteads: Deserted Rural Settlements in Wales*. CBA Research Report 148. York, Council for British Archaeology, 83–110.

Sayce, R. U. (1955–1956) The Old Summer Pastures. *Montgomeryshire Collections* 54, 117–145.

Sayce, R. U. (1957) The Old Summer Pastures Part II: Life at the Hafodydd. *Montgomeryshire Collections* 55(1), 37–86.

Silvester, R. J. (2000) Medieval Upland Cultivation on the Berwyns in North Wales. *Landscape History* 22, 47–60.

Silvester, R. J. (2006) Deserted rural settlements in central and north-east Wales. In K. Roberts (ed.) *Lost Farmsteads: Deserted Rural Settlements in Wales*. CBA Research Report 148. York, Council for British Archaeology, 13–40.

Silvester, R. J. (2010) Abandoning the uplands: depopulation among dispersed settlements in western Britain. In C. Dyer and R. Jones (eds) *Deserted Villages Revisited*. Hatfield, University of Hertfordshire Press, 140–161.

Thomas, C. (1992) A Culture-biological Model of Agrarian Colonisation in Upland Wales. *Landscape History* 14, 37–50.

Ward, A. (1997) Transhumance and Settlement on the Welsh Uplands: A View from the Black Mountain. In N. Edwards (ed.) *Landscape and Settlement in Medieval Wales*. Oxford, Oxbow Books, 97–112.

Withers, C. W. J. (1995) Conceptions of Cultural Landscape Change in Upland North Wales: a case study of Llanbedr-y-Cennin and Caerhun parishes, c.1560–c.1891. *Landscape History* 17, 35–47.

Field- and place-names

Charles, B. G. (1992) *The Place-Names of Pembrokeshire*. Aberystwyth, National Library of Wales.

Hooke, D. (1997) Place-Names and Vegetation History as a Key to Understanding Settlement in the Conwy Valley. In N. Edwards (ed.) *Landscape and Settlement in Medieval Wales*. Oxford, Oxbow Books, 79–96.

Hooke, D. (2003) Place-names and land use in coastal Ardudwy, with comparisons with the Conwy valley in North Wales. In T. Unwin and T. Spek (eds) *European Landscapes from Mountain to Sea*. Tallin, Huma, 139–145.

Morgan, R. (1998) *A Study of Radnorshire Place-Names*. Llanrwst, Gwasg Carreg Gwalch.

Morgan, R. (2005) *Place-Names of Gwent*. Llanrwst, Gwasg Carreg Gwalch.

Morgan, R. (2018) *Place-Names of Glamorgan*. Cardiff, Welsh Academic Press.

Morgan, R. and Powell, R. F. P. (1999) *A Study of Breconshire Place-Names*. Llanrwst, Gwasg Carreg Gwalch.

Owen, H. W. and Morgan, R. (2007) *Dictionary of the Place-Names of Wales*. Llandysul, Gomer Press.

Pierce, G. O. (1968) *The Place-Names of Dinas Powys Hundred*. Cardiff, University of Wales Press.

Pierce, G. O. (2002) *Place Names in Glamorgan*. Cardiff, Merton Priory Press.

Thomas, C. (1973) Place-Name Analysis in the Geographical Study of the Rural Landscape of Wales. *Studia Celtica* 8, 299–318.

Thomas, C. (1980) Field Name Evidence in the Reconstruction of Medieval Settlement Nuclei in North Wales. *National Library of Wales Journal* 21(4), 340–356.

Thomas, C. (1980) Place-Names Studies and Agrarian Colonization in North Wales. *Welsh History Review* 10(2), 155–171.

Wmffre, I. (2004) *The Place-Names of Cardiganshire*. BAR British Series 379. Oxford, British Archaeological Reports.

Welsh law

Jenkins, D. (1982) *Agricultural Co-operation in Welsh Medieval Law*. Cardiff, National Museum of Wales.

Jenkins, D. (trans. and ed.) (1990) *The Law of Hywel Dda*. Llandysul, Gomer Press.

Owen, M. E. (2009) The Animals of the Law of Hywel. *Carmarthenshire Antiquary* 45, 5–27.

Richards, M. (trans. and ed.) (1954) *The Laws of Hywel Dda ('The Book of Blegwryd')*. Liverpool, Liverpool University Press.

Wade-Evans, A. W. (trans. and ed.) (1909) *Welsh Medieval Law (Harleian MS 4353)*. Oxford, Oxford University Press.

Key site reports

Alcock, L. (1963) *Dinas Powys: An Iron Age, Dark Age and Early Medieval Settlement in Glamorgan*. Cardiff, University of Wales Press.

Allen, D. (1979) Excavations at Hafod y Nant Criafolen, Brenig Valley, Clwyd, 1973–74. *Post-Medieval Archaeology* 13, 1–59.

Austin, D. (1988) Excavation and Survey at Bryn Cysegrfan, Llanfair Clydogau, Dyfed, 1979. *Medieval Archaeology* 23, 130–165.

Barber, A., and Pannett, A. (2006) Archaeological Excavations Along the Milford Haven to Aberdulais Natural Gas Pipeline 2006: A Preliminary Report. *Archaeology in Wales* 46, 87–99.

Barker, P., Higham, R. and Clarke, P. (1982) *Hen Domen Montgomery: a timber castle on the English-Welsh border*. London, Royal Archaeological Institute.

Britnell, W. (ed.) (2001) Ty-mawr, Castle Caereinion. *Montgomeryshire Collections* 89, 1–242.

Brown, A., Turner, R. and Pearson, C. (2010) Medieval Fishing Structures and Baskets at Sudbrook Point, Severn Estuary, Wales. *Medieval Archaeology* 54, 346–360.

Caple, C. (2007) *Excavations at Dryslwyn Castle 1980–95*. Leeds, Society for Medieval Archaeology.

Courtney, P. (1991) Native-Welsh Medieval Settlement: Excavations at Beili Bedw, St Harmon, Powys. *Bulletin of the Board of Celtic Studies* 38, 233–256.

Cuttler, R., Davidson, A. and Hughes, G. (2012) *A Corridor Through Time: The Archaeology of the A55 Anglesey Road Scheme*. Oxford, Oxbow Books.

Fasham, P. J., Kelly, R. S., Mason, M. A. and White R. B. (1998) *The Graeanog Ridge: The Evolution of a Farming Landscape and its Settlement in North-West Wales*. Aberystwyth, Cambrian Archaeological Association.

Fox, A. (1937) Dinas Noddfa, Gelligaer Common, Glamorgan: Excavations in 1936. *Archaeologia Cambrensis* 92, 247–268.

Fox, A. (1939) Early Welsh Homesteads on Gelligaer Common: Excavations in 1938. *Archaeologia Cambrensis* 94, 163–199.

Hopewell, D. and Edwards, N. (2017) Early Medieval Settlement and Field Systems at Rhuddgaer, Anglesey. *Archaeologia Cambrensis* 166, 213–242.

Jones, I., Williams, D. and Williams, S. (2018) Early medieval enclosure at Glanfred, near Llandre, Ceredigion. *Archaeologia Cambrensis* 167, 221–243

Kelly, R. S. (1988) Two Late Prehistoric Circular Enclosures near Harlech, Gwynedd. *Proceedings of the Prehistoric Society* 54, 101–151.

Kelly, R. S., Lewis, J., Keeley, H., Chambers, F., Hillman, G. and Noel, M. (1982) The Excavation of a Medieval Farmstead at Cefn Graeanog, Clynnog, Gwynedd, Wales. *Bulletin of the Board Of Celtic Studies* 29, 859–908.

Lane, A. and Redknap R. (forthcoming) *Llangorse Crannog: The Excavation of an Early Medieval Royal Site in the Kingdom of Brycheiniog*. Oxford, Oxbow Books.

Redknap, M. (2004) Viking Age settlement in Wales and the evidence from Llanbedrgoch. In J. Hines, A. Lane and M. Redknap (eds) *Land, Sea and Home: Settlement in the Viking Period*. Leeds, Maney, 139–175.

Redknap, M. (2016) Defining identities in Viking age north Wales: new data from Llanbedrgoch. In V. E. Turner, O. A. Owen and D. J. Waugh (eds) *Shetland in the Viking World. Papers from the Proceedings of the Seventeenth Viking Congress Lerwick*. Lerwick, Shetland Heritage Publications, 159–166.

Schlee, D., Comeau, R., Parker Pearson M. and Welham, K. (2018) Carn Goedog Medieval House and Settlement, Pembrokeshire. *Archaeologia Cambrensis* 167, 245–255.

Silvester, R. J., Courtney, P. and Rees, S. E. (2004) Castell Blaenllynfi, Brecknock: a Marcher castle and its landscape. *Archaeologia Cambrensis* 153, 75–103.

Thomas, H. and Dowdell, G. (1987) A Shrunken Medieval Village at Barry, Glamorgan. *Archaeologia Cambrensis* 136, 94–137.

Vyner, B. E. and Wrathmell, S. (1978) The Deserted Village of Wrinstone, South Glamorgan. *Transactions of the Cardiff Naturalists Society* 98, 19–29.

Vyner, B. E., Wrathmell, S. and Wrathmell, S. (1981) The Manor and Township of Wrinstone, South Glamorgan. *Transactions of the Cardiff Naturalist Society* 9, 15–27.

Index

Page numbers in italics are figures.

PLATE 3.1. Long huts above Egryn, Llanaber.

PLATE 3.2. Field patterns on the Ardudwy coastal strip: Llanaber near Barmouth.

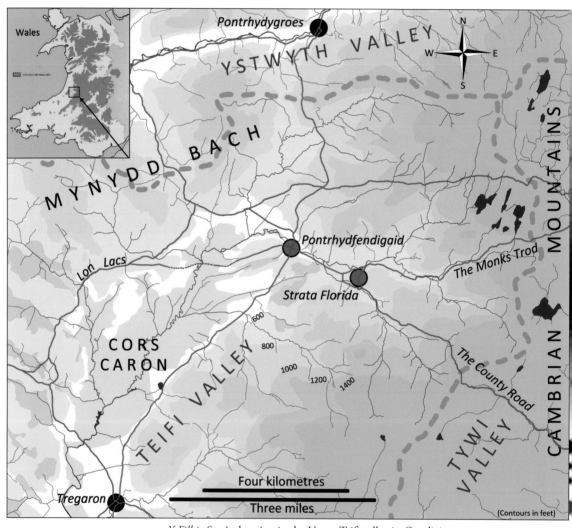

PLATE 7.1. *Y Filltir Sgwâr*: location in the Upper Teifi valley in Ceredigion.

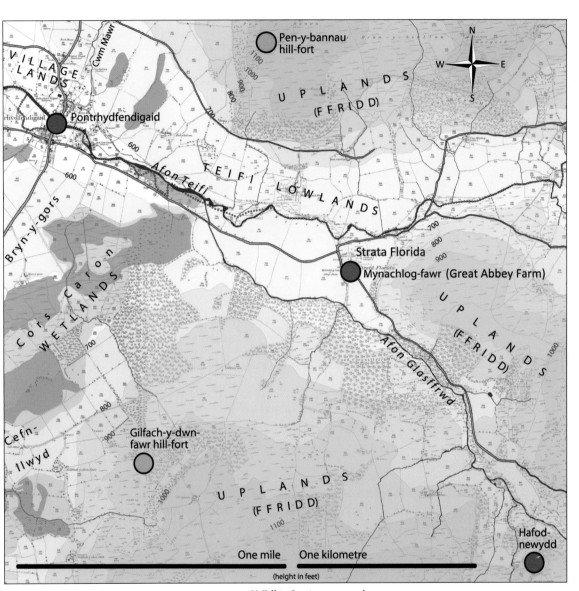

PLATE 7.2. *Y Filltir Sgwâr*: topography.

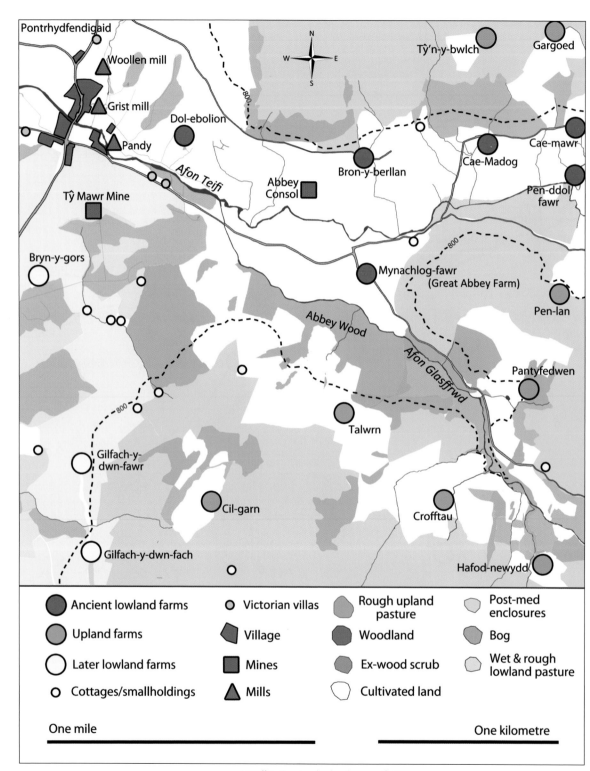

PLATE 7.3. *Y Filltir Sgwâr*: the landscape of 1886.

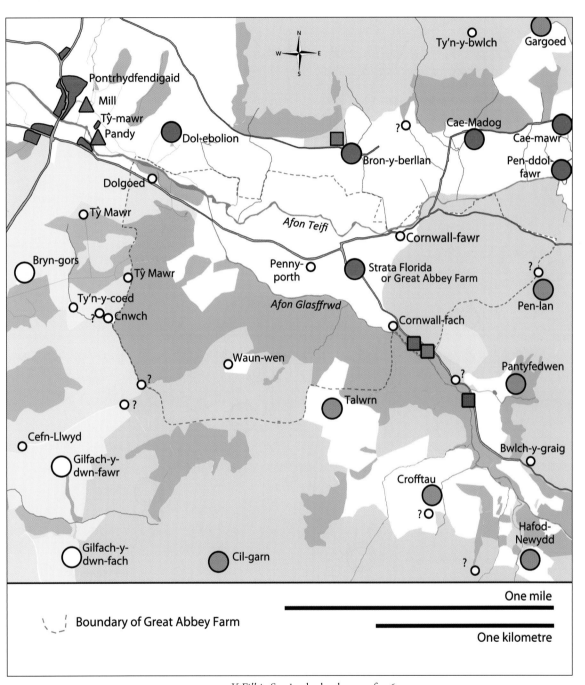

PLATE 7.4. *Y Filltir Sgwâr*: the landscape of 1765.

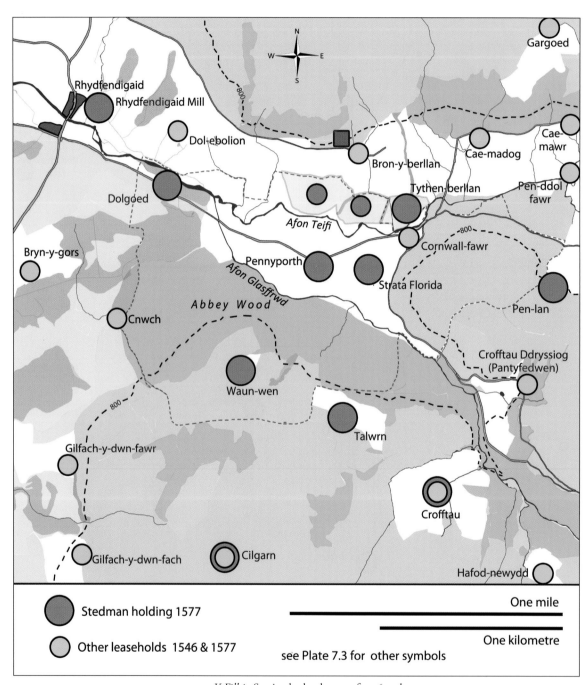

Rhydfendigaid
Rhydfendigaid Mill
Dol-ebolion
Bron-y-berllan
Cae-madog
Cae-mawr
Gargoed
Tythen-berllan
Pen-ddol fawr
Dolgoed
Afon Teifi
Cornwall-fawr
Bryn-y-gors
Pennyporth
Afon Glasffrwd
Strata Florida
Pen-lan
Abbey Wood
Cnwch
Crofftau Ddryssiog
(Pantyfedwen)
Waun-wen
Gilfach-y-dwn-fawr
Talwrn
Crofftau
Gilfach-y-dwn-fach
Cilgarn
Hafod-newydd

Stedman holding 1577

Other leaseholds 1546 & 1577

One mile

One kilometre

see Plate 7.3 for other symbols

PLATE 7.5. *Y Filltir Sgwâr*: the landscape of 1546 and 1577.

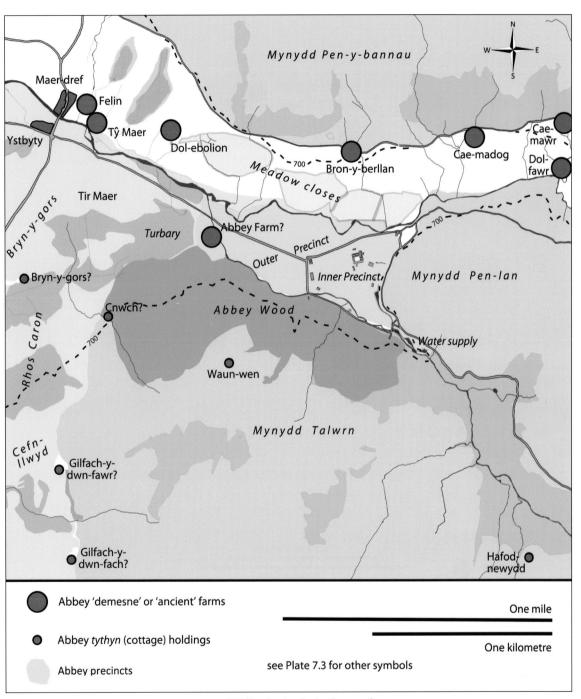

Maer-dref

Felin

Tŷ Maer

Dol-ebolion

Ystbyty

Mynydd Pen-y-bannau

700

Meadow closes

Bron-y-berllan

Cae-madog

Cae-mawr

Dol-fawr

Tir Maer

Bryn-y-gors

Bryn-y-gors?

Turbary

Abbey Farm?

Outer

Precinct

Inner Precinct

Mynydd Pen-lan

700

Cnwch?

Abbey Wood

700

Waun-wen

Water supply

Rhos Caron

Cefn-llwyd

Gilfach-y-dwn-fawr?

Mynydd Talwrn

Gilfach-y-dwn-fach?

Hafod-newydd

N
W E
S

Abbey 'demesne' or 'ancient' farms

Abbey *tythyn* (cottage) holdings

Abbey precincts

see Plate 7.3 for other symbols

One mile

One kilometre

PLATE 7.6. *Y Filltir Sgwâr*: the landscape of *c.* 1225.

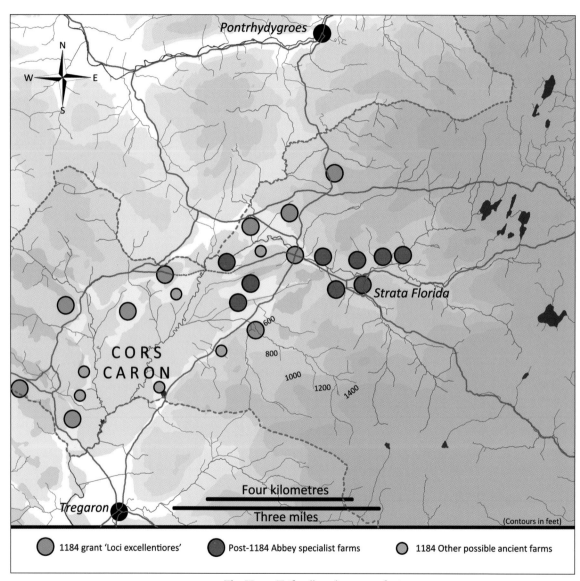

PLATE 7.7. The Upper Teifi valley: the grant of 1184.

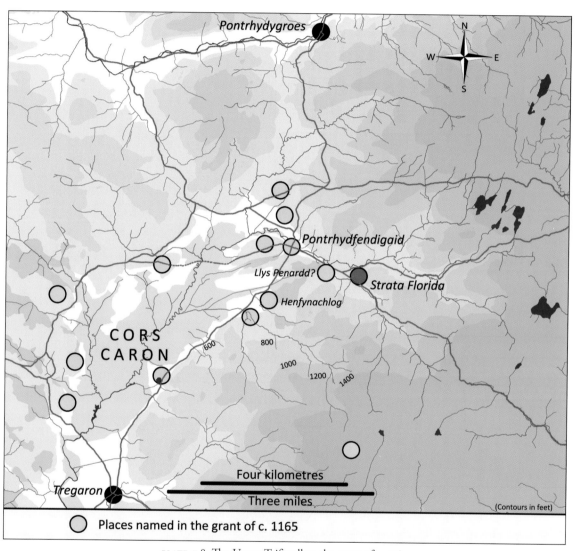

Places named in the grant of c. 1165

PLATE 7.8. The Upper Teifi valley: the grant of *c.* 1165.

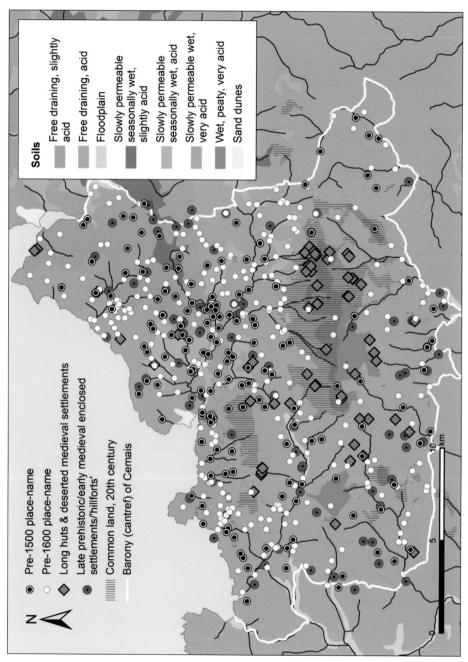

PLATE 8.1. Cemais: soils and settlement. Soil mapping taken from the Soil Survey Map of England and Wales 1983.

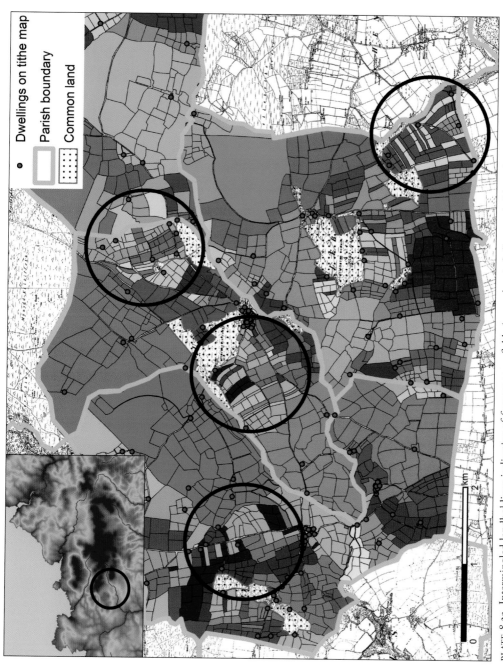

PLATE 8.2a. Intermingled landholdings indicative of former open fields (examples circled), recorded by tithe apportionments of 1839–1844 for the parishes of Little Newcastle/Casnewydd Bach (left), Puncheston/Casmael (centre), Morvil/Morfil (top right) and Castlebythe/Casfuwch (bottom right). Shown on the first edition Ordnance Survey map of 1888.

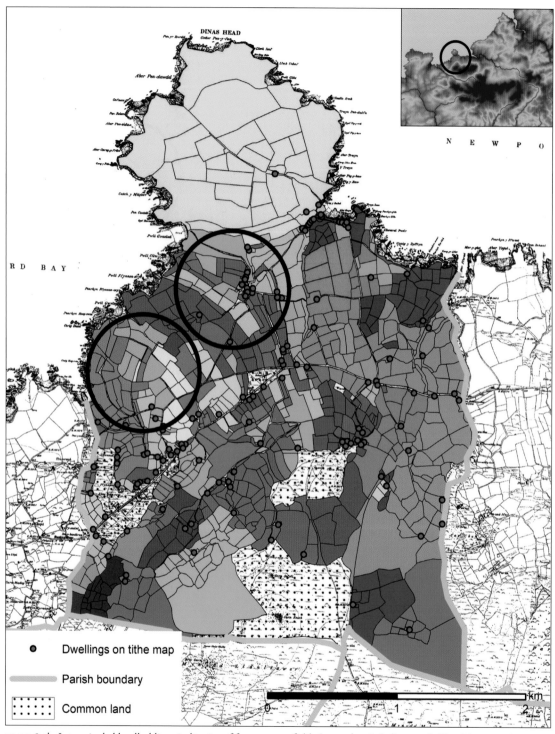

PLATE 8.2b. Intermingled landholdings indicative of former open fields (examples circled), recorded by tithe apportionments of 1841 for the parish of Dinas. Shown on the first edition Ordnance Survey map of 1888.

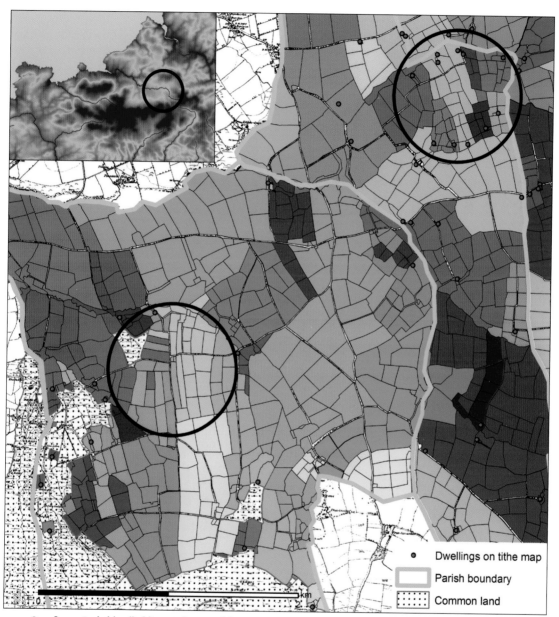

Dwellings on tithe map

Parish boundary

Common land

PLATE 8.2c. Intermingled landholdings indicative of former open fields (examples circled), recorded by tithe apportionments of 1837–9 for the parishes of Eglwyswen/Whitchurch (left) and Llanfair Nantgwyn (right). Shown on the first edition Ordnance Survey map of 1888.

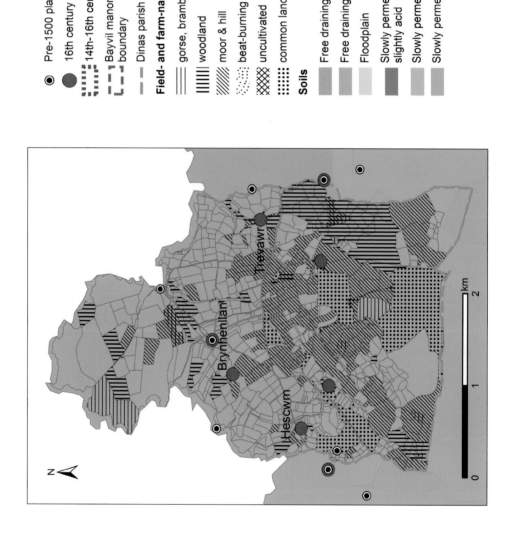

Pre-1500 place-name

16th century hamlets

14th–16th century shared pasture

Bayvil manor – approximate medieval boundary

Dinas parish boundary

Field- and farm-names

gorse, brambles, thistles, ferns

woodland

moor & hill

beat-burning

uncultivated

common land/cytir

Soils

Free draining, slightly acid

Free draining, acid

Floodplain

Slowly permeable seasonally wet, slightly acid

Slowly permeable seasonally wet, acid

Slowly permeable wet, very acid

Trefawr

Brynhenllan

Hescwm

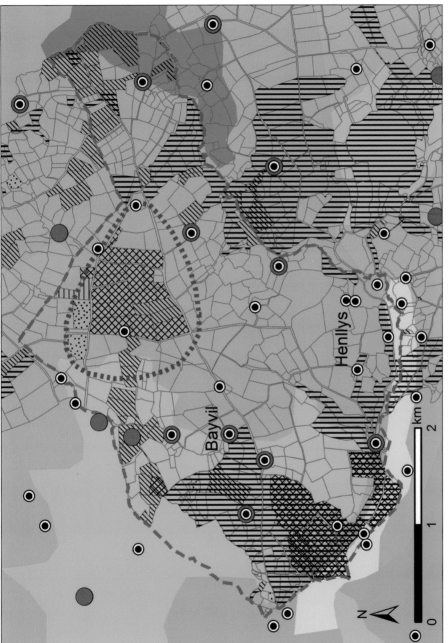

Plates 8.3 (Dinas, above) and 8.4 (Bayvil, below): Nineteenth-century field- and farm-names, and sixteenth-century hamlets in Dinas (above) and Bayvil (below), shown on the first edition Ordnance Survey map of 1888. Overlapping shading indicates differences between categories of field-and farm-names. (Sources: Tithe apportionments and maps of 1841-5; Charles 1992; Howells 1977; Soil Survey Map of England and Wales 1983.).

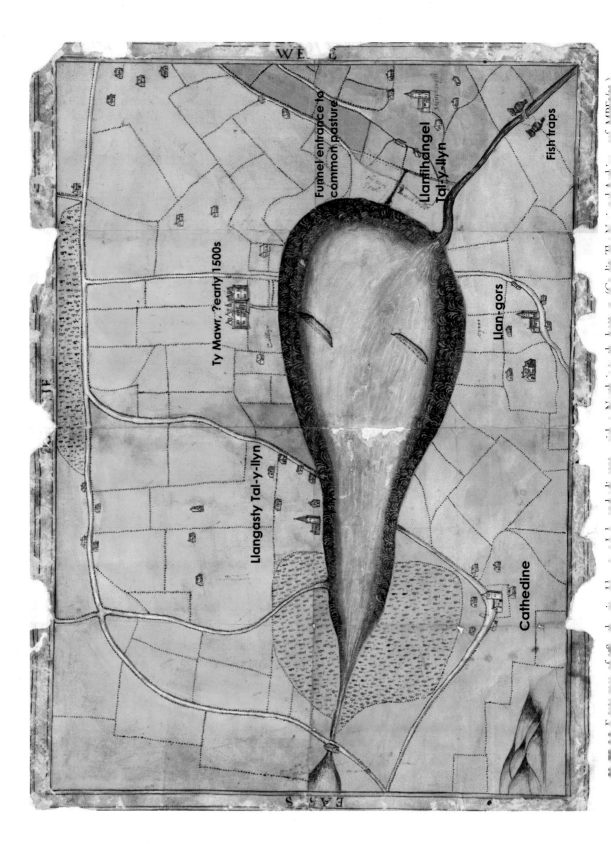

WEST

EAST

Funnel entrance to common pasture

Llanfihangel Tal-y-llyn

Fish traps

Ty Mawr, ?early 1500s

Llan-gors

Llangasty Tal-y-llyn

Cathedine